Twining

Twining

◇

Anastasia Salter

and

Stuart Moulthrop

Amherst College Press
Amherst, Massachusetts

References to internet websites (URLs) were accurate at the time of writing. Neither
the author nor Amherst College Press is responsible for URLs that may have expired
or changed since the manuscript was prepared.

Published in the United States of America by Amherst College Press
Manufactured in the United States of America

DOI: http://dx.doi.org/10.3998/mpub.12255695

ISBN 978-1-943208-24-1 (paper)
ISBN 978-1-943208-25-8 (OA)

Contents

Introduction

Why Twine?

In March 2020, classrooms around the world were abruptly shuttered and life moved online. In an interactive storytelling class at the University of Central Florida (UCF) that semester, we were in the middle of a unit on interactive fiction, working with Twine and discussing strategies for crafting hypertextual narratives. Twine is a platform for personal storytelling and individual disruption on an increasingly corporate web. The software, and the work it enables, is deceptively simple: the visual interface emphasizes approaching creation through metaphors of passages and links. Thanks to its combination of educator-friendly development decisions—the software platform is free to use, easy to access through a browser without installation, and well documented with a beginner-friendly learning curve—Twine makes frequent appearances in courses of this kind around the world. However, this association might suggest a tool for beginners, to be used and moved beyond. Twine is more than that—as a platform, it can be the destination as well as a tool for making the journey to creating interactive works.

We started that class meeting with a round of exquisite corpses (if you'll forgive the term): writing story beginnings on paper and folding away all but the last words and passing them around the room to take unexpected twists. The stories took dark turns almost immediately—the news was already grim, and Twine didn't present much of an escape. Each class meeting opened with an apology for the examples featured. So many of the most powerful works made in Twine draw us into moments of despair: Zoë Quinn's *Depression Quest*, with its simulation of the struggles of moving forward with clinical depression; Anna Anthropy's *Queers in Love at the End of the World*, which places the player in fleeting last moments with a lover; Michael Lutz's vision of horror and abuse in *My Father's Long, Long Legs*—the list goes on and does not include many of the escapist narratives still inextricably linked to our expectations of games. In the moment, some of these works became even more loaded, resonating differently as we played through our fears.

This is not to say Twine is only a tool for making depressing things or that Twine and hypertext must go hand in hand with crisis, struggle, and turmoil. However, Twine is a tool that particularly resonates for those with something personal to say, and Twine's importance and visibility on the web have often risen correspondingly with conflict (there is more to say about this in chapters T-4 and T-5). At a time when our technology is increasingly complex, sealed in tiny boxes and inscrutable to most of its users, Twine is transparent and open. At a time when our software is produced by large teams, with most of the production members hyperfocused on a project part, Twine allows a single person to develop an interactive experience holistically, without relying on any external specialist's knowledge. Twine is a tool for resisting the dominant interactive storytelling of our times and, as such, tends to be a tool for chronicling resistance and struggle.

But to return to the classroom the teaching of the theory and practice of interactive storytelling is an interwoven challenge of competing histories and terms. To gamers, the history has been written by mainstream game design companies and with increasingly cinematic visuals accompanying lavish environments. To electronic literature authors and scholars, it is a history told in competing platforms and continually deprecated tools, pushed to their limits for narrative experiments. To interactive fiction players and authors, it is a history of textual play and riddles, told in parsers and, sometimes, in hypertexts. Crafting a course in this area requires navigating these competing histories as well as students' own very different visions of what interactive storytelling should become.

Twine doesn't fit into any one of these histories—it moves freely among all three. Created by independent software developer Chris Klimas and released in 2009, Twine has gone through several iterations and includes a range of story formats that extend the underlying editor's capabilities to allow creators to build a wide variety of stories and other textual constructions. The second iteration of Twine, Twine 2, extended the accessibility of the platform by bringing a browser-based version of the development tool to users (Klimas). The things both Twine and Twine 2 allow users to make are united by their emphasis on choice, as Twine is at its heart a system for making passages and links that the user navigates to different ends. These choice-based systems can in turn become, in the hands of different makers, a platform for making games, crafting electronic literature, building simulations, documenting experiences, or telling interactive fictions. The resulting range of works confounds inclusion in the categories of "game" or "story," a false binary we will question throughout this work.

To return to our classroom, we were approaching Twine first through this lens as a user-friendly tool: at its base, Twine offers a graphical framework for making hyperlinked content, most often compacted into a single hypertext markup language (HTML) file (barring external resource files, such as images and sounds) for easy web distribution and longevity of access. Twine's tagline in the GitHub repository, where the history of the code is embodied in versions and iterations spanning years, describes it succinctly as "a tool for telling interactive, nonlinear stories" (Klimas). It is open-source and user-friendly, often recommended to newcomers to interactive making for whom code and procedural, rules-driven thinking is unfamiliar. In a classroom of students from different backgrounds, with varying knowledge of programming, Twine can be an equalizer—the quality of the story created has little to do with expertise in code but instead is driven by the honesty of the narrative and the crafting of the experience.

These are the Twine concepts we were working through together, offering players choices but then restricting them to produce manageable—and meaningful—narrative play. In that final, in-person meeting, we didn't know that we wouldn't be seeing one another for a long time, that our daily choices would be changing, as the restrictions and rules under which we operate were abruptly rewritten for public safety. We didn't know when we'd see the new fears of public spaces change—indeed, we still don't know. The broader landscape of the communities making interactive narratives is still shifting to adapt as I write this. The Game Developers Conference was canceled, with on-line talks replacing the largest annual gathering of the games industry. LudoNarraCon 2020 and NarraScope 2020, two celebrations of narra-tive video games and interactive fiction, respectively, moved online to streaming video rather than physical gatherings. We will address these types of gatherings, and their role in shaping Twine and the surround-ing community, throughout the work—while Twine exists online, such physical convenings have been a part of building Twine's influence.

It is thus no surprise that when the students' Twine stories were finally submitted online, weeks later, many of them dealt with COVID-19. The original final project for the class was simplified in favor of Twine's spiritual compatriot Bitsy, a graphical, web-based platform for small games with constrained, pixelated graphics and an emphasis on exploration and dialogue. The interactive stories of the rest of the semester frequently reacted to the moment—students built games about being confined in a room or dodging viruses in the one-way aisles of a grocery store; stories captured the claustrophobia of the home or invited players into social-isolation baking. Stress and fear and boredom fueled these interactive works, made for the browser, playable quickly, resonating with one another in exchanges through the class discussion forums.

One genre that persists in interactive fiction—particularly of the parser variety, where players input combinations of nouns and verbs to interact with a system, solve puzzles, and progress in a narrative—is the locked room. (One of our practical examples, *Twine Box* in chapter P-5, puts a twist on this theme.) A digital kindred of the physical escape room, the locked room in adventure games always presents the player with a variant on the same challenge: to get out. By contrast, the games that COVID-19 has inspired focus on the internal struggles of staying in. Within the locked room, players struggle with internalized anxiety, domestic tasks, and monotony. The threat of the external is ever-present, but the resistance of temptation and need to leave dominates. This theme recurs in the Twine games posted to events like the "Quarantine Game Jam." G. Deyke and Damon L. Wakes's *Quarantine Quest* entry in the jam (figure 1) opens with the real and moves quickly into the surreal, imagining nightmare scenarios and inviting the player to reflect through them (Deyke and Wakes). Games like these emerge in the moment, without the need for large investments in time or capital, and with no delay between the moment of completion and release.

This is where Twine excels—in the internal, the personal, and the immediate. We could take any large event and find similar traces—Twine games responding to the 2016 election in the US and to Brexit; Twine jams at the height of the cultural war of Gamergate; Twine games responding to incidents of police brutality—Twine games as protest, as documentation, as an emotional response to a moment. Twine is part of a growing category of tools that focus on allowing rapid procedural

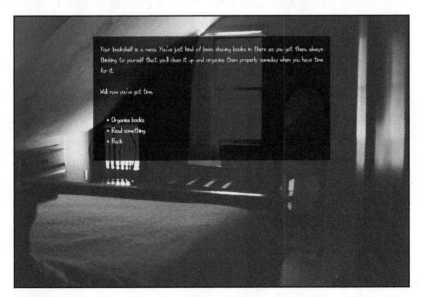

Figure 1: Killing time in the interior space of *Quarantine Quest* (Deyke and Wakes)

creativity, removing barriers of both hardware and knowledge. It also removes barriers in distribution, allowing for the rapid sharing of whatever is made, removing gatekeepers and creating an ease of "free" distribution (in the sense that any online trafficking is free). Twine's accessibility for making is key to its impact. Using Twine and Bitsy for remote coursework allowed us not to worry about the power of any student's computer: even students with Chromebooks or long-outdated machines could still load a web browser on even a limited internet connection and easily make, and play, the works these tools create. Twine is an ideal tool for this moment in teaching but also for this moment in living and making.

Defining Twine

When you first open Twine's interface to make something, you are presented first with a request to name your story, followed by the opening of the screen to a grid with a single, untitled passage waiting for editing. The interface immediately communicates the basic instructions: placeholder text reading "Double-click this passage to edit it" waits for a rewrite. This opening explicitly recommends a story, but works produced in Twine go under many names: games, interactive fiction, stories, websites, quizzes, resources, essays, and so forth. Klimas notes this "confounding" variety as a strength of the platform he hopes only increases: "I also want it to be even more confounding, that not only can the world be unable to decide whether things made with Twine are stories or games, but also whether they're sprawling commercial masterpieces or intensely personal stories. I want people—not gamers, not readers, just people—to experience something they love unabashedly and never realize it was made with Twine" (sub-Q).

Twine doesn't offer a blueprint for what these confounding works might become, but its interface does encourage certain approaches: the size of a passage box, and the very term *passage*, encourages creators to think and work in nodes. The omission of any fixed structure for the organization of links allows for any thought to become a connection, with works emerging as the creator moves from thought to thought.

Passages are easily reorganized and moved, but their position has no impact on the story structure, offering authors a flexible design board for rethinking as they work.

Because it defies such easy categorization, Twine as a platform sits among many fields of study that we will draw on throughout this volume. Twine works evoke commentary on literary and aesthetic choices as well as design elements that center interaction and play. In this book, we will draw on the disciplines of literature (electronic and otherwise), film and media studies, games and software studies, and perhaps others as needed to make sense of Twine's influence. We hope the variety of our discussion is less "confounding" than thought-provoking or revealing, but in the words of an old hypertext fiction, "there is no simple way to say" what Twine means to us and the worlds in which we work—which brings us to another complexity (Joyce). This book contains more than commentary. Meant for active exploration as well as critical understanding, the book pairs each chapter of reflection with a chapter of practical exercises. Whatever else Twine may be, it is first for us a means for making.

However, as we reflect on Twine in 2020 in a time of international social distancing, we are also reminded that Twine's making is situated. Twine is continually reimagined in dialogue with cultural forces—and as a result of its continual usage in resisting the corporate hegemony of the games industry and the social-media-dominated, commercially platformized web. Twine encountered a surge of critical attention and visibility in 2014, at the height of Gamergate, a cultural war driven by misogyny and a reductive, purist view of gaming that left no room for the type of game-making that Twine enables. This attention took what is still a community-driven tool within games and interactive fiction spaces and moved it dramatically into the spotlight in a way that similar platforms, such as Inform 7, have rarely been centered, forever associating Twine with the culture wars even as its influence extends beyond that moment. Laura Hudson drew the popular gaze to Twine with her article on the phenomenon in the *New York Times*, which highlighted Twine (and Zoë Quinn's game *Depression Quest*) as the spark that fueled the raging conflict. Hudson calls Twine "the video-game technology for all" and, in doing so, cements Twine's centrality to alternative, personal game-making (Hudson). This emphasis on Twine's influence in games communities can be viewed as a reaction to the lack of inclusivity in mainstream gaming spaces, as Carolyn Petit pointed out in her 2013 essay on Twine's importance: "When games are by the people—by women and gay people and poor people and the culturally marginalized and kids growing up in Iran and not just primarily by the people who are paid to make them by companies selling products designed to appeal to as many customers as possible—they will inevitably be for the people, too. Twine is a small but important step in this direction" (Petit).

To its developers, Twine is a platform for making hypertextual things—a platform whose capabilities are continually being extended and reimagined in light of users' creative interventions. To its critics and advocates, Twine is a tool for resistance and even revolution—for defiance and reimagining the future of genres of media production that were otherwise closed and stagnant.

In the introduction to the pivotal Twine-centered collection *Videogames for Humans*, merritt k calls Twine the force behind a "quiet revolution": "Taken up by nontraditional game authors to describe distinctly nontraditional subjects—from struggles with depression, explorations of queer identity, and analyses of the world of modern sex and dating to visions of breeding crustacean horses in a dystopian future—the Twine movement to date has created space for those who have previously been voiceless within games culture to tell their own stories, as well as to invent new visions outside of traditional channels of commerce" (merritt k).

That collection documents Twine's revolutionary potential through the words of many of Twine's most influential creators, including Anna Anthropy, Christine Love, Zoë Quinn, and many others whose work we encounter here. To call such creative forces "users" of software is reductive—these creators have contributed to the platform, directly and indirectly, and provided the blueprints of how Twine works can explore the poetics of choice and its absence.

As scholars, we are admittedly adjacent to this revolution, looking in at least partly from the outside—and, some might argue, looking down from the relative privilege and financial comfort of the so-called ivory tower (although in the wake of COVID-19, that same tower's foundations are shaking, if not collapsing). This positionality also impacted our approach to interviews, and we frequently relied upon existing material rather than ask for further time and resources from the creators whose work we engage here. We understand and acknowledge the limitations (and risks) of the academic gaze. Yet our relationship with Twine is still personal, and it is this thinking that guides our approach to Twine throughout the book: the histories we tell acknowledge our relationships with the platform, its creators, and the works herein. Our work with Twine is entangled with our own histories—this book was written alongside several years of reading, making, and teaching with Twine. The final manuscript was submitted during the first uncertain months of COVID-19-enforced social distancing, which in turn reshaped our collective relationship with the web. Scholarship is always driven by one's own perspective and position but is not always forthright about this connection. We argue here that Twine works demand personal and emotional engagement as well as theoretical and intellectual engagement and that, at times, these lenses are inseparable.

About the Book

This book is unlike a lot of academic projects. Its concerns range from autoethnography to close reading to something like critical code studies, from the abstractions of Wallace Stevens to the polychrome delights of "trash spinning." It is both a critical study and a guide to creative practice. The mixed nature of the work flows from our subject, which is both a tool for making and a made thing. Twine is an unlikely proposition—a software platform crafted entirely by volunteers, some of whom have never met in person, and a worldwide community of creators who explore and expand the platform. To understand this phenomenon, we do a kind of history, or tell stories, primarily about the decade from 2009 to 2019 but with inevitable references to earlier moments—and also the present, as current events are very much with us.

About that "us"—the book is written in two voices, both of whom will say "I" on some occasions and may speak of themselves in the third person, though generally, you will find a broadly inclusive "we." Though we wrote this book together in equal measure, we are different people, one a scholar in midcareer, the other an old hand closer to the end. To compare great with small, it is worth remembering the way Deleuze and Guattari open *A Thousand Plateaus*, observing that "since each of us was several, there was already quite a crowd" (Deleuze and Guattari 3). Like most people loosely aligned with the digital humanities—and there may be no other way to toe that line—we are by turns creative and reflective. We make things with various tools and platforms and think about the implications of what we and others have made. In some cases, the making and the thinking may be hard to tell apart, which is fine.

Above all, this book is a fusion of theory and practice. That is why we called it what we did: *Twining*, a noun derived from a verb, a name for an action or activity. The organization of this book encourages you to take up Twine's invitation. Each section alternates between reflection and making. The treatments of theory (broadly construed) are labeled as T-X and position Twine as a platform and examine its trajectory of influence across cultural forms and domains. The practical segments, labeled as P-X, start with the fundamentals of Twine making, then explore different techniques and trajectories drawing upon ideas from the Twine creators whose work is examined throughout. Each example of practice includes its source code and thus can be modified, prodded, and remixed for your own purposes. Access this source code directly through the project's GitHub repository, Twining, at https://github.com/AMSUCF/Twining.

Note that throughout this work, references and URLs are given to projects that are, like the web itself, unstable. The reference locations provided are the last available versions of those resources: in some cases, they can be accessed via the Wayback Machine, but in other cases, they are lost to the web. We hope through this work to play a small part in preserving this important history of contributions through our discussions, citations, and screenshots but acknowledge that even as Twine will continue to change, even the source code for these examples (and, indeed, GitHub itself) might eventually disappear.

The narratives and play-centered examples focus on the personal, literary, expressive potential of Twine, and we hope they provide seeds for your own making. Throughout, we also point to the resources already created and shared within the Twine community, such as the open-source Twine Cookbook (Cox). We cover a few of Twine's major technical variations or *story formats*, generally sticking with the Chapbook format and others currently popular among makers and writers, although those trends are subject to change as new voices enter the authorial sphere. Community resources like the Cookbook and similar online documents offer tools for taking your next steps in Twine making.

In the first theoretical chapter, T-1, we position Twine as a platform, looking at the influence of open-source ethos on development and positioning it in relationship to other tools both hypertextual and games-leaning. What makes Twine appeal to marginalized communities in the forgotten corners of the web, and how is this positioning distinct from the tools that have preceded it (and will, perhaps inevitably, follow)? How does Twine's relationship to code and not-code play an integral role in its reception and cultural rise? The practical section similarly introduces Twine but with a lens toward making, introducing the fundamental practices of passages and links and exploring the underlying assumptions of the code.

The first practical chapter, P-1, introduces the interface and operating framework of Twine, laying out basic concepts and nomenclature. Each practical chapter works through a series of exercises or projects. The series in chapter P-1 explores basic hypertext linking, moving from linear to multilinear examples, exploring some of the creative and cognitive challenges of linked writing along the way. The mechanisms introduced are sufficient to create an expressive work in Twine: indeed, some of the most powerful works created make no use of the more elaborate mechanisms of code and audiovisual enhancement covered in the later chapters.

The second theoretical chapter, T-2, takes an autoethnographical lens to Twine, unraveling the complexities of thinking of Twine as a tool for simultaneously making things and challenging culture. Twine

is intensely personal as a platform—the most lasting and powerful stories that have emerged from it are often raw, vulnerable, and passion-
ate. Our connection to it is similarly personal and grounded in both
our own histories with the web and hypertext and our communities of
practice. We begin by positioning Twine and this relationship, thinking through Twine as a tool and using our own lens to get at the "why"
of Twine: Why is Twine significant now, in a media landscape where
hypertext has become mundane? In the practical section of chapter
two, we dive into variation, examining Twine's take on the variable and
looking across the range of Twine's capabilities.

The second practical chapter, P-2, addresses the theme of variation
on several levels: the potential for variable text within Twine works,
the multiplicity of styles available to Twine writers, and the variations
of the software itself, ranging across story formats and scripting resources. The examples move beyond simple node-link replacement to
explore techniques in which Twine texts can change either between
readings or as we read them, in response to random selection or reader
choices. This chapter includes two projects using Harlowe, a story format with more robust scripting support.

The third theory chapter, T-3, takes up the (for some) uncomfortable question of how Twine works fit into literary traditions—if at all. It
works through commentaries on two Twine works, John McDaid's *We
Knew the Glass Man* (2019) and Porpentine's *With Those We Love Alive*
(2014). The first work looks back in irony toward high modernism, invoking the ghost of Wallace Stevens. The second work lives in a more
contemporary world of dark fantasy and the milieu of independent game
creation. These works are discussed both as narratives and as technical
achievements, with a detailed examination of parts of their code. To understand *With Those We Love Alive* as a game, it is compared to Valve's
classic *Portal* series, another story of mothers, daughters, and dungeons.

Chapter P-3 builds on the concepts of textual variation introduced
in the previous practical chapter to explore the idea of text generation:
assembling readable content by selecting from a set of components according to some logical procedure. The chapter introduces a primary
design pattern, the substitution grammar, which will be used in later

chapters. This chapter moves deeper into programming, considering a more ambitious use of variables in Chapbook as well as the inclusion of JavaScript code, an especially powerful affordance of this story format.

In chapter T-4, we turn our attention from the text to Twine's visual and dynamic aesthetics and the visual play at work in camp works built in Twine. Positioning this play with color, animation, and throwback web elements in relationship to camp, we consider the rise of Twine as a platform for queer storytelling and resistant play. Through an examination of works that have come to define Twine's influence, we note how the association of Twine with marginalized creators and the poetics of queer storytelling have shaped the platform. Given the dominant heteronormativity and transphobia of the wider games discourse, we note the importance of queer Twine as a point of departure and resistance.

Chapter P-4 explores the "too much"-ness of Twine, with projects exploring ways to add excess through movement, audiovisuals, and external JavaScript libraries such as Kate Compton's powerful procedural grammar, Tracery. In these exercises, we explore the practical side of developing camp Twine and explore the techniques Twine creators have used to break their players' expectations of the medium while incorporating aesthetic playfulness, visual extremes, and novelty.

In the last of the theory chapters, T-5, we bring together the insurgent impulses of camp Twine and the claims of literary legacy by looking at Twine works in a critical moment—both a moment of crisis (inevitably) and an opportunity for critical intervention or decision. The ultimate focus of this chapter is Anna Anthropy's game of apocalypse, *Queers in Love at the End of the World* (2013), which we examine through lenses including queer gaming and game narrative generally, reading it against Davey Wreden's art game *The Beginner's Guide* (2015) as well as other references in various media.

The final practical chapter, P-5, is devoted to projects that move beyond technique to concept. Its series of examples explore various ways stories and games made with Twine can call attention to and investigate their own forms and the nature of stories, games, and language itself. Using Chapbook exclusively, the chapter covers almost no new technical material but is intended instead to consolidate practical understanding and emphasize the connection between technical exploits and the development of meaning.

Following the last practical chapter is a conclusion that takes up skeptical questions about Twine concerning its aesthetics, its creative community, and its economic basis. Though acknowledging a mixed outlook, especially in the last area, the chapter offers three arguments for the continued development of Twine, based on the "cognitive mapping" of platform capitalism, the contribution of computational creativity to language, and, ultimately, on unabashedly personal investments in a multigenerational project.

Three supplementary sections round out the book: an interview conducted with Chris Klimas during our early research, an interview with Dan Cox, author of the Twine Cookbook and other key resources, and a bonus practical chapter that bridges Twine techniques to forms of web coding independent of that platform. While these techniques go beyond Twine, they demonstrate Twine's role as part of an ecosystem and its educational potential as a path to other web development platforms and approaches.

On a technical note, wherever possible, examples will be updated in the online edition of this work to reflect changing Twine standards. However, obsolescence is inevitable, and in that spirit, we hope to provide both the context and the way of thinking for working with Twine as well as code in the hopes that one of these things will outlive the other. When preservation is no longer viable, this work will serve as a record of the Twine that was and hopefully provide some inspiration for what comes after. The future of Twine will likely be more fragmented than its current iteration—already, different story formats within Twine require different syntaxes and focus on more specialized use cases or ways of thinking about making. Given that, it is important to attend to the specifics of the practical chapters and note the formats each example is coded to use.

As an open-source platform, Twine reflects its creators' dedication to making a tool that could be used widely and freely. This book is similarly open access, intended as a gift back to the Twine community.

We particularly hope that in the coming years, as Twine continues to serve as a platform for sharing and imagining the future, our words will in some way provide a starting point for new voices.

Finally, we want to express gratitude to a number of people who have helped us finish this project. We thank our editor at Amherst College Press, Beth Bouloukos, and the readers of our first draft, who have made the book substantially better, as well as the technical editorial team from Scribe Inc. for their detailed attention. Noah Wardrip-Fruin of the University of California, Santa Cruz, gave crucial feedback on parts of the manuscript. Colleagues and graduate students at UCF and the University of Wisconsin–Milwaukee have shaped our thinking and tested our code. Dan Cox's Twine resources and work, as well as his generosity in engaging with drafts and technical errors in this volume, have been invaluable. Any remaining errors are our own. Thank you to all the creative voices reflected here—and particularly to Chris Klimas for Twine itself.

Works Cited

Cox, Dan, ed. "iftechfoundation / twine-cookbook." 2017. GitHub. Accessed 2019. https://github.com/iftechfoundation/twine-cookbook.

Deleuze, Gilles, and Félix Guattari. *A Thousand Plateaus: Capitalism and Schizophrenia.* Translated by Brian Massumi. University of Minnesota Press, 1987.

Deyke, G., and Damon L. Wakes. "Quarantine Quest." itch.io, April 2020. https://gdeyke.itch.io/quarantine-quest.

Hudson, Laura. "Twine, the Video-Game Technology for All." *New York Times*, November 19, 2014. https://www.nytimes.com/2014/11/23/magazine/twine-the-video-game-technology-for-all.html.

Joyce, Michael. *afternoon, a story.* Tinker's Dam Press, 1986.

Klimas, Chris. "klembot / twinejs." Github, 2019. https://github.com/klembot/twinejs.

merritt k, ed. *Videogames for Humans: Twine Authors in Conversation.* Instar Books, 2015.

Petit, Carolyn. "Power to the People: The Text Adventures of Twine." GameSpot, January 21, 2013. https://www.gamespot.com/articles/power-to-the-people-the-text-adventures-of-twine/1100-6402665/.

sub-Q. "Developer Interview: Chris Klimas." August 20, 2015. https://sub-q.com/developer-interview-chris-klimas/.

Twine as Platform

We have introduced Twine, and indeed, Twine has more widely been studied, primarily through the works it enables. This raises a preliminary question: What is Twine for, and what do we call the things it makes? This simple question holds the shadow of a much larger history of definitional tension surrounding games and what "counts." More importantly, who gets to decide what—and, by extension, who—counts as part of the discourse of game design? The shadow of a history of misogyny, exclusion, racism, labor abuses, and general awfulness in video game culture looms large over this question. We will wrestle with Twine's place (and our own) in this history throughout our study of Twine, and if you engage in the making of Twine works as our practical chapters invite you to do, you, too, might find yourself facing questions of where your work fits—and what it should be called.

In academic circles, the desire for definitional clarity might be understood through the discourse of formalism or (broadly) the placement and understanding of a work according to its structure. And formally speaking, Twine works are near immediately recognizable unless their creators go through significant work modifying the final interface: while each story format (a set of rules that overlay Twine's central logic) has its signature interface design, the general structure of passage-driven, hyperlinked narrative holds. The two generations of the Twine editor are fundamentally similar, as the dominant meta-phors remain consistent, but they differ in the details. Rather like a branching Twine narrative, the history of Twine and its significance as a platform is a threaded, nonlinear tale, and how we tell it depends on where we begin in defining Twine works. This is no small decision, so before we make it, let me move toward a definition that will resist completion and finality as we move through this work. The front page of www.twinery.org offers a straightforward summary of the platform that notably makes no mention of games, a deliberate omission we will return to shortly:

> You don't need to write any code to create a simple story with Twine, but you can extend your stories with variables, conditional logic, im-ages, CSS, and JavaScript when you're ready.
>
> Twine publishes directly to HTML, so you can post your work nearly anywhere. Anything you create with it is completely free to use any way you like, including for commercial purposes.
>
> Twine was originally created by Chris Klimas in 2009 and is now maintained by a whole bunch of people at several different repositories. (Klimas, "Twine")

This initial definition suggests that Twine works are, most funda-mentally, stories. The reality is more complicated. Twine has been used recursively as a tool to build tutorials; rhetorically as a tool for argu-ments and essays; abstractly for poetry and generative art; and edu-cationally for making materials across disciplines, to name only a few instances.

More recently, the Twine Cookbook, maintained by Dan Cox, breaks down these features into usable demos across the many ver-sions, or formats, of Twine. The Cookbook notes that the terms used in Twine are intended to be not limitations but opportunities: "Anything made using Twine can be called by any name. They are no rules on naming conventions and everything from experimental games to more traditional novels can be created in Twine. Everything is welcome. In general, the Twine editor calls individual projects Stories" (Cox, "if-techfoundation / twine-cookbook").

When we call Twine a software platform for the development of games and interactive stories, we risk being simultaneously reductive and overgenerous with our description: not all things made with Twine fall into these easy categories, and as a software platform, Twine can make pretty much any genre of interactive text the user envisions. The term *software platform* evokes Lev Manovich's discussions of the power of "cultural software" in shaping (and allowing users to shape) culture, from Adobe Photoshop and Flash to Microsoft's Visual Studio (Manovich 3). Within this space, Manovich argues for the need for software studies focusing on a range of categories of application: within his hierarchy, Twine falls perhaps most easily into the category of "media software" or content creation software broadly (Manovich 24). It is in its resemblance to the tools of this category (graphical interface–driven metaphors of making) rather than the programming-driven category that Manovich describes as falling outside of this mainstream thanks to the dividing line of code: "Today, a typical professional graphic designer, film editor, product designer, architect, music artist—and certainly a typical person uploading videos to YouTube or adding photos and video on her/his blog—can neither write nor read software code. (Being able to read and modify HTML markup, or copy already prepackaged lines of JavaScript code is very different from programming)" (Manovich 31).

The dismissal of basic web development as "different" from programming in Manovich's parenthetical is notable, particularly as the book *Software Takes Command* was published in 2013—the same year public media attention was drawn to Anna Anthropy's "Twine revolution," where she offered an explanation of Twine's appeal that similarly put it in a category separate from programming: "This last year . . . people have really adopted Twine, which is a free tool for making text games. And aside from being free, it's really not programming at all—if you can write a story, you can make a Twine game" (Ellison).

Both Manovich and Anthropy draw a line around programming, a term that carries with it heavy baggage of gatekeeping and a recent history of exclusion (again, the shadow of who counts—and who owns—the culture of Silicon Valley and its global influence looms large). They focus their gazes on something else: the type of cultural software that allows anyone to make, presuming some foundational digital literacy. This association of Twine with the absence of programming is, of course, illusory: as you will experience in the practical chapters, Twine is entangled with code, and the code is at some level inescapable. "Code" itself has many layers of meaning and nuance: markup languages such as HTML primarily annotate and structure content, while scripting languages such as JavaScript center on interactivity. Twine adds its own layers over both, but in simplifying, it also imposes its own new structures and abstractions. While the graphical user interface (GUI) significantly draws the user into hyperlinked visual making, the passage boxes awaiting content must ultimately be programmed in that strict rules must be followed to ensure readability following the procedures of Twine's underlying machine. This contradiction is at Twine's heart: it is a piece of cultural software that allows a user to build complex interactivity toward many ends, and it invites the user into a rabbit hole of complexity where the entryway is paved with language, not code. As the user moves forward, Manovich's dismissal might even be reassuring: this disguised HTML, and precorralled JavaScript, is not programming at all.

This allure of Twine is, of course, not true at a fundamental level: Twine is code, and Twine-making is programming, but its structures are designed with user experience at the forefront. The tension between what Twine makes easy and what Twine makes possible is immense, and as is common to communally supported software projects, the complexity of entry to Twine has risen with its increased versatility even as the variety of entry points and tutorials available has also grown, complete with whole texts dedicated to learning Twine: Melissa Ford's *Writing Interactive Fiction* and Anna Anthropy's *Making Games with Twine*. Both of these books are notably aimed at the game development community of Twine.

Twine and Games

Though the definition of Twine provided on its own website omits the term *games*, a history of the platform that begins with usage (or starts in the tutorials, textbooks, and examples that have gained notoriety) cannot escape the term *games*. This term is hotly contested, all the more so as of 2019, as I type these words five years after the anniversary of Gamergate (whose specter haunts Twine and this work). In their provocatively titled book *Real Games*, Mia Consalvo and Christopher Paul examine the contested definitions of *game* and its impact on what gets studied, critiqued, and ultimately preserved: "Game studies academics are themselves variably interested in what constitutes a real game as a way to legitimate the field and define an area of study. What gets left out of structuralist arguments is the value judgment going into labels such as game or not game. If something is not a game, then it is decidedly less important from the field's perspective" (Consalvo and Paul xxv–xxvi).

In opening this volume, it is tempting to position Twine as a games platform and to categorize Twine works as games. Developing such a common framework would give us the language of games studies for addressing Twine's value—and critiquing its structures—but more urgently, it would also give us an easy case for Twine's significance. Such a claim would likely not go uncontested for long: in an entire volume dedicated to reclaiming and examining cases of "not games" ranging from Facebook games to walking simulators, Consalvo and Paul do not mention Twine or even interactive fiction. The "not games" they identify as edge cases are in many ways closer to gamelike expectations than Twine works. This is not to say there has been no intersection of this discourse: indeed, there is a fundamental awareness of formalism embedded in Twine. Twine creators have wrestled with the question of the platform's game-ness and, in doing so, give us an entry point into positioning Twine as a form.

The extremism with which the word *game* is regulated inspired the Twine metawork *Is This a Game?* released by the Game Police in 2013. The work asks users humorously to consider the degradation of language that might result if the player calls the work in question a game.

This "linguistic singularity" path, if pursued, results in the player faced only with the word *game* repeating meaninglessly. Commenting on the game's message, critic Steve Haske observed, "Meanwhile, you can choose to change your mind, rescinding your decision to call this thing a game. It creates an interesting food-for-thought Catch-22: if you opt out, then you haven't just played a game. If you don't, you may not have the 'game' experience you thought you would (though you can confusingly find an inherent design)" (Haske).

Figure 2 captures the rhetorical style of the game (or not game), which deliberately uses a mostly unmodified version of the Twine Sugarcane style sheet, capturing the aesthetic associated with Twine most widely at the time. The game later takes this a step further, demonstrating how its meaning eventually collapses under the weight of the word *game* by literally replacing all other previously displayed text and offering only the same word as a choice. While perhaps unsubtle, this work is very much a product of its time, offering a playable entry point into the controversy over whose work counts in the game world.

This controversy was not one with merely academic stakes. In the same year, the literal "game police" of Steam Greenlight were deciding

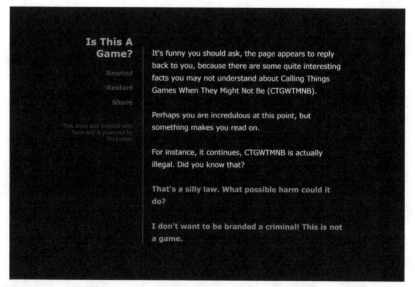

Figure 2: *Is This a Game?* escalates questions of formalism

whether a Twine game, *Depression Quest*, could be included on the game storefront. Being present on Steam opens up a market of opportunities for a designer, and Zoë Quinn's work, tagged by them as "interactive (non)fiction," would be the subject of hostility and debate. While the game was released in 2013 and had already been recognized as a game within independent spaces (including winning Best Narrative Game at Boston FIG and Official Selection at Indiecade 2013), one of the most popular discussion threads on the Steam Greenlight page asked, "Can this be counted as a game?" (Quinn).

Also in 2013, as questions of game-ness were rising around the independent-developer scene, critic Leigh Alexander offered a provocation on Twitter in defense of the type of experiences represented by *Depression Quest* and other works: "When people say games need objectives in order to be 'games,' i wonder why 'better understanding another human' isn't a valid 'objective.' . . . Games need 'challenges' and 'rules,' isn't 'empathy' a challenge, aren't preconceptions of normativity a 'rule'[?]" (Alexander). Alexander's tweet was not well received and escalated the debate as others joined in defending the formalist approach as essential to drawing lines to define the object of study.

Designer and critic Raph Koster responded to this provocation with a blog post entitled "A Letter to Leigh" that, among other critiques of noninteractivity, asked why the games don't in turn show more empathy for him as a player: "But I also find myself looking to the future, where I hope the games have empathy for the player, rather than the other way around, because it is a far harder artistic, and empathic, challenge to understand an opposing point of view than it is to present one's own. I'll be entertained by a rant I agree with, and angered by a rant I don't, but a debate is far more likely to change my mind" (Koster).

Darius Kazemi's "On Formalism" offers a playable response to that letter, taking a quote from Koster and centering it on the screen while offering a critique of Twine as a platform through code. It opens unassumingly, presenting as a classic Twine 1.X[1] work with the hallmarks of

---

1 For readers not familiar with this software naming convention, 1.X indicates any of several serialized releases in the first series of an application (1.1, 1.2.3, 1.999, etc.), 2.X indicates any release in the second series, and so on.

SugarCube (a story format for Twine with a side bar and restart button). Press "click to continue," however, and the screen breaks free. The passage starts to move, and the player's clicks turn into a weapon gradually reducing the words to nothing (as shown in figure 3). When the game was posted by Porpentine to the *Free Indie Games* blog in 2013, it inspired a debate about the definitions of interactivity and dialogue (Porpentine, "On Formalism").

In these critiques, formalism is a stand-in for the larger debate of where games begin and end—a debate that is used primarily to exclude and gatekeep—that also asks us to question our relationship with games and the assumptions that the very term makes us bring to our interactions with a work. Game designer Robert Yang's own blog post in response to Koster's (entitled, recursively, "A Letter to a Letter") further highlights the problematic aspects of Koster's claim, which Kazemi's work makes playable (while resisting "dialogue"): "I do think that you imply that this inability to separate content from form is an inherent (formal) weakness of personal games and the ways they mean things. That, because these games can't fit into a formalist frame,

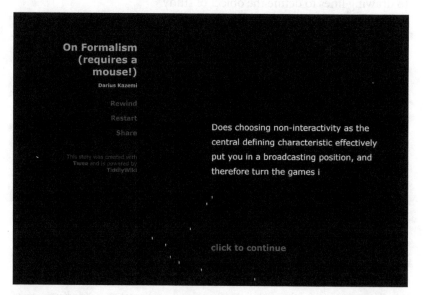

Figure 3: The weaponization and transformation of "On Formalism" after clicking

they are thus less gamelike. Instead, I'd argue that this is a weakness of a traditional formalist approach: mechanics are often boring / limit what authors can do with games. . . . 'Dialogue,' on an oppressor's terms, rarely results in empathy" (Yang).

In labeling something as a game, we might limit it; similarly, in labeling something not a game, we potentially exclude it, and its creators, from the discourse of games and what games might be. These challenges are worth pausing on here, as we operate with an awareness and interest in Twine's place as a hypertextual platform but also see the undeniable significance of claiming this platform in the name of games: not just for what it does for Twine but for what it does for games. It is no coincidence that these definitional debates accompany the cultural challenges to Twine, which we will examine in more detail throughout this book. Given these tensions, I want to stress that in examining Twine as a platform, we are not taking a formalist lens; instead, we want to consider how Twine's affordances have played a role in making certain types of experiments easier. To start with a simple claim, many of the games and experiences that have been made in Twine center on the personal, and the platform's affordances seem to map well to expressions that put the mechanics of choice—and denial of choice—at the forefront.

In her examination of the framing of Twine as a game platform alongside these tensions, Alison Harvey notes that the community's fundamental ethos plays a major role in framing the type of work produced: while many game tools offer tutorials based on shooting and conflict, Twine collections and tutorials place their emphasis on "a different set of preferred affordances" (Harvey 98). Look at the tutorials for Stencyl, GameMaker, Unity, and so forth: mechanics of movement, violence, and acquisition dominate the expressive palette, pushing early designers to imitate that which is already established (as broadening the vocabulary of a graphical game is a different challenge than empowering verbs in Twine). Similarly, game designer and Twine luminary Mattie Brice expressed her thoughts on games as objects in response to these debates:

There is much to be said in the way of a game's form. How is it structured, and how does that structure make a difference? Let's say someone submits something that doesn't look like a poem to a poetry contest. The judges don't necessarily go "This isn't a poem, therefore, it is not worth considering." Rather, the form itself critiques the established genre, it says "I'm a poem, and what are you going to do about it?" The formal genres in writing are for convenience only—ultimately, the kind of criticism needed for flash fiction, prose poems, short stories, novellas, and novels, is ultimately one in [sic] the same. Maybe everything is really just poetry. Boundaries, bones of old men before us, are only there to be transgressed. (Brice)

As a platform, Twine inherits this contradiction. It is structurally familiar and formally suggests so many antecedents that it does not at first glance appear transgressive—and yet it transgresses and transforms.

Transforming Hypertext

If we limit the lens of Twine as a platform to games, we ignore the other spaces that Twine has transformed, including hypertext itself and interactive fiction more broadly. Drawing on interviews with developers and community members as well as the embodied history of Twine within forums, mailing lists, and the code database, we will position Twine as a communal, open-source project. Positioning Twine alongside other platforms of the web (including precursors HyperCard, Storyspace, and Flash) offers insight into Twine's significance, which is not only a matter of interface and affordances. We will consider Twine's positioning within communities such as Glorious Trainwrecks, Tumblr, itch.io, and Philome.la and how the circulation and discourse within these spaces have shaped Twine's life-span and influence. Astrid Ensslin and Lyle Skains observe that Twine's rise is a rejection of exclusivity and platform control enabling a "writerly reader," or "(w)reader": this "(w)readerly empowerment through co-creation of narrative meaning cannot be imposed through forms, texts, and theories that imply exclusivity of access and assume that deconstructivist thought can be implemented through manifest literary materiality. Instead, movements like the Twine community and participatory social media writing have shown that genuine wreadership has to come from users themselves, driven by the aesthetic and social needs of their own communities . . . and the desire to get published as an experimental creative writer" (Ensslin and Skains). While Twine is "owned" in a sense—and, with the increased control of the Interactive Fiction Technology Foundation (IFTF) over its future, communally owned—it is not a closed or corporate platform, and its output is entirely open to reverse engineering, making it a purer form of hypertext in that it fundamentally compiles into open web standards.

Twine is responsive to its moment and the platforms that precede it: most of the earlier platforms are united by their reliance on proprietary, corporate-owned technologies. The web is littered with the unplayable or occasionally emulated remains of works built on these platforms: Apple's HyperCard, perhaps the first popular hypertext platform, vanished as the company shifted direction; Eastgate's Storyspace supported hypertext works sold on removable media that are now almost entirely unplayable; and so forth. The proprietary ecosystems and walled gardens of currently popular ecosystems for games and electronic literature, such as iOS and Android, are similarly fraught with demands for continual updates that, if unmet, render work unplayable. By contrast, the web's standards have been relatively reliable. It would be an exaggeration to say that HTML is still what it once was—open a browser source of the original HTML and HTML 5 and compare, and the tags are certainly similar, but the act of translation required is daunting. Fundamentally, we rely on this backward compatibility: we assume that all other platforms might fail us, but the web lives on. The dominant force in emulation is the Internet Archive: Jason Scott and his team have made it possible to reexperience many of the works created on platforms that have fallen by the wayside.

There are many visual entry points into hypertext, but most of them bring with them expectations of a corporate purpose or information architecture–driven organization system. Adobe Dreamweaver, with its drag-and-drop interface elements and GUI-driven editor, is in stark contrast to the playfulness of Flash. The WordPress interface (and similar content management systems) emphasizes a separation between form and content, offering modifiable themes and blocks of content that do not easily lend themselves to narrative. Meanwhile, opening up an .html file and starting from scratch can quickly become a logistical nightmare when it comes to tracking: nonlinear work requires fragmentation, and those fragmentations require significant marking with IDs (and tracking of past links) to navigate. In an early reflection on hypertext literacy, "Nonce upon Some Times," Michael Joyce notes that the "paradox" of hypertext relies on rereading, and that same rereading makes development difficult without a dedicated tool for visualizing the work:

> Hypertext fiction in some fundamental sense depends upon rereading (or the impossibility of ever truly doing so) for its effects. Yet in a sufficiently complex and richly contingent hypertext it is impossible to reread even a substantial portion of the possible sequences. Indeed for any but a reader who has consciously blazed his way through the thicket (breadcrumbs, in fact, have become a technical term for computer tools designed to keep track of the reading of hypertexts) it is unlikely that successive readings by a single reader will be in any significant way alike. Even in less vigorous hypertext systems such as current instantiations of the World Wide Web, bereft of the systematic memory that shapes possible readings, the linked surfaces of possibility themselves compound. (Joyce)

Joyce writes in the earliest stages of hypertext, before the link became utilitarian and familiar, so transparent as to become unremarkable. However, he draws our attention to the ways hypertextual linking can be playful, creative, and confounding, defying the utilitarian future of the web.

Reconsidering Joyce's concept of hypertext, and particularly his emphasis on defining the link, Emily Short notes, "From the perspective of more than twenty years later, many of Joyce's observations feel like first pen-and-paper cartographical attempts on a territory that has now been explored very extensively on foot" (Short). The type of nuanced links that Joyce and Short describe were not built into the initial Twine but evolved thanks to user-developers pushing Twine's utility forward.

Among those, one of the most significant developments is the cycling link, a structure that allows the user to click and replace a piece of text repeatedly from a set of options prewritten by the designer. (We retrace this evolution in the next practical chapter, concentrating on textual variation.) Porpentine documented the impact of Leon Arnott's cycling link macro in a blog post examining *Candy Ant Princess*, a game by Whisperbat that makes extensive use of the system to allow the player to make aesthetic choices that occasionally impact play. As Porpentine summarizes, this makes the difference between creating passages for every link and treating links as choices directly, as shown in figure 4 (Porpentine, "Live Free, Play Hard").

Though this will seem an odd observation in a book about Twine, in many ways, Twine appears unnecessary. It is an interface built on top of hypertext: everything that can be accomplished in Twine can be accomplished with HTML and JavaScript, albeit with more difficulty. Thus considered as a platform, Twine is not about the resulting work; it is entirely about the means of production. At the same time, Twine's particular mechanisms (the things that each generation, and each story format, makes easy) transform the resulting work, with cycling links as

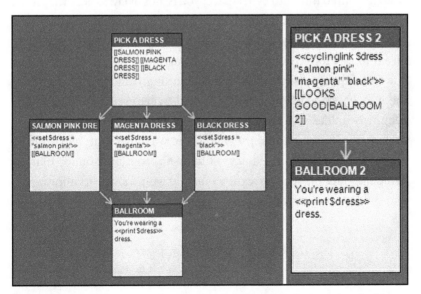

Figure 4: Choosing clothing in Twine 1.X with and without cycling links

just one example of the expanding vocabulary Twine offers with each iteration. Twine's tools allow creators to create new poetics of the link and particularly allow someone who might use Twine next to pick up and expand those poetics with relative ease. The consistency of the interface shapes the experience and the player's expectations for what a Twine work can be.

Twine's construction as a tool for facilitating a type of web production is far from unique. WYSIWYG (What You See Is What You Get) web editors have been around for almost as long as websites themselves, from the built-in tools of community hubs such as GeoCities and Angelfire to the unwieldy, mangled-code-generating FrontPage and Dreamweaver, but without the writerly metaphor that Twine's story assumption foregrounds. All this is a roundabout way of saying that what Twine makes easy is superficially simple but difficult in practice. The shortcuts are not just pragmatic code solutions but also visual navigation, and thus the most crucial element of Twine for many users is the GUI itself. To recall Steven Johnson's *Interface Culture*, the link is the center of hypertext, the first marker of meaning-making in digital navigation whose current ubiquity makes us forget its initial impact: "Ask any Web user to recall what first lured him into cyberspace; you're not likely to hear rhapsodic descriptions of a twirling animated graphic or a thin, distorted sound clip. No, the eureka moment for most of us came when we first clicked on a link, and found ourselves jettisoned across the planet. The freedom and immediacy of that movement—shuttling from site to site across the infosphere, following trails of thought wherever they led us—was genuinely unlike anything before it" (110).

It is this origin point of the link where we find Twine: a realization of the "freedom and immediacy" of Johnson's web, built on top of not a game interface but a hypertextual one that would shape its affordances and the expectations of its users going forward.

Contextualizing Twee

A short history of Twine starts not with Twine itself but with a scripting language called Twee, based on an earlier writing system called

TiddlyWiki, a tool for creating user-modifiable hypertexts, or wikis. Twee lacks the visual interface of Twine but encodes the fundamental underlying mechanics: it is the scripting language that precedes the graphical interface. In the interview he gave for this book (appendix I), Klimas described TiddlyWiki's self-modifying codex as too limited for the types of hypertexts he wanted to create—thus he set out to visualize a better tool, which would become Twee:

> I ran across this technology called TiddlyWiki, and it was this really clever thing where it was this self-modifying Web page. . . . You download it to your computer, you can edit it, it's like a wiki but there's no server component to it at all, and so it's like a very simple . . . DIY hypertext. And so I started editing and playing out stuff in there and experimenting with that medium . . . and it just got very disorienting, actually, to try to edit it from inside . . . where I'd click links, and follow them, and it's like—where am I? And so I'd get lost in my own stuff, and that was sort of the genesis: I want to build a tool that will help me do this better. (Klimas, appendix I)

In his oral history of Twee, Dan Cox notes that several derivative works perform a similar function, using output to bridge to other formats: Cradle, or UnityTwine (2015); Yarn (2015); Tweego (2013); Twee2 (2015); Entweedle (2015); and Entwee (2016); among others (Cox, "An Oral History of Twee"). The range of these should not necessarily be confused with influence—many of these projects are driven by the needs of their developers.

TiddlyWiki creator Jeremy Ruston remembers the allure of early web wikis that inspired his design of the system and particularly the idea of breaking out a single document model of development, which in turn would inspire Twee and Twine:

> The allure of the wiki for me was the feeling that it could eventually disrupt the prevailing paradigm of print-oriented documents and emails.
>
> After watching people use wikis for a few years, I noticed that power users made extensive use of the ability to open multiple wiki pages at

once in several browser tabs, making it easier for them to compare and
review pages, to copy text between them and to act as a sort of queue
of pages yet to be read.

 I felt that this ability to manipulate multiple pages at once was central to the ability to refactor a wiki, and it is generally accepted that a
wiki that is lovingly refactored tends to be more useful. And yet, standard wiki user interfaces have always been designed exclusively for the
presentation and manipulation of single pages at once. (Ruston)

The newest iteration of TiddlyWiki maintains that concept of nonlinear organization, inviting users with the question, "Have you ever
had the feeling that your head is not quite big enough to hold everything you need to remember?" (TiddlyWiki). This evokes similar nonlinear tools built around organization, such as Evernote and Microsoft
OneNote. The original Twee website maintained by Klimas in 2005
explains Twee's origin as emerging from his desire to have a text-driven
interface for working with TiddlyWiki:

Twee is a supersimple markup language for TiddlyWikis. It was invented when Chris spilled water on his laptop's trackpad, which
knocked it out of commission temporarily, and he still wanted to work
on his TiddlyWiki.

 In short, Twee lets you turn plain text files that look like this:

```
:: Twee [systemConfig]
Twee is a supersimple [[markup language]] for
~TiddlyWikis.
```

. . . into living, breathing TiddlyWikis. Right now, it allows you to target
the latest version of TiddlyWiki, TiddlyWiki 1.2.39, Twinkie, and iPods.
It also includes untwee, a tool that converts existing TiddlyWikis to
Twee source code. (Klimas, "Code and Other Oddments")

The legacy of the text version comes through in the earliest graphical iterations of Twine. In Twine 1.X, users were not by default introduced to the concept of incorporating Cascading Style Sheets (CSS)

and JavaScript into their work. Jane Friedhoff describes Twine's original user interface as using the "corkboard paradigm," which essentially means that Twine offers the same visual space and freedom as rearranging materials on a corkboard, including ease of movement and the ability to get a big-picture perspective. She notes, "This kind of visual, spatial practice is relatively rare in the coding world (outside of patching languages, such as MaxMSP), but it is very similar to the way many writers plan and organize their stories" (Friedhoff).

The passage interface did not distinguish between, or provide a specific space for, adding such code, leaving users to follow tutorials to incorporate "tagging" to mark special passages for this purpose. Twine 2.X is more elaborate in its initial assumptions and includes by default a separate style sheet and scripting area, with boilerplate guidance for incorporating CSS to properly link to the tags and structures of Twine. Twine 2's most dramatic innovation is the browser-based editor, which offers the next level of accessibility for users unable to install software. The 2.X editor is still not ideal for use outside of a desktop or laptop computer (similarly, Twine works are mobile-passable but only mobile-friendly when intentionally modified by the designer with the touchscreen user in mind). This shift reflects a shift in assumptions about the use cases for Twine, which have over time fallen more into classroom usage as well as general interest as an introductory development tool.

The story formats—or rulesets and paradigms that provide different ways of making in Twine (discussed in more detail in chapter P-1)—included in Twine 1.X are Jonah, Sugarcane, and Responsive. Later, SugarCube and Snowman would appear. By far the dominant story format for designers was Sugarcane (and by extension, SugarCube): the other two pushed more specific aesthetics onto users. The format called Jonah emphasizes the single page, requiring text that is designed to stretch and accrete rather than replacing one passage with another. Twine 2 removes the awkwardness of Twine's original distinction between a .tws source file and the .html output, removing the need for tracking and preservation of both the Twine editor's code and the browser's readable output. From a preservation standpoint, this strengthens Twine's longevity, as the final .html is its own complete archive. Notably, a tool for reverse engineering .html works in Twine 1.X now exists, which eliminates the need to have the source file in order to investigate the complete work. As a platform, Twine is thus continually expanding outward in the hands of its users. The Twine 2 Monogatari story format, for instance, allows users to build from the Twine syntax to create web-friendly visual novels (Pinheiro).

Twine's Spread

Traditionally, platform studies approaches have examined corporate-controlled ecosystems, usually regulated by the producer of the hardware or software in question (Bogost and Montfort). Open-source platforms raise different questions and simultaneously offer clearer attribution, thanks to the documentation of contributions on platforms such as GitHub and murkier ownership and control. Friedhoff notes that the lack of a regulated distribution model is essential to the success of Twine's more queer, erotic, political, and otherwise experimental titles that would likely not make it past the review standards of most other platforms (Friedhoff). Simply put, most Twine works would not—could not—exist in the wild without Twine's self-distributed, easily spreadable modality.

The Interactive Fiction Database (IFDB), an archive of digital writing now sponsored by IFTF, primarily chronicles work by designers who came in contact with or embraced the term *interactive fiction* for their work, while the curation blog *Free Indie Games*—founded by Terry Cavanagh and featuring several developers, including Porpentine—offers a counterhistory heavily emphasizing Twine from 2012 to 2014 (*Free Indie Games*).

Probing the history of Twine through the IFDB returns a few false starts: humorously, Anna Anthropy's Twine iteration of Nintendo Power's 1990 feature *Dragon Warrior Text Adventure* is listed under this date despite having been published in 2013. The game is primarily notable for its nostalgia (Nintendo Power and Anthropy). While this is one of the more extreme examples of Twine as a preservation/emulation tool, this trend continues in the second earliest publication noted: the 2006 entry for *Escape from the Crazy Place* refers to the 2017 version of what the authors call "a preposterous blob of literary jelly" that has previous lives in physical text, classic HTML, and the 2006 version in the Text Adventure Development System (TADS; Guest and Etheridge). The work is also an instance of collaborative Twine-writing, as its lead author describes in the Glorious Trainwrecks post announcing the Twine version:

> Written over 33 years, Escape from the Crazy Place is a sprawling TWINE game with over 90,000 words of text. It is also an example of exquisite corpse writing, combining the talents of around twenty different authors. Some wrote just a passage or two, others wrote dozens.
>
> This new TWINE version was originally intended to be a trimmed-down, more polished version of the 2006 TADS 2 version, but myself and my friends Loz Etheridge and Mark Bailey got a bit carried away, and somehow or other the 2017 version ended up being two-and-a-half times the size of the original. The game will continue to expand as I intend never to stop adding to it. (Guest)

TADS, originally released in 1988 and last updated in 2006, stands in contrast to Twine in its code-focused approach that resembles the programming language C. It also offers a different, code-grounded vision than another system often mentioned in the same breath as Twine: Inform 7. Created in 1993 by Graham Nelson, Inform 7 is Twine's most popular cousin in the interactive fiction arena. Inform 7 boasts the appeal of "natural language processing correlation between system and output" that has been noted in early interactive fiction platform studies: Alex Mitchell and Montfort note that both TADS and Inform, the dominant interactive fiction creation platforms as they were writing in 2009, are driven by software objects and that the model of object-oriented, category-driven programming, in turn, suggests a "simulationist" approach to design (Mitchell and Montfort). Mitchell and Montfort draw the term *simulationism* from the interactive fiction community, defined as "the tendency towards deeper and less abstract simulation of physical (and possibly emotional) properties of the game world, not for limited domains that the author has chosen, but as a general framework," with corresponding challenges for development: "Interactive fiction systems already face the problem of generating human-like text to describe situations arising in games. The list of objects in a drawer is generated from the underlying world model. The problem with simulationist IF is that this becomes a magnitude more complicated" (Mitchelhill).

Twine is the antithesis of this model. Originating in JavaScript (a non-object-oriented programming language that arguably has become more object-oriented as a result of increased pressures on web inter-activity), Twine lacks the strict structures and classes of its C-esque counterparts. While it is possible to build a world model within it that might be termed *simulationist*—see our discussion of Porpentine's *With Those We Love Alive* in chapter T-3—such development is not built into the system in the way that Inform 7 has responded to the needs of designers building complex world models.

Other platforms for the creation of interactive fiction are more prag-matic in their approach to potential users, recognizing that a knowledge of programming is required to progress in developing with their tools. To return to Inform 7, its system visuals are secondary to text, and the authoring of natural language follows the most orderly rules of coding: while the blank page of an open Inform 7 game might look like a Mi-crosoft Word document at first glance, freedom of writing style exists only inside the quotation marks that delineate strings. The rigor of the language is necessary for Inform 7's primary metaphors—the designer must first create the world and then define the rules by which the player might interact with that creation. Thus the structures of basic Inform 7 look like sentences but follow predetermined rules, as in this example:

The Office is a room. The description of Office is "Despite all your best intentions of cleaning, the office is covered in papers, none of them useful." The desk is a supporter in the Office. The laptop is on the desk.

Instead of booting the laptop:

```
say "The last thing you want to do is see the
state of your emails."
```

Note some of the conventions: quotation marks indicate a string, or a sequence of characters that the language will not attempt to parse and understand. All the other sentences must be readable to the parser: words such as *description* and *supporter* are defined in Inform and create certain properties. The "instead" rule allows the system to intercept certain verbs and respond—so if the player tries to type "boot the laptop," the phrase after it will appear to discourage them from continuing down that path of action. Once broken down, the structures and demands of the language on the writer become apparent immediately (even before the would-be creator descends into the more clearly programmatic metaphors of data structures, logic, and event-driven "scenes" that enable a complex state of play). Mitchell and Montfort end their analysis of Inform and TADS with a reminder that "it is useful to consider the less-than-obvious ways in which these systems might influence the shaping of stories and worlds" (Mitchell and Montfort). To extend this argument, I noted that it is necessary to consider the less-than-obvious ways in which these platforms are reconstructing game culture.

The original Twine macros reveal the code intensity behind the extension of links in the early formatting and syntax of Twine's vocabulary. To return to the poetics of the cycling link, the macro was described in its creator's introductory post on Glorious Trainwrecks as a simple enhancement: "This simply produces a link whose text cycles between a number of values whenever you click on it. It otherwise leads nowhere. You can use it as a silly clicky trinket, a cheap alternative to the <<replace>> macro, or (as detailed below) as an input interface element" (Twine).

In 2012 (right before Twine's rise on the scene), Montfort and Short noted in their examination of the state of interactive fiction that the move to the browser was driving pushes for change in platforms that typically had ignored and standardized the aesthetics of the user interface:

Presenting IF in a browser window generates its own new set of player and author expectations. Typography and text styling has for a long time been at best a secondary concern: interpreters on different operating systems present text in different ways, in different fonts, colors, and marginal arrangements. Traditionally, the tools used by the IF community have offered the author only limited control over this presentation. Portability across a large number of platforms (including small-screen mobile devices and computers being run with a screen reader by blind players) was often considered more important than the ability to craft a specific visual experience, and providing an attractive textual surface was often seen as the job of the interpreter creator rather than the author of a specific game. (Montfort and Short)

We return to this question of the interface in more detail later in this work, with chapter T-5's examination of Twine's entanglement with camp aesthetics. However, it is important to note that Twine's rise as a competitor to other interactive fiction platforms comes from both the ease of making and the ease of spreading work.

Open-Sourcing Twine

Placing Twine's history alongside this other most dominant platform for writing interactive fiction, Inform 7, illuminates their important differences as well as their fundamental similarities as platforms driven by their user communities. At NarraScope 2019, the first conference hosted by the IFTF, both Klimas and Inform 7 creator Graham Nelson offered "state of the platform" talks to audiences of players, developers, and scholars.

Klimas addressed the past and future of Twine for his audience. This moment was part of a shift in Twine's history, as Klimas documented some of the challenges of Twine as well as his hopes for the platform's future in the hands of the organization. At the core of his aspiration is Twine's commitment to open-source and open-access. The open-source nature of Twine has not been without its consequences. In 2018, Netflix released "Bandersnatch," a groundbreaking episode of its *Black Mirror* series in which suitably equipped viewers could select links to determine the unfolding of the narrative—an embrace of interactive video, or hypertext, or choose-your-own-adventure gaming, depending on perspective. Significantly, "Bandersnatch" also involved at least a glancing encounter with Twine. The "Bandersnatch" creative team has acknowledged using Twine, among other applications, in preparing the treatment (roughly speaking, the prototype) for the project (Rubin). Creator Charlie Brooker described Twine as the tool that assisted in his big-picture thinking for the episode: "Every time I had an idea I put it in a box, and you can move them around. It's a bit like making a giant patchwork quilt" (Rubin). In his NarraScope talk, Klimas reports reaching out to the "Bandersnatch" team but receiving only resounding silence. This reaction was probably predictable, given problematic claims of influence, authorship, and credit that crop up regularly in show business. There was, for instance, an ongoing lawsuit from the publisher Chooseco over the use of the choose-your-own-adventure concept, to which the company claims proprietary rights (Kaminsky).

Setting the "Bandersnatch" story aside, Klimas pointed to similar uses of Twine as a prototyping tool for professional, profitable endeavors ranging from the choose-your-own-adventure graphic novel *Romeo and Juliet* by Ryan North to the opening sequence of the game *Firewatch* but also pulled up a more stark testament to Twine's lack of financial support even as he showed this economic potential. (At the time, the Patreon to support Twine was at less than $800 a month.) This echoed discussions of financial realities in narrative games that are unavoidable: the conference opening keynote included shots of a game in progress, abandoned for being too expensive to viably complete. Nelson, speaking during the Q&A, noted, "I'm not doing anything to help that," reflecting on the type of ambitious game that the developer works on and the realities of the limitations of open-source tools: "We're making a really good box," but "every step you take along that road makes it harder to get access to what's outside" (Nelson).

Chris Klimas noted in his discussion at Narrascope that he is aware of the challenges that arise when the user drawn to Twine by the promise of no programming seeks more control over the logic of their play and hits the wall of code and assumptions that go with it. Reflecting on the question, "How do you assist people in getting over that wall?" Klimas

pointed to his then current work on the story format Chapbook, introduced at the conference. In his initial guide, Klimas planned a section
labeled "Advanced" but expected that it would need a disclaimer: "You'll
need to understand JavaScript." (We discuss JavaScript in passing in up-
coming practical chapters and in some depth in chapter P-3, where an
example explores the integration of JavaScript code within Chapbook.)

This decision reflects a constant tension at the heart of design work
on the platform: the balance of ease of use and capabilities. To again
evoke the spirit of the dearly departed Flash platform, the breakdown
of this balance can cause users to flee to new platforms or encourage
them to never upgrade—many users stuck with old versions of Flash
not just because of financial investment but because of the learning
curve that went with each iteration's significant extension of the base
feature set into a more and more algorithmic world. This resistance is
also a reminder of the incredible frustration that can await the artist
and writer in a world of ever-changing and proprietary tools; by contrast, the open-source tool offers the hope of consistency or at least the
promise of continued availability.

With that said, our venture into Twine as a platform will not be
without its challenges, and the interface underlies a greater complexity
than you might expect. Chris Klimas noted that even some of the most
fundamental functionality of Twine is more complex for the user than
it might at first appear: "Plugging images into Twine, which is a really
basic idea, is hard. You have to understand how URLs work. There's
the comfort and the size of the box" (Klimas, "Twine: Past, Present,
Future"). Twine's "box" of utility is continually growing, from the 2006
Twee with its off-putting lack of graphical interface, to the first Twine
GUI in 2009, to the 2014 Twine 2, which looked to the web as a work-
around for the frustrations presented by the walled garden of the Apple
Store and Android Market.

The reach of Twine is also increasing: Twine 2.3.1's downloadable
version (functional on Windows, Linux, and Mac) has reportedly ex-
ceeded twenty-five thousand downloads. The Twine community as of
Klimas's 2019 report included 3,000 members on a Discord chat and
2,300 on the unofficial subreddit. In his own assessment of Twine's

reach, Klimas observed three main groups using Twine, all with different needs. Creative professionals (mostly game designers) using Twine
as a prototyping tool, from the Netflix "Bandersnatch" team to the writers of the indie game *Firewatch*, rarely release those early iterations but
may acknowledge Twine in postmortems on their work. Educators such
as the authors of this book are the second primary user group, with
Twine's reach extending to classrooms in India and well outside of game
design programs (frequently as an alternative to the traditional paper-
writing research assignments of many disciplines). And of course, finally, Klimas noted the indie creators and the recognition their work
has brought Twine in a range of communities. These voices range from
those distributing work on itch.io and Steam to artists exhibiting at the
Whitney Biennial. Klimas observed that reaching (and keeping up with)
this audience presents its own challenges, offering, self-deprecatingly,
"I'm really not cool, and these people tend to be really cool."

The Twine platform was "adopted" as a recognized platform by
the IFTF, a decision driven by the need for maintenance and institu-
tional support. The Twine committee of the IFTF consists primarily
of the developers responsible for building the story formats and tutorials that power the Twine community: Leon Arnott, Thomas Michael
Edwards, Dan Cox, M. C. DeMarco, David "Greyelf" Tarrant, Colin
Marc (stepped down 2019), and Klimas. This team is notably less diverse than the set of indie artists we highlight throughout this work,
and tensions between the community and the guiding developers can
be high—as Klimas observed, people frequently blame an imagined
"they" for changes in Twine rather than seeing open-source projects
as authored by dedicated creators donating their time to the project.
Code authorship is visible when discussing an open-source project like
Twine, but in some ways, that leads to less of a sense of creative control.
The economics of this model are perhaps unsustainable: challenges include basic finances, such as paying to become a registered or "signed"
application to enable users to more easily install the Twine platform
on their computers. Other ambitious goals, such as modernizing the
development workflow to add a Twine package manager and collaborative tools, are likely out of reach and also raise their own questions:

If we cannot even easily define what Twine makes, who should—and will—decide where Twine goes?

In an inherently decentralized community, there are whole groups who use Twine but aren't part of the conversations about the future. The same challenges we face defining Twine's scope also make it difficult to plan its development road map, which, as Klimas noted, requires balancing the needs and requests of the experts versus the teachers and students working with Twine in classroom settings without code experience, who are thus perhaps less likely to post concerns and issues in GitHub. Even the decision about where to place resources changes the platform's reach. Klimas and collaborators abandoned a plan to move the Twine support forum to Stack Overflow, a popular website for coding support, given the emphasis on programming and the conventions that might be particularly daunting to newcomers. Previous community hubs, such as Google Groups and the Twine forums, have run into problems of spam and moderation, while gamer-favored platforms such as Discord and Reddit bring in whole new potentials for toxicity.

As we will argue throughout this work, Twine's in-betweenness is its strength: it is the source of the platform's influence and what makes Twine relevant in conversations ranging from the future of education to the unrealized potential of electronic literature to the need to transgress existing boundaries in games. As cultural software, it is itself hypertextual, linked into communities that may never themselves intersect. Its survival and evolution to this point, refusing to diverge toward a commercial approach, is both admirable and unusual and ultimately the source of Twine's revolution.

Works Cited

Alexander, Leigh (@leighalexander). "When people say games need objectives in order to be 'games,' i wonder why 'better understanding another human' isn't a valid 'objective.'" Twitter, April 8, 2013. https://twitter.com/leighalexander/status/321152113021448193.

Bogost, Ian, and Nick Montfort. "Platform Studies: Frequently Questioned Answers." *Digital Arts and Culture*, 2009. http://bogost.com/writing/platform_studies_frequently_qu_1/.

Brice, Mattie. "Triptychs." Mattie Brice's website, April 13, 2013. http://www.mattiebrice .com/triptychs/.

Consalvo, Mia, and Christopher A. Paul. *Real Games: What's Legitimate and What's Not in Contemporary Videogames*. MIT Press, 2019.

Cox, Dan, ed. "iftechfoundation / twine-cookbook." 2017. GitHub, 2019. https://github .com/iftechfoundation/twine-cookbook.

———. "An Oral History of Twee." Digital Ephemera, June 8, 2019. https://videlais.com/ 2019/06/08/an-oral-history-of-twee/.

Ellison, Cara. "Anna Anthropy and the Twine Revolution." *Guardian*, April 10, 2013. https://www.theguardian.com/technology/gamesblog/2013/apr/10/anna-anthropy -twine-revolution.

Ensslin, Astrid, and Lyle Skains. "Hypertext: Storyspace to Twine." In *The Bloomsbury Handbook of Electronic Literature*, edited by Joseph Tabbi, 295–310. Bloomsbury, 2017.

Free Indie Games (blog). "About." Accessed July 29, 2019. http://www.freeindiegam.es/ about/.

Friedhoff, Jane. "Untangling Twine: A Platform Study." Proceedings of the 2013 DiGRA International Conference, 2013, 10.

Guest, J. J. "Escape from the Crazy Place." Glorious Trainwrecks, February 21, 2017. https://www.glorioustrainwrecks.com/node/6547.

Guest, J. J., and Loz Etheridge. "Escape from the Crazy Place." Interactive Fiction Database, 2006. https://ifdb.tads.org/viewgame?id=ny5d87fqbeh3pnuz.

Harvey, Alison. "Twine's Revolution: Democratization, Depoliticization, and the Queering of Game Design." *GAME* 1, no. 3 (2014). https://www.gamejournal.it/ 3_harvey/.

Haske, Steve. "'Is This a Game?' Forces You to Contemplate the Philosophical Definition of Games." Complex, June 9, 2013. https://www.complex.com/pop-culture/ 2013/06/is-this-a-game-forces-you-to-contemplate-the-philosophical-definition -of-games.

Johnson, Steven. *Interface Culture: How New Technology Transforms the Way We Create and Communicate*. San Francisco, CA: Harper, 1997.

Joyce, Michael. "Nonce upon Some Times: Rereading Hypertext Fiction." *Modern Fiction Studies* 43, no. 3 (1997): 579–97.

Kaminsky, Michelle. "Chooseco, 'Choose Your Own Adventure' Trademark Owner, Sues Netflix over 'Bandersnatch.'" *Forbes*, January 14, 2019. https://www.forbes .com/sites/michellefabio/2019/01/14/chooseco-choose-your-own-adventure -trademark-owner-sues-netflix-over-bandersnatch/.

Klimas, Chris. "Code and Other Oddments." Gimcrack'd, March 28, 2006. https://web .archive.org/web/20060328165735/http://gimcrackd.com/etc/src/.

———. "Twine: Past, Present, Future." IFTF Narrascope Conference, June 15, 2019. https:// 2019.narrascope.org/pages/schedule.html.

———. "Twine Is an Open-Source Tool for Telling Interactive, Nonlinear Stories." Twinery.org, 2019. https://twinery.org/.

Koster, Raph. "A Letter to Leigh." Raph Koster's website, April 9, 2013. https://www
.raphkoster.com/2013/04/09/a-letter-to-leigh/.

Manovich, Lev. *Software Takes Command*. Bloomsbury, 2013.

Mitchelhill, James. "Simulationism and IF (Long)." Google Groups, October 1, 2005.
https://groups.google.com/forum/#!msg/rec.arts.int-fiction/o-Y2qK8_KLE/
Qrwmdv0L5k4J.

Mitchell, Alex, and Nick Montfort. "Shaping Stories and Building Worlds on Interactive Fiction Platforms." eScholarship, December 2009. https://escholarship.org/uc/
item/6pk7s4n6.

Montfort, Nick, and Emily Short. "Interactive Fiction Communities: From Preservation
through Promotion and Beyond." *Dichtung Digital* 41 (September 2012). http://
www.dichtung-digital.org/2012/41/montfort-short/montfort-short.html#10.

Nelson, Graham. "Opening Inform." *IFTF Narrascope Conference*, June 15, 2019.
http://emshort.com/narrascope/talk.html.

Nintendo Power, and Anna Anthropy. "Dragon Warrior Text Adventure—Details."
Interactive Fiction Database, August 2, 2013. https://ifdb.tads.org/viewgame?id=
vbs1pvv73c2p18i2.

Pinheiro, Haroldo de Oliveira. "haroldo-ok / twine-monogatari." GitHub, 2019. https://
github.com/haroldo-ok/twine-monogatari.

Porpentine. "Live Free, Play Hard: The Week's Finest Free Indie Games." Rock Paper
Shotgun, April 28, 2013. https://www.rockpapershotgun.com/2013/04/28/live-free
-play-hard-the-weeks-finest-free-indie-games-26/.

———. "On Formalism (Darius Kazemi)." *Free Indie Games* (blog), April 25, 2013.
http://www.freeindiegam.es/2013/04/on-formalism-darius-kazemi/.

Quinn, Zoë. "Steam Greenlight: Depression Quest." Steam, December 4, 2013. https://
steamcommunity.com/sharedfiles/filedetails/?id=200770535.

Rubin, Peter. "How the Surprise New Interactive *Black Mirror* Came Together." *Wired*,
December 28, 2018. https://www.wired.com/story/black-mirror-bandersnatch
-interactive-episode/.

Ruston, Jeremy. "History of TiddlyWiki." TiddlyWiki, September 23, 2014. https://
tiddlywiki.com/static/History%2520of%2520TiddlyWiki.html.

Short, Emily. "Links and Structures from Michael Joyce to Twine." *Emily Short's Interactive Storytelling* (blog), July 27, 2019. https://emshort.blog/2019/07/27/michael
-joyce-on-hypertext-links/.

TiddlyWiki. Accessed December 20, 2018. https://tiddlywiki.com/.

Twine, Leon. "Twine Macro: << Cyclinglink >>." Glorious Trainwrecks, January 28,
2013. https://www.glorioustrainwrecks.com/node/5020.

Yang, Robert. "A Letter to a Letter." *Radiator* (blog), April 10, 2013. https://www.blog
.radiator.debacle.us/2013/04/a-letter-to-letter.html.

From Links to Stories

◊ *Twining* is not simply a how-to book, so the step-by-step examples in this chapter are accompanied by comments designed to put practical learning in context. If for some reason you're more interested in the instructions alone, you'll find each action item set like this paragraph, boxed and marked with a special character. We'll use this convention for all the practical chapters.

Supporting materials for this chapter can be found online at https://github.com/AMSUCF/Twining. For most of our examples, you'll find two documents: a web page (.html), which is the finished version of the project, plus a plain text file (.txt) containing all the code we discuss. In projects with multiple pieces (or "passages," as you'll shortly learn to call them), we've indicated the passage to which the code belongs.

We're providing these resources as an invitation to tinker, play, and remix. There are two ways to make our code your own. The Twine 2 application allows you to import any published Twine file you find as a web page. The procedure is discussed later in this chapter. You can import any of our examples and see all the structure and code. On the other hand, if you want to work through our examples step-by-step, you may want to copy and paste from the text files to save yourself a lot of tedious typing.

Getting Ready to Write

You can access Twine via the web at www.twinery.org. There are two options: download a local copy or use the program online. We recommend downloading and installing if you can. The online version is fine for beginners, but it limits more advanced work (involving external files, for instance). Also, somewhat confusingly, the stories you build using the online tool are accessible only in the browser and computer you built them from. They are not stored on a server and the link cannot be shared, which can be problematic for newcomers.

Twine is available from Twinery at no charge, with versions for Windows (32- and 64-bit), Mac OS, and Linux. Installation is straightforward: download and run the appropriate installer. Twine will set up necessary files and permissions. You'll find a new folder named "Twine" in your Documents directory, where data files associated with your various Twine projects (called "stories" by default) will reside. An icon for the Twine application will appear in your list of programs and in the appropriate system folder where applications are stored.

On rare occasions, things don't go so smoothly. Depending on how your system is configured, you may encounter pushback from antivirus software. You might, for instance, see a warning about a supposed vulnerability called "WS.Reputation.1." Appearances to the contrary, this is not the name of a malicious virus code lurking in the Twine installer. "WS.Reputation.1" is a designation applied by makers of antivirus software to programs that serve small or niche audiences. Such programs, they imply, aren't circulated widely enough to have a reliable reputation. There are usually straightforward ways around any obstacles your antivirus software presents. At worst, you might have to open a quarantine folder, click on the Twine installer, and give it an exemption. You should only have to do this once.

We considered not mentioning antivirus problems. Most people will never run into them. If you do, you should feel safe using installers downloaded from Twinery. The Twine developers understand the risks of malicious software and maintain their code responsibly. It is at least ironic, and not a little insulting, to question their reputation. We tell this story because it highlights Twine's identity and ethos. You pay nothing for Twine—though you should consider making a contribution for its support. The program is nonproprietary, open-source software, supported and advanced by expert volunteers and a community of users. Twine belongs to a culture sharply different from that of giant corporations with hundreds of millions of sales. While you can use Twine for all sorts of things—journalism, education, research, and so on—it is designed for one basic task: telling complex, interesting stories. The rest of this chapter will help you get started with that.

Interface and Controls

Launch the Twine application by clicking on its icon. Since the installer may not place the icon on your desktop, you may need to look for it in the appropriate Applications folder on your system. After launching, you should see something like this:

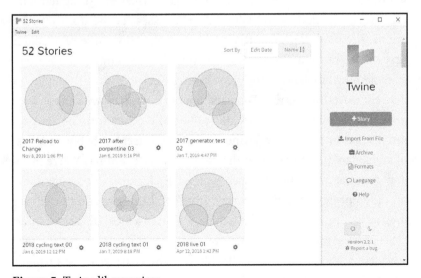

Figure 5: Twine library view

You're looking at a Twine library. This one has contents, but yours will contain no stories if you have done a fresh installation. The larger panel on the left will include a visual representation or thumbnail for each story you create. You can sort this collection in various ways. Each thumbnail is a square containing one or more circles. The circles stand for the subdivisions or *passages* in your story. They are arranged in a way that roughly imitates their layout in the Twine structure editor. (More about both passages and structure is just ahead.) Thumbnails can be helpful if you are trying to find a specific Twine story in a crowded library, but they are impressionistic.

To the right of the library panel, you'll see a stack of operators, or function buttons. The most important of these is the prominent green button labeled "+ Story." You'll use this operator to begin a new story. Next in the stack is "Import from File," which is a way to find and import existing Twine stories that may be located outside of your Twine folder. This function will be useful later in your Twine career, especially if you change computers or collaborate with other writers.

Below the import operator is "Archive," a function that creates a copy of your entire current library. You should use this tool early and often. Don't worry too much about storage space, unless your system is unusually constrained. Today's storage devices are designed with graphics and video in mind, and in many cases, Twine stories, which are mostly made up of words, take up only a tiny share of available space. Feel free to archive as often as you like. Remember to use a sensible naming convention for the resulting files.

Below "Archive" is the "Formats" operator, which shows all the *story formats* available in your Twine application. Story formats are presentational interfaces for Twine stories. Interfaces probably need less of an explanation today than they did in the last century. You're probably familiar with the way web pages can change as you view them on different devices and browsers. In effect, browsers and devices are interfaces. The contents of the web page exist in a file that various interfaces process for display. Something similar happens with Twine. Your story contents go into an output file, which Twine processes using a designated story format to determine what appears on the user's screen.

You are not required to choose a story format. The default format for Twine at this writing is Harlowe. A newer format called Chapbook will install as an inactive alternative. Chapbook is a simple, readable scheme designed to help people use Twine without encountering too much complexity—though it is quite good at supporting more advanced techniques. In our opinion, Chapbook provides excellent ways to move from simple to more ambitious creative uses. The material covered in the present chapter is the same for both formats, though we will rely largely on Chapbook in later practical chapters. Switching to Chapbook and making it your default story format is quite easy. We'll discuss it in the next practical chapter.

The "Formats" operator offers a choice of formats built into the Twine application. At this writing, that set includes Chapbook, Harlowe, and two even earlier formats, Snowman and SugarCube. You can find documentation and projects using these schemes online. Because Twine is an open-source application based on the core technologies of the web, anyone who wants to can build improvements and offer them to the world. Software never sleeps. The "Formats" operator allows you to add new formats as they are developed. Many Twine users do this seldom or never. At some point, though, a remarkably elegant and useful new format may give you the itch to switch.

Below "Formats" is an operator called "Language," which lets you localize Twine to any of thirteen national languages. Below this is a "Help" operator, which takes you to the wiki at Twinery. Continuing down the screen, after a small gap, we find two buttons marked by a representation of the sun (left) and moon (right). These buttons toggle the background and text colors used in any story format. In the dark theme, which is active by default, words appear in a light color against a dark background. The light theme reverses this arrangement. The choice of theme is largely a matter of preference. Some find the dark theme more dramatic, maybe suited to dystopian or gothic moods. Those less aesthetically inclined may find the dark theme hard to read in low light, preferring dark text against a bright background. This setup has worked pretty well for books, after all.

There are two text indicators at the very bottom of the stack. One identifies the version of Twine you are using, with a link to the credit screen for that build. Note—and please use—the included link for donations. Like public radio and TV, Twine depends on a combination of pride, love, and guilt. Every donation helps. The final item is a link to a bug-reporting channel, should you encounter anything in Twine that seems clearly dysfunctional. Use this link by all means—bug reports help everyone—but always ask yourself if the trouble could have been caused by some mistake in your use of Twine rather than the program itself.

Twine is nowhere near as complicated in its interface as some commercial products we use regularly, but it does have more than one menu of functions. We've just discussed the one that appears at the top level of the library view. Another will show up after you have opened a story file. You can access this menu by clicking on the name of your story, which appears at the lower left of your screen, or on the black triangle that may be visible next to your story name. (Longer story names make the triangle invisible.) When you unfold this menu, you will see nine options. We'll only discuss the last two, "View Proofing Copy" and "Publish to File." In fact, we'll defer "Publish to File" to the end of this chapter. "View Proofing Copy" produces a very useful printout of your story with the contents of each passage, including the script elements we will describe in later chapters. We're not quite sure how the passages are sorted in this report, possibly from graph position or order of creation, but they're all included, and each is set off by a dotted line. This draft view can be of great help if your story has very many passages or if you've lost your way in the process of composing.

Key Terms

Before we start doing things with Twine, we need to define some basic terms. A *story* is a Twine work, indicated in the library by a title and thumbnail. It is interesting to think of possible alternatives to this word. The strongest tension, of course, is between story and *game*, as we discuss in the theory chapters, but we could also consider other metaphors for branching texts. Labyrinths? Mazes? Webs? Weaves?

However, *story* is the word Klimas chose because Twine is first and foremost a storytelling tool. You may take this term loosely and think of your work as a news or feature story, or the kind of instructional story used in teaching, or the unfolding story-of-play that belongs to games, but everything tends to be some kind of story.

As we have seen in chapter T-1, Twine has a story of its own. Twine's relationship to earlier hypertext systems is complicated but close enough for some comparisons. Hypertext programs generally adopt a scheme called a *directed graph*—typically, a stylized tree made of boxes and lines—in which the reader's attention is meant to move from one division or *node* to another. Adapting this idea to literature, George P. Landow, the first theorist and rhetorician of hypertext, renamed nodes as *lexias*, deriving the term from the French literary theorist Roland Barthes, in whose work Landow found a conceptual basis for hypertext (Landow 2–3). Like early hypertext itself, the term *lexia* was eventually eclipsed by other usages, such as *page*, *post*, and *tweet*.

In many ways, Klimas's term for a textual unit, *passage*, represents a second coming of the lexia. A passage is a discrete body of material that may contain words, still or moving images, and sound cues. Passages are displayed one by one as a reader moves through a Twine story. (We don't yet know of a Twine story format that displays more than one passage at a time, or a good reason for building one, but never say never.) You can put as much or as little information into a passage as you like. Twine passages tend to be relatively terse, though some writers put multiple paragraphs into their passages. Long before Twine, the first hypertext writers faced a similar aesthetic problem: Why put a lot of text into a lexia if the point is to replace it with something else? A famous early hypertext paper contrasted "holy scrollers," who preferred longer, unbroken texts, to "card sharks," who thought the contents of a lexia should fit the dimensions of a file card (Halasz 838). Though the sharks still dominate, both traditions are still with us, often within single works. As Twine writers like Porpentine and Anna Anthropy show, varying the length of passages can be highly effective. There are no absolute rules about passage length. If you need a long passage, write one. Scroll if you want to—but don't consider it mandatory.

The last of our three crucial terms is *link,* the active aspect of any directed-graph system. We'll begin our practical work with Twine by describing how to make links, but before we get there, we need to explain what links essentially are. Links have become an invisible part of everyday life in the internet age. You use one kind of link, the type described by Hypertext Transport Protocol, or HTTP, every time you move from one web page to another—but what exactly are you doing?

The World Wide Web has led us to identify links with words or phrases set off in special colors or images that invite a click or tap. This sense comes into play every time we say something like "Go to the main Twinery page and follow the third link on the left." Such expressions may be inevitable, but they're also inaccurate. Visual traces are only one aspect of hypertext linking. We could also describe a link in terms of its underlying code—in, for instance, HTML:

```
<A HREF="www.twinery.org">Get your Twine
here!</A>
```

If we keep in mind the infrastructure that underlies any visible trace of a hypertext link, we begin to understand that links are, like all programming code, *hyperlinguistic* (Galloway 165). They are simultaneously meaningful in more than one mode. The HTML anchor tag (<A> . . . </A>) usually surrounds some readable text. That text is often meaningful as part of a sentence. The anchor tag itself has meaning as a bit of web coding, and that code in turn is significant to another piece of software, a browser application, which converts it into an expression in machine language. When your computer receives this machine instruction, it retrieves and displays the indicated information.

Links are more than just markers on a screen. In the most complete sense, a link is a transition—an action or event—associated with multiple signatures or traces: the immediate words of the text, to which the link is *anchored*; the underlying code that specifies what the link will do; and a third aspect that we have not yet explored, which we will discuss in greater detail later in this chapter.

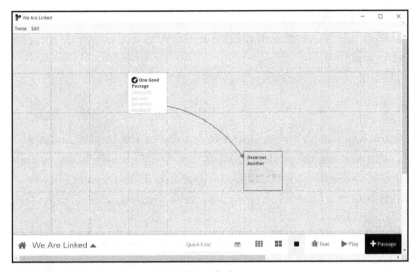

Figure 6: Two passages connected by a link

In terms of the hypertext graph, which we will call *structure*, the link is represented by a line with an arrow at one or both ends, showing the possibility of transition from one passage to another. Hypertext systems do not always display graph structure—consider the World Wide Web—but graphical mapping can be very important in building complex narratives like hypertexts and games.

To summarize, when we say *link*, we may refer to any or all these aspects:

1. Some anchoring text or image
2. Underlying software code
3. A representation in the story's structure map
4. An action, typically replacing one passage with another

The most important item in this list is the last. As the poet and designer Johanna Drucker says, digital writing is always "more event than entity" (Drucker 31). The point of a hypertext or other kind of digital fiction is that it allows things to happen, often in response to choices by a reader/player. In a sense, all language—certainly all storytelling—is a happening of some sort. In Twine and systems like it, this active aspect of the text is particularly central. This distinction will be important as we shift our conception from literary texts to games, which must be actively played.

Example 1.1: A Simple, Circular Story

Action requires planning. Stories need to be written, and digital stories have to be designed or structured as well. You'll eventually divide your time between the words of your story and its logical layout, but everything begins at that primary, verbal level—what you choose to say—so let's start there.

> ◊ Launch Twine if you haven't already.
>
>   A dialogue box will open asking for a title. You can call this story anything you like, though we recommend calling it *The Ostrich*. Click that green button on the right labeled "+ Story." At the title prompt, enter "The Ostrich."

Here's what your screen should look like—a view into the Twine structure editor:

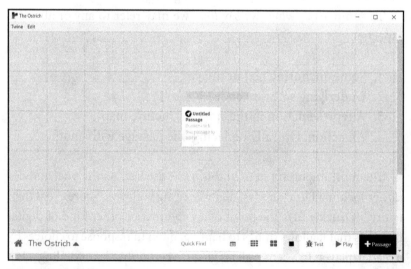

Figure 7: Beginning a new story

The background of the structure editor is a grid system with two scales, or rules, bold and fine. These lines are just a visual convenience for people who like to line things up neatly. They don't affect the function or underlying code of your story. Within this grid is "Untitled Passage." Below the title, you can faintly see the message "Double-click this passage to edit it"—which is a bit like the label on that bottle Alice finds in Wonderland—*Drink me.* Who could resist?

◊ Double-click the untitled passage.

When you double-click the passage, the structure editor is replaced by the passage editor, which is a specialized text processor. It looks like this:

Figure 8: Passage after opening

Here's where we'll begin writing, but first have a look at the elements that sit above the editing window. The first is a title bar. Every passage needs a title, preferably a *unique* title, for reasons that will become apparent shortly. (In fact, you can give two passages the same name in Twine, but this is a bad idea unless you know what you are doing.)

Below the title bar is a space where you can add *tags* to your passage. Tags are further ways of identifying the passage and can be used to sort, group, and otherwise process them. If the main title is a tag's given name ("Chris"), a tag might be its family name ("Klimas"). So if our Chris passage has relations, they might all be tagged as Klimases. There are other ways to use tags, including in more sophisticated, code-intensive operations, but this is a starter example, so we won't add any tags.

> ◊ Type "the last thing" into the title area.

Now that we know what we're writing, let's get ready to enter some text. As you'll see, there's a small twist to negotiate here, but we can begin sensibly enough by blanking out the existing text before adding our own.

> ◊ Select (drag over) the phrase "Double-click this passage to open it," then press "Delete" on your keyboard.

You might expect this operation to yield a nice, blank writing area. It doesn't. Out of their desire to make their program superfriendly, Twine's developers have decided to display a page of hints every time you begin editing. This quick reference includes directions about formatting text, working with special symbols, making links—the subject to which we are coming—and some advanced topics. This is all very useful information, though we wonder if you really need to see it every time you start to write. Go ahead and erase these notes before entering your own text—and don't worry, you can find all this information on the Twine wiki by clicking the "Help" button.

> ◊ Place your cursor to the right of the bullet (•) in the text editing area. Type any character.

The helpful page disappears, and you have a blank space in which to write. Well, almost blank—for some reason, that bullet character remains. Don't worry, though, it won't appear when your text is displayed.

> ◊ In the writing space, enter the following text:
>
> ```
> . . . on this of all mornings, the last thing
> anyone wants to see is an ostrich.
> ```

This text is a recommendation, not a requirement. Feel free to write other words as you move through this example. Just be sure to put in links where they are specified. We're coming to those.

> ◊ Click on the "X" at the top right of the editing window.

The editing window will close, returning you to the structure editor, where you should see a passage named "the last thing," with the sentence you just typed visible inside the square. In the upper left corner of the square, you should see a small, circular icon in green and white. This icon, which looks to some people like a rocket ship, marks the passage from which play will begin.

With only one passage, we don't have anything like a real Twine story or a hypertext yet. The magic begins with a second passage. We're going to add one now. You might expect to repeat the process we used to create our first passage, and in fact, you could do so—but if we use that method, we'll miss an elegant and charming aspect of Twine.

> ◊ Double-click your passage. In the text editor, add a pair of square brackets on either side of the word *ostrich*, making your text look like this:
>
> ```
> . . . on this of all mornings, the last thing
> anyone wants to see is an [[ostrich]].
> ```

Use right and left square brackets—the keys to the right of the letter *P* on your keyboard—not parentheses or curly braces. Twine looks for these specific characters and won't recognize substitutes. Also, if you are following closely, you'll put the period outside of the right set of brackets. There's no great harm if you get that detail wrong. (In later examples, however, precise punctuation may matter quite a bit.)

> ◊ Click the "X" to close this passage . . . and behold!

Treasure this moment. It's your first step into hypertext. It is also your first experience of a very beautiful thing: Twine automatically creating a new passage to complete a link. Most people take this little transaction for granted, but some early hypertext systems did not include this feature. The World Wide Web makes no attempt at all to manage structure. For these reasons, Twine's automatic link creation makes an old hypertext writer smile. It's a sweet hack. More important, creating passages automatically makes building complex structures a fluid, coherent process, giving a major boost to creativity.

If you look at the structure editor now, you'll see two passages (boxes), with a curved, arrowheaded line between them. Structurally speaking, you now have the beginnings of a genuine Twine story.

> ◊ Double-click on the "ostrich" passage to edit its text. Set your cursor to the left of the first line and type the following:
>
> ```
> But here it is, maybe slightly larger than
> life, in the middle of your Auntie Integer's
> sunroom. A flightless bird with eyes the size of
> [[gumballs]].
> ```

As you may guess, typing those double brackets around the word *gumballs* automatically links the "ostrich" passage to a third passage called "gumballs."

> ◊ Return to the structure view; open this new, blank passage; and enter a third paragraph:
>
> ```
> Once, for an entire week between the ages of
> two and two-point-one, your entire vocabulary
> ```

> consisted of the word "gumball," which became the
> name of every person and object as well as
> the lone verb in your dramatic revision of the
> human language. Now, somehow, the occurrence of
> this word makes you vaguely [[uncomfortable]].

If you do this right, you'll summon up a third link to a fourth passage, which is automatically titled "uncomfortable."

> ◊ Open that passage and enter a last chunk of text:
>
> "!!!" says the ostrich, also apparently
> unsettled.
>
> But you speak Human, not Ostrich. You take a
> step closer.
>
> "!!!," the ostrich reasserts.
>
> You carefully blink each of your eyes in
> succession, an old trick for stabilizing
> realities. It is unmistakably an ostrich;

This time we didn't end with an automatic link. That's because we're going to join this fourth passage back to the first one—ironically called "the last thing." Doing this will let us demonstrate a second powerful technique for making links in Twine.

> ◊ At the end of your text in the current passage, following the
> semicolon, add the following text:
>
> [[and . . .->the last thing]]

Here you see a second way to define a link in Twine: by adding the symbol -> (a two-character rendering of an arrow) plus the name of an existing passage. Links made in this way can run anywhere you like, not just from new to newer but into and among existing passages as well. The name of the destination passage ("the last thing") must be spelled exactly as it appears in the structure graph, and unlike destinations in HTML links, it is not placed in quotation marks.

Our first story, *The Ostrich*, is now complete. Properly assembled, it forms a simple loop. To see how the loop works in practice, we'll need to play it through.

Playing through the Story

Twine provides two main ways of checking the operation of a story, each associated with a button you will see to the left of the "+ Passage" button. Moving from right to left, the first of these is "Play." To its left is "Test." The "Play" button shows the story pretty much exactly as it will appear to your reader. "Test" adds debugging tools, which become useful as you begin building more ambitious things.

◊ Click the "Play" button.

You should find yourself looking at the text you wrote in the first passage, called "the last thing." If you are using the Harlowe story format (still the default at this writing) and did not change from dark to light themes, the letters will be light-on-dark. If you have switched to Chapbook, you'll see something resembling a printed page. The final word of the passage, *ostrich*, should appear in a style that indicates the starting point of a link: blue in Harlowe or underlined in red for Chapbook. If any of these details are wrong, click the "X" in the upper right corner of the window to return to the structure view. Reopen the problematic passage and check what you wrote.

Suppose you found a mistyped character in the third of our four passages ("gumball"). After you make the correction, you can press the "Play" button again and move through the story from the first passage. With only four passages, this is just mildly annoying, but once your stories stretch to dozens of passages, you won't want to return to the top. Fortunately, Twine allows you to make any passage the start of the story. Let's make "gumball" the beginning.

> ◊ Return to structure view if you are not there already. Hover over the "gumball" passage. A row of buttons appears. Slide your cursor down and to the right, then click once on the button marked with three dots (. . .). A menu appears. Choose the first option, "Start Story Here."

The "gumball" passage now has the green rocket ship, indicating that it is the start of the story. If you use the "Play" or "Test" buttons now, you'll automatically begin with "gumball." Resetting your start passage can be essential in building longer stories—but be careful. If you change the start passage for editing purposes, *remember to change it back*. When you export or publish your Twine story, whatever passage is currently marked as the start will become the entry point. If you send out a story and readers complain that it seems to start in the middle, that might be because you forgot to reset the start passage. (With hypertext, though, you can always say you wanted things that way.)

> ◊ Use the "Start Story" procedure to set "the last thing" as the start passage again. Then play through the entire story, following the single link at the end of each passage. Visit all four passages and make sure the final link takes you back to "the last thing."

Our *Ostrich* story shows one legitimate use of Twine, but not the best or most interesting. *The Ostrich* has only one reading sequence. Even if we move the start point, the reader will always follow the same path around the loop. Every passage has only one exit, leading inevitably to the next. *The Ostrich* is the sort of story we might find on printed pages, which is fine, but Twine can do more than imitate print.

It is tempting to say this story is not a hypertext, but that claim could be controversial. Theodor Holm Nelson, who invented the term, insisted that "hypertext is the most general form of writing" (Nelson 3/2). According to Nelson, writing in fixed succession—the paragraphs of a newspaper story, for instance—artificially limits language. Even without computers, writing tends toward multiple arrangements or sequences. You can open a book to any page you like. To return to newspapers or web pages, think of the way your eye might drift from one story to an item in another column or space, then back again. For Nelson, multiple sequences are the natural order; linear chains, like our *Ostrich* story, bury their heads in constraint, ignoring other possibilities.

What happens if we explore those possibilities? Doing so would lead us away from the conventions of single-stream media (books, film, video) in the direction of other things, including hypertexts and computer games. This turn has obvious creative consequences, but it can also be a technical matter. We can measure how hypertextual a story is in terms of *link density*, the ratio of passages to links. *The Ostrich* has a link density of 1.0, with exactly one link per passage. Other values are possible. Consider a story with five passages and a total of seven links among them. That story has a link density of 5 to 7, or 1.4. We might say that a true hypertext should have a link density greater than 1. We might also say that link density will generally fall somewhere between 1.0 and 2.0—which may seem strange, considering there is no formal constraint on the number of links you can put into a passage. However, not all constraints are formal. Consider the following example.

Example 1.2: *Overflow*

◊ Start a new story in Twine. Name it *Overflow*. Create a new passage, title it "Overflow," and type in the following text:

```
Let me make one thing perfectly clear: I am
in no way responsible for whoever or whatever
devoured the sun.
```

◊ Type double square brackets around each word in the sentence. (You can either include or exclude the colon and period, as you like.) You should end up with something like this:

```
[[Let]] [[me]] [[make]] [[one]] [[thing]]
[[perfectly]] [[clear:]] [[I]] [[am]] [[in]]
[[no]] [[way]] [[responsible]] [[for]]
[[whoever]] [[or]] [[whatever]] [[devoured]]
[[the]] [[sun.]]
```

◊ When you are finished typing, click the "X" in the upper right corner to return to structure view. Consider the results.

Twine will happily anchor a link on every word in a sentence or every word in a passage. You could even . . .

```
[[l]][[i]][[n]][[k]] [[e]][[v]][[e]][[r]][[y]]
[[c]][[h]][[a]][[r]][[a]][[c]][[t]][[e]][[r]]
```

. . . if you were entirely mad. Of course, Twine will generate a destination passage for everything you link. In the case of *Overflow*, we end up with a total of twenty-one passages—the original plus twenty possible successors. Think for a moment about the time it will take to write unique text for each of those twenty passages (as we've actually done in the completed version in the digital version of this book). Now consider writing at least one outward link from each of those passages. And what if every successor passage needed *more than one* link out? Before you knew it, you'd have a completely unmanageable project. One early hypertext writer, Shelley Jackson, encountered this problem while working on her celebrated fiction *Patchwork Girl* in 1995. She began by making links at will, starting threads and branches that expanded in all directions. After a while, she found the proliferation of links downright monstrous. In a later interview, she called the resulting structure map a "Brillo pad" of tangled lines. So much for the first draft. "I erased all the links," she said. Then she started over with a more careful approach (Jackson).

Link explosions can be troublesome. Yet strangely, there are at least two important digital fictions in which each word in every lexia behaves like a link: Michael Joyce's *afternoon* (1990; the first thing called a hypertext fiction) and Judd Morrissey and Lori Talley's *The Jew's Daughter* (2000). In the Twine era, Porpentine's *Howling Dogs* contains at least one passage in which every word is linked. How did these writers manage to avoid the Brillo pad of madness?

If every link system implies a conceptual tree or bush, the answer to explosive growth is simple: cut back the excess. Trim judiciously. Think topiary gardens, not jungles. Let's consider a more sensible example.

Example 1.3: *The Reign of the Two Doors*

◊ Start a new story called *The Reign of the Two Doors* (holding nose for pun). Enter the following text in a new passage also called "The Reign of the Two Doors":

```
You find yourself in the two-door universe. It
was slightly less expensive than the three- or
four-door models and all we could afford.
```

◊ Below the text you just entered, enter the following:

```
[[Go through the left door->Not Right]]

[[Go through the right door]]
```

Before going on, let's introduce a useful Chapbook feature designed especially for the kind of story we're telling here. It's called a *fork*. A fork is a visual device for presenting a small set, usually a pair of links. If you're using Harlowe, don't worry—the fork is convenient but not essential.

> ◊ Add a greater-than sign, or right angle bracket, before each link, like so:
>
> ```
> >[[Go through the left door->Not Right]]
>
> >[[Go through the right door]]
> ```

The angle bracket notation creates the fork. Its visual effect is subtle but pleasing: a fine line appears between the two links. The online Chapbook guide (https://klembot.github.io/chapbook/guide/) provides advanced information about restyling the appearance of forks. You can include this effect or not, depending on your taste.

As you can see, this story is written in an idiom many Twine fictions share with parser-based interactive fictions and the kind of multipath novel usually called "choose your own adventure." The reader/player is addressed in the second person. For scene-setting, we use the present progressive tense. Link anchors, which substitute for command-line typing in interactive fiction, use the imperative mood and describe some action—in this case, movement through space carried out by the reader/player's persona.

Each of our twin links uses one of the main linking styles available in Twine. The leftward exit names a specific destination passage that, since it does not previously exist, will now be created. The rightward link calls into being a passage named for its anchoring text.

Looking at the structure graph, you'll see that we have two fresh passages to deal with: "Not Right" and "Go through the right door." Let's handle the second of these ("Not Right") first:

> ◊ Open the passage called "Not Right" and enter the following text:
>
> ```
> You find yourself in the Place of No Winning. It
> is a simple room with, of course, two doors.
> ```

```
[[The Init Door->The Reign of the Two Doors]]

[[The Exit Door->The Reign of the Two Doors]]
```

The point here is that both doors from this passage lead back to the start point, closing a loop. There are two doors because this is a two-door universe. If you'd prefer one, that's fine. The reference to winning (or its opposite) is a matter of judgment. Maybe the player wants to stay in the loop. Who are we to say?

◊ Open the passage called "Go through the right door" and enter the following text:

```
Advancing boldly through the dexterior portal,
you find yourself in another version of the same
stupid room. Someone is trying to make a point,
you suppose.

[[Left! Maybe it will work this time->Not
Right]]

[[Right!]]
```

For the record, *dexterior* is not an actual word, though maybe it should be. By now, you should grasp the general design of this story: there are two links (or doors) from every passage. So far, at least, one of them always leads to the so-called fail passage, locking the player into the loop. However, there is a bit more to the story.

◊ Return to structure by closing the current passage. Open the new passage called "Right!" and type the following text:

```
Right. Always take the door on the right. You
get it now.
```

```
[[Always right->The Reign of the Two Doors]]

[[Left Behind]]
```

In this passage, we do the perhaps all-too-predictable thing, ca-priciously breaking the left/right pattern. The first link leads back to the beginning, while the second, left-hand door leads on. This is an entirely voluntary decision, of course. You could be kinder to your player/reader and avoid such perversity. When it comes to link pat-terns, the rules are up to you.

◊ Return to structure. Open the new passage called "Left Behind" and type the following text:

```
Moving at last through the door the writer
apparently doesn't want you to take, you begin
to float above the confines of the labyrinth,
leaving fools behind.

Rise up, you lovely winner.
```

Players of Davey Wreden's metagame, *The Stanley Parable*, will recog-nize the two-door controversy (Wreden, *Stanley Parable*). This rising-up business is an abject steal from Wreden's next offering, *The Beginner's Guide*, which we'll address in the conclusion of this book, even though it is not a Twine work. The player's upward motion expresses a univer-sal figure or trope. Given a loop or labyrinth, there are three possible actions: make your way to the center, find some way out, or rise above the whole thing. It is no coincidence that we find ourselves referring to a video game and reaching beyond the realm of hypertext fiction (and indeed Twine). The current generation of Twine creators think of them-selves as game developers as well as storytellers, and they occupy the same social and economic space as independent game developers. As we'll see in chapter T-2, they're part of the conflicts that come with that contested space. Many Twine stories are explicitly designed as games, with rules, consequential decisions, winning and losing outcomes, and even scoring systems. Porpentine's *Ultra Business Tycoon III* (Porpentine, *Ultra Business Tycoon III*) and Seth Alter's *RocketJump-ification* (Alter) are excellent examples.

For some, Twine works belong entirely within the game world. Others see Twine works as hypertexts encompassed within a larger group of creative products called *cybertexts*. That term was coined many years ago by Espen Aarseth, who went on the become one of the founding theorists of computer games. Cybertexts include games but also any other undertaking without a fixed sequence of presentation, where "non-trivial effort" is required to experience the work (Aarseth 2). There's much more to say about Twine stories and games both here and in the chapters that follow, but for the moment, there's more to say about our example, both as story and as hypertext.

The Reign of the Two Doors has a respectably hypertextual link density of 2.0: there are two ways out of every passage. Yet it requires no more than six passages, since, in five of those passages, only one link runs to a nonexisting passage, expanding the structure. (In the "Not Right" passage, both links bend back to the beginning.) You can build as many links as you want, provided many or most do not expand your inventory of passages. This is the technique used by both Porpentine in *Howling Dogs* (Porpentine, *Howling Dogs*) and Joyce in *afternoon* (Joyce). In the former, the overlinked passage presents a field of linked words that mainly go to the same place, except for the one that doesn't. Joyce uses a different but similar technique in which a few words in each lexia will "yield" a connection to a specific other lexia (Joyce). Every other word in the lexia is implicitly linked to a default destination. This design was made possible by a clever feature of Storyspace (Bolter, Joyce, and Smith), the early hypertext system for which *afternoon* served as the test file.

The third example mentioned earlier, *The Jew's Daughter* (Morrissey and Talley), arrives at universal link coverage very differently. In Morrissey and Talley's story, which is, in fact, less a hypertext fiction than an example of digital text generation, clicking any word on the current screen feeds the word to a program that composes a new passage beginning with that word. This revolutionary technique goes beyond predefined passages and links, but you may want to keep it in mind even so. Because it offers access to programming resources like JavaScript, Twine allows you to work with dynamic, variable, and even logically generated text. These are more advanced subjects, so we reserve them for later chapters, beginning with P-3.

Our *Reign of the Two Doors* example shows that it's possible, even with basic tools, to manage links and story structures, avoiding explosive overload. Links and linking strategies take a wide variety of forms. *The Reign of the Two Doors* shows what we might call *navigational* linking, tied to the movement of a virtual character or point of view through a described space. A close cousin of this approach is *procedural* linking, where the anchoring text describes an action involving the persona: "You shut the door"; "The ostrich says nothing"; "The Twinebot emits another burst of story," and so on. Also quite popular is *conversational* linking, where the anchors are options for responsive speech. For instance,

```
The high commissioner shoots you an arctic stare
and says, "Twine. Really?" You answer:

[["It is the way among my people."->Way]]
[["Who said anything about Twine?"->No Way]]
[["Hey, is that an ostrich?!"->Way Out]]
```

All these linking strategies—navigational, procedural, and conversational—share a common feature of composition. They divide the visible space of the passage into two parts: an upper section that advances the story and a lower part that contains the link anchors (perhaps set off as a fork). We could say the upper part is definitive or diegetic, reporting what happens or has happened in the world of the fiction, while the lower portion is hypothetical, consisting of language still in play. We'll call this arrangement a *bifold* construction.

The alternative, which we'll call a *unified* construction, brings the links directly into the diegetic text. Here is a thumbnail example:

```
Every morning, [[the old man->Hubert]]
comes to search our [[trash bins]]. He is
impeccably dressed and obviously from the
[[Ministry->Darkness]].
```

As you can see, this passage consists only of narration—strictly speaking, the direct report of an unidentified narrator. There is no second-person address and no reader/player persona. There are link anchors, but they fit into the diegesis instead of pulling away from it, as is often the case in the bifold scheme. These features give the example a stronger resemblance to conventional literary fiction than to interactive fiction or choose your own adventures. The unified or in-line treatment of links was a signature of early hypertext fiction, whose writers sometimes set themselves (perhaps regrettably) against the older interactive fiction tradition of parser-based games.

Very roughly speaking, bifold construction accentuates the game-like qualities of Twine stories, while the unified approach plays to literary interests; but this distinction can never be absolute. In the 1980s and '90s, some hypertext writers said of their work, "This is not a game" (see McDaid). In the following decades, however, stories and games inevitably converged. In a later hypertext from the web era, one of us revised the claim, declaring, "This is not not a game" (Moulthrop). Today's Twine writers dispense with single and double negatives alike. Klimas's use of "story" notwithstanding, many Twine creators call their products games and even "videogames," as in merritt k's groundbreaking and essential anthology, *Videogames for Humans* (merritt k).

However controversial the claim to game identity may be, it will not go away. Twine stories can be games, and Twine games tell stories. One interest or the other may dominate, but both will be present. In fact, many Twine writers exploit this dynamic, alternating the two types of construction, writing some passages in the double-decked way and others with the all-in-one pattern. Two of the most impressive Twine stories, Porpentine's *With Those We Love Alive* and *Howling Dogs*, display this strategy. Know and consider your options. Nothing requires you to address a player persona (the eponymous "you"). Likewise, no law says that Twine stories have to imitate print fiction. At its best, Twine allows us to explore the spaces between those alternatives, refining a new art form as we go.

Example 1.4: *Don't Think of an Elephant*

Here's a fourth example exploring what can happen if you let your links mingle with the rest of the text.

◊ Start a new Twine story. Title it *Don't Think of an Elephant*.

◊ Add a new passage. Title it "Don't Even Think." In this passage, type the following:

```
At dawn, the [[Elephant Men->Elephant]] will
come for your skull. But meanwhile, as Uncle Jed
always told you, [[the night]] is as long as you
want it to be.

Just, you know, don't think. You know. Of it.
```

◊ Close the text editor and return to the structure editor. You should see two links running from your first passage—one to a new passage called "Elephant" and the other to "the night."

◊ Open the "Elephant" passage and enter the following text:

```
Hyperintelligent pachydermatoids from an
exoplanet we haven't found yet are here to
avenge humanity's crimes against the elephants.
Evidently, they will be satisfied with just one
trophy. That would be you.

Why they chose you remains a mystery, though
it could have something to do with the illegal
```

> safari they caught you on. And that elephant gun
> with the smoke coming out of it.
>
> The senior Elephant Man asks if you have any
> [[last words]].

Yes, this is one of those tales about exoplanetary pachydermatoids. This story also appears to have a link density of 2, like another example we might recall. If this story follows the earlier pattern, we might expect it to have two tracks: one leading to happiness and the other, otherwise. Let's finish the darker destiny first.

> ◊ Open the passage called "last words" and enter the
> following:
>
> Evidently, you don't.

There are no links from this passage. It is in every sense a dead end. With the less fortunate outcome covered, let's see what lies along the other track.

> ◊ Return to the structure editor and find the passage titled "the
> night." Open it and enter the following:
>
> As, for instance, that first night in the
> Algarve, when Georges-Marie said, "La, but it is
> [[so big->Elephant]]!"
>
> Meaning the room, or the bed, possibly. But you
> [[flattered]] yourself.
>
> ◊ Back to structure. Two links, as always, one already pointing
> conveniently back to "Elephant." The other runs to a new pas-
> sage called "flattered." Open that one and enter this text:

> "Not the [[Hermes->Elephant]]," Georges-Marie
> objects. "It flatters not the slightest. Goes
> immediately into wrinkles. And the gray does
> nothing for you."
>
> This was on the night train to St. Petersburg.
> You remember the cocktails with prices in
> Korean, the waiters in their tricorn hats, the
> endless fields of [[elephant grass]].

As in *The Reign of the Two Doors*, we're throwing some curves. The general rule here is to avoid any word or phrase that makes us think of an elephant—references to things of a large scale or a gray and baggy suit. But now there's this link to "elephant grass." Remember, in *Two Doors*, this was where we challenged the player/reader to win by reversing logic. Think we'll do the same now?

> ◊ Open the passage titled "elephant grass" and enter the following:
>
> Oh dear. You meant to say
> "[[potatoes->Elephant]]."
>
> [[Oops->Elephant]].

Sometimes Twine stories are simply cruel. Save the elephants.

With a couple of exceptions—the additional passage on the way out and the tragi-farcical ending—this story is structurally identical to *The Reign of the Two Doors*. Instead of explicitly revealing the logic of its links, however, this story works by implication and association—as language tends to do, especially literary language. Perhaps this difference represents a step away from the idiom of games, at least games of a certain kind. But we could as easily say that it connects logical play with wordplay. That might be a promising match, at least in stories more graceful and sophisticated than this one.

Exporting and Sharing Twine Stories

One last detail needs attention before we finish with the basics: how to make your Twine story available to friends, strangers, editors, and teachers. There are many options for circulating a story, but before you can circulate, you must first export your work. *This requirement applies even if you are using the online version of Twine.* Stories you build online are accessible only using the current browser and computer: they are stored locally to your computer. If you send the web address (URL) of an online Twine story, recipients will not be able to view it, as the material is not stored online.

◊ In the structure editor, look at the bottom left area of the window. You should see an icon that resembles a house. Click this icon to return to your library. In the library, find the thumbnail that represents the story you wish to export. Next to the title and time stamp for each thumbnail, you'll see an icon that looks like a gear wheel. Click this icon to reveal a menu. The third item in this menu is "Publish to File." Select that item.

At this point, your operating system will go into its usual file-saving routine, asking you where you want the results to be stored. *Pay close attention.* In Windows and Mac OS, saved files usually default to a Documents folder. Be sure you know how to find that folder. When in doubt, change the destination to the desktop, where items are immediately visible.

Click the "Save" button in the file-saving dialogue to complete the process. Twine now creates a single file containing your story plus everything a web browser needs to display it. This file is saved as a web page, with the file extension *.html.*

Why a web page? you may ask. Why doesn't Twine use binary code or some arcane, proprietary format? Like the World Wide Web and HTML, Twine is noncommercial, open-source software. It uses free, accessible resources. For all its limitations, HTML/HTTP is for most of us the most convenient hypertext platform available. Exporting Twine stories as web pages means they can be uploaded to a web server and displayed either remotely or locally in virtually any browser.

The other advantage of HTML is accessibility of code, for those who are motivated and prepared to read it. The file format for every web page is plain text, which can be read by built-in text processors such as Notepad (Windows) and SimpleText (Mac OS). You do need to know what you're looking at, which in the case of Twine stories is not just basic HTML but also quite a bit of JavaScript. JavaScript is an auxiliary coding language (or scripting language) developed to extend the function of web browsers. Much of the magic of Twine depends on JavaScript.

If you are not a programmer, you don't need to concern yourself with any of the underlying code for your story. All you need to know is that Twine pages require JavaScript to function, so your server and browser must be configured to allow for this. We've encountered at least one academic course management system that prohibits script-enabled web pages. Hopefully, that won't happen to you. Talk to your teachers or your system administrator if it does. If the prohibition has no exceptions, there are work-arounds.

With export complete, you are ready to show your file to others. The simplest way to do this is via email, again provided your email system allows you to send web pages as attachments. Any browser application can read a web page immediately without going through a server. All your friends and teachers need to do is download the attachment and open it as a local file.

If you want a wider world to experience your work, you can upload your HTML file to a web server. There are plenty of free web hosts (Wix, Weebly, etc.). Many schools offer server access for students. Always remember that information shared on the web can be seen by nearly anyone in the world, so don't include sensitive details, names of private persons, or other things that violate common sense. You might also want to think about the audience you have in mind for your Twine story. If the story contains material that might disturb or trigger some people or might be inappropriate for young children, include a disclaimer at the beginning.

Works Cited

Aarseth, Espen J. *Cybertext: Perspectives on Ergodic Literature*. Johns Hopkins Press, 1991.

Alter, Seth. *RocketJump-ification*. Subaltern Games, 2013. Accessed June 6, 2020. https://subalterngames.itch.io/rocketjumpification.

Bolter, Jay David, Michael Joyce, and John B. Smith. *Storyspace* [hypertext system software]. Eastgate Systems, 1990.

Drucker, Johanna. *What Is? Nine Epistemological Essays*. Cuneiform Press, 2013.

Galloway, Alexander. *Protocol*. MIT Press, 2004.

Halasz, Frank. "Reflections on Notecards: Seven Issues for the Next Generation of Hypermedia Systems." *Communications of the ACM* 31, no. 7 (1988): 836–52.

Jackson, Shelley. "Interview Part 5: Thinking outside the Screen." In *Pathfinders*, edited by Dene Grigar and Stuart Moulthrop. Nouspace Press, 2015. https://scalar.usc.edu/works/pathfinders/shelley-jackson.

Joyce, Michael. *afternoon, a story*. Eastgate Systems, 1990.

Landow, George P. *Hypertext 2.0*. Johns Hopkins University Press, 2006.

McDaid, John G. *Uncle Buddy's Phantom Funhouse* [hypermedia novel]. Eastgate Systems, 1993.

merritt k, ed. *Videogames for Humans: Twine Authors in Conversation*. Instar Books, 2015.

Morrissey, Judd, and Lori Talley. *The Jew's Daughter*. Self-published, 2000. http://www.thejewsdaughter.com/.

Moulthrop, Stuart. "Reagan Library." *Little Magazine* [CD-ROM edition], 1999.

Nelson, Theodor H. *Computer Lib/Dream Machines*. Microsoft Press, 1987.

Porpentine. *Howling Dogs*. Alien Dovecote, 2012. http://slimedaughter.com/games/twine/howlingdogs/.

———. *Ultra Business Tycoon III*. Alien Dovecote, 2013. http://slimedaughter.com/games/twine/tycoon/.

———. *With Those We Love Alive*. Alien Dovecote, 2014. http://slimedaughter.com/games/twine/wtwla/.

Wreden, Davey. *The Beginner's Guide*. Everything Unlimited, 2015.

———. *The Stanley Parable*. Galactic Café, 2011.

CHAPTER T-2

Twine (R)evolutions

Works built in Twine hearken back to early electronic literature, evoking HyperCard and Eastgate hypertext fictions, but their relationship with these established digital forms is not straightforward (as we'll discuss further in chapter T-3). The reception and definition of Twine as a platform recalls the many debates of definitions surrounding electronic literature. Works in Twine have been included in interactive fiction competitions, displayed at independent games festivals, and built as part of interactive story jams. However, despite Twine's link to hypertext fiction, it has not been as visible in the electronic literature community. In an interview in *Guardian*, designer and writer Anna Anthropy has called attention to the works in Twine as part of a "revolution," noting that they offer a solution to some of the dehumanizing aspects of mainstream games: "I think that what I want to see more of in games is the personal—games that speak to me as a human being, that are relatable, which is the opposite of the big publisher games that I see. People who are creating personal games aren't hundred-person teams, they are people working at home, making games with free software of their own experiences" (Ellison). Key Twine works evoking this personal literary construct include Nora Last's *Here's Your Rape*, Finny's *At the Bonfire*, Anna Anthropy's *Escape from the Lesbian Gaze*, and

Zoë Quinn, Patrick Lindsey, and Isaac Schankler's *Depression Quest*. We examine these works (and many others) as part of "Twining"—a practice, event, and platform that challenges the existing discourse of several disciplines—and further invite the reader to engage in their own personal making, subversion, and reflection. *Twining* will, like Twine itself, intertwine theory, practice, and poetics—we will weave together principles of making with an examination of the many Twines. Twine is simultaneously punk and childish, new and retro, a return to nineties hypertext and a procedurally driven rejoinder to web 2.0's toxic "real self"–driven social spheres of performance and harassment.

What follows is an autoethnography positioning Twine as a force for culture, documenting and at times wrestling with the emergence of Twine as a piece of cultural software—a history of encounters, people, interfaces, and aesthetics that situate Twine's significance as a platform with queer, feminist, and punk leanings. We apologize in advance for what it does oddly but would argue that this oddness is necessary for embracing what makes Twine Twine. As such, in this chapter, we diverge into the "I," drawing on Anastasia Salter's point of view (again, with apologies and trepidation). In this rapid, personally situated history, we consider Twine as a tool of disruption and invite you to join us in asking, Why Twine?

Welcome to the Neighborhood

The appeal of Twine is the appeal of a GeoCities neighborhood (my first virtual "home" was in Area 51—for those unfamiliar, that was once the designated space for science fiction fandom and home to many writers of another important form of electronic literature—fan fiction). My GeoCities site was populated by animated GIFs "adopted" from online artists, webrings links to other preteens and teenagers with rambling, and confessional web pages filled with fandom, and most of my early writing (such as it was) was done in the collaborative, free-form space of a role-playing chatroom in my first fandom. (Which fandom is irrelevant and omitted here for self-preservation. OK, it was *Mummies Alive!*) Thankfully, any and all record of this appears to have been erased by the death of the old-school web (reader: do not view this as a challenge, please). These websites gave birth to the similarly aesthetically challenged chaos of MySpace, which similarly featured the web-1.0 look of clashing backgrounds, bad animation, and lots of flashing and moving parts—an aesthetic shown in figure 9, which we will revisit in chapter T-4.

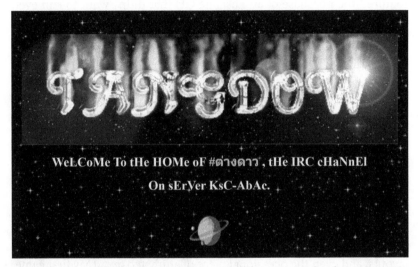

Figure 9: A typical '90s website, https://geocities.restorativland.org/Area51/Atlantis/2782/. Mine was worse.

By contrast, Facebook is boring, uniform, and tiresome, with a panopticon of profiles, all the same and algorithmically monitored. Interactive fiction constructed in parsers has always felt similarly off-putting to me—colorless and gray. Inform 7 has the cookie-cutter visual look of corporate web 2.0, despite its decidedly rebellious lineage. Twine, on the other hand, is the discordant, frequently visually dissonant development tool that seems to have grown up on GeoCities, MySpace, and LiveJournal.

But back to GeoCities: when I was happily linking my site to others through webrings and banner exchanges, I was not particularly aware that hypertextual narratives were a thing (or even a thing other people did), and that is something I suspect I have in common with many of the writer/designers who discovered Twine. On reflection, I was participating in their ilk—the interwoven narratives of self-inserted characters appearing and reappearing in fan fiction traded and rewritten had its moments. While I was generationally of the right age to grow up on graphic adventure games and a few text-game holdovers, I would not discover hypertext fictions and electronic literature until a college class directed me to the appropriate corners of the web and required the purchase of an Eastgate CD that didn't want to run even then. That disk, Deena Larsen's beautiful work *Samplers* (1996), is still on my shelf for posterity's sake alongside many other unplayable pieces. As a platform, Eastgate's Storyspace was immediately off-putting to me: anything that can't be shared freely online or found in a computer software store seemed to me (raised on fan fiction) inaccessible. Hypertext fictions seemed better-suited to thrive when made open on the web and lived alongside GeoCities in nineties venues, including *New River*, *Postmodern Culture*, and *Iowa Review*.

Prior to Twine, I built hypertextual narratives and scholarly projects the old-fashioned way, with tons of files and links. Built in Notepad and featuring the correspondingly horrific coding styles of the 1990s and early 2000s, these projects usually had inline styles, overly complex table layouts, and even the occasional piece of animated text. (My first game, built rebelliously as a JavaScript vocabulary quiz for a class board game assignment, featured an entry portal so complicated that no one could find it until I wrote out a detailed instruction manual.) I left this style of web development behind for years, lured in by the world and tools of graphical game development. For years, the idea of teaching something like Twine in the game design classes where I would teach primarily Flash, XNA, and Unity would have seemed laughable—getting students to care or see text-based games as relevant was nearly impossible. In an interactive narrative course I later developed, I brought in Inform 7 in a pre-Twine concept, and students struggled with both the text emphasis and the idea of making games that were this complicated. The graphical world seemed to have won.

But something happened. Flash died. I wrote it a eulogy, slightly early but quickly proven final, released during the same year as Gamergate. More on that later (Salter and Murray). Gaming changed: it needed a new disruptive platform, a space for metacommentary like the Flash games that used to mock the standards and norms of console games and mainstream gaming. And similarly, those displaced, alienated, and boxed-in by web 2.0 would start looking for tools to break out—tools that would be accessible and would, most importantly, allow for rapid circulation and distribution outside of gated platforms, software installations, and expense. Twine would make a place for itself as that platform.

What follows is my highly biased, timeline-jumping, woefully incomplete narrative of why I think that is.

The University of Baltimore, or How I Accidentally Was Present for the Birth of Twine*

*(But Mostly Missed It)

I started my doctoral program at the University of Baltimore (UB) in 2007. I ended up in a class with a cohort of interesting fellow students, including Chris Klimas, who would later be known as the creator of Twine. We had some conversations about interactive fiction, but I did not, at the time, realize I was talking to someone who would redefine the term. Chris Klimas introduced himself to our cohort in September 2007, noting that he came from a background that mixed computer science and creative writing: "I've had webby kinds of jobs for the past six years which started off kind of amorphous, but by now I think I've figured out I'm a web developer, not a designer. The line can be a fuzzy one. . . . In general, I'm good at code but not so much design. . . . Lately I've been writing hypertext. . . . If you're curious, I post my stories on gimcrackd.com" (Klimas, IDIA student introductions). I still have slides and emails from projects we collaborated on at UB, including an orientation game designed for, of all things, a Motorola Razr phone. The pace with which technology would advance was not foreseeable even to us, immersed as we were in its potential. Looking back at these projects, Chris's (and for that matter, my own) growing interest in accessibility in design is apparent.

The TweeCode/Twine Google Group dated from 2006 to 2018, at which point it was superseded by other Twine forums. Prior to Chris Klimas's own enrollment at UB, he was working on Tweebox 1.1, which was decidedly focused on interaction over aesthetics, but the discussion in the Google Group suggests he was starting to think about interface: "Right now the color scheme's pretty bland. This is sort of intentionally so—I didn't want it to be too distinctive—but even so, it would be nice to offer a couple of color variations. Either that or allow people to tweak the colors right from Tweebox, though that might be a bit too much complexity to give your average person" (Klimas, "What I'm Thinking About").

The "intentionally" bland look of this early Twine story format, Jonah, is not so different from the default look of the corporate web—but that would change. In an interview with Gamasutra, Chris Klimas cited the influence of the interaction design courses we both took at UB on Twine's move away from the computational interface to a graphical one: "[Twine] might have been my graduate thesis, originally, if I had the patience to complete one. . . . At the time, I had been experimenting with ways to create hypertext that were strongly code-oriented. I was studying interaction design, so Twine was my attempt to make something that would be friendly to people who were writers more than coders" (Alexander). I'd also suspect the impact of Eric Roberts's course on learning and interactive media, which we took together with others from the cohort. Sadly, nearly all records of that class are, for me at least, lost to time and poor memory.

The Twee documentation (which dates from Klimas's time at UB in 2009) reflects how different Twine was in this early, grad-school incarnation. It's decidedly geared toward hypertextual narrative, not games: "Keep in mind that hypertext is best described as a medium, not a genre. There can be hypertext fiction, nonfiction—even poetry. But in this document we'll talk about hypertext prose" (Klimas, "What Is Hypertext?"). Likewise, the discourse of the design documentation is grounded in electronic literature: "Links are the glue between passages. They are the equivalent of being told to turn to another page in a nonlinear book; in gamebooks, for example, you do this to make decisions for the main character" (Klimas, "What is Hypertext?"). But this isn't the only possible kind of link. Deena Larsen describes a whole taxonomy of links in "Fun Da Mentals: Rhetorical Devices for Electronic Literature." The original "Fun Da Mentals" includes a coloring book section entitled "Drowning in the Distance" that invites the reader to connect imagery and passages with any tool that enables linking. Twine appears currently on the list of recommended tools alongside a number of other open-source tools for manipulating and remixing content (Larsen).

The barriers to entry for the original Twee were high, but that was not uncommon. At the time, the shift to accessibility in tools-focused discourse in the digital humanities was only beginning its rise, along with increased interest in bringing these types of platforms to new users. Both Chris and I were part of this interest and on the outskirts of the digital humanities community—where, in 2011, the reader called *Defining Digital Humanities* would include an essay where Stephen Ramsay observes that "learn to build" might be more useful than "learn to code" as a call for action in the digital humanities (Ramsay). He particularly points toward the usefulness of the THATCamp model in the sharing of methods of building—a space that Twine itself was heading toward, albeit slowly.

THATCamp Games

The Humanities and Technology Camp—THATCamp—is a peculiar institution, worthy of its own book that will hopefully someday be written. It is an informal "unconference" gathering of digital humanists, convened by anyone with the will to organize and embrace the low- or no-cost model. It appears repeatedly in the stories of early digital-humanities community formation, best chronicled in the *Debates in the Digital Humanities* volumes (Gold and Klein). THATCamps vary wildly. Many THATCamp agendas included sessions about games, with enthusiasts such as myself sharing favorites and preaching their potential value to humanists everywhere, but for most, the very idea of games in the classroom still seemed challenging and out of reach.

In 2011, I co-organized the first THATCamp Games with Amanda Visconti at the University of Maryland, College Park. The camp was held in January 2012 during a snowstorm, with participants primarily including games scholars and digital humanists. Twine was so far under the radar at that point that even Klimas didn't discuss it: he offered a workshop on Flash game development with Flixel, an unrelated precursor of sorts to Twine in (relative) accessibility and usage if not in aesthetics. However, 2-D game development of this kind was a very different proposition than what would develop in Twine—Chris's boot camp description noted that "you should have some previous experience with object-oriented programming" (Salter and Visconti). The other boot camps were similarly positioned. Darius Kazemi foreshadowed the growing significance of HTML5 with a session on the Akihabara framework for 2-D games in HTML, which required programming experience; Bridget Blodgett (also from UB) focused on text-based games using Inform 7; John Murray looked at the Kinect Software Development Kit; James Morgan and Marek Kapolka looked at GameMaker 8 (back when there was a free version); and Todd Bryant shared strategies for modding *Civilization IV* (Salter and Visconti).

Looking back over the open schedule, many of the participants were looking for something like Twine—sessions on games and literature, narrative design, games for teaching arguments, queering games, and games and gender all foreshadowed Twine's eventual significance in educational games discourse. Twine was introduced but not yet dominant—reporting back after the event, Carly Kocurek, a game researcher and historian, noted, "I came back from THATCamp excited to play more with some of the tools I'd had the opportunity to work with, but also excited to spend some time with the tools I heard about but didn't get an opportunity to fiddle with hands-on at THATCamp Games: Flixel, Unity, Inform 7, and Twine, among others" (Kocurek).

Another attendee and designer, Sukey Argfored, posted observations on Inform 7 that echoed both its allure and the problems I've seen with it in class: "The nuts and bolts of creating a game in Inform 7 may be simplified for non-programmers, but they are still far too complicated to really learn in an hour and a half session" (Argfored).

We really should have held a Twine boot camp, but it says a lot that here, on the brink of 2012, even Chris Klimas himself didn't propose one for this venue. The explosion of Twine games (which would in turn help push the open-source project forward and create many of the resources on which Twine developers currently rely) wouldn't happen until a little later. I started at this time pointing people to Twine, but more the digital humanities crowd than the games crowd: in my own world of graphics-focused coursework, with students demanding better ways to build zombie shooters, there didn't seem to be a place for Twine in educational games discourse—yet. For small projects and subversive gameplay, we had Flash, which was highly visual, relatively quick and well supported, and easy to circulate on all the pre-iPhone platforms we could imagine.

Glorious Trainwrecks and the Intervention of Anna Anthropy

While our THATCamp-ers were learning Inform 7, elsewhere, others thinking inventively about games were discovering Twine. The main page of Glorious Trainwrecks opens with a provocation: "This site is about nothing, if it is not about getting off your ass and creating. Wikipedia claims that [people] used to stage trainwrecks (with empty trains, of course) for the amusement of the general population. Would the world not be a better place if we brought this tradition back?" (Glorious Trainwrecks). The site turned ten years old in April 2017, and since 2008, the moderators have maintained a list of rapid game development tools on which Twine features second (after Klik N Play, a graphical game tool currently described as "free, terribly buggy, doesn't work on 64-bit, beloved by all"). The parenthetical for Twine is more positive: "free, open-source, creates web-based text games with a nice no-programming GUI interface." The list was last updated in 2012 and still links to Gimcrack'd, Chris's now defunct site that used to host the Twee wiki as well as his own work. Leon Arnott (maintainer of the Harlowe story format) turned the site into a resource for Twine poetics and practices with a series of blog posts dating back to 2012 and covering topics including Twine page transitions and CSS tricks, adding in external libraries such as jQuery and extending the built-in JavaScript support with more dynamic elements.

Glorious Trainwrecks is home to one facet of the rapid game-making community that wasn't Twine's initial audience but would come to define it, as Chris credited in our interview:

> I initially thought of [Twine] as this thing that was for . . . serious writing, I guess, though serious writing is obviously a loaded term. It wasn't that I thought [Twine work] was somehow better than a game, it was more that I couldn't see how you build a game out of it, originally. And then everybody came along and proved me wrong, basically. And that was the other piece of it. I had zero awareness of the indie game scene at the time. That was the thing that Anna Anthropy really recognized, I think. I honestly credit her. . . . We'll go fifty-fifty for Twine's success. Because she saw something and was in a digital community I had no relationship to. (see appendix I)

In June 2012, Anna Anthropy was interviewed in Rock, Paper, Shotgun by Cara Ellison, who published the interview as a Twine game: after a nod to GameMaker (which has since gone very commercial), Anna Anthropy plugged Twine: "The other thing I recommend to people who are making games for the first time is Twine, which is a really simple tool for making basically choose your own adventure sort of things—very simple text stories—click here to do this—and it makes games as web pages that you can put online" (Ellison). This, along with similar Anna Anthropy interviews and posts, was the introduction to Twine for many.

My interest in Twine had already been piqued by these discussions, and I was rapidly working on my own (woefully bad) experiments. I found inspiration and discovered a better entry point into the community after a post from Porpentine in the Twine Google Group on August 11, 2012: "i've been working in Twine for a while and recently discovered this group. Just posting a collection of the games i've made along with my favorites from other people in the indie game scene to show that Twine isn't dead. There's a variety of tones and styles on display here so there's sure to be something you enjoy" (Porpentine, "collection of Twine games from me and other people"). The list included many of Porpentine's own works, as well as Kitty Horrorshow's horror and a number of romantic and historical vignettes. Many of these remain powerful, teachable works, and they also demonstrated early on Twine's range—from "surreal" to "dripping horror" and beyond. I am a fan of *Batman Is Screaming*, described here by its creator as "tiny, surreal"—it presents the strangest merger of fan fiction tropes, Twine, and body horror I've yet seen. It remains understudied, probably because of the connection to that "other" woman-driven, frequently queer, online community of storytelling: fandom. More on that and other unusual works later.

Many others would find Twine during this surge thanks to Porpentine, who would quickly become one of Twine's most respected creators. In an essay she has since deleted that we quote here for its formative influence and power, Porpentine described the appeal of Twine's blank page as something other than the white page of the word processor. She particularly noted the value of Twine's original aesthetics, which I still appreciate myself—the black background of Twine 1.X's default story format lends itself to a certain atmosphere, while the chunked passage formats encourage thinking through fragments rather than confronting the whole. As she observed,

> So many people tell me their stories start to get personal no matter how they start out.
>
> Twine's default color scheme is blue on black, not black on white. Black on white is daylight, it's mundane. Twine invites us to write our secrets into the night. We can make it light in a line of CSS, but that the default is inverted feels non-trivial to me.
>
> More significantly, when we write in natural language, as opposed to code, we're in the element of the diary, the notepad, the confessional.
>
> Our engines shape our output. We can't pretend that the history of game design has been designing on a blank canvas or a white page. The history of game design has been working with a canvas that

screams at you and changes shape and rejects your strokes if they aren't just right—working with machines. (Porpentine, "Creation under Capitalism")

Published in November 2012, this essay exemplified everything that would make Twine important. Prior to my focus on Twine, I was interested in another tool that has this "personal" element, Adventure Game Studio. However, Adventure Game Studio is far more difficult for development, and the graphical narratives made with it frequently take their lead from commercial adventure games of the past rather than from text-based games. It and other genre-driven engines force the user/creator into a certain trajectory, demanding the embrace of dominant mechanics, while Twine offers the freedom of the creator-defined verb—the link—over any other interface.

Twine down the Rabbit Hole

As Twine became hip among the alternative gaming community, I was inspired by its throwback aesthetic to start playing with it not for game-making but for scholarship. The first time I used Twine for my own scholarly work was in the construction of *Alice in Dataland*, a project that began as part of Anvil Academic's abandoned (as far as I know) *Built Upon* series in digital scholarship. I combined Twine with other old-school hypertextual play throughout the project, using animated GIFs, simple canvas animation, and procedural play on classic forms such as Montfort's procedurally generated poem *Taroko Gorge*—all to explore Alice's rabbit hole as a metaphor for remediation, remediated.

The project was not at all what the editorial board of Anvil Academic had in mind—their vision of digital humanities scholarship was data-driven, database-heavy, and "modern," not web-nostalgic. A year after the initial announcement of my project and others being accepted, the editorial board posted a commentary on the project's failure, though that commentary foreshadowed something larger: the failure of the entire series, which as of 2020 has not published a volume, perhaps due to their emphasis on "production values: sophistication of interface design, complexity and power of the underlying software engine, and other features that (intuitively, at least) fall under the heading of technology rather than scholarship or intellectual content. The lone author, in other words, working without the support of a digital scholarship lab, finds it hard to compete when work is evaluated both for its technical sophistication and its intellectual content" (Moody). This is certainly accurate; particularly the demands of data-intensive work and complex development have only grown in overhead.

But such commentary also echoes some of the criticisms frequently aimed at Twine—criticisms that can be one of the platform's most important virtues. The lone creator, making work in hypertext, may release on games platforms but will never have work that echoes the technical style of their storefront companions. Twine creators frequently don't find a home for their games alongside the corporate marketplaces, which similarly forefront "production values" but instead have played a role in shaping new spaces for personal games. Similarly, I found my lone, strange Twine scholarly project a more suitable home in *Kairos*, a journal dedicated to multimodal rhetoric and thus full of experimental digital scholarship exploring the form. Here I found the same echoes of what Twine-makers were noting in games: Twine games, intensely personal, developed by the "lone author" in most cases, were easy to reject, to label as not-games—and would become central to the discourse of game or not game that was about to become much more than an academic debate.

Gamergate, or How Twine Helped Fuel a Culture War

In 2013, Zoë Quinn released a Twine game called *Depression Quest*. Quinn also broke up with an abusive boyfriend. The two events together would fuel the outbreak that we now call "Gamergate," which was essentially an onslaught of toxic masculinity, online warfare, and misogyny that would send several of its targets into hiding while fundamentally changing the discourse of gaming culture and game studies as a field. It put some academics into a hostile spotlight, fueled by the rhetoric of "saving" games from the onslaught of "feminists" and "social justice warriors" bent on ruining games for cisgender, hetero-sexual white men.

The outcomes are a testament to the deep understanding on the part of Zoë Quinn's ex of what makes men on the internet angry. The still-unfolding incident has been well documented elsewhere, but Twine's role as an inciting platform, and eventually a platform for commen-tary and resistance, is not so well known. Quinn recently published a detailed account of their experiences in and after Gamergate in Crash Override, covering both the roots of the movement in domestic abuse and the calculated attacks of their ex-partner and the years of coordi-nated harassment that followed. In that work, Quinn never mentions Twine but does discuss the works it enabled (they used Twine for both *Depression Quest* and the Crash Override resources they later devel-oped for victims of similar attacks).

During Gamergate, Klimas came under attack as the developer of Twine and alerted me when my name showed up with his in the discus-sion on Gamergate forums. I'd already linked the affordances of Twine to the Gamergate movement in some early talks where I'd been working through the significance of *Depression Quest*—as Quinn's work drew attention to the ways their ex used the existing groups of misogynistic, angry white supremacist groups (the same Donald Trump's campaign would tap into only a few years later), I was interested in what it was about Twine itself, not just the content produced on Twine, that added fuel to that culture war.

As a result of giving a talk of this kind at a conference that also included an inclusivity-focused Wikipedia edit-a-thon, a participant would put Zoë Quinn's work on Wikipedia. Thus Klimas's name and mine would become linked by the research of the same aforementioned posters mentioned. The initial message from Klimas (with the appro-priate title "quinnspiracy"), dated October 2, 2014, directed my atten-tion to an *Escapist* magazine forum, where my name had popped up as part of an elaborate conspiracy. For a while, I screenshotted mentions (and put all my accounts under two-factor authentication as a preemp-tive defense mechanism), but it amounted to very little other than a message from a colleague: "Wait, you're part of a vast conspiracy to bring down gaming from the all-powerful throne of academia and you didn't tell me?! I am so disappointed in you. Thanks for the heads up."

The conspiracy post noted my overlap with Klimas at UB as well as the presence of Twine in my courses, linking us in an elaborate conspiracy:

> In summation, you have an edit-a-thon hosted and facilitated by a Wikipedia admin who has been found editing for hire in the past. During that edit-a-thon someone registers an account at Stierch's urging and creates a bio for Zoe Quinn, less than an hour after Stierch writes some mocking edits on her page about video games linking to some social justice-style attack on gamer culture. Stierch protects Quinn's article from deletion but does not remove blatantly promotional language. The edit-a-thon was taking place at the university where the creator of Twine, the software Quinn's game uses, works and one of the other participants in the event that included the edit-a-thon attended the same university as the creator of Twine at the same time as the creator of Twine where she wrote about emerging software useful for creating interactive fiction and has since promoted Twine heavily in her work and at seminars. It is definitely a very shady situation. (link deliberately omitted)

I apologize for the rather lengthy quote, but I believe it demonstrates something essential in how the Gamergate discourse twisted community—among both academics and game-makers and those of us in-between—into conspiracy. The same story would later be added to the Gamergate wiki as part of the entry on Wikipedia. Clearly, I could have started and ended the history of my own involvement with Twine here. Whoever did this research paid more attention to my timeline than I had, though, in some ways, this autoethnography is its own rejoinder—a history focused on connections, not manipulation.

It was around this time that my entire scholarly focus changed.

This sounds like an exaggeration, but it's really not. Since Gamergate, I've cut down on my participation in games-centered research and spaces and instead focused on electronic literature, social media, and particularly how open platforms and communities can provide spaces for resistance and expression. Taking a step back from games also meant looking at the culture I'd long been part of as a so-called geek and examining the role we'd collectively played in shaping this moment.

This political bent started to inform my Twine workshops and my larger scholarship, which I shared in a session entitled "Lit Misbehaving" at the Modern Language Association (MLA) convention in 2014. The Digital Rhetoric Collaborative write-up of the session noted this focus: "Given the sexual harassment that women encounter when trying to form an identity as a game developer, Salter suggested that Twine has potential to change the definition of games and enrich the voices we hear in the gaming community" (Sullivan). Such write-ups (and indeed, my own work and the work of other feminist scholars at this moment) insufficiently grounded the importance of trans women and queer creators in leading the way, an omission in my own early work that I hope to remedy in this project.

Amplified by the hashtags of the conference and the realities of the moment, that year's MLA panel also ended up the subject of a weird blog post and YouTube video (edd77) designed to encourage criticism from the Gamergate loyalists, of which my personal favorite is a line-by-line repost of the account with commentary from cool_boy_mew reproduced in part here: "All in all, the feminists are the ones invading our space and making everything worse in their passage. These so called 'heroes' of feminism are completely toxic and the feminists academics are a complete mess. . . . We are not the monsters you make it out to be. If anything YOU are the monster. I've never seen so much bullshit disguised by a supposed drive to do good" (Irvine).

So obviously, after this type of scintillating commentary, I and all the other "monstrous" feminists in games gave up and went home.

Twine during Gamergate

Twine didn't quiet down after Gamergate started—it got louder. Several game-makers used it to comment on the moment, with one of the most powerful coming from D. Squinkifer via their game *Quing's*

Quest VII: The Death of Videogames. The game was released as part of Ruin Jam 2014, a jam "open to anyone and everyone who has been, is being, or plans to be accused of ruining the games industry" (Sandel). The game (shown in figure 10) featured an over-the-top narrative inspired by classic adventure games, featuring a narrator exiled from Planet Videogames following the Gamergate-analogous Culture War.

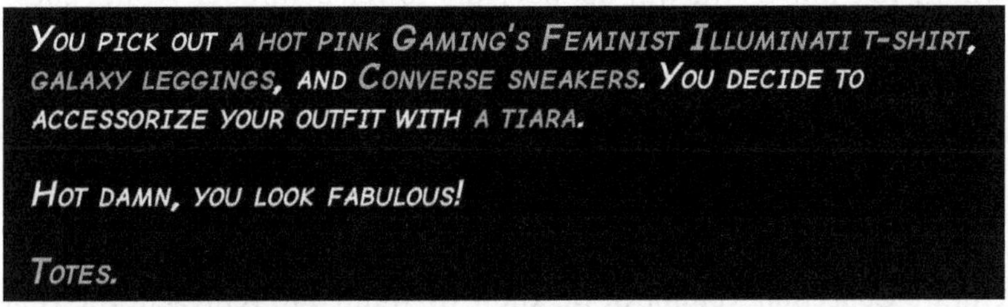

> YOU PICK OUT A HOT PINK GAMING'S FEMINIST ILLUMINATI T-SHIRT, GALAXY LEGGINGS, AND CONVERSE SNEAKERS. YOU DECIDE TO ACCESSORIZE YOUR OUTFIT WITH A TIARA.
>
> HOT DAMN, YOU LOOK FABULOUS!
>
> TOTES.

Figure 10: Like many people, I went out and bought the T-shirt

2014 was also the first year Twine entries outnumbered parser interactive fiction pieces in the annual XYZZY finalists. The shift from the relatively obscure influence of the parser, with its resemblance to the command line and its reliance upon an understanding of a verb-based interaction system, was received with mixed reactions at the time. While both hypertext and parser-based interactive fiction already had—and continue to have—a long history, this shift also served to bring new voices to the competition. As Klimas commented, "There is no doubt that Twine and its kind represent a different paradigm of interactive fiction. But I think there's more opportunity here for devotees of parser IF than there is ill omen. Easy for me to say, right? I created Twine. Of course I think this is a positive development" (Klimas, "War, Pestilence, Famine"). Six years later, the mix of tools suggests that Chris was correct and there is no winner—Twine and Inform 7 coexist, both bringing different opportunities to interactive fiction.

During this time of fallout and increased Twine visibility, I was invited to serve as part of the editorial board for the "Electronic Literature Collection—Volume 3," or ELC3, the latest volume in a series of compendiums compiled by the Electronic Literature Organization (ELO).

I wasn't quite sure what I was doing there, so I decided to make the most of it and get Twine represented within the discourse of electronic literature. This includes *Quing's Quest VII*, despite—in fact, in part because of—the dig at electronic literature within its text: when the player suggests migrating to "planet hypertext," a character responds, "Is that even a real planet, comrade? I thought it was a satellite. Is it inhabitable, even?" (Squinkifer). The game is no kinder to academia: "You'd be willing to climb all the way up that ivory tower, comrade? Wow, I guess we're in a more desperate situation than I thought."

Despite this skepticism of an admittedly often-closed ivory tower, several Twine authors agreed to be part of the collection, as shown in the index of the Twine keyword. We addressed our goals in including these works in the introduction to the volume: "In the *Electronic Literature Collection Volume 3*, we knew we wanted to represent the vital work happening in Twine, which hadn't really existed as a platform at the release of the ELCv2. However, this posed many challenges, including the problem of asking people who perhaps wouldn't identify with this research community or even the label 'electronic literature' to include their work in an ongoing open-access space. While most Twine works are released for free, several creators have been working to find ways to receive at least some payment for their work, or to leverage projects towards a career" (Boluk et al.).

The careful wording of this statement reflects some of my own unease about potentially colonizing Twine work by annexing it as "electronic literature." While Klimas clearly had that framework in mind while creating the tool, it is far less visible in the current work or ongoing communal discourse. The Twine works featured reflected some of the works that had most influenced my own view of how games could be reimagined. *Quing's Quest VII* appears alongside Anna Anthropy's *Hunt for the Gay Planet* and Porpentine's *With Those We Love Alive*, both of which we will discuss at length in later chapters.

In an interview following the publication of the ELC3, lead editor Leonardo Flores commented on how this type of work challenges existing definitions of electronic literature: "We also need to account for the ubiquity of computing and digital media. In the early days of the field, the distinction between print and digital writing was a convenient and rhetorically powerful trope. But now that most contemporary writing is already 'born digital' (though designed for print-based interfaces) its digitality has lost power as an indicator. This raises a few questions: how much of an engagement with digital and electronic media is enough for something to be considered e-lit? And what distinguishes e-literature from computationally intensive works such as videogames? How e-literary is a work of e-lit?" (Offenhartz and Flores).

I appreciated the double-sidedness of this disruption. The question of Twine's inclusion had the potential to challenge definitions of electronic literature with the same force as it has challenged the definition of games. Positioning Twine in the sphere of electronic literature—a space we both, with various levels of comfort, inhabit—can be reductive but also valuable for expanding the dialogue around the form. To revisit the early discussion of Twine as a platform and particularly that lingering question of "What is Twine for, anyways?" one way of understanding Twine is through Flores's lens of third-generation electronic literature—a tool for disrupting some of the field's assumptions and points of entry.

Teaching Twine

Throughout these various shifts in the tides of electronic literature and games and their corresponding rocking of Twine's boat, I spent a lot of time teaching Twine. Workshops that I used to teach with board games to avoid procedural barriers to design were rethought in Twine, and I introduced the tool to hundreds of students in the large courses I taught at UCF. My workshops have primarily reached humanities educators and librarians, who in turn often take Twine to their students in various disciplines.

Alexis Lothian commented on Twine's usefulness for teaching after using Twine with her students following an introduction in one of these workshops, noting that "Twine's structure of branching choices lends itself really well to explorations of the ways that our day to day choices are limited by dominant power structures" (Condis). She offered the example of a game exploring the experience of a nonbinary student continually asked to fit themselves into gendered boxes that made no room for them—a metaphor of play that particularly resonates with me, as most games (and spaces) still make no space for those of us more comfortable in-between.

Questions of accessibility more broadly are encoded in the choice of Twine over other more visual platforms. Former IFTF board member Flourish Klink noted that the organization's first two goals are to build a program to help sustain the Twine community over the next twenty-plus years and seek solutions for making interactive fiction games more accessible to people with disabilities: "There are many game genres that are difficult to make accessible . . . not because of any failure on the part of the developers, but because they simply require sight. On the other hand, it should be easy for [players with disabilities] to play an interactive fiction game . . . because interactive fiction is usually developed by indies who don't have experience with accessibility, sometimes that falls by the wayside. We plan to create resources to help those developers, and to work with projects like Twine, Inform, etc to make sure they have good accessibility tools" (Francis).

I explored this in a collaboration with UCF faculty and students engaged in a cultural exchange program with students from a school for low-vision students in Russia. They developed a game that combined large text and audio narrations—recorded themselves—with keyboard input replacing the need to touch a particular quadrant of the screen.

Working with Twine is usually part of my prototyping or rapid development workflow rather than my more complex work, simply because most things I want to make ultimately demand breaking out of some of the Twine aesthetics. I also resisted Twine 2.X initially (but have now embraced it), in part thanks to the aesthetic changes—the online editor in particular is too cheerful for me. I've spoken to others quietly about the use of Twine to create works that have no particular audience. The fragmented form lends itself to journaling or exploration.

I am continually impressed by the ability of writers to use Twine to respond to moments movingly and quickly. A recent standout that quickly sparked discourse among academics is *September 7th, 2020,* a stark work by Cait S. Kirby, released in the summer following the initial wave of COVID-19. It places the player on a reopened campus, confronting day-to-day challenges:

> You raise your hand. Your professor motions that it will be a few minutes. She's trying to answer other questions, but each question takes longer than usual due to masks and social distancing.
>
> While you're waiting, you look around. You see that a neighboring student is not wearing a mask.
>
> Do you motion for the student to put their mask on or pull your own mask tighter? (Kirby)

By asking the player to make impossible choices in the position of a high-risk student, the work pushes back on the choices universities are already making for students in the name of preserving a traditional experience of education. It is the best of Twine: personal and cultural, making an immediate impact in a charged moment of debate.

As we move out from the personal and gaze on Twine as a cultural object, we believe this divergence provides a useful framing to remember: Twine is personal, and our relationship with it is continually reshaped by the moment in which we use it. Twine is a platform but also a happening, and what's happening around Twine influences the expectations of those who pick it up and renew it. The future (and present) of Twine is in this trajectory of influence. As we will discuss later, Twine works now emerge into interfaces and forms ranging from print books to Netflix films to Unity games. Twine can be a beginning and an end (as we examine in chapter T-5, which delves further into queer Twine, camp, and the evolution of the GeoCities aesthetic), and it can be a beginning to new ends and new platforms.

Works Cited

Alexander, Leigh. "Game Creation for the Masses: What's Next for Twine." Gamasutra, October 9, 2014. https://gamasutra.com/view/news/227313/Game_creation_for _the_masses_Whats_next_for_Twine.php.

Argfored, Sukey. "THATCamp Games: Inform 7." *TeLS Webletter*, January 21, 2012. http://www.telswebletter.com/2012/01/21/thatcamp-games-inform-7/.

Boluk, Stephanie, Leonardo Flores, Jacob Garbe, and Anastasia Salter, eds. *The Electronic Literature Collection*. Vol. 3. Cambridge, MA: Electronic Literature Organization, February 2016. http://collection.eliterature.org/3/.

Condis, Megan. "Composition Games: An Interview with Dr. Alexis Lothian." *Unwinnable*, August 6, 2016. https://unwinnable.com/2016/08/08/composition-games-an-interview-with-dr-alexis-lothian/.

edd77. *Anastasia Salter on the Video Game Industry*. Accessed September 2019. YouTube video, 6:16. https://www.youtube.com/watch?v=K-JBZ3fKVzQ.

Ellison, Cara. "Anna Anthropy and the Twine Revolution." *Guardian*, April 10, 2013. https://www.theguardian.com/technology/gamesblog/2013/apr/10/anna-anthropy-twine-revolution.

Francis, Bryant. "Interactive Fiction Foundation Formed to Aid Twine, IFComp Growth." Gamasutra, June 30, 2016. https://www.gamasutra.com/view/news/276226/Interactive_Fiction_foundation_formed_to_aid_Twine_IFComp_growth.php.

Glorious Trainwrecks. March 29, 2018. https://www.glorioustrainwrecks.com/.

Gold, Matt, and Lauren Klein. "Debates in the Digital Humanities." *Debates in the Digital Humanities*, 2019. https://dhdebates.gc.cuny.edu/.

Irvine, Spencer. "Too Few Feminists in Video Games, Says Professor." Accuracy in Academia, January 23, 2016. https://www.academia.org/too-few-feminists-in-video-games-says-professor/.

Kirby, Cait S. "September 7, 2020." Accessed June 16, 2020. https://caitkirby.com/downloads/Fall%202020.html.

Klimas, Chris. IDIA student introductions, September 18, 2007.

———. "War, Pestilence, Famine, Death, and Twine—Chris Klimas." Chris Klimas, April 22, 2014. https://chrisklimas.com/blog/2014-04-22-129/.

———. "What I'm Thinking about for 1.1." Google Groups, December 4, 2006. https://groups.google.com/forum/#!searchin/tweecode/Right$20now$20the$20color$20scheme$27s$20pretty$20bland%7Csort:date/tweecode/BDKuEUy3nYc/wpid6eJzOTkJ.

———. "What Is Hypertext?" Twee Reference, October 1, 2009. http://twee-twine-doc.tiddlyspot.com/.

Kocurek, Carly A. "THATCamp Games Postmortem." *Carly A. Kocurek* (blog), February 14, 2012. http://www.sparklebliss.com/thatcamp-games-postmortem/.

K10blogger. "Info: A Look Back at the '90s Internet." *Info* (blog), April 23, 2011. http://randominfok10.blogspot.com/2011/04/look-back-at-90s-internet.html.

Larsen, Deena. "Fun Da Mentals: How to Read and Write Electronic Literature." Fun Da Mentals, 2008. http://www.deenalarsen.net/fundamentals/.

Moody, Fred. "The New Digital Divide | Anvil Academic." Anvil Academic, October 23, 2013. http://anvilacademic.org/the-new-digital-divide/.

Offenhartz, Jake, and Leonardo Flores. "Electronic Literature in 2016: Definitions, Trends, Preservation, and Projections." Entropy, February 1, 2016. https://entropymag.org/electronic-literature-in-2016-definitions-trends-preservation-and-projections/.

Porpentine. "collection of Twine games from me and other people." *Tweecode Google Group*, April 11, 2012. https://groups.google.com/g/tweecode/c/Jv_D7kx7CAo?pli=1.

———. "Creation under Capitalism and the Twine Revolution." Nightmare Mode [Archived], November 25, 2012. http://nightmaremode.thegamerstrust.com/2012/11/25/creation-under-capitalism/.

Ramsay, Stephen. "On Building." In *Defining Digital Humanities: A Reader*, edited by Melissa Terras, Julianne Nyhan, and Edward Vanhoutte. Ashgate Publishing, 2013.

Salter, Anastasia, and John Murray. *Flash: Building the Interactive Web*. MIT Press, 2014.

Salter, Anastasia, and Amanda Visconti. "THATCamp Games." THATCamp Games, January 22, 2012. http://thatcampgames.org/tcg-2012.

Sandel, Caelyn. "Ruin Jam 2014." itch.io, September 14, 2014. https://itch.io/jam/ruinjam2014.

Squinkifer, D. *Quing's Quest VII: The Death of Videogames*. Self-published, September 1, 2014. https://games.squinky.me/quing/.

Sullivan, Rachael. "Session 754 ~ Lit Misbehaving: Responding to New and Changing Modes of Production." Digital Rhetoric Collaborative, February 3, 2014. http://www.digitalrhetoriccollaborative.org/2014/02/03/session-754-lit-misbehaving-responding-to-new-and-changing-modes-of-production/.

CHAPTER P-2

Variation

If there had been computers and the internet in ancient Rome, they would most likely have been dedicated to Mercury—emissary, messenger, trickster. The planet named for this deity moves both backward and forward across the sky. The element called Mercury is quicksilver, a physical puzzle, fluid and solid at the same time, hard to hold. All these attributes can be applied to computational media. The great designer Alan Kay thought of personal computers as a "metamedium," a technology capable of mimicking or assimilating others (Kay and Goldberg). The theorist Lev Manovich has developed this insight to unfold the cultural impact of software (Manovich 23). These ideas build on an aphorism of H. Marshall McLuhan, who declared that the content of one medium is always another medium (McLuhan 10). Alphanumeric text is a container for language, and technologies like Twine bring text into the metamedium of software. Words like *contain* and *content* may suggest a static situation, like the nesting of Russian dolls, but actual experience is more complex and organic. The embedding of text in digital media more resembles the way very early microbes were assimilated by slightly newer microbes, eventually becoming the mitochondria in animal cells. Which is to say, it's more about biology than physics, involving complexity, development, surprises. *It's alive!*

These remarks bring us to the limits of theory, at least for present purposes. This practical chapter introduces possibilities beyond the basics covered in chapter P-1. The seven projects described here explore *variation* in Twine, both in how we use the software—looking at various approaches to textual variation—and in the software itself, surveying a variety of formats and structures available in the Twine world. In this book, we generally prefer Chapbook, the story format and coding environment best suited for learning Twine. The last two of our examples shift to Harlowe, a more powerful and somewhat more complex alternative. As in the first practical chapter, each exercise is a recipe you may follow as closely or loosely as you like. If you carefully type or copy-and-paste the components, each project should work as described within your local or online instance of Twine. Alternatively, you might read through the project descriptions, pick up their basic concepts, and adapt them to your own ideas.

We're all about variation here. Michael Joyce, the first person to write something called a hypertext fiction, famously said that, unlike print, "electronic text replaces itself" (Joyce 232). Reflecting on that remark, the critic N. Katherine Hayles wrote of "flickering signifiers," bringing the contingency of the moving image to the aesthetics of literary writing (Hayles). These insights originated in the days of cathode-ray tube monitors, when the flicker of screen refresh was more noticeable than it is in high-definition displays we use now. Yet the pixels that form our words still replace themselves many times per second under the control of software that can instantly recompose the screen matrix. These changes may come in response to our desires, or they may result from a glitch or accident—and there is a third possibility, a software program whose methodical rearrangement of elements produces something unforeseen. This is the technique we will explore in this chapter. We specialize in surprises.

◊ As in other practical chapters, action items will be boxed and set off with the symbol you see at left, in case you want to skip the contextualizing discussion (more's the pity) and go straight to keyboard practice. We fondly hope you will read the context passages at some point—ideally before you start building things—but we're just the writers.

Supporting materials for this chapter can be found online at https://github.com/AMSUCF/Twining. See our discussion at the beginning of chapter P-1 about using the .html and .txt files to follow along or adapt our code to your own purposes.

At this point, we need to say something more about story formats. For the first five examples in this chapter, we will be using Chapbook. We'll switch back to Harlowe for the final two. To change formats, launch Twine but do not open a story (stay in library view). Click on the "Formats" option in the right-hand column. You should see a radio-button list of all available formats. Click the button next to Chapbook—the highest numbered version if there is more than one. This designates Chapbook as your default story format. Every story you create from this point on will have Chapbook as its format. Existing stories in other formats will not be affected. They will still run in Harlowe, SugarCube, or whatever format you made them in. Likewise, you can change the format for any story during development—though that isn't a good idea if you've already begun to code.

Speaking of coding, you'll find that the examples in this chapter, and the chapters that follow, increasingly involve various forms of code. We'll start with CSS, a key element of web page coding, moving on to the native instruction set of Chapbook and its more powerful adjunct, JavaScript. We hope you won't feel stressed about coding. We'll make our way in small and gradual steps, with what we hope will be useful explanations at each step. There is an entire section devoted to error-checking and debugging at the end of this chapter.

Example 2.1: *Loki on the Links*

Before we get into deeper waters, let's spend some time on the most basic kind of variation that is possible in the Chapbook format: changes to the story's visual appearance, using its main CSS. Style sheets are sections of a document (sometimes independent documents themselves) containing instructions to the web browser specifying how the elements of a page should look. Though we speak of stories and passages in Twine, remember that Twine is delivered through a browser in the form of a page.

The simplest demonstration of this technique might involve simply resetting text color and page background (red text on magenta, midgray on deep black, blue on bluer, and other questionable choices). However, remember our discussion of hypertext links in the previous chapter, where we raised the possibility of links that are not visibly marked, as in Joyce's *afternoon*. We can do something similar with CSS in Chapbook. Hence the name of our example, *Loki on the Links*, which, we promise, does not involve the god of deceit playing golf with the god of thunder. (Unless that's where you think it needs to go. Just imagine the mulligans.)

◊ Open the Twine application on your computer or connect to the online version at www.twinery.org. As before, check your story formats to be sure Chapbook is present and selected. If it is not already selected as the default format, make it so. Start a new story. Set its format to Chapbook if it isn't that way by default. You can name your story anything you like. Name the first passage "Loki's work." Here's some suggested text:

```
The trickster has done it again, hiding the
hypertext links. Some words lead to [[Asgard]],
some to [[Midgard]], but which? [[Ship]],
[[hammer]], [[meadhorn]], [[goatsbreath]]. You
feel a [[thunder]] coming on.
```

If you test this story, it will come up in the usual way—black text on a white background. The linked words will display red underlining. We'll leave the text and background alone, but prepare to go all Loki on the links.

There are several ways to work with CSS in Twine. There is a link in the left-hand pop-up menu that reads "Edit story stylesheet." There's also the possibility of making a special passage and assigning it "CSS" in its tag field. Both of these mechanisms work for other story formats like Harlowe, but Chapbook has its own way of doing things—as does SugarCube, whose CSS features we discuss in chapter P-4.

To change the page styling in Chapbook, first return to the structure view. Hover your mouse over the starting passage of your story, the one with the green rocket. In the pop-up menu, click on the black triangle or arrowhead, which happens to be the "Test" button. You should see something like this:

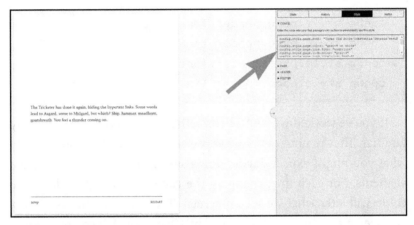

Figure 11: Test view in Chapbook

Two things about figure 11: First, the large arrow has been added as a visual aid. Also, the state shown here is one step ahead of our current progress. Once you've brought up the "Test" interface, locate the four tabs at the top right. Click on the one marked "Style." Below the tabs, you should see an option marked "CONFIG," with a rotated triangle. (If it's not rotated, click on the triangle to make it so.) Below that is a text window containing several lines of code. See where that large arrow is pointing. Drag over all the lines in that text window, being careful to select every character. Then do whatever you normally do to copy text (CTRL-C, Apple-C, right-click "Copy," etc.).

For insurance, open a word processor or (preferably) a text editor and paste in the lines you copied. It might be a good idea to save this document somewhere convenient like your desktop. Here's what you should have in that saved file:

```
config.style.page.font: "Iowan Old Style/
Constantia/Georgia/serif 18"
config.style.page.color: "gray-9 on white"
config.style.page.link.font: "underline"
config.style.page.link.color: "gray-9"
config.style.page.link.lineColor: "red-8"
config.style.page.link.active.color: "red-8 on
red-0"
config.style.page.header.font: "16"
config.style.page.header.link.font: "small caps"
config.style.page.footer.font: "16"
config.style.page.footer.link.font: "small caps"
```

If you've worked with CSS before, these lines should look vaguely familiar. They're not exactly what you see in web coding, but they do what you might expect, laying down specifications for several page elements. For each line, changing the value on the right side of the colon will alter what we see on-screen. The idiosyncratic style sheet you see here is the default installed by Chapbook. We can override it by installing a copy at a key point within the starting passage of our story.

◊ Your story will have eight passages if you're using our suggested text. Seven radiate out from "Loki's work." We'll largely ignore the child nodes—you can fill them in yourself if this project sparks your imagination. Open "Loki's work." Reselect all those "config" lines you copied and set aside. Paste them in *ahead* of the prose you entered in our first step. At the end of your inserted lines, on a separate line of their own, type two dashes:

```
--
```

Have a cookie or maybe a drink. You have just created your first *variables section* in Chapbook. A variables section, sometimes also called a variables block, contains programming instructions that will not appear on the screen. There's no formal term for the visible part of the passage code. In a web page, it would be the body, so we'll call it the text body. We'll be doing quite a lot with variables and the simple instruction set that comes with Chapbook, so you'll see more variables sections as we go.

Meanwhile, back to the one you just inaugurated. The instructions you pasted in provide a basis for the variations we desire. Let's get to work.

> ◊ Find the line for config.style.page.link.font. Change its right-hand value from "underline" to "none." (Keep the quotation marks.)

Now run your story. The red underline under the linked words has disappeared, so we've made the first step toward tricking up our links. However, if you hover over one of the linked words, you'll see that the word itself turns red. We can fix that.

> ◊ Find the line for config.style.page.link.active.color. Change its right-hand value from "red-8 on red-0" to "gray-9." (As before, keep the quotation marks.)

Run your story again. We've now gone about as far as we can, using Chapbook's config scheme alone, to disguise the link words. We've replaced red styling on the active link with an Open Color text color, "gray-9." The effect isn't perfect. If you're watching closely, you'll see that the system cursor still changes shape as the reader passes over a linked word.

At this point, our technical tinkering raises a question of design. Maybe these two levels create just enough uncertainty. Perhaps we just want our reader/players to look very carefully at the words as they pass over them. (Which suggests we might be doing something interesting with spelling or typography later in the story.) Or maybe we don't want to make the game aspect of our story too hard. At some point, many if not most technical decisions become design decisions.

For the true child of Loki, there is a way to suppress the cursor change on link hovering, though it involves levels of JavaScript that go beyond Chapbook and Twine. A bit of web searching should reveal those secrets, and we leave that sleuthing and experimenting to you. As for the rest of our story, that's also yours to imagine. Those seven second-level passages spurring out from "Loki's work" suggest the infamous Brillo pad problem we discussed in chapter P-1, but maybe you can find a way to manage them. Maybe it is a golf game after all.

Example 2.2: *The Daily*

This project makes up for the sprawl of its predecessor by staying within a single passage. It shows how, working in Chapbook, we can set conditions for the display of certain bits of text using a *modifier*.

> ◊ With Chapbook as the default format, create a new story and name it *The Daily*. (You can name it anything you like, really.) When the story opens, double-click on the supplied first passage and begin editing. Change the name of the passage to "Good Day!" (In the past, we've used systems that ruled out exclamation points and other special characters in the names of elements, but Twine is civilized about this.) In the text area of the passage, type the following:
>
> ```
> {now.weekdayName}
> ```

This is a strange expression, prosaically speaking, so let's give it some context. The main expression is enclosed in *curly braces*. In Chapbook, curly braces mark an *insert*, which is where code comes into contact with expressive text. In this case, we're inserting a variable called a *lookup object*. This variable exposes certain information that is available to Twine through the web browser—in this case, the name of the day of the week on which you are reading this story. The *now* object encodes a lot of useful information about the time of access, including the current time in hours, minutes, and seconds (no milliseconds—sorry). Though it's not important for this project, it's worth knowing that any information obtained in this way is accessed only once when the object is accessed, which for our purposes means when the passage is opened. JavaScript users may be familiar with similar lookup objects that can be accessed by web pages on the fly. Chapbook doesn't support that kind of dynamism. You get only one peek at the time, so don't plan anything that involves second-by-second updates, unless you're ready for advanced JavasScripting. If you're willing to wait twenty-four hours for things to change, it's all good.

◊ Skip a line after the first line and type the following:

```
[if now.weekdayName === "Sunday"]
Our story begins with a dreadful hangover.

[if now.weekdayName === "Monday"]
Our story opens with a deep sense of dread. Not
again.

[if now.weekdayName === "Tuesday"]
Our story starts out with a certain doomed
resignation.

[if now.weekdayName === "Wednesday"]
Our story figures it might as well get on with
itself.

[if now.weekdayName === "Thursday"]
Our story begins restlessly, eager to be over.

[if now.weekdayName === "Friday"]
Our story wants to know if it's 5:00 yet.

[if now.weekdayName === "Saturday"]
Our story will get back to you after this round
of drinks.
```

This seems a good time to point out that the lines following the *[if]* clauses are arbitrary and replaceable. Apologies if drinking and drudgery aren't things you can or wish to laugh at. Substitute other forms of daily variation if you'd like.

As you've probably figured out, this mélange of code and prose presents a different line for each day of the week. In Chapbook, anything inside square brackets is a *modifier*. In this case, we're using seven *if* modifiers to check the value in *now.weekdayName*. This example shows some notable features of Chapbook's coding style. First, notice that a modifier is a self-contained, one-line expression. There's no need to wrap the line that follows in any kind of markup. By rule, every line following a modifier is subject to the conditions of that modifier (in this case, the *if* test) unless another modifier occurs. There is a special modifier called *[continue]* that can be used optionally to disengage the previous modifier from subsequent text. We don't need to use it here because each of our modifiers terminates its predecessor, and each modifier only applies to a single line.

Also, note the triple sequence of equal-signs. If you've written any JavaScript, you probably remember that a double equal-sign is used in that language to evaluate a variable. The == symbol asks if the expression on the left side is equal to the expression on the right. Because Chapbook uses the double equal-sign for another purpose, we need to triple up. JavaScript, Java, and C programmers take note. At some point, you'll probably slip up and type == where you need ===. See our remarks on debugging at the end of this chapter.

Finally, a word about the usefulness of this example, which is admittedly dubious. People have written games and stories in Twine and other systems using weekday-sensitive expressions, but it's a highly specialized effect. We're showing it to you here partly to make a point about testing your code. You *could* spend 168 hours seeing if your story works as intended. Or you could change the name value in the first modifier to "Monday," then "Tuesday," then "Wednesday," and so forth, checking each time. You can change your code any way you want in testing. Just remember to change it back.

Example 2.3: *Our Story Unfolds* (Stretchtext)

Here's another relatively simple, one-passage project. We confess to having had some fun with the writing. Also, despite the Badger State references, for some reason, this is a Western.

◊ Check to be sure Chapbook is your default story format, make any necessary changes, and create a new story. Name the default passage "Our Story Unfolds." (Or anything you like.) In the text area of the passage, type the following:

```
Sheboygan Slim made a {reveal link: 'remark',
text: 'rude and uncalled-for observation about
the dubious parentage of the Kenosha Kid, not
omitting to cast doubt upon the breeding of the
horse he rode in on'}.
```

Let's contextualize. We're using an *insert* here—curly braces—and the type of insert is a *reveal link*. This expression places within the passage text a clickable link that replaces the initial argument—in this case, the word *remark*—with whatever follows the *text* attribute. You can use double quotes in place of the single ones used here, just be sure to close your quotes before the final curly brace. Leave the period outside of the insertion.

You can write as much or as little text as you want. Word-for-word replacements are often very effective, though in this case, we're implementing a concept called "stretchtext," in which one word or phrase is replaced by something longer. The name *stretchtext* was invented by Ted Nelson, who coined the word *hypertext*.

◊ After the first line and insert, add the following:

```
The Kid {reveal link: "replied.", text: "allowed
as how this being a free country, every honest
feller was entitled to his opinion, but wouldn't
```

```
the gent be more comfortable in some part of the
territory where the Kid's bowie knife wasn't
hard up against his fifth rib?"}
```

By now you probably understand how this structure works. Notice that we pulled the terminal punctuation into the initial argument because we're changing it from a period to a question mark when the second reveal happens. Small details like this matter in Twine works.

All you need to do at this point is test. Your initial state should look like this:

Sheboygan Slim made a remark.

The Kid replied.

Clicking each link unfolds its associated text. One limitation (or flaw) of this example is the possibility of a player opening the second link before the first. Perhaps you can think of a way to use this bug as a feature: could you write a stretchtext that rewards reading from the bottom up?

Example 2.4: Seamus, or Progress

This example is literally a shaggy-dog story. We have known an actual Seamus, though he never told the joke in question. There are two passages here. We use the *[if]* modifier and another lookup object, *passage. visits*, to control access to the second passage.

◊ Check to be sure Chapbook is your default story format, swap it in if necessary, and create a new story. Name the default passage "This Is Where You Are." (This name is referenced in a link, so change it at your own risk.) In the text area of the passage, type the following:

```
[if passage.visits === 1]
You are in a dimly lit room filled with gray
shapes.

[if passage.visits === 2]
You are in a dimly lit room filled with gray
shapes, one of which is moving.

[if passage.visits === 3]
You are in a dimly lit room filled with gray
shapes, the largest of which is moving rapidly
toward you.

[if passage.visits === 4]
You are in a dimly lit room filled with gray
shapes, the largest of which is human-sized,
covered with fur, and leaping onto your chest.

[if passage.visits > 4]
You are in a dimly lit room with a big, friendly
Irish Wolfhound. Down, Seamus. Nice doggie!
```

That's a fair amount of typing. There's yet more to add to this first passage, but let's discuss the stack of modifiers first. They may look familiar from example 2.2, where we set up story openings for each day of the week. Here we're deploying five variations for the text of "This Is Where You Are." One replaces another each time the player clicks the link at the bottom of the passage (to which we are coming). This effect depends on the lookup object *passage.visits*, which is a very handy feature of Chapbook. The story format code silently maintains a record of every passage you visit during a given play session, including the number of times you return. The variable in question gives us access to that count. At this point, you may be wondering where we go when we leave "This Is Where You Are." In fact, you go nowhere:

◊ Add the following to what you have typed previously:

```
[[Ticktock ->Next]]

[if passage.visits < 5]
[[Ticktock ->This Is Where You Are]]
```

The workings of these new lines require some explanation. As you can see, they are both standard, destination-specific hypertext links of the kind you learned in chapter P-1. However, they have some peculiarities. The first link, which leads away from the present passage to one called "Next," is governed by the fifth of those modifiers you typed in the first step, the one that reveals its text only when *passage.visits* is greater than four. This may create some confusion for those who are used to *if* structures with parentheses or braces that mark off what they affect. (Thanks to Noah Wardrip-Fruin for pointing this out.)

In Chapbook, a modifier applies to everything that follows until another modifier occurs. A modifier can apply to multiple lines even when separated by spaces. If we wanted our first "Ticktock" link to be independent of the test *passage.visits > 4*, we could put *[continue]* on a new line immediately following. However, we want to offer the reader a link to a new passage only if the visit count is five, when all the preceding variations have been presented, so we don't break out of the *if* modifier for the first of our two links.

We disengage the first test with a second test, this time for a value of *passage.visits* less than five. Chronologically, this may look strange, since we're previously covered the end of the game; however, the logic of the instructions (as we've written them, anyway) demands this bit of backwardness. This second condition covers the first four loadings of the page—because indeed, this page is designed to be loaded five times in succession. The second link has the same anchoring text as the link above it—the phrase "Ticktock"—but its destination is not the external passage "Next" but the present passage "This Is Where You Are." It is perfectly acceptable in Twine to link a passage to itself. When the visit count reaches five, it is replaced by the first link.

For the first five turns in this story, the player remains at the passage "This Is Where You Are" and each time sees a link at the bottom labeled "Ticktock." For a while, it just returns us to the same place, updated. On the fifth click, "Ticktock" leads to the passage "Next." Using the same text for the loop links and the eventual escape is a design decision. In the grand tradition of interactive fiction, where the difference between "twisty little passages" and "little twisty passages" has been celebrated (Montfort 92–93), we could have made the second link text "Tick Tock" (with a second capital *T*), or "Tock Tick," or maybe "Ding!" We're trying to be subtle here.

It only remains to write that next passage, which we admit is more than a little ridiculous:

◊ Create a new passage named "Next" and enter the following text:

```
_Have I ever told you the one about the priest,
the optician, and the Belgian national anthem?
Seamus inquires.
```

Yes, well, a talking wolfhound. Doubtless, you can think of something better. Finish and test. Your first four clicks should advance through the sequential descriptions. The fifth should take you to the second passage.

In closing, we will note that this example shows how you can develop multiple moments or beats of your story without making a transition between passages. Structurally, this suggests a way to reduce the number of passages in stories and possibly a means of keeping thematically related bits of your writing in the same unit of the map.

Example 2.5: Seating Chart

In our fifth project, we'll demonstrate a classic technique from games and simulations: the consequential combination of two variables. This pattern of logic has a clear application to real life, assuming you consider social etiquette and the seating of dinner guests a part of real life. More to the point, this example shows how to get extensive variation, and thus replayability, from a relatively compact structure. We'll also learn some things about the way Chapbook handles variables.

◊ Be sure Chapbook is your default story format, make it so if necessary, and create a new story called *The Seating Chart* (or what you will). Name the default passage "Table 12." The name will be used in a link, so change it with care. There's a fair amount of typing in the initial passage, so let's get some simple prose out of the way first. Type the following:

```
You've almost finished the seating chart for
the Bunstables' annual beet roast and Scrabble
tournament. Just two places remain at table 12.
```

◊ So much for the setup. Now let's get to the action. Skip a line and enter the following, being very careful to differentiate between curly braces and square brackets and to close all sets of quotation marks.

```
In the first seat, let's put {cycling link
for: "gent", choices: ["someone","Lord
Magnavox","Nasty Louie","Cousin Sue"]}.

And on the left, {cycling link for: "lady",
choices: ["someone else","Lady Splatt-
Simple","Violet Femme","Second Cousin Laraine"]}.

[[OK then! ->Decision]]
```

We're using an insert here called a *cycling link*, which creates a special kind of hypertext link. Instead of sending us to a new passage, this link replaces its current anchor with the next in a list, continuing through the list each time it is clicked and cycling back to the start. This is an enormously useful design element with great potential for both text variation and the kind of consequential choices upon which games depend. However, a cycling link is also quite complicated syntactically. It will break if you forget the colon after *choices*, which we do all the time. It will break insidiously if you forget the colon after *for*, introducing your variable. That is, the cycling element will work, but your variable will not be assigned a value. You need to be very careful when typing out a cycling link.

You can write cycling links without specifying a variable if you simply want to allow for changes in readable text. We want changes to have consequences, so we have a variable. Every time the link anchor changes, its value is stored in the variable specified by the *for:* argument. In the first instance here, we have a choice of four people for the *gent* variable. We get four more choices for *lady* in the second construction. (We apply these quaint gender categories with irony—Cousin Sue counts as a gent—but if the binary is unacceptable, feel free to use different categories: left/right, north/south?) The value of the respective variables will be whatever the player has made it when she clicks "OK then!" and heads to the next passage.

We'll get to that passage in a moment, but let's first discuss what you might do with a cycling link. Two sets of four options yield sixteen possible seating pairs, each of which you might treat differently. Of course, remembering the example of our overlinked sentence in example 1.2, you're not required to respond to every possibility—as you'll see, we're only interested in a few pairings and will write a generic response to cover those not featured. This strategy of selection makes it possible to expand the range of choices far beyond 4 × 4; though going to something like 12 × 12 or 16 × 16 might well be excessive.

What do we intend to do with the pairings we've singled out as special? There has to be a moment of reckoning, but that moment won't necessarily come in the next passage. Instead, we'll give our player a pause to reflect.

◊ Twine has already created for us a passage called "Decision." Open that passage and enter the following text:

```
You have seated {gent} next to {lady}.
```

All we're doing in this line is confirming the choices the player made through the cycling links in the previous passage. We store the seating assignments in variables called "gent" and "lady," respectively. We use two *variable inserts* to bring their values into the visible text. With the variables announced, we offer an initial response to the player's choices.

◊ Skip a line and enter the following:

```
[if gent === "someone" || lady === "someone
else"]
You do realize 'someone' is not an actual
person, right?

[if gent === "Lord Magnavox" && lady === "Lady
Splatt-Simple"]
They'll SO enjoy reminiscing about how he threw
her younger brother from that balloon.

[if gent === "Nasty Louie" && lady === "Violet
Femme"]
Now THERE'S a pair.

[if gent === "Cousin Sue" && lady === "Second
Cousin Laraine"]
Oh dear. Cousins.
```

Here we have a series of *[if]* modifiers, very similar to those you have seen in previous examples. Note the use of Boolean operators. *And* (&&) means both conditions must be met for the following text to be revealed. *Or* (||) shows its text if either condition is met. In terms of the story, we've decided that the most interesting pairs are Lord Magnavox and Lady Splatt-Simple, Louie and Violet, and the two cousins. We've kept the list small to spare you typing; you can probably see how it could be expanded. Notice that we haven't accounted for pairs that contain only one of our interesting parties (e.g., Lord Magnavox and

Second Cousin Laraine). We'll need to do that in the final passage. But first, let's finish "Decision."

> ◊ Skip a line after the previously mentioned text and enter the following:
>
> ```
> [continue]
> [[Hmm ->Table 12]]
>
> [[Outcome]]
> ```

The *[continue]* modifier, which can also be written *[cont]* or *[cont'd]*, terminates the modifier that precedes it, which in this case is the test for the two cousins. As we've noted, conditional-display modifiers apply to all the text that follows them, even after skipped lines, unless another modifier occurs. That's why we have *[continue]*. If we didn't use it here, our final links would appear only when both cousins were selected. The links themselves are the standard type. It's worth noting that we give players an option to rethink their selections at this point, in a (perhaps feeble) effort to lend the game dramatic tension. Uncertainty can be fun . . . so long as it's temporary. Let's proceed to the moment of truth.

> ◊ Twine will have created a new passage called "Outcome."
> Open it and enter the following text:
>
> ```
> happy: gent === "Nasty Louie" && lady ===
> "Violet Femme"
> veryHappy: gent === "Cousin Sue" && lady ===
> "Second Cousin Laraine"
> unhappy: gent === "someone" && lady === "someone
> else"
> veryUnhappy: gent === "Lord Magnavox" && lady
> === "Lady Splatt-Simple"
>
> --
> ```

Once again, you are looking at a variables section, as in example 2.1. In the last few examples, we've dealt only with variables that are automatically created as part of other structures like the cycling link insert. However, you can also make your own variables, which you do simply by assigning them a value, using a colon. Remember those crucial two dashes that divide the variables from the text body.

We create four variables here, reflecting four pairings with which we're either happy, very happy, unhappy, or very unhappy. The way we do this may need some explaining, especially if you're familiar with variables from other programming and scripting languages. In Java-Script, for instance, we might approach the current design problem by giving a specific value to a single variable, as shown in the following code excerpt. *Don't enter this code—it's for comparison only.*

```
//DO NOT TYPE THIS CODE INTO YOUR STORY!
var outcome = 0
if(gent == "Nasty Louie" && lady == "Violet
Femme") outcome = "happy"
if(gent == "Cousin Sue" && lady == "Second
Cousin Laraine") outcome = "very happy"
if(gent == "someone" && lady == "someone else")
outcome = "unhappy"
if(gent == "Lord Magnavox" && lady == "Lady
Splatt-Simple") outcome = "very unhappy"
```

There are more elegant ways to implement this logic in JavaScript (e.g., a *switch* statement), but the point is that Chapbook won't allow anything like them. That's because we can't use *if* conditions in the variables section. The *[if]* modifier can only be used to conditionally reveal text, and that can happen only in the text section of the passage, not up in the attic where we keep the variables. We can speculate that Klimas made this rule to minimize complexity in Chapbook. It keeps the system simple for those who aren't ready for a lot of logical maneuvers—and crucially, it allows a relatively simple work-around, which Chris kindly explains in the Chapbook guide.

As you see in the material you did enter, in the code block before the JavaScript example, we can render *if* tests unnecessary. Instead of defining four states of a single variable, we create a variable for each state and build our conditions into the definitions of the variables. This compromise keeps things simple but allows for sophistication—one of the best features of Twine.

◊ With the variables section done and dusted, we can move on to the text portion of the passage. Below the double dashes that close the variables section, enter the following text. You can skip a line after the dashes if you like, though it is not required.

```
[if happy]
We're sure {gent} and {lady} will get on like a
house afire.

[if veryHappy]
Bringing {gent} and {lady} together is the only
decent thing you have ever done.

[if unhappy]
We're sure something happened, but no one can
remember what.

[if veryUnhappy]
The evil encounter between {lady} and {gent}
was the first step toward disaster.
```

We can use *if* conditions here because we are in the main text body, not the variables section. Chapbook allows us to do conditional checking for the presentation of text—and for that purpose only. This code should be very familiar: it's a series of *[if]* modifiers providing tailored responses for each of the four privileged outcomes we've laid out. We slip in the values of *lady* and *gent* where they're interesting and omit them where they're not (the generic case). Each text will come up if its pairing condition is met—but what happens if the player makes a match we haven't provided for (for instance, Nasty Louie and Lady Splatt-Simple?) Type on.

```
◊ Skip a line and enter the following:

[if !happy && !veryHappy && !unhappy &&
!veryUnhappy]
The evening was neither triumph nor disaster.

[continue]
{restart link, label: "Start over"}
```

When it precedes the name of a variable, the exclamation point means "not." In Chapbook, the "not" condition is met either if the variable contains the Boolean value *false* or if the variable has not been assigned a value. The condition we match here is compound—all four must be false or empty. If so, we assume the choice was one in which we're not especially interested, and we cover ourselves with an evasive answer. At the end, we have our now familiar *[continue]* modifier, then a structure you haven't seen, the *restart link* insert. This link has the same effect as clicking the "RESTART" link in the Twine application: it wipes out the values of all variables, including *passage.visits*, and gives us a fresh start.

This example shows what we can do with the simple affordances of Chapbook, but it also reveals some limitations of that story format. For the sake of exploration, the final two examples in this chapter will set Chapbook aside in favor of Harlowe, an earlier and in some respects more powerful alternative. There are good reasons to be familiar with more than one format. The best way to learn any coding practice is by reading other people's code. At this writing, much of that existing code uses Harlowe. When you look into these other practices, you may find some of them appealing. Remember, though, that it is not possible to mix Harlowe and Chapbook code structures. (Maybe someday a story format will permit this. Who knows?) You must declare your story format before beginning a story. Let's see what happens if we declare differently.

Example 2.6: *The Changing Room* (Harlowe)

◊ Create a new story in Twine and name it *The Changing Room* or anything else you'd prefer. Open your story. Along the bottom line of the Twine window, immediately to the right of the story title, you'll find a triangle. Click it to expand a menu. The third item of this menu is "Change Story Format." Select that item and you will see a list of available formats. If you've set Chapbook as your default, it will appear as the current format for this story. Switch to Harlowe by clicking its radio button. If you have multiple versions of Harlowe available, choose the one with the most recent release (e.g., Harlowe 3.1).

◊ Now create a new passage and name it "Changing Room." Notice the Twine authoring interface is unaffected by the change in story formats. Story formats only affect the way Twine code is passed to a web browser for display. However, Twine being an open-source, user-built system, each format comes with its own dialect of code. The Twine world is a bit like Europe—you can step across a border and find the language very different from what you speak back home, so there's a reason to learn multiple languages. Consider the following experience a lesson in language immersion. Enter the following text into "Changing Room":

```
You (either: "are","find
yourself","awaken","begin to
exist","materialize") in (either: "the UNREADY
ROOM","the CHANGE EXCHANGE","a SHIFTY SORT
OF LOCATION","a PLACE of POSSIBILITIES","ZONE
UNKNOWN").
```

At first glance, Harlowe might not look all that different from Chap-book. There's the same in-line mix of programming structures and nar-rative prose. Looking more closely, you'll see that Harlowe uses different characters for demarcation—parentheses instead of curly braces and square brackets. Both of those markers also occur in Harlowe, though not in the present instance. The structure you're seeing here is called an *(either:)* macro. Macros are a bit like inserts in Chapbook—they allow for textual variation according to logical conditions.

The *(either:)* macro allows the writer to create a list of elements from which Twine/Harlowe will *automatically select an item at random*. As we'll see in chapter P-3, the same thing can be done in Chapbook, but not as elegantly as in this holy macro. As you will surmise, we are inor-dinately fond of *(either:)*. It's among the simplest ways we know, in any coding idiom, of quickly creating a planetary cloud of language, spinning it up, and seeing what rolls out. There is only one thing about *(either:)* we can't completely applaud—its name. In English, the prepo-sition *either* should only be used with two alternatives—either my way or the highway. Include a third option and you need another preposi-tion. Strictly speaking, this macro should have been called *(one of:)*, and in fact, there's a structure with that name, and a very similar func-tion, in the interactive fiction language Inform 7, to which we assign grammatical bragging rights.

Name-wince aside, consider the power of *(either:)*. Here we've ap-plied it to the main verb clause and predicate of our opening sentence, but we could give any word similar treatment. While that might once again cast us back to example 1.2 and its attempt to link all the words, an extensive use of *(either:)* is more feasible. It's only a matter of writing some quick lists. Let's do a bit of that now.

◊ Skip a line and enter the following:

```
There is a(either: " zither","n astrolabe","n
Earthkey"," chef's hat"," trilobite"," ghost
weasel") to the (either: "left","right","nor
theast","windward") of a(either: " large","n
```

```
obvious"," cryptic"," throbbing") (either:
"snowman","theater critic","armoire","pyramid","
tank trap").
```

Needless to say, you don't have to use the words provided here. Come up with your own absurdities, by all means. Though do note the way we've finessed the a/an problem in the first and third instances, adding a space before words beginning with a consonant and a letter *n* with a trailing space for words beginning with a vowel. You might also notice that the option list in an *(either:)* macro can be as long or short as you want and that every list is independent—though you will need to think about possible combinations in case of hookups that are ungrammatical or unintentionally obscene.

```
◊ Skip a line and finish the passage:

You can see (either: "a blank wall","an [[Open
Door!->Done]]","nothing of interest","a wall
that is blank","a blankish wall of a wall","a
wall of blankness","the blankest wall in the
world","an unsatisfying wall") here.

[[Change the world . . .->Changing Room]]
```

The macro at the start of this fragment should pique your interest. The second option includes a link to another passage. Yes, you can include a link as a possible selection in an *(either:)* macro. Since this is one of eight options, and since selections from an *(either:)* are effectively unpredictable, it's possible to run through quite a few iterations before the link appears. It's also possible for a player who doesn't expect the appearance of the link to overlook it when it does show. In other words, this is a questionable bit of design. You might want to treat your player with greater respect.

Finally, you'll notice that the link at the bottom of the passage connects to the passage itself, functioning as a refresh button. As we've said, that's OK. All the *(either:)* macros operate when the passage is reentered. The place reconfigures itself. The 1:8 lottery for the exit link is run again—if the player comes up lucky, it's possible to move on.

> ◊ The second passage, "Done," will not be generated automatically because its link structure occurs within a macro. You'll need to create it and enter within it the following text. Using French is optional:
>
> ```
> Plus ça change.
> ```
>
> ```
> [[Try Again ->Changing Room]]
> ```

Example 2.7: Carousel

We'll stay with Harlowe for our final example, which uses another tasty macro called *(live:)*. Like its corresponding structure in Chapbook, the *[after]* modifier, *(live:)* defines a span of time between the opening of the passage and some further transformation. In Chapbook, we're limited to the display of text. Harlowe offers much more range, allowing us to trigger any other macro after the delay. That includes the intriguing macro *(go-to:)*, whose counterpart in Chapbook is undocumented and not officially supported. The *(go-to:)* macro allows a code-defined transition from one passage to another *without player action*. In the sweet, meticulously turn-based world of Chapbook, that would be outrageous.

Let's be outrageous. We'll apologize later.

> ◊ This project has five smallish pieces. After starting a new story and setting its format to Harlowe, you might want to create all five passages. You can name them numerically, "01" through "05." (The zeroes are just for show, and in fact, you can name your passages anything you want, as long as you use the correct names in your *(go-to:)* macros.) Open "01" and enter the following:

```
Room 01

The Eye of Imus (click: "Eye") [(set: $hasAmulet
to false)]

(live: 2s)[
    (if: $hasAmulet is false)[(go-to: "02")]
]
(stop:)
```

All our rooms will follow the same pattern. They will contain an object—in this case, the Eye of Imus. (Doesn't bear thinking about.) For each of these objects, its main noun will be the subject of a *(click:)* macro, which plants a special hyperlink on the word or phrase supplied. When activated, this link *sets the value of a variable*. We say this with emphasis because it's something you can't do in Chapbook, at least not in such a direct way. Harlowe allows authors to set and reset variable values within the passage, independent of passage transitions. This means that the experience of a Harlowe-based story—for instance, Porpentine's *With Those We Love Alive*, discussed in the next chapter—can be much more eventful than in basic applications of Chapbook. Possibilities for action abound.

Curiously, the action here sets the value of a Boolean variable, "$hasAmulet," to false. (In Harlowe, variable names begin with a dollar sign.) You might expect a click on the name of a mystical object to activate that object or perhaps add it to our inventory. We could have provided for these possibilities, but as you'll see, we only care about that amulet. The other four items are MacGuffins.

Below the "Amulet" line, you'll see the *(live:)* macro. The argument "2s" means two seconds. That's all the time the player is allotted in any of the passages, which all contain a variant of this macro. After two seconds, we perform a test on "$hasAmulet," and if it is false, we execute the *(go-to:)* macro and flip to the second passage (or room). You'll see a *(stop:)* macro on the final line here. This macro terminates the previous *(live:)*. Theoretically, the timer will continue to run if we don't do this.

◊ Passages 02, 04, and 05 are nearly identical to 01, so let's
write them in next. Then we'll come back to the crucial passage 03. Open each passage in turn and type in the following
text. The only changes are the names of the mysterious objects
and the destination passages in the *(go-to:)* macros.

For passage 02

Room 02

```
The Stone of Blarney (click: "Stone") [(set:
$hasAmulet to false)]

{
(live: 2s)[
   (if: $hasAmulet is false)[(go-to: "03")]
]
(stop:)
}
```

For passage 04

Room 04

```
The Chalice of Malice (click: "Chalice") [(set:
$hasAmulet to false)]

{
(live: 2s)[
   (if: $hasAmulet is false)[(go-to: "05")]
]
(stop:)
}
```

For passage 05

```
Room 05

The Charm of Bracelets (click: "Charm") [(set:
$hasAmulet to false)]

{
(live: 2s)[
   (if: $hasAmulet is false)[(go-to: "01")]
]
(stop:)
}
```

We've already explained the code contained in these passages. As you've probably figured, they form a loop or carousel, spinning the player from room to room with only two seconds in each destination. More about this dubious design later, but first a technical concern raised by Dr. Wardrip-Fruin, who we should note has a graduate degree in computer science. He wonders, "What will happen if the word 'Eye' [in the first passage] isn't clicked within the first two seconds? Will we be testing an undefined variable?" (Wardrip-Fruin). This question shows the difference between actual expertise and whatever goes on in our heads. It also shows the way Twine and Harlowe make life easy for foolish experimenters. As best we can explain, with recourse to the debug view that comes with Harlowe, the *$hasAmulet* variable doesn't exist for Twine until something is clicked, at which point its value is either *true* or *false*. We do indeed test for these values in the subsequent passages, but thanks to Harlowe's JavaScript roots, it has no qualms with nonexistent variables. It gives the software equivalent of a shrug and moves on.

However, do not expect such generous treatment from other software entities, including Chapbook, which may report an "unexpected error" when asked to do something with a variable not previously defined.

Now back to the outlandish design of this project. Why two seconds per passage? We chose that number arbitrarily for purposes of demonstration. It's almost certainly too short, and it raises uncomfortable questions about ableist game design. Lots of people have trouble reading short bursts of text in a few seconds or may need more time to execute a manual response. Arguably, we don't need more games like this one, even (or maybe especially) as a parody. We offer the example with the perhaps foolish hope that its autotransition mechanism may be used for more humane purposes. See, for instance, Anna Anthropy's *Queers in Love at the End of the World*, about which we will have more to say in the conclusion of this book.

◊ For whatever it may be worth, let's finish the Carousel of Story by entering the following text into passage 03:

```
Room 03

The Amulet of Immobility (click: "Amulet")
[(set: $hasAmulet to true)]

{
(live: 2s)[
   (if: $hasAmulet is false)[(go-to: "04")]
   (else:) [Congratulations, you have stopped
   the Carousel.]
]
(stop:)
}
```

There are only two small variations here. Clicking on "Amulet" sets "$hasAmulet" to true, which deactivates the machinery of dislocation. In recognition of this fact, we set an *(else:)* macro below the *(if:)*, catching the happy condition and reporting the same.

And so we have whirled our way from Chapbook to Harlowe and from simple hypertext to dynamic games. In the next chapter, we take a similar journey, this time on the theoretical and critical side, considering how Twine's various trajectories intersect the grand arcs of literature and culture. Bring the amulet.

Before you go, however, there's a subject we need to discuss at the risk of raising some anxiety—and you thought you'd heard That Talk. We need to say some things about debugging. Code requires close attention to both details of expression (syntax) and arrangement of instructions (logic). You may need some practice to work up this kind of attention. Even for experienced hands, mistakes are inevitable, so let's consider how to manage them.

Debugging

There are basically two ways things can go wrong with a Twine project. Sometimes a story works, meaning it does not report any fatal errors but doesn't work as intended. This is usually a problem of logic or design. We'll talk about those problems in a bit. First, let's discuss the more common and annoying source of trouble, which is often typographic—you forget a character or type the wrong one. The result, in the current version of Chapbook, is what we call the Pink Screen of Pain:

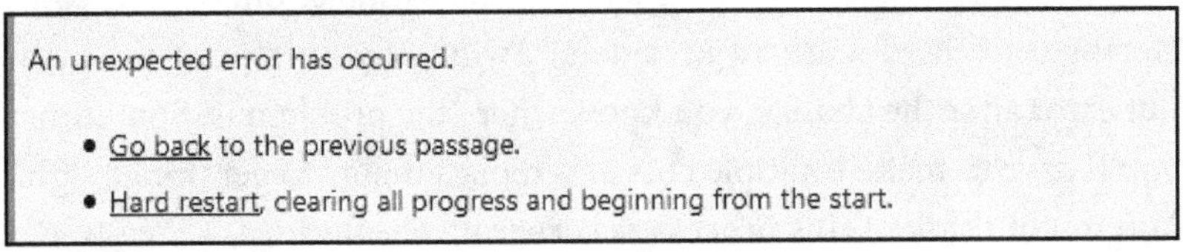

```
An unexpected error has occurred.

  • Go back to the previous passage.
  • Hard restart, clearing all progress and beginning from the start.
```

Figure 12: "Unexpected error" report in Chapbook

When code is not written properly, Chapbook reports an "unexpected error"—now *there's* an irony!—which can be as useful as your mechanic saying "that wasn't good" as smoke pours out of your car. The error window does include two links, "Go back" and "Hard restart," that sometimes prove useful, though in many cases (for instance, when there is no previous passage), they don't help at all. In most cases, you'll need to dig through your code to find technical or syntactical mistakes.

If you use the "Test" feature instead of "Run," Chapbook will open a debugging window that may offer a more detailed error report. For instance, it might say something like

```
SyntaxError: missing ] after element list
```

This hint alerts us to look for structures that use square brackets and take the form of lists, including arrays. As a general rule, you should look closely at (parentheses), [square brackets], and {curly braces}; try not to mix them up; and make sure that each left-hand character has a right-hand counterpart. In the case of expressions where both [] and {} are required, such as the cycling link in Chapbook (example 2.5), you may want to have a reference document like the Chapbook guide open in your browser. We often forget even basic syntactical forms if we haven't written code for a while. You don't need to memorize rules if you can look them up.

If your code contains several complicated expressions, and thus multiple openings to error, here's a technique to try. Suppose you have a pair of variables containing extended lists in the form of arrays with lots of typographic complexity. Open a document in a word processor or (preferably) text editor and cut one of the variables out of your code, storing it in the document outside of Twine. If your story runs without error after the change, you know where the problem is. Sometimes you'll have to make multiple cuts and replacements to get things right. You might think of this process as *cornering the bugs*.

Once you've dealt with each all-too-expected error, you can move on to the more mysterious problems of logic. The only way to solve these is to think through your code and its consequences step by step. An example of that thinking occurs at the end of example 2.7, where we mention a critical note on our code given by an experienced software designer. He caught a legitimate flaw in our design by mentally inspecting the state of the system at a certain moment of operation. You may find yourself thinking in code after a while. (If you start dreaming in code, maybe you need a break.)

Talking about debugging is essential, though as we said, it may raise anxiety. The best nonchemical antidote to anxiety is playfulness.

Screwing up code on your local device is unlikely to have terrible consequences in the larger world. Yes, it can darken your mental weather, but hopefully, that weather is changeable. So fail boldly if not better. No error is ever unexpected. You're going to foul things up. There's a reason that programmers use the names *foo* and *bar* for test variables—as in FUBAR, effed up beyond all repair, which is the fate of most complicated systems sooner or later. Fixing those systems can be pleasurable. Eventually, you may even learn to smile at your mistakes. They have value. Often we need to make mistakes to investigate and learn. Try to experience the pink screen without pain—frustration may be unavoidable. The root word of *error* means *wandering*, which can also mean *exploring*. There's plenty of that still ahead.

You still have the amulet, right?

Works Cited

Hayles, N. Katherine. "Virtual Bodies and Flickering Signifiers." *October* 66 (Autumn 1993): 69–91.

Joyce, Michael. *Of Two Minds: Hypertext Pedagogy and Poetics*. University of Michigan Press, 1995.

Kay, Alan, and Adele Goldberg. "Personal Dynamic Media." In *The New Media Reader*, edited by N. Wardrip-Fruin and N. Montfort. MIT Press, 2003, 391–404.

Manovich, Lev. *Software Takes Command*. Bloomsbury, 2013.

McLuhan, H. Marshall. *Understanding Media: The Extensions of Man*. McGraw Hill, 1964.

Montfort, Nick. *Twisty Little Passages: An Approach to Interactive Fiction*. MIT Press, 2003.

Wardrip-Fruin, Noah. Personal correspondence. April 28, 2020.

Twine and the Question of Literature

Legacy?
PÍÍÍÍÍÍÍÍÍÍÍÍÍÍÍÍÍÍÍÍÍÍÍÍt!
—Xalavier Nelson Jr.

Whoever

Twine is generally described as a tool for telling stories that involve what Espen Aarseth calls "non-trivial" engagement or, as it is familiarly known, interactivity (Aarseth, *Cybertext* 2). Writers using Twine have made and continue to make compositions of striking vision and sophistication, covering a range of expressive possibilities. There are richly conceived science fiction stories like Jedediah Berry's *Fabricationist Dewit Remakes the World* (Berry) and Tom McHenry's *Tonight Dies the Moon* (McHenry). There are deep excursions into fantasy, such as Kevin Snow's *Beneath Floes* (Snow), Porpentine's *Howling Dogs* (Porpentine, *Howling*) and *With Those We Love Alive* (Porpentine, *With Those*), the latter a subject of this chapter. Some works interrogate terms and techniques of interactive storytelling, as in Michael Lutz's *My Father's Long, Long Legs* (Lutz), which visually tunnels into narrative, and D. Squinkifer's *Quing's Quest VII: The Death of Videogames* (Squinkifer), which asks hard questions about the putative ends of play. Twine writers have created parodic tours de force, including Porpentine's *Ultra Business Tycoon III* (Porpentine, *Ultra Business Tycoon III*), Kris Ligman's *You Are Jeff Bezos* (Ligman), and Jon Bois's *Bill Belichick Offseason Simulator* (Bois).

The appeal of Twine crosses literary generations, as in the work of John McDaid—to which we are coming—or Richard Holeton's Twine-based autobiography (Holeton). Resonance and references can implicate nondigital work as well. *Tonight Dies the Moon* opens with a sardonic quotation from David Barthelme; *Howling Dogs* begins with a long passage from Kenzaburo Oe; *You Are Jeff Bezos* is both a striking piece of social commentary and an homage to Kafka's *Metamorphosis*.

This chapter asks a controversial question: *Can Twine works be thought about as literature?* In some ways, the obvious answer might be no. Many if not most Twine creators call their works games, not fictions, essays, or plays.[1] As Astrid Ensslin and others have pointed out, game and story need not be exclusive categories, and the categorization itself can be questioned (Ensslin). Darius Kazemi, Twine writer and game critic, has wisdom on this point:

> I guess what I'm trying to say is: if games AREN'T working for you as a tool for creative expression, don't give up on games, but also try some other stuff. Don't try and bend ideas to fit into the mold of "game." MAYBE try and bend "game" to fit to your idea, that might work (I'm thinking of Twine games here, which bend the concept of game so much that it makes traditional game designers cranky that the authors have the audacity to use the word "game." This also works in the other direction: please think about whether your Twine game should be an essay instead.) (Kazemi)

Arguably, Twine works bend more than just the concept of *game*. They ring changes on culture generally and writing in particular. For

---

1 The term *poem* might remain in play. Porpentine refers to Pierre Chevalier's *Destroy / Wait* as a "poem" in a comment. Anthropy has a category for "Game Poems" on her website. Outside of the Twine world, Bogost has published a series of Atari games meant to be understood as poems (Bogost).

that reason, they are hard to write about. As we have said, one of the things that makes this book such a strange combination of impulses is the way Twine sits between cultural identities—story and game, art and entertainment, personal statement and commercial production. Categories are not good tools for thick description. The emergence of Twine as a creative platform, itself part of a software subculture that includes things like interactive fiction, the demoscene, e-poetry, and metagaming, is, as Johanna Drucker says of all digital writing, less entity than event (Drucker). The event is still in progress.

Twine creations are many things. Their frequent use of meaningful choices brings them very close to games, as some have defined them.[2] They may include images, sound, and temporal effects that make them comparable to film.[3] For the most part, though, Twine works use words to describe characters and tell stories. This begins to look like literature, though the recognition may be more of resemblance than identity.

As our epigraph from independent game designer Xalavier Nelson Jr. reminds us, people who make things like Twine games often distrust terms like *legacy*. These creators are part of an active, vital art movement that lives very much in its early century moment, still unfolding and far from conclusion. And yet, as Nelson went on to say in the same talk, "I'm going to DIE one day"—not for a long, long while, we hope, but the sentiment is as real as it is universal (Nelson). We all live in time, bringing anxieties to any moment. The discomfort is twofold: legacy points backward as well as forward. We inherit as well as bequeath. The problem of the timeline can't be dismissed, even with a much-extended *Pffft*.

Trying to wind Twine works around some traditional literary axis may be as risky as filing jazz under American popular music or calling the Marvel Cinematic Universe (MCU) cinematic. Those descriptions

---

2 See the discussion of this criterion in Juul's *Half-Real*, Myers's *Games Are Not*, and Consalvo and Paul's *Real Games*. The question of what is and is not a game has been vexed by the Gamergate culture war. Here as elsewhere in this book we refer to various constructions nonexclusively. Meaningful choices are one way to define games, but not the only way.

3 See chapter T-5, where we discuss Claudia Lo's reading of *Queers in Love at the End of the World* via slow cinema.

are valid, but they need unpacking. Technically and aesthetically, the digital fantasies of the MCU lie a long way from the heyday of smoke-filled movie houses and celluloid film.[4] It might be more accurate to say, as film theorists have largely decided, that digitally rendered works redefine cinema (Gaudreault and Marion 154). As for jazz, it is every bit as American as chattel slavery. It is the signature of a nation that should never have been, or ever again be, dedicated to whiteness. Both cases teach us this: time keeps running, but there's no escape from history.

Over multiple generations, any art is a dynamic system. Its state will change both in gradual increments and abrupt, shearwise jolts. Such disruptions involve both memory and forgetting, and their tension generates waves of irony. My first lesson in this effect came when I was very young, listening to a song by Paul Simon called "A Simple Desultory Philippic (or How I Was McNamara'd into Submission)." First written in 1965 and revised for the album *Parsley, Sage, Rosemary and Thyme*, the song is a broad, talking-blues send-up of Bob Dylan (Simon and Garfunkel). In an unmistakable twang, Simon reels off topical jokes on the way to a final epiphany:

> *I've paid all the dues I'm going to pay*
> *'Cause I learned the truth from Lenny Bruce*
> *That all of my wealth won't buy me health*
> *So I smoke a pint of tea a day*

I probably heard these words in 1969 or 1970. Like many products of the sixties, the "Philippic" aged too fast. Even then, it needed decoding—Lenny Bruce, celebrated bad boy of standup; Robert S. McNamara, major architect of the Vietnam war; tea, another word for pot; but what else was Simon going on about? At that moment, Dylan the protest-hero felt even more mythical than the recently broken-up Beatles. My barely teenage self couldn't process the cultural grudge, and the second part of the song made things murkier:

---

4 The exquisitely classical screen kiss that ends *Avengers: Endgame* proves this by exception.

I knew a man, his brain was so small
He couldn't think of nothing at all
Not the same as you and me
He doesn't dig poetry
He's so unhip that when you say Dylan
He thinks you're talking about Dylan Thomas
Whoever he was

Though it probably explains a lot, please set aside the tiny tragedy of a seventies teen learning stale material. Focus instead on Simon's cultural unpeeling—"Dylan Thomas, whoever he was"—but remember, no internet. In 1970, if you were lucky and relatively privileged, a parent or teacher might tag the Welsh poet (1914–53) and quote something more interesting than "Do not go gently." You could then appreciate the shade in Simon's lyrics, the way they call out a counterculture hooded in historical blindness. At the very least, you could feel the divide between old world and new, even as, confusingly, you sensed *the truly hip* denied it.

History favors convergence. Fifty years later, we had the hyperirony of Bob Dylan's 2016 Nobel Prize for Literature, desultorily accepted a year later, which put the business of 1965/1966 in rather a different light. Dylan/Thomas: "assuming that's a distinction you observe, heh heh," to quote that other prophet of the terminal sixties, Thomas Pynchon (Pynchon 411). Cultural fissures inevitably appear, displacing now from then, but countervailing forces bend toward atonement.

What, you may ask, do these vinyl memories of the very late sixties have to do with Twine writing, born and bred in the next century? It is a question of history, if not legacy. The Twine platform and the writers who distinguish it are at least convergently millennial, but the story to which they belong begins well before 2001. The code resources on which Twine is based, HTML and JavaScript, date from the late 1980s and mid-1990s. The internet protocols that underlie them were indeed mid- to late-sixties productions (see Galloway). There is a history here.

Art tends to involve precedents. The kind of storytelling commonly done with Twine has three main ancestors: game books (choose-your-own-adventure stories), parser-based text adventures

(interactive fictions), and hypertext fictions. A popular novel with op-
tional reading schemes was published in 1930 (Hopkins and Webster).
Game books for younger readers became broadly popular in the 1970s
(Nikolajeva). Interactive fiction made its debut in procedural narratives
like *Oregon Trail* in 1971 (Rawitch, Heinemann, and Dillenberger) and
Colossal Cave Adventure (Crowther) five years later.[5] Hypertext fiction
began in the mid-1980s with Judy Malloy's *Uncle Roger* (Malloy) and
Michael Joyce's *afternoon: a story* (Joyce, *afternoon*).

Opinions differ about whether these works belong to literary history. At a certain point in the early history of digital fiction, it was
fashionable to accuse them of debasing literature (see most notoriously
Birkerts). Nonetheless, figures associated with hypertext, such as Joyce,
Shelley Jackson, and John McDaid, have identified mainly as fiction
writers. Montfort aligns interactive fiction with the ancient poetic genre
of the riddle (Montfort 14). Aarseth argued for an "ergodic literature"
that includes interactive fiction and word-based virtual environments
(Aarseth, *Cybertext*). After the turn of the century, however, Aarseth
helped establish the independence of computer games from literature and other prior arts (Aarseth, "Computer Game Studies").

These uncertainties also affect the Twine world. Some influential Twine
creators moved into game design after bad experiences in college creative
writing programs and game-design academies (see Anthropy's comments
in *Rise* 95). After Gamergate, Twine work has been strongly associated
with independent, insurgent game creation, especially queer gaming. As
merritt k says in the indispensable manifesto/anthology *Videogames for
Humans*, "Many of the figures who have risen to prominence in Twine
circles are trans women. That trans women are recognized as the leaders
of an artistic scene is a fact worth appreciating in its own right" (merritt k
12). We will say more about these connections to resistant and alternative
culture in the rest of the book, especially chapter T-4. The present chapter
looks the other way across this divide, connecting Twine works at least
tentatively to a literary ethos—though with the present very much in mind.

---

5   As Salter points out, this millennium-adjacent cohort is often described as "the *Oregon
Trail* generation." See https://mashable.com/2015/05/21/oregon-trail-generation/.

In this, we are responding to another point raised by merritt k, who hopes to promote "more communication and crossover between fringe game design and literary communities" (merritt k 18). Communication never comes without the risk of misunderstanding or disrespect, especially in a cultural crisis. We need also to remember Brice's poignant survey of the literary landscape, already cited but worth repeating here: "Boundaries, bones of old men before us, are only there to be transgressed" (Brice). This chapter unearths various bones and pays some attention to old men, real and imagined. It does so, we hope, in the spirit of connection merritt k evokes—though this is hard. Reaching across historical gaps creates that effect Jacques Derrida punningly called "hauntology." In doing hauntology, we need "to learn to live *with* ghosts, in the upkeep, the conversation, the company, or the companionship, in the commerce without commerce of ghosts. To live otherwise, and better. No, not better, but more justly. But *with them*. No *being-with* the other, no *socius* without this *with* that makes *being-with* in general more enigmatic than ever for us. And this being-with specters would also be, not only but also, a *politics* of memory, of inheritance, and of generations" (Derrida xviii).

Ghosts pose a serious problem for rationalist-materialist theories of existence—much the same problem, Derrida also taught, that lies in language itself. There is no "genuine *being-with* the other," no way past the enigma of otherness—*whoever he was*—and yet we persist in naming names. We tell ghost stories. Like cinema's illusion of motion, the act of naming invokes false presence and dubious ancestries. Unto every Dylan, there will be some Thomas—doubtful if not doubting, and technically speaking no relation, except that in language and literature, there is nothing but relation, however vexed. The house of Twine is haunted.

Final Fictions and Delta-T

Postmodern haunting is complicated. Our ghosts no longer show up in the Dickensian holiday three-pack, but come instead in trickier, fractal numbers. The return of the repressed may cross hauntological registers in strange, Escher-like loops. These radical effects are captured in a work called *We Knew the Glass Man*, written by John G. McDaid and crafted in Twine with the assistance of his son, Jack McDaid (McDaid, *Glass Man*; all other citations of this work are given in the text by passage name). The title, which refers to Wallace Stevens's "Asides on the Oboe," names an ancestral presence of literary modernism whose effect on the work we will explore (Stevens). In its own way, McDaid's *Glass Man* recapitulates the Dylan/Thomas logic, folding Stevens's modernist abstractions over other cultural signatures—science fiction, psychedelics, occultism, garage-band rock, and, crucially for our purposes, Twine.

There is a literal haunting in the work. To echo our earlier catchphrase, the signature of *Glass Man* might well be "whoever he was," with notable slippage under the pronoun. The question applies most directly to Tyrell Rand Walker, the main haunt of the story. Walker ("Ty") was a friend of the unnamed narrator from their days at Syracuse University. As old readers of Sunday comics will recognize (see Falk and Herman), his surname might as well be Phantom, the Ghost-Who-Walks. His given name echoes the maker of the replicants in Ridley Scott's *Blade Runner* and in shortened form suggests connection or binding ("tie"). The middle name remains mysterious—Ayn Rand? Janice Rand from *Star Trek*? "Rand" for *random* (as we will see)? This guesswork seems appropriate, as Mr. Walker is made of mysteries. He seems to have died six times under different circumstances. These details are given in various funereal passages of *Glass Man*:

1. Drowned in the surf off Cape May, New Jersey ("Unitarian Church in Fayetteville")
2. Fell to his death from a water tower while tripping on acid ("Eighteen"; see also the passage "Remain in Light," where the same scene ends without the fall)
3. Drove into a tree in Prospect Park, Brooklyn ("It Was Quick")
4. Blown up on TWA Flight 800, July 17, 1996 ("Beach at Coney Island")
5. Suffocated in his sleep by a fire that destroys 219 Clarendon Street ("A Jar in Tennessee")
6. Died at home of undisclosed causes in 2016 ("Cemetery of Last Resort")

This narrative uncertainty registers how, in every sense of the phrase, *times have changed*. Heterocosms, inconsistent or causally divergent world-models, were popular in the last century. We could point to postmodernist fictions, from Virginia Woof's *Orlando* to Mark Danielewski's *House of Leaves*, or just as plausibly to popular entertainments, from *Rashomon* to *Spider-Man: Into the Spider-Verse*. In this new century, multiversal thinking seems to be on tap wherever stories are told. Hypertext fiction is certainly part of this phenomenon, and Twine along with it. Because hypertext usually implies a graph, we might begin by reading from the map:

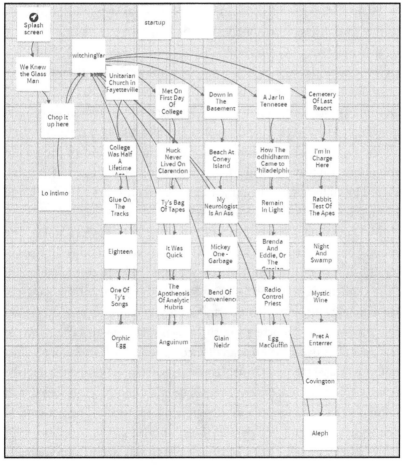

Figure 13: Structure map of *We Knew the Glass Man*

This is the story structure of *We Knew the Glass Man* as it appears when the output HTML file is opened in Twine. Much can be learned about the design of the story from this graph. There is an initial track from "Splash Screen" (far left) to a passage from which many lines emanate, with an equal number returning. This passage is called "Nighttime in the Switching Yard," echoing the title of a Warren Zevon song. Zevon is another of the whoevers haunting this story. To the left of the Switching Yard lie five linear tracks, each containing at least one of the death scenarios (the first track includes both "Unitarian Church in Fayetteville" and "Eighteen"). At far left are two passages without linking lines—and though they are important, we will pass over them for the moment.

Each of the extended tracks ends with a passage that loops back to the Yard. These ends-of-the-line have numinous names: "Orphic Egg," "Anguinum," "Glain Neidr," "Aleph," and the definitive "Egg Mac-Guffin." Each passage begins with the same sentence, then diverges. They describe a relic passed down to Ty Walker from Arthur "Buddy" Newkirk (more about him presently). The nature of this object is hazy: it is an ancient Greek magic stone, a Druidic talisman (twice), a chip off the Egg Stone of Glastonbury, or a totem of unknown properties and origin, vaguely recalled. The echoing endpoints round out the plan shared by all five lines—begin with a reminiscence, arrive at death and a funeral, finish with the arcane object.

McDaid alludes more than once to Jorge Luis Borges's story "The Aleph," but the structure of *Glass Man* also recalls another Borgesian model: the "heap of contradictory drafts" that is the talisman of "The Garden of Forking Paths" (Borges 24). This literary assemblage, the fantastic novel from which the story takes its name, appears to violate causality—major characters vanish suddenly, change unaccountably, or reappear after dying. The apparent inconsistencies are intentional, illustrating a radical theory of time: "Unlike Newton and Schopenhauer, [the novelist] did not think of time as absolute and uniform. He believed it an infinite series of times, in a dizzily growing, ever spreading network of diverging, converging and parallel times" (Borges 28).

In much the same way, McDaid's *Glass Man* seems ontologically incoherent. Ty Walker dies in 1981, or 1996, or 2016. He meets his fate outside of Syracuse, in Brooklyn, on a doomed airliner headed for France. Readers run into all these possibilities as they move from passage to passage, which brings us to the navigation scheme of *Glass Man*.

Once readers have passed from the Switching Yard onto one of the five linear tracks, there are two mechanisms for movement through the text: a button or pair of buttons to the left of the body text[6] and a linked expression at the end of the passage. The buttons are marked with a three-dot sigil, either ∵ or ∴. These symbols are conjunctions from symbolic logic that mean *because* and *therefore*, as hovering glosses on the buttons indicate. In a work that plays fast and loose with causality, these linear operators are inevitably ironic. The operator buttons allow movement either back to the previous passage (*because*) or to the next in the current line (*therefore*), but this arrangement does not imply cause and effect. Setting these buttons aside, the reader can advance to the next destination by clicking an expression that occurs at the end of the body text:

$$\Delta t^7$$

Like the pseudological buttons on the left, this in-text operator carries a double sense. In physics, delta-t indicates change over time—and indeed, clicking this button does advance the timeline of the current reading, though it may as easily take us back to something we have seen as forward to unread material. Linear references are misleading in this text. There is another way of understanding "change" and "time," if we factor in Borgesian possibilities. In addition to *in*, *over*, or *through*, we might also consider *of*—a change of time, time-streams, or continuities. Both "The Garden of Forking Paths" and *We Knew the Glass Man*

---

6 The appearance of these buttons is governed by one of the two unlinked passages in the story structure—the lower one that appears blank. It actually contains JavaScript instructions that assign the buttons their symbols and functions.

7 The Δt expression has its most famous literary use in Pynchon's *Crying of Lot 49* (1966), where it is associated with end-stage alcoholism (delirium tremens, or the DTs) and a possible visionary experience. McDaid alludes to this dark magic at several points in *Uncle Buddy's Phantom Funhouse*. Δt is also the logotype of McDaid's personal brand, Torvex Communications—as might be expected of a science fiction writer with a recurrent interest in time travel.

humanize post-Newtonian time. Borges evokes the tragedy of a descendant who must assassinate the man who tells him about the greatness of his ancestor. McDaid offers a more prosaic tragedy, suspected senile dementia:

> My neurologist, Dr. George Zanniger, is an ass. The kids, convinced that my memory is shot, set me up with an appointment. In unctuous doctor-speak, he spooled out his "As we get older," speech. Reviewed my med list. Made me touch my nose. Stand on one foot. Take the god-damned Montreal Cognitive Assessment. Yes I can count backwards from 100 by sevens. Draw a watch. Recite the Invocation of Mnemosyne: Face Velvet Church Daisy Red.
>
> He wrote me up for a brain MRI, which will almost certainly show absolutely nothing. Modern medicine is the apotheosis of analytic hubris. If I recall counterfactuals, if there are acausal lacunae in my narrative timeline, it is not beta amyloid or TIAs. ("My Neurologist Is an Ass")

And so we arrive at another variation on *whoever he was*: our nameless narrator, beset with plaques or brain bleeds—or a condition best diagnosed in the Twilight Zone. If we follow his insinuation, he is not just "unstuck in time," in Kurt Vonnegut's phrase, but adrift across a series of timelines (Vonnegut).

The narrator of *Glass Man* is haunted by stories, or the sketchbook approximation of stories, or maybe by narrativity itself. Just as plausibly, though, we can trace his problems to bodily jeopardy, the fraught experience of an aging man in an old house. Hauntings often involve houses, and this is especially the case with *Glass Man*—though as Huckleberry Finn might say, you will not fully appreciate the reference unless you have read *Uncle Buddy's Phantom Funhouse* by Mr. John McDaid.

The *Funhouse* is an artifactual hypernovel consisting of paper documents, audio tapes, and a set of digital files created with Apple Computer's long-obsolete HyperCard application (see Moulthrop and Grigar). It was published by Eastgate Systems as a multimedia assemblage in 1993 (McDaid, *Uncle Buddy's*). Prefiguring both the surreal architecture of *House of Leaves* (Danielewski) and the unpeopled spookiness of *Gone Home* (Gaynor), *Funhouse* incorporates a digital memory palace, a hyperlinked image that maps its software components onto regions of an old house. As in *Glass Man*, there are multiple dimensions to this hauntology. The virtual house and its textual contents are conveyed to the reader as the literary estate of a vanished writer, Arthur "Buddy" Newkirk, described as a relative we may not remember because of "lapses of memory or other unspecified divergences" ("READ ME FIRST"). The Newkirk of *Funhouse* is a contemporary of the Syracuse crowd, front man and songwriter for the punk band called the Reptiles. In *Glass Man*, he is an older, semilegendary science fiction writer whom Ty's friends regard with some awe, whose main role involves passing the MacGuffin to Huck. What this revisionist history means for the ficto-biography of John McDaid is perhaps of interest mainly to his fans. Suffice to say that the twenty-first-century Twine work *Glass Man* is haunted by prior art, especially hypertextual experiments from three decades back. In a sense, all Twine works share this haunting, whether they know it or not.

Hypertext linking—the association of words, phrases, and images with code that replaces or transforms the initial text—operates in *Funhouse* through the HyperCard "stacks" that make up its digital archive. Although there are sequential links in most of these stacks, there are also disruptive and digressive links on words, phrases, or images, making the experience of reading *Funhouse* polylinear. In *Glass Man*, hypertext is applied less fancifully, with most passages limited to the linking scheme already described. This limited connectedness points away, perhaps, from the experimentation of the mid-1990s toward older conventions of print fiction.

That shift may be related to the conceptual basis of the work. *Glass Man* was published in an ongoing project of the literary journal *cream city review* called *i0*, showcasing works in which print and digital elements are equally important. A page-bound version of McDaid's story appears in the print edition of the journal. In design and execution, *We Knew the Glass Man* is a hybrid, bridging the domains of book and software, haunted equally by technology and literature.

In this sense, the major ghost of *Glass Man*, Thomas to its Dylan, is the modernist poet Wallace Stevens.[8] McDaid takes as an epigraph the opening of "Asides on the Oboe," a short poem written in 1940 and published in the collection *Parts of a World* (Stevens). For what it's worth, Harold Bloom considers this volume "Stevens' most underrated book" (Bloom 136). The poem is nearly contemporary with Borges's "Garden of Forking Paths," published in 1941, though the texts are related (if at all) only through the idea of a "final," or as Stevens would later say, "supreme fiction":[9]

> *The prologues are over. It is a question, now*
> *Of final belief. So, say that final belief*
> *Must be in a fiction. It is time to choose.*

That last sentence stands out—maybe perversely so, if we think for a moment like a certain hard-core traditionalist. Stevens is a model of erudition and "quiet authority" on whose work critics like Bloom, J. Hillis Miller, and Helen Vendler have honed their critical insights (Vendler). He is the acknowledged master of difficulty and abstraction. According to Vendler, when a colleague complained of not understanding Stevens's writing, the poet replied, "That doesn't matter; what matters is that I understand it" (Vendler). In other words, Wallace Stevens is not a writer to take literally.

Yet when Stevens's injunction to choose occurs in a work of digital fiction, it has to be taken that way. An important part of the ancestry of Twine and other platforms for branching narrative lies in game books

---

8   McDaid's overt engagement with Stevens inevitably recalls Jessica Pressman's important thesis about "digital modernism," in which contemporary writers "[adapt] literary modernism as a means for challenging the status quo of electronic literature and our assumptions about it" (Pressman 303). However, Pressman has in mind "works [that] use central aspects of modernism to highlight their literariness, authorize their experiments, and situate electronic literature at the center of a contemporary digital culture that privileges images, navigation, and interactivity over narrative, reading, and textuality." Her primary example is the cine-poem *DAKOTA* by Young-Hae Chang Heavy Industries, very distinct from the narrative emphasis of hypertext fictions and Twine games.

9   This phrase comes from "Notes toward a Supreme Fiction," published in *Transport to Summer* (1947).

or choose-your-own-adventure stories, where the "time to choose" comes at the end of every narrative unit, as it does in *Glass Man*. The cultural gulf between Wallace Stevens and game books is about as great as anyone could imagine. There are those who lament that divide and those who have tried to erase it.[10] Notable among these is Aarseth, whose study of procedural narrative is based partly on *The Money Spider*, a game-book from the 1980s (Aarseth, *Cybertext* 69–70). McDaid's cultural politics align with the levelers, which makes his appropriation of Stevens odd and at least partly ironic. "It is time to choose," but despite the simplicity of the sentence, its application to McDaid's story is deeply complicated—and perhaps not so literal after all. In *Glass Man*, both time and choice defy simple understanding.

Ty Walker has six histories and six catastrophes. There is no clear way to differentiate one from another. The deceptively linear structure of the work tilts toward seriality but leaves the reader and narrator in a state of haunting or defective memory. Which time? What time? How do we choose among them? McDaid's story is fundamentally anxious, yet if we turn to Stevens, we find the opposite, a movement toward final clarity. There is considerably less uncertainty about its central figure:

> *In the end, however naked, tall, there is still*
> *The impossible possible philosophers' man,*
> *The man who has had the time to think enough,*
> *The central man, the human globe, responsive*
> *As a mirror with a voice, the man of glass,*
> *Who in a million diamonds sums us up.*

"The man who has had the time to think enough" can be applied to McDaid's story, but with questionable results. Ty Walker has apparently had several worlds and times, and we can wonder if the narrator will ever be able to think enough about this enigma. The "central man" of

---

10 See the much more nuanced account of contemporary canon formation in Fishelov's *Dialogues with/and Great Books* (Fishelov).

the Twine story is elusive, more impossible than possible. In the poem, by contrast, the philosophers' man unfolds in a series of symbols: a globe, a mirror, diamonds. The globe is encompassing, the mirror reflective, but the key lies in that cascade of diamonds, shattering light into a constellation of difference. Somehow this explosion of information "sums us up." What can this mean?

McDaid's ghost story complicates such questions, warning that the reference of any "us" becomes unstable across the timelines. Are we the ones who mourned Ty at Coney Island, or came to the funeral in Fayetteville, or watched him slip off the tower outside of Syracuse? Recall Derrida: "No *being-with* the other, no *socius* without this *with* that makes *being-with* in general more enigmatic than ever for us." If we apply this hauntology to the texts in question, we might ask if the first-person plural of 1940 includes a twenty-first-century reader. How was it ever possible to sum up then and now into an "us?" What does it mean to know the Glass Man in the context of a fracturing that is not metaphoric but actual?

Considering this essential question—which is the question with which this chapter began—we come to a major difference between old and new, one with important implications for understanding Twine work in relation to literary tradition. The crux comes at the end of Stevens's poem, after its lament about the disruption of the idyll of "jasmine scent" by "death and war":

> It was not as if the jasmine ever returned.
> But we and the diamond globe at last were one.
> We had always been partly one. It was as we came
> To see him, that we were wholly one, as we heard
> Him chanting for those buried in their blood,
> In the jasmine haunted forests, that we knew
> The glass man, without external reference.

To know the Glass Man, for Stevens, is to operate "without external reference." These are his last words on the subject. Knowledge of the impossibly possible central man must be internalized, unworldly, something outside of image, association, and language. In sharp contrast, McDaid's fiction strains toward externalities, arguably on two levels.

The first reach toward external reference can be found within the story world, in those talismanic stones at the end of each timeline. In their mystic associations, they express a yearning for enlightenment and presence. At a crucial point, we get a unified vision of the stone:

> The stone was unremarkable in that it was veridical. Obstinately truthful. It just was. In the words of my philosophy professor Fernando Molina, who received dharma transmission from Clarence Irving Lewis, it stood, oblivious, beyond any assortment of qualia in my consciousness, a *Ding an sich* forever beyond direct experience. Oh, I could have some epistemically lazy notion that I knew about the stone, but Lewis would have slapped me into clarity: there was no sense in which I could make reliable, testable predictions about future experience. For pragmatic phenomenologists—which is how I had been trained—I was stuck in a bracketed reality, with the stone regarded as real. But any ontic claim was beyond me, denied by the stone's veridical centeredness, its *da stehn* while around it, the rest of the cosmos revolved. ("Nighttime in the Switching Yard")

This centrality is a setup, betrayed to variation. The stone's fixed placement is belied, narratively speaking, by what comes if we follow the links. The centering moment occurs in that deeply nested passage called "Nighttime in the Switching Yard." The cosmos of the fiction revolves or circulates around this point, the main junction from which the death-tracks radiate and to which they return (see figure 13). That pattern reinforces the withdrawal of the thing-in-itself. At the end of each track, the stone is painted with a different mythology, until the reader clicks a locally final Δt and returns to the Yard. Returning reasserts the stone's centrality. There may be "veridical centeredness," but there are also stories, and these accounts create tissues of difference. Every such departure rules out any final "ontic claim," dissolving certainty into a blur of possibilities. Relic becomes tchotchke, Egg Stone devolves to Egg

MacGuffin. After all, *Glass Man* belongs to consumer culture, which is less a matter of object-oriented ontology than a cargo cult.

The reach toward external reference within the story goes to pieces, but there is a second plane of externality in this fiction that also demands attention. The reference, in this case, is the text itself as a technical object. Although this suggestion might seem outlandish for traditional, page-bound literature, it is always appropriate for digital fictions and is explicitly framed here. Naming a key passage "Nighttime in the Switching Yard" calls out the operative metaphor. It reminds us that we are in a system of circulation, variation, and control. As noted, the title points to Zevon's song, a funked-up railroad blues about a midnight train that "runs both ways," much like the recirculating fiction of *Glass Man* (Zevon). The song closes with these words:

> *Listen to the train*
> *Listen to the track*

Taking "listen" in its metaphorical sense of *attending* or *considering*, we might indeed ask how the tracks laid out around "Switching Yard" shape our sense of its curious system of stories and what mechanisms are at work in the Yard.

The first notable thing about the "Switching Yard" passage is its count of hypertext links—six instead of the three that occur in most other passages—and the fact that five of these links are anchored on phrases within the body text, as in familiar hypertext fiction. Each inline link points to the start of one of the tracks, by which the Switching Yard lives up to its name as a junction point. The sixth link, anchored on the Δt symbol, does something more interesting. Here is its underlying code (written in the Harlowe story format):

```
(set: $rand to (random: 1, $passageList's
length))
(set: $randTarget to ($rand) of $passageList)
<div class="deltat">[[Δt|$randTarget]]</div>
```

The two *set* macros generate a random integer between 1 and the length of a variable called *$passageList*, then use this variable to select an item from *$passageList*. *$passageList* is an array, a special variable whose components can be selected individually. The list itself is defined in the other of those two unlinked passages at the far right of the map in figure 13, the one with the title "startup." It contains the following:

```
(set: $passageList to (array: "Unitarian Church
in Fayetteville","College Was Half A Lifetime
Ago","Glue On The Tracks","Eighteen","One Of
Ty's Songs","Orphic Egg","Met On First Day Of
College","Huck Never Lived On Clarendon","Ty's
Bag Of Tapes","It Was Quick","The Apotheosis
Of Analytic Hubris","Anguinum","Down In
The Basement","Beach At Coney Island","My
Neurologist Is An Ass","Mickey One--
Garbage","Bend Of Convenience","Glain Neidr","A
Jar In Tennessee","How The Bodhidharma Came
to Philadelphia","Remain In Light","Brenda
And Eddie, Or The Grecian Urn","Radio Control
Priest","Egg MacGuffin","Cemetery Of Last
Resort","I'm In Charge Here","Rabbit Test Of
The Apes","Night And Swamp","Mystic Heated
Wine","Aleph","Pret A Enterrer","Covington"))
```

The array *$passageList* includes the names of all passages in the five tracks. The scripting of the Δt link thus reveals a double articulation. A reader of *Glass Man* could proceed methodically through the in-line links in the Switching Yard, entering each of the five timelines successively as they loop down and back, but those attracted to the mysterious Δt will have a different experience. They will drop into the textual system at unpredictable points, often in the middle of an extended meditation, able to grasp what is going on only after returning to the Switching Yard several times. They may thus see the system as doubly disrupted, both by its unstable narrative contents and by the possibility of arbitrary leaps into randomness. Listening to the track—reading what its script ordains—suggests less a railroad than a pinball machine, a tool for indeterminacy.

What can we do with this understanding of the digital text as an "external reference" for McDaid's Man of Glass? For one, we can conclude that all the drifts and divergences of Ty Walker's history ultimately fall within an intentional system, one that ties understanding to circulation, repetition, and contradictory memories. For another, we can recognize the importance of *contingency*, the activation of outcomes not expected or foreseen, to the meaning of this work. Embracing contingency identifies *Glass Man* as a special kind of sign system, one that has been defined as "a semibounded and socially legitimate domain of contrived contingency that generates interpretable outcomes" (Malaby).

This definition was not written for literary texts, and yet *Glass Man* satisfies its terms. Realist fictions are inherently "semibounded," being invented accounts of plausibly real experiences—an effect accentuated by the contradictory fictions of *Glass Man*. There is certainly a claim to social legitimacy, however ironized, in the invocation of Stevens. How the work delivers "contrived contingency" should be clear. On the last point, "interpretable outcomes" are what *Glass Man* relentlessly reproduces through its rippling self-disruptions. These terms that *Glass Man* fits so well were proposed by the anthropologist Thomas Malaby as a contribution to the theory of play. Here is his complete sentence: "A game is a semibounded and socially legitimate domain of contrived contingency that generates interpretable outcomes" (Malaby 96).

The striking correspondence between McDaid's Twine fiction and Malaby's definition of *game* raises an ultimate question about its "external reference." What if we can know the Glass Man only through play? What if we say, in our networked, algorithmic moment, that final belief must be in a *game*?

Malaby's definition is designed to break down the "exceptionalism" that separates play from other human experiences (Malaby 96). Stricter theories of games would fail *Glass Man* on several points: it lacks evaluative feedback, differentiated outcomes, and, above all, causal logic (Juul 29). Yet with a certain suspension of disbelief, we might find in

McDaid's Twine story elements of active engagement. If, following the Borgesian logic, we are dealing not with a disordered narrative but with limits of conventional/Newtonian time, then we can understand the repeated link signature Δt as a matter of practice—time for change; change the time. "There is a Hand to turn the time," as Pynchon says just before the end of *Gravity's Rainbow* (Pynchon 760), though in the case of *Glass Man*, the act is more click than crank, and the agency is not mystical but human. In this gamelike, second-person context, the Hand belongs to you. You find the time to choose; your engagement turns over the time-streams.

However, even by the most generous standard, McDaid's fiction counts as a minimal game, at the limit of formal requirements, like the "minimum labyrinth" imagined in "The Garden of Forking Paths" (Borges 25). Its print-digital hybridity registers a link to conventional poetry and fiction, the Dylan Thomas side of the old Philippic. To the extent that it flirts with choice-of-adventure fiction, the overture is at least partly ironic. Yet the external reference of *We Knew the Glass Man* does make an important statement with respect to Twine and literature. It points toward writings more fully identified with games—for if final belief must still be in a fiction, the nature of that fiction is in play.

Δt, everybody.

With Those We Love Still Alive

Although it was published five years before *We Knew the Glass Man*, Porpentine's *With Those We Love Alive* seems in many ways the younger work: produced by a writer under thirty, untroubled by specific poetic hauntings, and, above all, written in a way that weaves the intersecting lines of fiction and game into an inviting moiré (Porpentine, *With Those*). *With Those We Love Alive* takes us to a dark-fantasy city ruled by a nightmarish, insectoid empress who lives on human sacrifice. Despite its frequent horrors—warning for "abuse" is given at the outset—the game has the immersive potential of a darkly lucid dream, complemented by Brenda Neotenomie's entrancing soundtrack. Play begins with a striking promise: "Please remember: nothing you can do is wrong" ("please").

This statement overturns a major convention of computer game design, in which wrong options usually far outnumber those that are in some way right (see Juul, *Art*). In contrast, Porpentine offers blanket indemnity as we begin "living this life." McDaid's temporally unstable ghost story implicitly asks *whoever he was*, but that is not the only existential question we can find in Twine works. For stories that converge with games, the foundational questions include *Who will you be at the end of play? Who are you this time?*

Character configuration is a mainstay of games, from tabletop role-playing systems to console epics and massively multiplayer online universes (see, e.g., Voorhees). *With Those We Love Alive* has its own way with this convention, offering the player/reader at the outset three queries: birth month, "element," and eye color. These factors seem arbitrary, very different from those in other games (races, tribes, professions, moral axes). The arbitrariness of the options continues the iconoclasm of the opening message. Although *With Those We Love Alive* is not a print-digital hybrid like *Glass Man*, it takes up a similarly liminal position between story and game, though on its own terms.

The birth month question is resolved by choosing from a table of links. For the other two factors, Porpentine uses an implementation of cycling text: clicking a word or phrase replaces it with the next item in a list, the last option looping back to the first.[11] A conventional, transitional link ("Yes") locks in the current selection and advances to the next passage. This naming sequence tells us something important about Porpentine's craft. Electronic text replaces itself, but nothing says the replacement has to be simple or instantaneous. Links may trigger scripted instructions as well as direct transitions. Though passage-to-passage transitions are common enough in *With Those We Love Alive*, the naming sequence reminds us that Porpentine has other options.

---

11 We have encountered cycling links in the practical chapters and will come to them again, but we should point out that this feature in Chapbook is notably streamlined in comparison to the older constructions Porpentine uses.

After the third query, we come to a link that will reveal our name. If we choose to be born in the first month, taking petal as our element and brown as eye color, we are called "Sparna Jarndot." Dialing in the seventh month, tears, and green eyes names us "Cade Ophigloss." Twelfth, fur, and gray yield "Langloss Umdas." Every configuration of Porpentine's three variables produces a unique name. There are twelve possibilities for month, six for element, and ten for eye color (including "Heterochromic" and "Nothing here describes my eyes"). Multiplying 12 times 6 times 10 gives us 720 possible names. To a nonprogrammer, this number might suggest a maximalist or brute-force approach, a series of 720 if/then conditions. Porpentine actually uses a more efficient scheme, but the impression of large scope is correct—*With Those We Love Alive* is notably bigger than *Glass Man*, as is clear from its structure map:

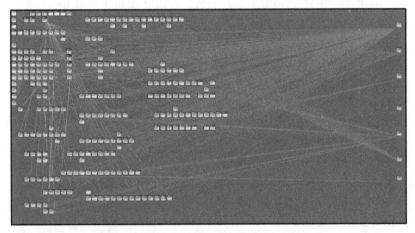

Figure 14: Structure map of *With Those We Love Alive*

There are 267 passages here, compared with 38 for *Glass Man*. References to print works have limited usefulness for Twine, but the difference between short story and novella gives a rough measure. The map comparison can also be deceptive, however. Though there is a dense tissue of linkage among the passages, there are also many more passages without link lines than in McDaid's structure. Passages of this kind often contain code, as we saw in *Glass Man*'s Switching Yard, and can also be invoked as in-line elements in dynamically assembled passages. Both strategies are used here. *With Those We Love Alive* is both broad and deep, making intensive use of scripting.

A short digression is needed at this point. In just a few years as a Twine creator, Porpentine has produced an extraordinary range of work. *With Those We Love Alive* is among her more formal, literary efforts. Chapter T-4 looks at works that are more spontaneous, personal, and in-the-moment. Perhaps inclining toward this side of her aesthetic, Porpentine has called her process "trash spinning" (Kaye; see further discussion in chapter T-4), but that term is hard to square with *With Those We Love Alive*. The way Porpentine transforms storytelling in this work seems anything but discardable. There may be a lot of "spinning" going on here, but the machinery behind it is impressive.

Noah Wardrip-Fruin, another pioneering maker and theorist of digital writing, has written about an "ELIZA effect," in which computer programs appear larger and more complicated than they actually are (Wardrip-Fruin, *Expressive* 23). The term refers to a script used in an early experiment in interactive text generation, undertaken in the mid-1960s by the computer scientist Joseph Weizenbaum. ELIZA mimicked the speech strategies of a Rogerian therapist so successfully that users of the program, interacting via teletype, behaved as if talking to a human doctor (Wardrip-Fruin, *Expressive* 32). Despite this striking functionality, the code for ELIZA is remarkably simple. It exemplifies a programming concept called *elegance*, in which compact expressions yield versatile results.

Porpentine's naming system is notably elegant. Looking at the code embedded in the "Name" passage reveals a chain of *if* conditionals, but only 30, not 720. The script uses the month selection to choose one of twelve first names (everyone born in the first month is a "Sparna"), the "element" factor to set the first syllable of the surname, eye color the second. A few lines of code produce a large range of variations.

Games produce "interpretable outcomes," in Malaby's phrase, and gamelike stories do the same. They can be understood as subjects of interpretation, or texts. In the case of the naming ritual, the reader may wonder about larger determinative effects. Will Sparna Jarndot have the same options in the game as Caromine Melovir or Mia Hexador? Do names matter, and if so, how?[12]

Reading a story/game hybrid requires a different procedure than reading a print/hypertext hybrid such as *Glass Man*. In *Cybertext*, Aarseth distinguishes between *scripton*, a sign presented to a reader or player for interpretation, and *texton*, the arrangement of systematic signs whose activation produces readerly experience (Aarseth, *Cybertext* 62). The multiparagraph, page-like passages of McDaid's story foreground the scriptonic, aligned with traditional close reading. In contrast, Porpentine's passages tend, at least on first presentation, to be terse and mainly descriptive, a common feature of some textual games. Here, for instance, is the initial description of the empress's city.

> The streets are narrow, winding, mazelike. Ropes span between buildings like enormous spiderwebs blanketing the city.
> The temple is this way, across the dry canal.
> The dream distillery is surrounded by scaffolding.
> Return to the palace. ("City")

Like McDaid's Switching Yard, passages like "City" and "Palace" are routing points, meant to be encountered many times during the game. The metaphorical narrative train runs both ways, out to other parts of the story and back. However, the trips we take in this text are subject to more complex manipulation. In *Glass Man*, the Switching Yard remains constant in expression and function. In Aarseth's formalism, the work has "static dynamics" (Eskelinen 45). In *With Those We Love Alive*, however, the switchyards can and do change during play, both in visible text and invisible logic. This is what Aarseth calls "intratextonic"

---

12 The syllables of the surname are written directly to the screen and are thus purely local, but the given name is recorded in a variable, so it could be used in other passages (which it is) and affect deeper logics of the game (though it doesn't). Salter points out the resemblance of this logic to that used in meme generators, image-based name generators, and other recent code crazes.

dynamics, indicating a program that can be flexibly configured. We can understand this by looking at the code for "City":

```
The streets are narrow, winding, [[mazelike]].
[[Ropes]] span between buildings like enormous
spiderwebs blanketing the city. <<if $dead_
person is "city">>A dead person is watching you
from a window.<<endif>>

The [[temple]] is this way, <<if $day gte
21>>across the [[flooded]] canal.<<else>>across
the [[dry]] canal.<<endif>><<if $day gte 14 and
$day lte 17>> [[Black petals]] cover the temple
steps.<<endif>>

<<if $day lt 7>>The dream distillery is
surrounded by [[scaffolding]].<<else>>The
[[dream distillery]] has a gruesome pull for
you.<<endif>>

[[Return to the palace|Palace]]
```

There are ordinary links here, as in McDaid's Yard, but also several items enclosed not in the double square brackets of standard hypertext, but in two pairs of angle brackets: << >>. These are in-line TwineScript statements, two *if* conditions and an *if/else*. They refer to values stored in the variables *$dead_person* and *$day*. If the value in the first variable is "City," the narration includes that ominous, undead watcher. The other conditions test for values in *$day* and adjust the description of the scene accordingly ("gte" and "lte" mean greater-than- and less-than-or-equal, respectively). The greatest value of *$day* mentioned here is 21, implying that *With Those We Love Alive* spans at least three weeks of in-game time, although other scripts could extend that range. Notably, the conditional block includes links that will not otherwise be seen. If we have been through at least seven game-days, for instance, the scaffolding comes off the Dream Distillery and a link to the corresponding passage asserts a "gruesome pull." This switching yard never sleeps; it remains in operation around the clock, constantly reconfiguring expressions and affordances as we conduct our in-game life.

If we want to understand the literary dimensions of Porpentine's work, we need to appreciate the way her code entwines—pun very much intended—with the words that evoke its world. We cannot rely solely on scriptonic readings, looking only at what appears at any given moment of the game. This level of language overlooks mechanisms of generation and control not presented to the reader. These mechanisms make a difference to reading because they make or generate differences in the text presented. Any momentary configuration exists in relation to other possible expressions.

With Those We Love Alive goes quite far in exploring the possibilities of Twine's first-generation release.[13] The work includes third-party JavaScript extensions that add a routine for cycling text, visual effects, and an audio handler for the soundtrack. Making these miscellaneous resources work seamlessly within one's own design takes considerable effort. In this case, we might say that Twine work at its best is as much like producing as it is like songwriting—art forms that have notably converged in the last half century.

Reading code requires us to account for linkage and dependency as well as local effects. We can see how $dead\_person$ and day work in the "City" passage, but in what other structures are they implicated? Both variables are introduced (declared) in a special passage called "Story-Init," whose instructions are performed when the game begins. This placement means they are accessible and alterable from any passage in the work. The variables are eventually reset by code attached to a passage called "sleep_process," activated when the player-character returns to her room and decides to sleep. Here is its script:

---

13 *With Those We Love Alive* was written using some version of the first release of Twine, probably in the 1.4 series.

```
<<set $weather = random(1,7)>>

<<set $tasted = false>>

<<if $day neq 1>><<set $dead_person = either("ga
rden","workshop","city","lake","balcony","temple
")>><<endif>>

<<if $hormone_day is 7>><<set $hormone_need =
true>><<set $hormone_day = 0>><<endif>>

<<set $day += 1>><<set $hormone_day += 1>><<set
$energy = 1>>
```

Using the *either* macro to make a random selection from a given list, the *$dead_person* variable distributes possible encounters over six locations in the story, repositioning the ominous figure while we rest. The crucial variable *$day* is incremented. We also see five variables not previously discovered: *$weather*, *$tasted*, *$energy*, and the related pair *$hormone_day* and *$hormone_need*. The first randomly assigns weather conditions. The second records whether the player has sampled the liquor of stolen dreams in the Dream Distillery. The *$energy* variable determines the player's ability to perform tasks in her workshop. As we can see, the game applies both historical and budgetary constraints, which brings us to *$day* and the two *$hormone* variables, which need more detailed discussion.

As the name indicates, *$day* keeps time for the game, incremented whenever we return to our chambers and click a link commanding the player-character to sleep. Sleeping is pivotal in *With Those We Love Alive*, in terms of diegesis, gameplay, and the game's overall concept. When the sleep link is clicked, the screen fades momentarily to black. A story transition may occur during sleep if *$day* or some other variable reaches a crucial value. If no transition occurs, we fade back to "Chambers." This curious process is the equivalent of McDaid's Δt, the command with which we turn the time, but time here has a distinctive character. The visual effect and the possibility of repetition make the sleep action more organic than discrete. In terms of story, the sleep mechanism ties time to our in-game body. Ludically, it connects progress to elective player action.[14]

The two $hormone variables relate to a major feature of our in-game life: we play as a person in transition, dependent on "estroglyphs" to maintain hormonal balance. As we will see, this is only one aspect of Porpentine's complex treatment of embodiment, about which there is much more to say both here and in chapter T-4. For the moment, we should note that cycles of our fictional body belong to a systematic representation of self and other, a cybernetic *world model*. The game creator and theorist Michael Mateas refers to "playable models" (Wardrip-Fruin, *How Pac-Man Eats*). Likewise, Montfort identifies world-modeling as a primary constituent of the form (Montfort). More recently, we have come to think about such models in and out of games in terms of algorithms, those often-unseen mathematical abstractions that govern digitally connected life.

Computer games are perhaps uniquely suited to comment on this aspect of modernity, especially when they operate satirically. One particularly strong example in this line is Valve Software's *Portal*, a geometrical puzzle game oddly cross-bred with an in-house parody of *Half-Life* (Swift). Bo Ruberg uses *Portal* as the basis for a remarkable "too-close reading" of the game's queer gender dynamics, to which we will return (Ruberg 56–83). Reading without the lens of queer theory, Michael Burden and Sean Gouglas extol the game's "algorithmic experience" in ways that resonate with *With Those We Love Alive*. As they see it, *Portal* presents

the tension between the cold, hard certainty of algorithms and the creativity and freedom of an art. It is the tension between the algorithm's simplification of complex concepts versus the need for problematization and criticism. It is the tension between a world without questions

14 This rest-to-advance pattern is also used in *Howling Dogs*, where it is explained more directly to the player.

and the inquiry that art embodies. It is the tension between knowledge that emerges from the algorithms of the scientific method and the
human knowledge encountered in art. All videogames are algorithms,
and therefore, *Portal* is an algorithmic exploration of human struggle
against algorithmic processes. The game's very nature is an adherence
to rules. Art's very nature is to challenge rules, to the point of defying
definition. (Burden and Gouglas)

In this view, *Portal* counts as art because it establishes a world-
model and concomitant story—the player-character's struggle against
a homicidal AI—that satirically pits the algorithmic regularity of game
software against the antinormative impulses of art. As Burden and
Gouglas see it, *Portal* bends the nature of the computer game back
upon itself, yielding important insights into the human experience of
technology.

Setting aside obvious differences of platform and context, we can
find parallels between Burden and Gouglas's definitive art game and
With Those We Love Alive. Both are intensely algorithmic, intricately
tied to logical constraints and performance measures. Both are haunted
by dangerous maternal presences. Though the mute empress of Porpentine's game shows none of the chatty ex-humanity of Valve's GLaDOS,
their homicidal regimes are similar. Artistically speaking, both texts
display edgy relationships to their primary genres. Valve satirizes the
paranoid fantasy of *Half-Life* through the cartoonish antics of Aperture Labs. Porpentine gives us a game in which "nothing you can do
is wrong," challenging mainstream game design. It might follow, then,
that *With Those We Love Alive* also constitutes a work of algorithmic art,
pitting machinic procedure against human striving and desire. Since
the primary medium of this work is written language, we might make a
strong case for integrating *With Those We Love Alive* with at least some
version of literary history, one that unifies story and game.

Two eminent critics of writing and technology, N. Katherine Hayles
and Alan Liu, have independently proposed replacing the old name
literature with more expansive terms—"the literary" (Hayles 4–5) or,
as Liu has it, "the future literary" (Liu 8). Perhaps *With Those We Love*

Alive offers a harbinger and model of this future, but to fully understand its prophetic potential, we need to examine more fully its curious moral precept: *nothing you can do is wrong.*

We have earlier called this claim iconoclastic. It can also be simply baffling even to the strongest reader. In an important early review of *With Those We Love Alive*, Emily Short begins with a classical reference. She quotes a quatrain from the *Bhagavad Gita* in which Porpentine seems to have found her title:

> *Better to live on beggar's bread*
> *with those we love alive,*
> *than taste their blood in rich feasts spread,*
> *and guiltily survive*

The lines suggest a convenient moral axis for the game, a call to re-nounce worldly pleasures in favor of ascetic discipline. But *With Those We Love Alive* is not that kind of game. As its unseen structures suggest, it does require a kind of discipline, the regular round of rest and glyph application. Likewise, any careful gameplay could be interpreted as a renunciation of bad paths to reach the good, but this game/story eludes such reductive conclusions. This is not in any way a game of withhold-ing or avoidance. We are "living this life," and in it, we face certain choices. One such decision point particularly bothers Short:

> The player has a choice: to be a person, one with others, or to be separate and alone. This choice is presented in isolation, before we understand how it will constrain us. In what follows, we discover its importance. If we choose to be one with others, we are then forced to participate in the eradication of the princess-spores, going around stomping the new-formed creatures to death. We can show them mercy only if we have determined to separate ourselves from the rest of humanity. I did not like stomping them to death, and I did not like declaring myself separate from all other people, and I also feared letting them live to perhaps become new Empresses (but the world building here is so allusive that it is hard to know for sure what will

happen if they survive). The entire passage disturbed me regardless of which way I played it. (Short)

Cognitive dissonance may be baked into algorithmic art, where human-centered impulses collide with logical procedures. We can separate ourselves from the monster-aligned human community, or we can join the massacre of the empress's "mewling" daughter-spores, which is like treading to death several litters of kittens. The moral axes in this game are darkly drawn and complicated. We are often forced to choose without a full grasp of the consequences.

Short is understandably displeased. "After this sequence," she notes, "we are invited to draw an icon representing what we feel about this turn of events. My icon was a ball of spikes" (Short 2014). This inscription is one of many that players of *With Those We Love Alive* are invited to draw on their bodies over the course of the story. Short reflects on the procedure:

> This was a strange and striking mechanic. It is arguably inconvenient, in that it restricts the contexts in which you can play this (probably not at work, or on the bus, or right before a job interview) and it asks the player to do something rather intimate in response to the game. It incorporates a sensual experience, the touch of pen on skin, and it asks the person drawing to think about how they would inscribe certain ideas. And where to inscribe them: I not only found myself thinking about how I would draw a symbol representing, say, "chasm," but also where on myself I would put that symbol in order to carry the most weight. Our bodies are geographical; there are places on the skin that mean "vulnerable" and parts that mean "strong" and parts that mean "receptive, empathetic"; places that are scarred or calloused. (Short)

The "intimacy" Short finds in this body-drawing has been elsewhere suggested as a general aesthetic of Twine works. Laura Hudson quotes the designer and critic Cara Ellison in praise of "mechanics of intimacy" that stand in sharp contrast to the kinetic and objectifying mechanics of commercial game design (Hudson MM46). Porpentine's invitation to engage the "geographic" body offers a clear instance of this approach.

Short is pragmatically skeptical about body-drawing—*you can't play this at the office*—but we may want to set aside this objection. Perhaps this transgressive story/game is not meant to be safe for work. When she asks players to ink their flesh, Porpentine calls for a radical commitment of *presence*. Drawing on our bodies asks us to be present both to our personal geographies, as Short insightfully observes, and to the fiction/game/mechanism in a way that is outlandish and perhaps excessive, even if the ink washes off. Porpentine's glyph-play reorients and reasserts the human with respect to the textual machine.

To grasp the full significance of this aesthetic move, we need to return to the critical discussion of *Portal*, but with an update and spoiler warning. We need to consider the last word of the *Portal* saga (so far), the end of *Portal 2* (Weier). Ruberg revealingly notes that "*Portal* is a game about a woman moving inside another woman," exploring lesbian and domme/sub themes in the relationship of GLaDOS and Chell (Ruberg 80). If we factor in the second game, we can see the entire trajectory of this weird/queer pairing (see Moulthrop). In the ultimate scene of the second game, Chell is offered a truce by a restored GLaDOS. She is free to "go make some new disaster," in the words of the closing-credits song (Weier, *Portal 2*), but she will have to do this somewhere other than Aperture Laboratories. Before this moment, we have learned that the human seed of GLaDOS's personality was Chell's mother, an innocent abducted into the system. We watch GLaDOS purge the last traces of this maternal presence from her cores, leaving us with a flicker of suspense—will the now thoroughly inhuman AI kill us off at last? Instead, GLaDOS sings a moving operatic aria ("Cara mia addio") and sets Chell free—but not before declaring that she will replace human test subjects with robots from now on.

In the last frames before the credits, Chell walks through not a transdimensional portal but an ordinary door that slams behind her. Ruberg reads Chell's exit from the first game as an expulsion from the monstrous/maternal body, but it is tempting to take the final act of the second game more literally (Ruberg 77–79). The door reopens to eject the lost, beloved Companion Cube from the first game, then shuts again forever. Chell turns away, and the last thing we see through her eyes is an endless, post-Anthropocene prairie. The impression is less of birth or release than separation and exile. Jonathan Coulton's closing song this time is "Want You Gone," a breakup ballad. As in the first game, the credits roll over a company document. In *Portal*, it was a gleeful performance evaluation. In the second game, the form reads, "NOTICE OF TERMINATION." Chell is given her life back but she is dismissed from employment. The murder-science machine doesn't need human beings anymore.

At first, there may seem little in common between this moment in *Portal 2* and Porpentine's inky mechanic of intimacy. Perhaps we could say that each disruptively winds computer games around a different medium and genre. *Portal 2* replaces gameplay with cinema or machinima—something we will see again in chapter T-5; *With Those We Love Alive* moves from the procedurality of story-game to the free space of embodied writing. These lines of flight do not apparently converge—and that is precisely the point. The *Portal* saga's collision of algorithm and human desire ends in separation. There may be a ghost in the final version of its machine, but its lone human subject is cast into the wilderness. *With Those We Love Alive*, in sharp contrast, keeps humanity in the picture, reasserting embodiment in the face of the machine. Porpentine extends the reach of her imagination to our bodies—and remembering that promise that we can do no wrong, to bodies that are implicitly beloved.

In the song that ends the first *Portal*, GLaDOS dedicates the "triumph" of her test regime for "the people who are still alive," a phrase that unwinds into several threads of meaning. In one sense, it refers to Chell, who has managed to avoid all the murderous traps; more metaphorically, it also includes the player who has cleared the final level in a nondead state; most directly, it applies to GLaDOS herself, denying defeat to set up the sequel.

As Ruberg notes, *alive* is the keyword of Valve's epic (Ruberg 81). Of course, it also has pride of place in Porpentine's title. Perhaps we can use the slippery logic applied to this term in Valve's game to unwrap the enigma of Porpentine's opening promise. In playing the story-as-game, we may well do things that prove to be wrong: such is the algorithmic experience. The world-machine is morally broken, and we are constrained by its flawed conception—but never absolutely. Porpentine creates a fictional enclosure that is semibounded, a permeable membrane. Her game does not exclude our humanity but promotes our presence as embodied selves. The poet Stevens in his day aspired to a knowledge "without external reference." In another century, in the vastly different techno-social context of her generation, Porpentine comes to the opposite conclusion. By being present to her text, we become the beloved who are still alive, and in this corporeal presence, offering our bodies as scriptable surfaces, nothing we can do is wrong. As Ruberg would put it, games awaken and serve our desire for alternative solutions, for a range of experiences not bound by traditional norms (Ruberg 11). As embodied in *With Those We Love Alive*, perhaps this achievement defines "the future literary" or a literary future, at least if we believe that writing-as-art remains a human enterprise—so long, we might say, as we have skin in the game. So long as that remains the case, maybe nothing we can do with our imaginations, as poets or as game-makers, can ever be wrong.

Works Cited

Aarseth, Espen. "Computer Game Studies, Year One." *Game Studies* 1, no. 1 (July 2001). http://gamestudies.org/0101/editorial.html.

———. *Cybertext: Perspectives on Ergodic Literature*. Johns Hopkins University Press, 1997.

Anthropy, Anna. *Rise of the Video Game Zinesters*. Seven Stories Press, 2012.

Berry, Jedediah. *Fabricationist Dewit Remakes the World*. Self-published, 2015. http://www.makoian.com/jedediah/fabricationist/FabricationistDeWit.html.

Birkerts, Sven. *The Gutenberg Elegies: The Fate of Reading in an Electronic Age*. Farrar, Straus and Giroux, 1996.

Bloom, Harold. *Wallace Stevens: The Poems of Our Climate*. Ithaca, NY: Cornell University Press, 1974.

Bogost, Ian. *A Slow Year*. Self-published, 2010. http://bogost.com/games/aslowyear/.

Bois, Jon. *Bill Belichick Offseason Simulator*. SBNation, 2015. https://www.sbnation.com/2015/3/31/7979801/bill-belichick-offseason-simulator.

Borges, Jorge Luis. *Labyrinths: Selected Stories and Other Writings*. Translated by Donald Y. Yates. New Directions, 1962.

Brice, Mattie. "Triptychs." Mattie Brice's website, accessed September 21, 2019. http://www.mattiebrice.com/triptychs.

Burden, Michael, and Sean Gouglas. "The Algorithmic Experience: 'Portal' as Art." *Game Studies* 12, no. 2 (2012). http://gamestudies.org/1202/articles/the_algorithmic_experience.

Consalvo, Mia, and Christian Paul. *Real Games: What's Legitimate and What's Not in Contemporary Videogames*. MIT Press, 2019.

Crowther, Will. *Colossal Cave Adventure*. Self-published, 1976.

Danielewski, Mark. *House of Leaves*. Pantheon, 2000.

Derrida, Jacques. *Spectres of Marx*. Translated by Peggy Kamuf. Routledge, 1994.

Drucker, Johanna. *What Is? Nine Epistemological Essays*. Cuneiform Press, 2013.

Ensslin, Astrid. *Literary Gaming*. MIT Press, 2014.

Eskelinen, Markku. *Cybertext Poetics: The Critical Landscape of New Media Literary Theory*. Continuum, 2012.

Falk, Lee, and Andrew Herman. *The Phantom the Complete Sundays Volume 6: 1957–1961 (Phantom, the Complete Sundays 1957–1961)*. Hermes Press, 2019.

Fishelov, David. *Dialogues with/and Great Books*. Sussex Academic Press, 2010.

Galloway, Alexander. *Protocol: How Control Exists after Decentralization*. MIT Press, 2006.

Gaudreault, Andre, and Philippe Marion. *The End of Cinema? A Medium in Crisis in the Digital Age*. New York: Columbia University Press, 2015.

Gaynor, Steve. *Gone Home*. Fullbright, 2015.

Hayles, N. Katherine. *Electronic Literature: New Horizons for the Literary*. University of Notre Dame Press, 2008.

Holeton, Richard. *Dream Book*. Unpublished Twine work, 2020.

Hopkins, Doris, and Mary Alden Webster. *Consider the Consequences*. Century Company, 1930.

Hudson, Laura. "Twine, the Video-Game Technology for All." *New York Times*, November 19, 2014. https://www.nytimes.com/2014/11/23/magazine/twine-the-video-game-technology-for-all.html.

Joyce, Michael. *afternoon, a story*. Tinker's Dam Press, 1986.

Juul, Jesper. *The Art of Failure: An Essay on the Pain of Playing Video Games*. MIT Press, 2013.

———. *Half-Real: Video Games between Real Rules and Fictional Worlds*. MIT Press, 2005.

Kaye, Finch. "Beautiful Weapons." New Inquiry, June 25, 2013. https://thenewinquiry.com/beautiful-weapons/.

Kazemi, Darius. "Fuck Videogames!" Tiny Subversions, 2013. https://tinysubversions.com/fuckvideogames/#slide1.

Ligman, Kris. *You Are Jeff Bezos*. Self-published, 2018. https://direkris.itch.io/you-are-jeff-bezos.

Liu, Alan Y. *Laws of Cool: Knowledge Work and the Culture of Information*. University of Chicago Press, 2004.

Lutz, Michael. *My Father's Long, Long Legs*. Correlated Contents, September 23, 2013. http://correlatedcontents.com/misc/Father.html.

Malaby, Thomas. "Beyond Play: A New Approach to Games." *Games and Culture* 2, no. 2 (2007): 95–113.

Malloy, Judy. *Uncle Roger*. The WELL, 1986.

McDaid, John. *Uncle Buddy's Phantom Funhouse*. Eastgate Systems, 1993.

———. *We Knew the Glass Man*. cream city review, 2019. http://io.creamcityreview.org/43-1/McDaid/WeKnewtheGlassMan_v1.1.html.

McHenry, Tom. *Tonight Dies the Moon*. Self-published, 2015. https://tommchenry.itch .io/tonight-dies-the-moon.

merritt k, ed. *Videogames for Humans: Twine Authors in Conversation*. Instar Books, 2015.

Montfort, Nick. *Twisty Little Passages: An Approach to Interactive Fiction*. MIT Press, 2003.

Moulthrop, Stuart. "Deep Time in Play." In "Small Screen Fictions," *Paradoxa* 29 (2018): 123–44.

Moulthrop, Stuart, and Dene Grigar. *Traversals: The Use of Preservation for Early Electronic Writing*. MIT Press, 2017.

Myers, David. *Games Are Not: The Difficult and Definitive Guide to What Video Games Are*. Manchester University Press, 2017.

Nelson, Xalavier, Jr. "A Very Normal and Encouraging Keynote." NarraScope 2020, Interactive Fiction Technology Foundation, keynote address, May 28, 2020. Online. https://www.youtube.com/watch?v=cXdAZip75j4.

Nikolajeva, Maria. *Children's Literature Comes of Age: Toward a New Aesthetic*. Routledge, 2015.

Porpentine. *Howling Dogs*. Self-published, 2012. http://slimedaughter.com/games/twine/howlingdogs/.

———. *Ultra Business Tycoon III*. Self-published, 2013. http://slimedaughter.com/games/twine/tycoon/.

———. *With Those We Love Alive*. Self-published, 2014. http://slimedaughter.com/games/twine/wtwla/.

Pressman, Jessica. "The Strategy of Digital Modernism: Young-Hae Chang Heavy Industries' DAKOTA." *Modern Fiction Studies* 54, no. 2 (2008): 302–26.

Pynchon, Thomas. *Gravity's Rainbow*. Viking, 1973.

Rawitch, Don, Bill Heinemann, and Paul Dillenberger. *The Oregon Trail*. Minnesota Educational Computing Consortium.

Ruberg, Bo. *Video Games Have Always Been Queer*. New York University Press, 2019.

Short, Emily. "IF Comp 2014: With Those We Love Alive (Porpentine, Brenda Neotenomie)." *Emily Short's Interactive Storytelling* (blog), accessed September 21, 2019. https://emshort.blog/2014/10/16/if-comp-2014-with-those-we-love-alive -porpentine-brenda-neotenomie/.

Simon, Paul, and Art Garfunkel. *Parsley, Sage, Rosemary and Thyme*. Columbia, 1966.

Snow, Kevin. *Beneath Floes*. Bravemule, 2015. http://www.bravemule.com/beneathfloes.

Squinkifer, D. *Quing's Quest VII: The Death of Videogames*. Self-published, September 1, 2014. https://games.squinky.me/quing/.

Stevens, Wallace. *Parts of a World*. Alfred A. Knopf, 1943.

Swift, Kim. *Portal*. Valve Software, 2007.

Vendler, Helen. "Wallace Stevens' Voice Was 'Life-Saving.'" *New Republic*, November 18, 2013. https://newrepublic.com/article/115628/helen-vendler-wallace-stevens.

Vonnegut, Kurt. *Slaughterhouse Five*. Delacorte Press, 1969.

Voorhees, Gerald. "The Character of Difference: Procedurality, Rhetoric, and Roleplaying Games." *Game Studies* 9, no. 2 (November 2009). http://gamestudies.org/0902/articles/voorhees.

Wardrip-Fruin, Noah. *Expressive Processing: Digital Fictions, Computer Games, and Software Studies*. MIT Press, 2009.

———. *How Pac-Man Eats*. MIT Press, 2020.

Weier, Joshua. *Portal 2*. Valve Software, 2011.

Zevon, Warren. *Night Time in the Switching Yard*. Asylum, 1978.

CHAPTER P-3

Generation

In 2009, the year of Twine's debut, the poet and computational linguist Nick Montfort visited Taroko National Park in the Republic of China, the site of a famously splendid gorge on the Liwu River. Take a poet to the wilderness and the result is usually a nature poem. Crossing that exposure with computer science yields what is arguably a new kind of nature poem. Written (we could also say "coded") during the flight home, Montfort's *Taroko Gorge* is a poetry generator; you can read (watch?) the work at nickm.com/taroko_gorge (Montfort, *Taroko Gorge*). Its compact rules weave several sets of words into a richly impressionistic account of Montfort's hike through the gorge—which is to say, a poem—but the program runs on an endless loop, continually scrolling from bottom to top, adding lines that are apparently unique, made fresh every few seconds. This feature turns the nature poem into something like a simulation. *Taroko Gorge* captures in words the basis of natural beauty: an endlessly surprising permutation of given elements.

As we suggested in chapter P-2, electronic writing has a particular affinity for permutation, which brings us to a second important aspect of *Taroko Gorge*. Like the community of Twine developers, Montfort believes strongly in open-source software. He shares his poem-making code with anyone who wants to adapt it. Another poet, J. R. Carpenter, has written a collection called *Generation(s)* consisting of her own reworkings of Montfort's earlier programs (Carpenter). Something similar, though less overtly organized, happened with *Taroko Gorge*. Friends and family of Montfort began swapping out the vocabulary in Montfort's program and restyling the poem in evocative and sometimes parodic ways (e.g., *Tokyo Garage* and *Takei, George*). The web page for the poem includes a table of intervening authors with links to their versions. Montfort ritually crosses out each name and reasserts his own at the bottom of the list—less an exercise of ego than a playful recognition that authorship isn't what it used to be.

Taroko Gorge is not a Twine work, but perhaps a first cousin. It is written in Python, a language popular with web coders. Montfort has written other works in JavaScript, the specialized programming language that provides an infrastructure for Twine. However, the idea of generated text, language programmatically assembled by combination or random selection, belongs to every branch of the software family. It is present in the naming ritual at the beginning of *With Those We Love Alive*, discussed in the last chapter and imitated in one of our practical exercises in this one. As another of our examples will show, text generation can be used to make static poems as well as endless simulations. Most important for our purposes, exploring this practice will show us more about the affordances and limitations of Twine, building on our encounter with textual variation in the previous practical chapter.

> ◊ As in other practical chapters, action items are boxed and set off with the symbol you see at left, in case you want to skip the contextual discussion. Examples in this chapter use Chapbook exclusively.

Supporting materials for this chapter can be found online at https://github.com/AMSUCF/Twining. See our discussion at the beginning of chapter P-1 about using the .html and .txt files to follow along or adapt our code to your own purposes.

Example 3.1: Mad Computer Libs

If we want to seem serious and dignified, we can describe the subject of this example as a *substitution grammar*, borrowing a scientific term from computational linguistics. However, like many serious and dignified things, our subject here is actually rooted in party games. In 1958, a pair of comedy writers, Leonard Stern and Roger Price, published *Mad Libs*, a book containing phrases, sentences, and paragraphs for which the player was meant to supply missing words, as outrageously as possible. In the "Mad-Mad" era of cocktails and party games, the book was a huge hit, even though it was hardly original. A generation earlier, the surrealists invented a practice called the exquisite corpse, in which standard patterns of language were intentionally disrupted by sharing a text with multiple authors, imposing new rules for each new writer, or allowing each writer to see only the most recent fragment of the text.

Though neither the surrealists nor the comedians knew it, they were working at the margins of computer science. In 1952, a British researcher named Christopher Strachey created a program to generate love letters (Wardrip-Fruin). Its sentence-template mechanism was closer to Mad Libs than the surrealist game, and the title of our first project reflects that fact (along with a glancing homage to Ted Nelson's *Computer Lib/Dream Machines* of 1974, the manifesto of our movement). Give your fingers a good flex before digging in. There are five passages, each with a fair number of words to type.

◊ Create a new story and call it anything you like. We'll be using Chapbook, so select that story format if it is not your default. Create a new passage and name it "Step 1." This name is referenced in a link, so change it with caution. In the new passage, enter the following text:

```
propNoun: 'Somebody'
--
Type a proper noun: the name of a real or
imaginary person, place or named thing, e.g.,
```

```
'Louise Pringle,' 'Jimmy One Nose,' 'H.M.S.
Winnebago.'

{text input for: 'propNoun'}

[[Next ->Step 2]]
```

We're working here with a Chapbook feature you haven't seen yet, the *text input* insert. As you may suspect, this insert creates a box into which the player is expected to type something at will. When the player leaves the "Step 1" passage, the contents of the input box are stored in the variable *propNoun*. The initial value we assign in the variables section shows up in the text-entry box and can be used as a default if the player declines to type anything.

◊ Create another new passage and name it "Step 2." It's very similar to "Step 1," except we're looking for an adverb this time.

```
adverb: 'furiously'
--
Type an adverb, e.g. 'triumphantly,' 'softly,'
'twice.'

{text input for: 'adverb'}

[[Next ->Step 3]]
```

◊ Create another new passage and name it "Step 3." Enter the following text:

```
verb: 'ignores'
--
Select a verb:
```

```
{dropdown menu for: 'verb', choices: ['avoids',
'wrangles', 'removes','finagles','blasts','enjoys
','terrifies','exhausts','tickles','amuses']}

[[Next ->Step 4]]
```

We could have kept on with the *text input* insert, but for the sake of exploration, we'll instead use the *dropdown menu* insert. It does pretty much what you'd expect, creating an expandable menu from which the player is expected to select. Obviously, it imposes more constraint than free input, a move you may want to make from time to time, even in such a minimally structured game. As with text input, we assign an initial value ("ignores") to the key variable. This word comes up as the default selection. Each time the player selects a word, it is assigned to the *verb* variable. The final selection (or default, if no selection is made) is passed on when the player clicks the "Next" link.

```
◊ Create another new passage and name it "Step 4." Enter the
following text:

org:  'the Modern Language Association'
--
Select a civic organization:

{dropdown menu for: 'org', choices: ['Friends of
Linda','the Ancient Order of Voles', 'the Liars
League', 'International Mothers Helpers','Men
with Hats','the Committee of the Hole']}

[[Next -> Step 5]]
```

Again, this step follows the pattern of the one that preceded it: another dropdown menu, this time listing civic organizations. Feel free to shorten, expand, or modify this list. This project does not test for specific selections.

> ◊ We're almost done. Create another new passage and name it
> "Step 5." Enter the following text:
>
> ```
> enders: ["in bed","for a limited time","in
> stores everywhere","as seen on TV","in your
> loudest dreams","where not prohibited by law"]
>
> ender: enders[Math.floor(random.fraction*enders.
> length)]
> --
> {propNoun} {adverb} {verb} {org} {ender}.
>
> [[Play again? ->Step 1]]
> ```

The variable *ender* adds a final phrase to our basic noun-adverb-adjective sentence. Coming unforeseen, it's meant to add a punchline, like the phrase people insufferably recite after reading the contents of a fortune cookie—"in bed." (It's still technically a punchline even if it's dumb.) Joke-theory aside, have a look at the code with which we deliver this final phrase: it contains a trick you haven't seen before, which you will encounter again in the next project. The variable *enders* is an array, a list of values (in this case, strings) to which we can refer by number. The variable *ender* contains a selection from the array, using a complicated but powerful expression:

```
enders[Math.floor(random.fraction*enders.length)]
```

With a little variation, this is the same syntax used in JavaScript to make a random selection from an array. We're deliberately mixing JavaScript and Chapbook syntax.[1] In JavaScript, we indicate an item of

---

1 Twine is built on JavaScript, so its relationship to various Twine dialects, like Chapbook coding or Harlowe scripting, somewhat resembles that of an older language to English—JavaScript : Chapbook || Latin : English. This is an imperfect analogy, but it does help explain what's going on when we blend JavaScript and Chapbook syntax. It's like dropping a Latin phrase into an English sentence, exempli gratia.

an array by using the array name, followed by a number or expression in square brackets. The first element of the array is *enders[0]*, the second is *enders[1]*, and so on. The expression used here resolves to an integer value between 0 and its maximum range, inclusive of 0 but excluding the maximum. The *floor()* function of the Math object, which rounds a fractional value down to the next lowest whole number, comes from JavaScript. The *random.fraction* lookup is from Chapbook—the corresponding JavaScript would be *Math.random()*. Likewise, *enders.length* calls on the built-in *length* property of JavaScript arrays. When we wrote the first draft of this chapter, this technique was not documented; we discovered it by experiment. Since all Twine formats communicate with JavaScript, it's always worth probing for hidden connections—we'll see another in example 3.5. Sometimes the attempt is futile. It's not always possible to mix JavaScript and Chapbook features—some of our later examples in this chapter will explore the limits—but in this case, it works to welcome effect. We'll give more details of this technique in the next example.

First, though, we invite you to give our Mad Lib generator a few spins. You can of course break and abuse its grammar rules all you want. The next examples are more severe, if not more serious.

Example 3.2: Subject-Verb-Object Generation in Chapbook

◊ This example is quite compact, consisting of a single passage and one line of code in the text body. All the typing comes in the variables section. Create a new story and name it anything you like. (We suggest *S-V-O* as a handy nickname.) Start a new passage and name it "Sentence me." You can change this name if you want, provided you reflect the change in the final link. Here are the complete contents of the lone passage. Type away!

```
subjs: ["Edgar","The cat","Edgar
the cat","Gorgomon","Stephane
Grapelli's typewriter","An
```

```
astrolabe","Mrs. Macaleister","An implausible
gravy"]

theSubj: subjs[Math.floor(random.fraction*subjs.
length)]

verbs: ["eschews","thrashes","adores","invalidat
es","steals","withholds","accuses","dethrones"]

theVerb: verbs[Math.floor(random.fraction*verbs.
length)]

objs: ["Niall","the planet Mercury","Episode
Three","our better angels","Stephane Grapelli's
typewriter","furiously","space and time","to no
discernible purpose"]

theObj: objs[Math.floor(random.fraction*objs.
length)]
--
{theSubj} {theVerb} {theObj}.

[[Again! ->Sentence me]]
```

All the hard work comes at the top, in the variables section. We define three arrays and three string objects, each one containing a random selection from one of the arrays. There's one array/string pair each for subject, verb, and object. We've already discussed the hybrid Chapbook/JavaScript selection mechanism that made its first appearance at the end of example 3.1. There's no difference in that structure here. The Chapbook expression *random.fraction* resolves to a decimal between zero and one, which is exactly the same as the JavaScript *Math.random()* function. Multiplying by the length of the array gives us a fractional number between zero and the length of the array. So *random.fraction* might give us a value of 0.356792. Suppose our array has seven items. Multiplying that number by a value between 0 and 7, say 4, gives us 1.427168. Only integers can be used as array selectors, so we need to do some rounding.

We use the JavaScript *Math.floor()* method to convert this decimal to the next lowest integer. That's because the numbering of arrays begins with zero and stops one short of the array's length value. If the array *Joey* has seven items, they'll be as follows:

```
Joey[0]
Joey[1]
Joey[2]
Joey[3]
Joey[4]
Joey[5]
Joey[6]
```

There's never a *Joey[7]*. Rounding down keeps us safely within the range.

With the array selections conveniently stored in our three respective string variables, all we need to do is deliver them, which we do with a line of three variable includes on the other side of the two dashes that close off the variables section. *Et voilà.*

Example 3.3: S-V-O in JavaScript

This example is something of a digression, so we won't go through the process of breaking it down for sequential construction. You can do the typing if you like. Even though you'll be typing in JavaScript, set your story up with Chapbook. That may seem odd, but it's time to reveal an important Chapbook affordance: *you can include extended bits of JavaScript code in Chapbook passages.* We'll take some first steps with this technique in the next few examples. If you're interested in going further, be sure to read the final section of this chapter, where we offer some important technical considerations.

It's been possible to include JavaScript in Twine projects from early on, but in version one of Twine, this code had to be entered in specially marked passages. Twine 2 lets you put JavaScript directly into story passages. You do this with the *JavaScript* modifier, which is just what you see on the first line. You will use a *continue* modifier eventually to switch back to standard Chapbook mode.

◊ Here's the text to type, if you're inclined:

```
[JavaScript]
t=""
subjs = new Array("Edgar","The
cat","Edgar the cat","Gorgomon","Stephane
Grapelli's typewriter","An
astrolabe","Mrs. Macaleister","An implausible
gravy")
verbs = new Array("eschews","thrashes","adores"
,"invalidates","steals","withholds","accuses","
dethrones")
objs = new Array("Niall","the planet
Mercury","Episode Three","our
better angels","Stephane Grapelli's
typewriter","furiously","space and time","to no
discernible purpose")

t = subjs[Math.floor(Math.random()*subjs.length)]
+ " "
t += verbs[Math.floor(Math.random()*verbs.
length)] + " "
t += objs[Math.floor(Math.random()*objs.length)]
+ "."

write(t)

[continue]
[[More ->Tales from the Script]]
```

The basic architecture of this example is similar to that in 3.2: we set up three arrays, containing subject nouns, verbs, and object words or phrases. We make selections from the arrays using the three-step procedure explained earlier—generate a fraction, multiply by the array length, round downward.[2] The delivery mechanism is different. Variables defined in JavaScript can't be passed into Chapbook—this is the first of those functional limitations we'll need to explore. Chapbook allows only one thing to be done with a JavaScript variable, at least without some serious programming: you can pass it to a custom method called write(). This method, which should not be confused with the JavaScript / document object model (DOM) method called *document. write()*, does for the JavaScript variable what the Chapbook insert does for Chapbook variables. It writes the value into the visible text of the Twine passage. The value we write here comes from the variable *t*, which we use to build up our sentence one word at a time.

If you run this JavaScript-inflected example, you'll see the same output as in example 3.2: a subject-verb-object sentence. Since we can achieve the same end without wading into JavaScript, you may ask why we led you on this tour. There's a reason. In working with random selections, you'll sometimes want or need to do things that are not possible in Chapbook. We'll come to one of those cases in our next example.

Example 3.4: Nonrepeating Randoms and the Knuth Shuffle

Let's start by identifying a problem:

Tell us your story
I am a red wheelbarrow painted orange
Shake the boards and howl

---

2 For consistency, we are using the JavaScript generator for a random fraction, *Math. random()*. However, we have accidentally discovered that it is possible to substitute the Chapbook alternative, *random.fraction*, even inside a JavaScript modifier!

I am a red wheelbarrow painted orange
Shake the boards and howl
I am a red wheelbarrow painted orange
I am a red wheelbarrow painted orange
Struggle to define existence

Does this look like something someone has written? If so, we might wonder about all that repetition: two of the eight lines occur twice, and a third appears in quadruplicate. Maybe this is the work of a neo-minimalist poet who is really into repetition. Maybe these are lyrics from a song and the repeated lines are connected to something that makes sense musically. Or maybe this is just output from a bad text generator.

Let's suppose the generator in question works at the sentence level: our next example (3.5) will feature one of those. Perhaps this sentence-level generator just needs more sentences to draw from, though it's also possible its random-selection tool has a basic flaw.

The fundamental tools for generating random numbers in Chapbook are variations on an object named "d" for "die," the singular of "dice." There are variants for integer ranges of 4, 5, 6, 8, 10, 12, 20, 25, 50, and 100. We've already seen *random.fraction* in use, where it does the same thing as the JavaScript *Math.random()*. All these mechanisms have the same weakness: like physical dice, they can produce the same number twice (or more) in succession. In the Chapbook guide, Klimas alludes to Tom Stoppard's play *Rosencrantz and Guildenstern Are Dead*, which opens with a coin flip that stubbornly refuses to produce tails. A tenfold run of heads is vanishingly unlikely in both the real world and software (1024:1 against); but *d.8* returning back-to-back threes is much more probable. The odds may look long at 64:1, but software often involves repeated and rapid iteration—not to mention a thing called luck.

◊ In this example, we'll eliminate the possibility of repeating numbers for a defined range of random selections. This can't be done with Chapbook tools, so we'll turn to JavaScript. Create a new story in Twine using the Chapbook format. (We'll embed our JavaScript in a Chapbook story.) Create a single passage and give it a useful name. We call our version "Loopy." Start with these lines:

```JavaScript
[JavaScript]

sourceArray = new Array('Sunday','Monday','Tuesd
ay','Wednesday','Thursday','Friday','Saturday')
```

This bit should look familiar: it's a standard array declaration. We use the days of the week because they're a familiar sequence. The technique will work with a list of any kind.

◊ Next, we'll enter some more variables:

```
trackArray = new Array()
trackArray.push(99)
rNum = 99
```

The first of these lines creates an empty array called *trackArray*. The second line uses the *push()* method to place the number 99 into the first (and so far, only) position of *trackArray*. In the third line, we declare a variable called *rNum* and give it the value 99. The number 99 is essentially arbitrary: we need to use the same number both for the first array item and for *rNum*, but that number could be anything.

◊ Next, we'll write a JavaScript *function*:

```
function randy(){
    while(trackArray.includes(rNum)){
    rNum = Math.floor(Math.random()*sourceArray.
    length)
    }
trackArray.push(rNum)
return sourceArray[rNum]
}
```

A function (also referred to as a *custom method*) is a group of statements introduced by the keyword *function* and a set of parentheses. The *function body* is then defined within a set of curly braces. The statements within a function have a special status. They are not immediately put into effect (executed) but are held in reserve until the function is activated or *called*. Statements in a function can be called multiple times, often from diverse parts of a longer program.

This function contains a crucial piece: something called a *while loop*. We're using JavaScript in order to access this structure—*Chapbook does not include any kind of loop*. By contrast, there are two types of loops in JavaScript: limited loops, usually *for loops*, that run a specific number of times, and indefinite loops, which run as many times as needed until their stop conditions are met. The indefinite loop we're using here runs *while* we're waiting for a certain outcome. *While loops* are enormously powerful. They are, in fact, the only way to prevent repetition in a random-number sequence.

Programmers tend to be wary of indefinite loops because, in theory, they can turn into loops of a dangerous third kind: *infinite loops*. Unless you are trying to outwit a being of pure energy on *Star Trek*, infinite loops are bad.

Properly written, an indefinite loop is harmless. At the dawn of computing machinery, indefinite loops were avoided because they are inefficient, and computing cycles cost real money back then. In the not-too-distant future, as we recognize the energy impact of all our irresponsible computing, opinion may once more turn against these structures—though the worst offenders are cryptocurrencies and porn. For the moment, concern is muted. Use *while* while you can.

Our magic loop runs under one condition: the value of *rNum* occurs somewhere within the array *trackArray*. If this condition is true, we execute the line contained within the loop, which generates a random value for *rNum*. This is, by the way, the reason we set *rNum* initially to a number we also push into *trackArray*. We need a match in order to get our first generated random. Once we have that number, the loop then checks if this value is in *trackArray* already—in other words, if our number is used or unused. If the number is fresh, the loop terminates. Outside of the loop, we push our guaranteed-unique number onto the tracking array and return the value in *sourceArray* (a day of the week) that corresponds to that number. When a function returns a value, it is fed back into other parts of the script or program.

Our little program eliminates repetition by sorting our original array into a nonsequential pattern. This is like shuffling a deck of cards. In fact, the scheme upon which this program is very loosely based is called the Knuth shuffle algorithm, named for the computer scientist Donald Knuth, author of the classic textbook *Literate Programming* (Knuth). Once we've established the basic principle of shuffling, we can proceed to action.

◊ Here's the last of the JavaScript:

```
for(var i=0; i<sourceArray.length; i++){
    write(randy()+'<br>')
    }
```

This is that other sort of loop, a *for loop*. It runs seven times (the length of our source array) and calls our unique-selection function (*randy()*) each time. Because we embed the call to *randy()* in a *write()* statement (which you'll remember from the previous example), the result of the selection is made part of the visible text.

◊ All that remains is the final Twine link, allowing us to replay the whole business:

```
[continue]
[[Again ->Loopy]]
```

If you haven't made any mistakes, this example should display the seven days of the week in a differently randomized order every time you reload its single passage. Why is this outcome significant? Well, each of these seven-day sequences is both random and nonrepeating;

in the second of our next pair of examples, you'll see why that matters. For the moment, though, let's try a fresh approach to text generation.

Example 3.5A: Situation Reports (Passages)

◊ Create a new story using Chapbook. Call it anything you like. This example is surpassed only by our too-many-links experiment (1.2) for number of passages. There are eleven in all, so the setup will involve a little tedium. You can spare yourself some repetitive strain by first creating ten new passages. Name each one numerically from one to ten—we won't count from zero this time. Open each passage in succession and enter the corresponding sentence from the following list—one sentence to a passage. Do not include the numbers in the passage text:

```
1. The specimen emits radiation in the X-band.
2. The density of the specimen appears to be
increasing.
3. The specimen does not respond to repeated
perturbation.
4. Whoooo da good specimen?!
5. The specimen may be entirely anechoic.
6. The density of the specimen has in fact
decreased.
7. Attempts to ascertain the origin of the
specimen are ongoing.
8. We were briefly unable to locate the specimen.
9. The specimen may have assimilated Technician
Anderson.
10. The specimen has no observable effulgence.
```

Remember when we promised an example of text generation at the sentence level? Well, here it is. More significantly, this generator also works at the *passage* level, which is an interesting way to operate in Twine.

◊ There's just one more passage to build now. Create a new passage and name it "Readout." Let's start with its variables section:

```
passages: ["1","2","3","4","5","6","7","8","9",
"10"]

passage1: passages[Math.floor(random.
fraction*passages.length)]
passage2: passages[Math.floor(random.
fraction*passages.length)]
passage3: passages[Math.floor(random.
fraction*passages.length)]
passage4: passages[Math.floor(random.
fraction*passages.length)]
passage5: passages[Math.floor(random.
fraction*passages.length)]
--
```

The first variable we create is an array called "passages." It simply stores the numerals from 1 to 10 as strings. Why not an array of numbers, you may ask? This is because passage names must be strings.

We've also set up five variables, each assigned a random selection from "passages"—in other words, a selection of five passages out of our set of ten. Yes, we can pick the same passage more than once. I am a red wheelbarrow painted orange. We'll fix this in the next example. You may wonder why we used a series of numbered variables instead of an array. While we could type out a five-item array in the same way we built our ten-piece array in the first line, all those randomizations would create typographic chaos, with their tricky embedding of elements. In JavaScript, we'd use a *for* loop to fill our array by repeating the random-number assignment five times. However, Chapbook has no loops at this writing. (Who knows if they'll be added later.) When you have a relatively small number of items, sometimes a simple series of variables will do.

```
◊ Now for the finishing touches, which follow
directly after the -- that closes the variables
section:


Situation Report {now.date}:
{embed passage: passage1}

{embed passage: passage2}

{embed passage: passage3}

{embed passage: passage4}

{embed passage: passage5}

[align right]
[[Update ->Readout]]
```

And there it is, a tiny bit of sci-fi horror in five sentences, making use of a very important Chapbook insert called *embed passage*. As the name suggests, this modifier copies the contents of the specified passage into the present passage at the point indicated. Using SugarCube and Harlowe, Twine writers have already developed similar techniques into a very fine art. Random selection among a range of passages—ideally a much larger set than the present ten—can be a powerful tool for building an unpredictable structure. It's interesting enough if all we're doing is scooping up one sentence at a time, but there's no reason the embedded passage can't contain Chapbook code like our S-V-O substitution grammar from example 3.1. We'll demonstrate that idea in example 3.6. Randomly choosing output *from a set of independent generators* could produce very surprising and potentially delightful results. Or maybe just the opposite. Such is the challenge of art.

Example 3.5B: The Horror . . .
the Nonrepeating Horror

Meanwhile, let's take on a more approachable challenge: modifying our passage-based generator so it won't pick the same passage twice. We already know how to do this for selections from an internal array. Now we'll adapt our JavaScript code to integrate the Chapbook-based passage selector from the previous example.

> ◊ Set up a new story using Chapbook. We'll be using JavaScript within Chapbook—with an interesting twist or two.

Like 3.5A, this is a big one: eleven passages. There are two ways to go here. Since the ten embeddable passages are identical to those in 3.5A, you could start by duplicating and renaming your version of that story. If you take this work-saving option, open the passage called "Readout" and delete its contents. Then you're ready to go. If for some reason you enjoy tedious typing, then start a fresh story and repeat the procedure in the first step of example 3.5A: make ten new passages and enter a sentence in each. Whichever way you go, we'll assume you have eleven passages, each containing a sentence, and a passage called "Readout" with no contents. Ready?

> ◊ We'll start by entering a variables section in our new version of "Readout":
>
> ```
> ep1:  ' '
> ep2:  ' '
> ep3:  ' '
> ep4:  ' '
> ep5:  ' '
> --
> ```

You may ask yourself, *Hey, aren't we supposed to use JavaScript for this thing? So why do we have a Chapbook variables section?* It turns out that Chapbook has an originally undocumented quirk—if you declare a variable first in Chapbook and *then declare it again in JavaScript,* you can do more than pass the value of the variable for screen display. Using this exploit, we can compute a value for a variable using JavaScript, then pass it to a Chapbook insert. (Klimas confirms this is permissible; he just overlooked the possibility when he wrote the first version of the Chapbook guide.) While we're asking skeptical questions, you might also ask why we're using five separate variables instead of an array. It turns out our JavaScript pass-through exploit doesn't work with arrays, at least at this writing. Oh well.

◊ With our obligatory Chapbook work out of the way, let's get started on the JavaScript. Enter the following:

```
[JavaScript]

sourceArray = new Array('01','02','03','04','05'
,'06','07','08','09','10')

trackArray = new Array()

trackArray.push(99)

rNum = 99
```

These lines should look familiar from example 3.4. They're the standard setup for our Knuth shuffle implementation. The source array contains the names you gave to the arrays that contain our sentences.

◊ Here's the next piece of our JavaScript:

```
for(i=0; i<5; i++){
    while(trackArray.includes(rNum)){
    rNum = Math.floor(Math.random()*sourceArray.
    length)
    }
```

```
trackArray.push(rNum)

if(i==0) ep1 = sourceArray[rNum]
if(i==1) ep2 = sourceArray[rNum]
if(i==2) ep3 = sourceArray[rNum]
if(i==3) ep4 = sourceArray[rNum]
if(i==4) ep5 = sourceArray[rNum]
```

This is our *while loop* again, this time wrapped not in a function but in a *for loop* with five iterations. As before, we push our guaranteed nonrepeating value onto *trackArray*. That's why we use a series of *if* tests to route our successive selections into five distinct variables whose values can be passed back to Chapbook.

```
◊ The remainder of the project is pure Chapbook. The struc-
tures should be familiar:

[continue]

{embed passage: ep1}

{embed passage: ep2}

{embed passage: ep3}

{embed passage: ep4}

{embed passage: ep5}

[[Again ->Readout]]
```

The *continue* modifier shifts us back to Chapbook mode. The embed inserts pull in the contents of the passages whose names were selected (without repetitions!) in our JavaScript shuffle maneuvers. That's the project. It has all the advantages of passage-based generation without the flaw of inelegant repetition. The JavaScript-Chapbook trick play shows again why it's worth tinkering with code, especially when it's young. Software sometimes doesn't know its own strength.

Example 3.6: Free Verse, or You Get What You Pay For

Two examples back, we promised a project that uses embedded passages that generate text through local computation. Ideally, we'd try embedding a passage containing something like our S-V-O sentence generator. Though we have something else in mind for this example, let's think through the S-V-O experiment first.

◊ To try later: set up a Chapbook story, create passages named "bedfellow" and "testbed," and copy the Chapbook S-V-O code from example 3.2 into "bedfellow." In "testbed," type the following:

```
{embed passage: 'bedfellow'}
{embed passage: 'bedfellow'}
{embed passage: 'bedfellow'}
```

Lo and behold, you can embed the same passage more than once![3] Since "bedfellow" generates a plausibly fresh sentence each time it's accessed, you should end up with three unique pieces of nonsense. The world needs more nonsense.

With this conceptual exercise behind us, let's turn to something more concrete and hopefully less nonsensical: a genuine free-verse

---

3 At this point, a certain bad thought may come into your head: *What if I write a passage for embedding, which in turn embeds the passage that embeds it?* In other words,

Passage A embeds passage B
  Passage B embeds passage A (which embeds B, which embeds A embedding B, and so forth)

The saints in heaven cry when you do this. Also, your browser and JavaScript make Twine knock it off after about a thousand iterations. Now you don't have to try this thing, right?

generator. *Free verse* is poetry without constrained rhyme or meter—low-hanging fruit for demonstration purposes, though you could build out the technique shown here to write more demanding forms, such as haiku, sonnets, or villanelles. As in example 3.5A, we'll work at the level of complete lines. That decision raised the specter of repetition in the earlier example, but as you'll see, we have no such worries here.

◊ Set up a Chapbook story called anything you like (ours is called *Free Verse*). Create seven passages in that story. Name the first one (the default starting passage) "Versify." Name the others "Opener," "Middle 1," "Middle 2," "Middle 3," "Middle 4," and "Finisher." Open "Versify" and enter the following:

```
{embed passage: 'Opener'}
{embed passage: 'Middle 1'}
{embed passage: 'Middle 2'}
{embed passage: 'Middle 3'}
{embed passage: 'Middle 4'}
{embed passage: 'Finisher'}

[[Again ->'Versify']]
```

No mysteries here: our main passage embeds all six subsequent passages in sequence, without any random choices. That business happens in the embedded passages themselves.

◊ Open "Opener" (that was awkward) and enter the following:

```
r: random.d6

open (r === 1): 'something I heard no one say'
open (r === 2): 'now this'
open (r === 3): 'between some dreams I thought I
heard'
```

```
open (r === 4): 'you might not believe this'
open (r === 5): 'this much the night allowed
me'
open (r === 6): 'a spider spun this for me once'
--
{open}
```

This is a reasonably simple structure. To the variable *r* we assign the results of the *random.d6* function, which is an integer between 1 and 6 inclusive. Next, we take a variable called *open* and assign it a value based on *r*. In Harlowe or JavaScript, we would use *if* statements or perhaps a *switch* construction, but we've learned to work differently in Chapbook (see example 2.4). We give the variable name, enclose the condition we want to match in parentheses, and after a colon, we give the value we want the variable to have if the condition is met. In example 2.4, we used this technique to create a scoring scale. Here it's a randomizer. (Notice we're using one of the whole-number random functions from Chapbook, this time without any funny business.)

After we close the variables section, we simply insert the variable. Chapbook automatically knows which permutation has been chosen. It's worth noting that when we perform the insertion here, the action effectively migrates to our main action passage, "Versify," where the present passage ("Opener") is embedded. Anything made visible in an embedded passage is made visible in the embedding passage.

◊ As you may guess, the remaining five passages are versions of "Opener" with different text. Here's "Middle 1":

```
r: random.d6

m_1 (r===1): 'water is a silence'
m_1 (r===2): 'a silence has come upon the
waters'
```

```
m_1 (r===3): 'we are the sum of waters'
m_1 (r===4): 'drink your water in silence'
m_1 (r===5): 'the silence of waters'
m_1 (r===6): 'water is never really silent'
--
{m_1}
```

◊ Enter the following in "Middle 2":

```
r: random.d6
```

```
m_2 (r===1): 'imagine the invention of water'
m_2 (r===2): 'every moment is the beginning of
invention'
m_2 (r===3): 'the spark of nothing less is
this'
m_2 (r===4): 'for seeing the word so far'
m_2 (r===5): 'having carried words no further'
m_2 (r===6): 'water could not be silent'
--
{m_2}
```

◊ Enter the following in "Middle 3":

```
r: random.d6
```

```
m_3 (r===1): 'quantify your blessings'
m_3 (r===2): 'render your account'
m_3 (r===3): 'spill out that bag of content'
m_3 (r===4): 'say what you contain'
m_3 (r===5): 'read the bill of particulars'
m_3 (r===6): 'gather up the washing'
--
{m_3}
```

◊ Enter the following in "Middle 4":

```
r: random.d6

m_4 (r===1): 'dreams beasts sex'
m_4 (r===2): 'monkeys jewels and fabulous
stories'
m_4 (r===3): 'a rock a mandarin a twisted pike'
m_4 (r===4): 'larks crows kingfishers calumets'
m_4 (r===5): 'gazettes and galley proofs'
m_4 (r===6): 'whelks whales and waterfowl'
--
{m_4}
```

◊ And finally, enter the following in "Finisher":

```
r: random.d6

finish (r===1): 'and that was something said'
finish (r===2): 'and nothing more of time'
finish (r===3): 'and then the rain came'
finish (r===4): 'until we end our song'
finish (r===5): 'or this and nothing more'
finish (r===6): 'the machine stops'
--
{finish}
```

We'll just say one more thing about this project: the writing doesn't aim at artistic merit, but it does stumble closer to seriousness, or at least coherence, than our other efforts. We do this to suggest the possibilities of this free-verse generator, or something like it, as a genuine literary device—or perhaps a gateway experience. Computational poetry is an established and flourishing field. Substitution grammars are just the beginning. More advanced work can involve N-gram text generation, operations on large digital text bases, and various forms of machine learning. If you want to know more about the history of computational poetry, check out Chris Funkhouser's *Prehistoric Digital Poetry* (Funkhouser, *Prehistoric*). For recent trajectories, see his *New Directions in Digital Poetry* (Funkhouser, *New Directions*), as well as the website of the School for Poetic Computation: https://sfpc.io/.

Example 3.7: Game of Names (after Porpentine)

We'll finish with one from the heart. The naming ritual at the beginning of Porpentine's *With Those We Love Alive* creates a moment of high enchantment. We've discussed its mysteries in the previous critical chapter. Here we'll subject it to shameless imitation, partly for one more demonstration of the creative possibilities of Twine, and mainly because we think (well, one of us does) that making up character names is huge fun.

> ◊ Create a new Chapbook story and call it what you will. Make two passages. Name the starter passage "Choose Your Time." Name the other one "Your Name Will Be." Let's start with the variables section in the first passage. Open "Choose Your Time" and type the following:
>
> ```
> theDays: ['Scum','Monster','Tomb','Weed','Thirst
> ','Fear','Scatter']
>
> theSeasons: ['Waking','Making','Darkening','Ni
> ght']
> --
> ```

We make two arrays, one for the seven days of a fantastical week, the other for four eldritch seasons. This is less detail than Porpentine works with; we need to keep things manageable for demonstration purposes.

◊ After closing off the variables section with the required double dashes, add the following to "Choose Your Time":

```
Today is a {dropdown menu for: 'theDay',
choices: theDays}day in the season of {dropdown
menu for: 'theSeason', choices: theSeasons}.

[[So it is; who am I? ->Your Name Will Be]]
```

It's our old friend, the dropdown menu. We could have used cycling links as in the Porpentinian original, but no one likes a robotic imitator. Going with the *dropdown menu* insert also allows us to demonstrate a small but useful trick: you can define your menu options as an array, up in the variables section, then simply reference the array as the argument to "choices" within the insert. If for some reason you have a long menu of choices, this separation might be convenient.

◊ Open the second passage, "Your Name Will Be." This passage has a long variables section, which we'll break into pieces. Start with this:

```
firsts: ['Drag','Mars','Mol','Bren','Hal','Dom']

seconds: ['rak','ra','della','bim','bang','rica'
,'dottir','goth','gren','thing']

thirds: ['Hamble','Rumble','Storm','Mountain','R
iver','Valley','Moose','Squirrel']

fourths: ['hand','mind','foot','body','thumb','w
easel','love','song']
```

We have four arrays, each containing options for syllables in a four-syllable name. We'll have two kinds of names—some that are generated from these arrays, and another set arrived at differently.

◊ Here's the next piece of the variables section in "Your Name Will Be":

```
nameFirst: firsts[Math.floor(random.
fraction*firsts.length)]

nameSecond: seconds[Math.floor(random.
fraction*seconds.length)]

nameThird: thirds[Math.floor(random.
fraction*thirds.length)]

nameFourth: fourths[Math.floor(random.
fraction*fourths.length)]

id: nameFirst+nameSecond + " " +
nameThird+nameFourth
```

The four sequential variables receive random selections from the syllable arrays. The combination of these variables is assigned to the variable *id*. Note that the plus sign (+) works here as a *concatenation operator*, simply sticking together some strings. That's because JavaScript (and Chapbook) automatically changes the function of the plus sign when a string is involved. (If only numbers are involved, "+" signifies mathematical addition.)

◊ One more push to complete the variables section:

```
id (theDay==='Monster' && theMonth==='Waking'):
'Slam Danghandle'
id (theDay==='Weed' && theMonth==='Making'):
'Leah Romavant'
id (theDay==='Tomb' && theMonth==='Darkening'):
'Gnowth Marvydink'
id (theDay==='Thirst' && theMonth==='Night'):
'Crassa Foomstoffer'
```

```
id (theDay==='Fear' && theMonth==='Waking'):
'Blastgret Stimsocket'
id (theDay==='Scatter' && theMonth==='Making'):
'Meera Upfallen'
id (theDay==='Scum' && theMonth==='Darkening'):
'Kristel Vannafoy'
id (theDay==='Monster' && theMonth==='Night'):
'Markie Mistmother'
--
```

Don't forget the dashes closing the variables section. Here we have another instance of conditioned variables, as in examples 2.4 and 3.6. We single out eight combinations of day and season for special names not made from the syllable sets. We throw in this feature arbitrarily, but it does add some stakes to the naming game. There are twenty-eight permutations of days and seasons and eight special names, giving a 2:7 chance of obtaining one. If there were a story attached to these two passages, maybe a character with a special name would be treated differently than one with a generic, generated name. Or maybe, as in *With Those We Love Alive*, the name would essentially be a MacGuffin, elaborately generated but not otherwise consequential. Creativity is all about choices.

◊ The rest of the second passage is simple:

```
[align center]
Born on a {theDay}day of the {theMonth} month,
you are:

~~{id}~~

[continue]
[[Try again? ->Choose Your Time]]
```

Finish and test. Who will you turn out to be?

So ends our encounter with text generators. Like other applications of Twine, they may be silly, serious, or somewhere in between. They can incline toward the party-game fare of Mad Libs, to the revolutionary aesthetics of the exquisite corpse, to the endlessly iterative fascination of *Taroko Gorge*. Whichever way you turn, you'll be working with a system fundamentally dedicated to possibility, variation, contingency, and play. Chapter T-4 looks at the cultural implications of that iconoclastic, radically playful turn.

Technical Notes on JavaScript and Chapbook

This chapter has introduced the JavaScript modifier, opening the door to hybrid constructions. If you'd like to explore that path, you may want some experience with JavaScript first. Our bonus practical chapter presents a series of projects that work exclusively with JavaScript without touching Twine. They might be a good place to start, and of course, commercial guides to JavaScript authoring are abundant. An excellent resource for creative applications is Montfort's *Exploratory Programming for the Arts and Humanities* (Montfort, *Exploratory*). What follows here is fairly detailed and is meant primarily for those who have become interested in doing more ambitious things with JavaScript and Twine.

A subject of great concern to modern programmers is *the order of operations*—just when the computer processes your instructions. In Chapbook/JavaScript hybrids, you need to consider this issue in arranging your code. Let's say you have two custom methods or functions, A and B. Method A invokes method B. In browser-based JavaScript, you can place the definition of B after A in your code. Not so with Chapbook, which in our experience will throw a pink fit if you refer to a method you haven't previously defined.

The order of operations also has implications beyond the structure of code. If you've worked with JavaScript in web pages, you may have encountered a situation where a script's behavior depends on where it is placed within the page code. The "HEAD" division is usually safe, but not always—if, for instance, your script needs to interact with an element that is dynamically added to the page by another script. The browser needs to load related elements before your script operates on them. A similar problem can arise with Chapbook if you write a script that changes a page element and do not either (a) make the script dependent on a user action, such as reloading the page, or (b) delay the first execution of the script by using *setTimeout()* or *setInterval()*. These are advanced topics that go beyond the purview of this book, but we thought we'd mention them in case Twine starts complaining that you've tried to modify a "null" object.

Finally, a general note about the Twine/JavaScript relationship. As we've noted, it's incestuous. Twine runs in JavaScript, so its hybridized structures are always a little . . . kinky. On occasion, you may find that JavaScript instructions, especially those with compound and complex syntaxes, don't behave as expected. JavaScript in Chapbook is not quite the same as JavaScript in a conventional web page. However, these instances are rare, and we can do a remarkable range of things without running into difficulties. As we've said, you can see more of those possibilities in the bonus chapter at the end of this book.

Works Cited

Carpenter, J. R. *Generation(s)*. Traumawien, 2010.

Funkhouser, Chris. *New Directions in Digital Poetry*. Bloomsbury, 2012.

———. *Prehistoric Digital Poetry*. University of Alabama Press, 2007.

Knuth, Donald. *Literate Programming*. Cambridge University Press, 1983.

Montfort, Nick. *Exploratory Programming for the Arts and Humanities*. MIT Press, 2016.

———. *Taroko Gorge*. 2009. https://nickm.com/taroko_gorge/.

Nelson, Theodor H. *Computer Lib/Dream Machines*. Mindful Press, 1987.

Wardrip-Fruin, Noah. "Christopher Strachey: The First Digital Artist?" Grand Text Auto, August 1, 2005. https://grandtextauto.soe.ucsc.edu/2005/08/01/christopher -strachey-first-digital-artist/.

Queer Twine and Camp

Twine is inarguably situated in queer discourse: some of the most influential designers and games produced with Twine are narratives that center trans identity, dysphoria, coming out, and coming of age as queer. Play with pronouns, bodies, monstrosity, and eroticism is common, particularly in the works of leading designers such as Porpentine, Anna Anthropy, Christine Love, and many more. There are two ways we might talk about Twine as queer. The first is straightforward and thus overly simplistic: Twine is a platform made rich by queer stories. If we were to define a Twine canon, it would be impossible to do so without including rich narratives of trans bodies in sci-fi horrors, of lesbian cowgirls finding romance, of queers in love at the end of the world—can we imagine making such a claim about any other game platform? This distinction alone is enough to place Twine works firmly on the margins of how gaming is generally discussed, even in scholarly circles, where an increased interest in queer gaming has permeated. What is subtext elsewhere is firmly text in Twine—while it is possible to construct depictions of unnuanced, heteronormative relationships, the platform itself seems to challenge such depictions and asks authors to reconsider binary choices for richness of exploration. And this aspect, perhaps, leads us to a less straightforward reading of Twine as queer.

Given its origins in open-source, its insistence on a nostalgic interface that recalls early hypertext even as it dismisses such antecedents, and its extreme potential for an over-the-top aesthetic that recalls the days of GeoCities, is Twine itself a queer platform?

The early web was delightfully queer: a walk down memory lane through a 1999 feature in the *sexualities* category suggests that "the gay, lesbian, bi, transgendered and other anti-gender communities were ahead of the game here," noting the existence of a 540-page "tome the size and shape of a computer manual" by Jeff Dawson in 1998 entitled *Gay and Lesbian Online: Your Indispensable Guide to Cruising the Queer Web* (Gauntlett 327). It is hard to imagine such a guide today—indeed, it is hard to recall the type of mind-set that would have a writer typing out websites such as the lengthy URL to For Queer Mice, a website appropriately housed in the WestHollywood neighborhood of GeoCities (Gauntlett 328).

Twine is a throwback to this aesthetic, drawing on what artists Olia Liana and Dragan Espenschied define as a type of digital folklore language in their unusual and important volume documenting the types of web art practices that often go derided or unremarked: "Users' endeavors, like glittering star backgrounds, photos of cute kittens and rainbow gradients, are mostly derided as kitsch or in the most extreme cases, postulated as the end of culture itself. In fact this evolving vernacular, created by users for users, is the most important, beautiful and misunderstood language of new media" (Espenschied and Lialina). The examples these artists draw on emphasize the feminine and the decorative, two intertwined aesthetics that already attract derision.

In the introduction to their mix of theoretical and pragmatic examinations of this user-powered web, Liana and Espenschied further note that the attention to the history of dominant technologies means "we have studied the history of hypertext, but not the history of Metallica fan web rings or web rings in general," a reminder that is particularly compelling given whose web is centered by this divide (Espenschied and Lialina).

Notably, popular coverage of these same artists' project to delve into the GeoCities archives and share their findings on Tumblr has come with headlines like "Remember the Hilarious Horror of Geocities" (Chan). This derision dismisses the investment of individuals working in the web in a tradition not so removed from outsider or visionary art, which is defined by the American Visionary Art Museum as "Art produced by self-taught individuals, usually without formal training, whose works arise from an innate personal vision that revels foremost in the creative act itself" ("American Visionary Art Museum"). The personal web page embodies shaping webrings, building coordinated background sets and buttons to avoid HTML defaults, crafting animated GIFs, and optimizing resolution to account for limited modem bandwidth.

These individuals were the original artists-in-residence of the web. Artist Richard Vijgen draws our attention to the spatial metaphors of GeoCities through his project Deleted City, which he described in an interview as capturing the settler mind-set that GeoCities encouraged: "The idea that in the beginning, cyberspace is an empty space that has to be populated, was I think easily linked to this idea of America being an 'empty' continent. . . . They provided web space with a story, with a narrative" (Howard). Notably, the most popular of the communities was Heartland, which suggests a GeoCities with a highly normative main street: "With an emphasis on 'parenting, pets, and home town values,' the Heartland neighborhoods (including 41 suburbs with names like Plains, Meadows, Prairie, and Woods) also spoke to Geocities' immense popularity with a specific demographic: wealthy, white, and American, those with the disposable income to become some of the net's first users" (Howard).

Step outside of "Main Street," however, and the neighborhoods change dramatically: WestHollywood offered the forthright listing: "Gay, lesbian, bisexual and transgendered" (GeoCities, "GeoCities— Neighborhoods"). Notably, this same neighborhood was at the center of an early case of online censorship when CyberPatrol blocked the entire community rather than reviewing its content: "The blocking of West Hollywood raises the issue of whether it is possible to filter the Internet at all" (Wallace, "There Goes the Neighborhood"). The pages linked in one archived WestHollywood neighborhood hub tell a different story, to list just a few:

Lesbian Epiphanies
GENDER is so confusing. ??
The Wonderful Homepage of Two Huge Indigo Girls Fans
(GeoCities, "Geocities WestHollywood LGBTQ")

Such pages are arguably as much a part of the history of hypertext as any novel associated with the history of electronic literature, yet most of this work goes undocumented outside of the work of a few web historians, and the aesthetic expression of early queer hypertext (and the communities it enabled) is typically treated separately from the literary potential, despite the many impromptu literary journals and narrative-driven spaces within these neighborhoods (see figure 15), particularly on the fandom side. Such pages often included personal touches along with vivid color and images. These pages, taken collectively, demonstrate a number of early solutions to personalizing what was once more appropriately called the home page: boring line rules were replaced with GIFs, including the examples here of a rainbow bar or a spider moving across the page. Visitor counters tracked one's impressions, often accompanied by guest books for leaving comments. Under-construction GIFs of every variety reminded the viewer to return to

Figure 15: An example of a literary home page in WestHollywood, emulated from 1996 (Twilite909)

appreciate changes. Tiled backgrounds allowed for smaller images to serve as the basis of extensive patterns. And of course, the deeply personal nature of the web is well reflected in the contact information and personal collection of links that appear on these pages.

To call these pages evidence of a camp aesthetic in the early web would be oversimplifying matters—however, the decorative elements here, taken to an extreme, produced pages that live on for their visual infamy as a testament to what hypertext can do.

Aesthetically, a classic model of hypertext in electronic literature leaves much of the lifting to the words. The literary model and heritage we've discussed thus far emphasize hypertext not on interface (though it is certainly present) but on structure, and several of the early platforms and iterations of hypertext reflect that preoccupation. While early Storyspace novels integrated graphics and works like Shelley Jackson's *Patchwork Girl* (1995) demonstrate the platform's ability to integrate graphics and use visualizations to make the linking structures more visible, the emphasis is on text first (see figure 16).

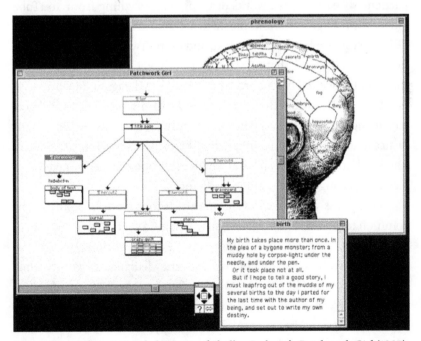

Figure 16: Different visual elements of Shelley Jackson's *Patchwork Girl* (1997)

By contrast, web-based hypertext is more inherently multimediated, and authors experimenting with the web as a platform frequently exercised their greater aesthetic control. For example, Jackson's *My Body* (1997) integrated image maps, although many of the other aesthetic choices of these works were functional. For example, *My Body* incorporates small image fragments illustrating each page of the body as the reader navigates the work, then uses the standard practice of highlighting active and visited links in different colors to demonstrate what the reader has already explored. The work uses some of the affordances of hypertext, such as image backgrounds, to create the tiled repetition of the brushstrokes.

As a medium grounded not in text but in hypertext, with the markup that entails, and adopted not necessarily by makers of "literature" but by makers driven by games and interactive media, broadly conceived, Twine is a platform where aesthetic restraint is not so dominant. Indeed, one of Twine's defining characteristics is the ability to harness layered, multimedia expressions of emotion rapidly, and remixing is particularly easy for live works drawing on everything from YouTube videos for backgrounds and music to a digital art heritage of animated GIFs, vector graphics, blinking text, and more. Twine thus offers a technological throwback that recalls the age of GeoCities and an interface that points back to HyperCard. The use of HTML tags and in-line style hearkens back to when the web was filled with animated GIFs and personalizing a page with everything from animated GIFs to elaborate fantastical backgrounds and blinking line-break bars was simply the norm. The modern web has its own aesthetic: Facebook does not give users leeway to change a color, much less a font.

This expressive space allows Twine artists to work in an aesthetic uncommon to games: camp. Mark Booth homes in on the challenge of defining camp: "The key to defining camp lies in reconciling its essential marginality with its evident ubiquity, in acknowledging its diversity while still making sense of it" (Booth 66). Susan Sontag suggests that camp is frequently intertwined with the decorative, "emphasizing texture, sensuous surface, and style at the expense of content," explaining that "the hallmark of Camp is the spirit of extravagance" (Sontag 59). Jack Babuscio notes that Sontag obscures the queerness of camp, which is essential to the camp of hypertext and Twine: "Camp is ... in part, a reaction to the anonymity, boredom, and socialising tendencies of the technological society. Camp aims to transform the ordinary into something more spectacular. In terms of style, it signifies performance rather than existence" (Babuscio 122).

Twine has been positioned as an outsider platform, a connection Matt Kirschenbaum suggested in his survey of the field in 2017: Twine seems aligned with punk and disruptive, in spaces ranging from academic to industry. The saga of *Depression Quest* (perhaps the most influential Twine game in history) is a testament to the power of Twine to anger. Feminist and queer code studies invite us to ask if there is something about Twine that is responsible for this potential—does the platform's emphasis on accessible disruption make it inherently queer or feminist? Making such a claim is significantly risky and potentially painfully reductive. David Halperin warns against a normalization that pulls queer back into an abstraction: "A generic badge of subversiveness, a more trendy version of 'liberal'" (Halperin 341). Certainly, Twine's subversiveness is well documented. A case can be made that Twine's ease of use and distribution is the key to this subversion, and Leonardo Flores sets Twine forth as part of the third generation of literature, with an emphasis on accessibility: "The software tools at their disposal are varied and increasingly lower the barrier to entry, with programs like Twine, Unity, Javascript Libraries, simple and free publication platforms (like Cheap Bots, Done Quick! and Philome.la), and social media apps like Vine, Instagram, Snapchat, GIPHY, and others" (Flores). Such tools notably include many free corporate platforms appropriated for the purpose of personal creativity.

Alongside these other tools of the third generation, Twine evokes what Kathi Berens refers to as the "Try it Yourself" model of e-literary intention: "As the technical barrier-to-entry lowers, a wider range of people are empowered to 'try it yourself' making digital art. They 'reject or are unaware of' e-lit's aesthetic of difficulty. 'Try it Yourself' doesn't prescribe an aesthetic. It discloses an intention" (Berens). Porpentine invokes a similar intention in an interview entitled "Beautiful Weapons," where she notes both Twine's accessibility and the role of herself and other queer designers in making it popular. Porpentine describes Twine in the interview in terms of conflict:

> Twine is guerrilla warfare. It is cheaply-made pipe bombs and land mines that can proliferate and crop up in the dominant space. Besides being easy to create, it is not enough that our art be beautiful. It must be a beautiful weapon. We must ensure that our art is weaponized and can destroy other things.
>
> We can flood sites and the Web with our games because it's so easy to upload and share. There's just no obstacle to playing them—you just load it like a webpage. We're competing now with AAA games. That's what I mean by weaponization. It's hard to argue with that kind of viral, proliferating, breeding spirit. (Kaye)

This discussion of Twine's accessibility allowing for the ease of pro-liferation is notably part of the essential appeal of modern hypertext and is what distinguishes web-driven hypertext from the platforms associated with electronic literature. Platforms such as StorySpace forefronted the literary (as discussed in chapter T-3): this is not to say that such platforms can't be similarly accessible for creation, but their models of distribution are more tightly controlled, and the obstacles to their proliferation and play are intensely different. Twine offers no obstacles—a concept can be built, circulated, and played without spe-cialized knowledge, which lends itself to expressive works that can be rapidly experienced and responsive to immediate discourse.

In this, Twine is an heir to Flash but without the baggage of a browser extension. While Flash certainly brought an era of weird ca-sual games and experimental electronic literature with it, the corporate control of the platform and the need for an installed extension always limited its scope and eventually its life-span (Salter and Murray). Flash emerged because hypertext was seen as insufficient to the task of play and marketing—Twine is a rebuttal and a reminder of how much native web technologies can accomplish.

The open-source aspect of Twine is particularly resonant with its use for queer and disruptive play, which Adobe's ownership of Flash (and the cost of development software) inherently hindered by tying it to corporate economic models that similarly make the iOS and Android app stores less queer-friendly spaces. Twine's queer potential has previously been described primarily in terms of this type of democratization: Alison Harvey notes that the queer alternatives Twine provides for game-making are emerging in part due to its lack of alignment with "games" as a construct: "Because Twine was not conceptualized as a technology of game-making, assumptions about what these kinds of tools do are not embedded in its structure and paratexts in the same way as other dedicated digital game design programs" (Harvey 97). This returns us to our opening discussion of Twine's formalism: the mechanics most associated with dominant game genres—violence, acquisition, and conquest—are absent from the platform's affordances. They are possible but not embedded or default.

With that said, it is impossible to separate the history of queer Twine from the history of queer gaming, particularly given the number of Twine works examined here that make explicit interventions in gaming discourse. Similarly, it is not in the realm of electronic literature where most Twine works seek to make their intervention but instead in the broader context of the web and games. Matt Kirschenbaum's jest of Twine as punk occurred before its counterpart, an apparent number-one hit of electronic literature born of Twine: the special episode of the Netflix series *Black Mirror* called "Bandersnatch," discussed in chapter T-1. The mundane focus of "Bandersnatch" on a cis, straight white man as a lone-wolf game designer is the epitome of traditional games discourse and does not seem to easily mesh with a discussion of Twine's punk potential. Instead, it emphasizes exactly the qualities that many Twine creators react against. Yet this is not an inherent refutation of Twine's potential as a disruptive force—rather, it is a reminder that the goals of the creators and particularly the role queer designers have played in shaping Twine's aesthetics and its impact cannot be separated from our discussion of Twine's potential for influence.

The queer creators who have shaped Twine have claimed a different aesthetic place for the platform. Thus I argue that Twine is not punk; it is camp. It is the potential of the web, and its history, for decorative and dramatic play; it is the invitation to excess and personal style; it is frequently too much and does not collapse under the weight of style. Its emphasis on in-line tags allows users to jump from blinking text to rumbling to marquees and everything in between in the space of a single passage. This is not to say that all work in Twine is camp (it isn't) or that Twine is uniquely a queer game platform (it's not, nor is it the only home of queer gaming.) However, its fundamental embrace of the aesthetics of an early, defiantly personal web makes Twine an invitation to explore style and decoration, and the resistant narratives queer Twine creators have produced have embraced camp as a form of defiance against the painfully traditional masculinity associated with gaming.

Camp and Porpentine

No work better demonstrates Twine's potential for glorious excess and camp than Porpentine's *Cry$tal Warrior Ke$ha* (2013), a tribute to the named pop artist whose anthem "Warrior" plays in the background when the game is launched. One reviewer describes that album as demonstrating "Ke$ha's willingness to experiment with everything, up to and including hitherto unexplored corners of the kitchen sink. There's *Animal*'s scuzzy synthpop, classic rock, EDM and, on occasion, dubstep. In 'Crazy Kids' we get all the above with bonus cut-and-paste points, completely changing between genres like a light switch" (Nellis). The music blasts the moment you open the browser to Porpentine's *Cry$tal Warrior Ke$ha*. Hover the mouse over a link, and the bold turquoise lettering is replaced by larger, bright-pink letters with a tiled, animated GIF of a pink star flashing repeatedly behind the words. The story (set at a concert from the artist's perspective) quickly moves into the absurd and fantastical as an attack interrupts the performance and Ke$ha's internal monologue responds:

your elite bodyguards/back-up dancers are undone.

it wasn't just an energy attack. whoever did this had chrono magic.

the time bomb didn't kill them. it scattered them to distant lonely worlds of time, temporal backwaters. they could be the kid you meet on the street, the old woman hobbling through her garden. (Porpentine, *Cry$tal Warrior Ke$ha*)

Porpentine frequently introduces the supernatural elements of her narratives with similar matter-of-fact introductions. However, in this iteration, they are also evocative of the imagery of Ke$ha's album and concerts, both infamous for theatricality and excess that the game captures through rhythmic, spaced lines in a bold color palette (see figure 17).

The game was announced on Porpentine's Tumblr in 2013 with the message, "THIS GAME IS 100% CANON." The original post received 287 notes (mostly hearts and reblogs) with comments including "The greatest game so far in 2013" and "Play this now" (Porpentine, "POR-PENTINE"). The release location of Tumblr is particularly significant given Tumblr's role as a hub for queer culture and particularly transgender, genderqueer, and gender-nonconforming community building during this time (Fink and Miller). The community building and role of queer trans aesthetics in shaping Tumblr follows a trend of shifting from platform to platform as corporate policies make some spaces

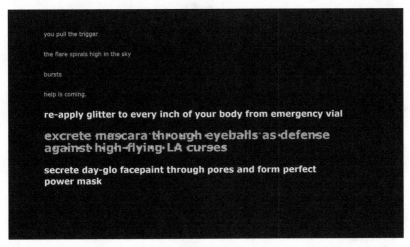

Figure 17: A pivotal moment of conflict in *Cry$tal Warrior Ke$ha* (Porpentine)

uninhabitable for queer discourse: the people reshape the platform, and through their influence, "the website becomes a laboratory for erotic experimentation, a canvas for the collective depiction of trans desires, and a living archive of sexual attraction" (Fink and Miller). This reimagining of space recalls Kara Keeling's framework of queer as resistance in software: "Queer offers a way of making perceptible presently uncommon senses in the interest of producing a/new commons and/or of proliferating the senses of a commons already in the making" (Keeling).

While the experience of *Cry$tal Warrior Ke$ha* is short (about fifteen minutes or less), it is memorable. Notably, this game made Amanda Wallace's Storycade list of three recommended games to introduce people to Twine. Wallace's description of the game highlights the message about popular culture and particularly its resistance to the antifan, noting that just as the protagonist "fights off crowds of haters," so too can the game be used "to point out when someone is going too far with their pop-culture hatred" (Wallace, "3 Twine Games").

This emphasis on fighting back against haters, and particularly those who would limit her artistic expression, is not just a theme of Ke$ha's music but also a pivotal part of her career. One poignant review notes that the game thus has ongoing, and changing, resonance thanks to the singer herself:

> The year is 2013, and this is long before Dr. Luke and the rape allegations became common knowledge, back when Kesha was simply a pop princess crossed with a glitter encrusted party girl. Back when she sang about brushing her teeth with a bottle of Jack, back when she sang to the misfits and the bad kids. Back when she wasn't held in contractual limbo, unable really to sing at all.
>
> Because the character in Porpentine's game isn't the Kesha of 2016. She's the 2013 Ke$ha, who was still suffering in silence. Who was the symbol for at least one developer, of being capable of facing down the haters and surviving. Of smiling while doing it. (Hudgins)

This postassociation is particularly powerful given the similar narratives of abuse and silencing of women that would play out in the games industry, changing the game's significance and keeping it in the minds of many players. Porpentine's more literary games, from the darkness of *Howling Dogs* (2012) to the bleak meditation on suicide in *Everything You Swallow Will One Day Come Up Like a Stone* (2014) and the psychologically haunting body horror *With Those We Love Alive* (2014), attract the bulk of her critical enthusiasm and praise. *Cry$tal Warrior Ke$ha* is something else: a game that demands the player be immersed in a world of pop music and feminist glitter just to play, a game that's lyrical components defy the nonfan to even comprehend. Yet it deserves as canonical a place as Porpentine's other works, in part thanks to its crucial role in cementing an essential part of Twine's aesthetic potential—excess. Mat Jones goes even further in his review of the game: "It's not very long and it'll change your entire life. You'll view everything from this moment on as taking place post-CRY$TAL WARRIOR KE$HA world and ensure that any Game Of The Year list you produce from now until after the universe consumes itself maintains a special place for it in any Top Ten. All of time freezes in place and yet existence carries on, morosely, as we've already reached the apex of human achievement—perhaps that of any living being known or unknown. We've limited reason to carry on" (Jones).

It is impossible to talk about the game without positioning this excess in relationship to the hypermasculinity of the games industry—notably, the game appears on Zoë Quinn's "Top 10 Games of 2013," released on Giant Bomb just as the attacks on her would bubble up. They describe the game as "best played outloud in a group of friends so that you can collectively feel like badasses as you shout out MANTIS VICTORY SCREAM together" (Quinn). As a Gamergate snapshot, this captures the significance of the game in indie discourse—unsurprisingly, the comment thread devolved rapidly, with one moderator asking that people cease from posting attacks with the note "Also, I don't see any mention of feminism in Zoe's list, so I'll be treating any mention of it as off-topic, irrelevant, and distracting from a conversation that should be happening about the games" (Quinn). While the height of harassment would not start until August 2014, the toxicity was already well seeded.

Another succinct review captures the game's essence and puts it firmly in conflict with AAA game development expectations: "I finally played Cry$tal Warrior Ke$ha. CWK is the Saints Row 3 of twine games, but it's better because it's not full of a bunch of generic side missions masquerading under the guise of absurdist premises. Instead CWK is part a fuck you empowerment statement and part the greatest Magical Girl video game I've ever played. It not only made me appreciate Ke$ha, but it made me appreciate myself" (M).

The empowerment seeded in *Cry$tal Warrior Ke$ha* is not simply narrative or text—it is a defiance that runs through the game's entire over-the-top design. The game is bold and attention-demanding, the soundtrack designed to blast and impossible to ignore or silence without removing much of the contextual meaning. The color choices are bold and tacky; the imagery straight from Ke$ha's album covers; and the continual moments of animation and flashiness are certainly worthy of a "magical" girl. Some of the characteristic elements of camp twine emerge from an examination of *Cry$tal Warrior Ke$ha* and its legacy: an emphasis on the decorative and the excessive; an unapologetically queer thrust to both narrative and design; and an embrace of multimedia that can feel discordant or cacophonic.

Porpentine's work also embraces camp in process and discourse. In an interview, Porpentine discusses her approach to hypertext and making with Twine as "trash-spinning," emphasizing spontaneity and emergence of meaning through the act of creation:

> I've always just called it trash-spinning. Just like rolling up trash. But most of my games are just spontaneous improvisations where I roll up everything in my environment and I wad them together. They're a big, crystalized trashy ball of everything that's happened to me over the 24 hours or 48 hours in which I made the game. Like conversations, or you'll notice how I incorporate all of the music I'm listening to in my games. It's just very organic. Then I try to turn it into a weapon, something people can feel. How can my emotions be transmitted to another human being? A dart of nausea, arousal, triumph, crying, even radical, transformative joy. (Kaye)

This description of "radical, transformative joy" is, we would argue, at the heart of what Twine brings to the web—the very traits that Porpentine describes as allowing for "trash-spinning." Porpentine's approach has inspired others, particularly thanks to her role in amplifying the platform through Tumblr and other queer, indie, and experimental communities online. Her work is definitive of Twine's camp potential, but it is also in conversation with a number of other creators who perform similar radical, transformative acts with their work.

Much of the radical work of Porpentine is less grounded in recognizable popular culture and moves into more speculative, and surreal, territory. Porpentine's compilation of Twines works, "Eczema Angel Orifice," includes a number of contemplations on bodies. Unlike *dys4ia* (Anna Anthropy's original "empathy" game), Porpentine's work centers the physical and emotional experience through metaphor. Porpentine described her embrace of the inhuman in an interview: "A lot of my games have been kind of submerged. . . . They're written from a very dissociated perspective where the point of view is almost smeared into the environment. They have trouble conceiving of themselves as a person" (Muncy).

Porpentine's *Girlwaste* draws on the aesthetic of the retro web, zines, and low-res art and particularly embodies this reckoning with the physical body through a submerged, inhuman self. The color palette is initially reminiscent of the stark red, lined landscapes of Nintendo's Virtual Boy, while the "movement" recalls the earliest graphical RPGs, offering the player arrows to navigate on the search for estrogen (see figure 18). The lines of the body moving are emotionally charged, and the transparency works to craft a sense of incompletion and disconnection. The player encounters others who help her out on the quest, such as a "slimebabe" who "is not from this layer." The monstrous bodies accompany your personal need: selecting "ache" raises the text "Your glands rumble. Icicles of withdrawal pierce through the reverberation."

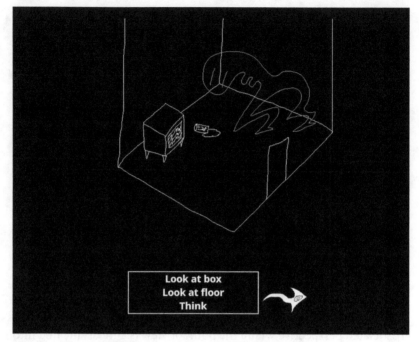

Figure 18: Representative graphics from Porpentine's *Girlwaste*

Queer, Camp Twine in the Wild

Another significant example, Christine Love's *Even Cowgirls Bleed* was released on Tumblr around the same time as *Ke$ha* (2013 being the height of Twine camp, perhaps?)—she posted with an important warning: "I was not feeling great that day" (Love). In an interview, she elaborated on the origin points: "The whole thing is based off something that happened to me with a girl in real life. It left me feeling pretty shitty, and . . . well, here's the thing about crying yourself to sleep: it seems like it'd work eventually, but mostly it just gives you insomnia. . . . So after the second or maybe third night of that, I decided I was sick of crying and decided to funnel those feelings into something productive" (Johnson).

The emphasis on sorrow rather than joy places a catharsis at the heart of the game that leads in a far darker direction than the bright colors immediately suggest. The game chronicles a lesbian romance between two cowgirls amid conflict, featuring an interface that removes all the black and white usually associated with Twine in favor of shades of orange and red. One reviewer describes how Christine Love breaks the expected Twine interface to draw the player in:

> During the passages where nothing much is happening, the "Holster" button alternates between either side of the screen, mimicking the in-game description of you anxiously tossing your pistol from hand to hand. And when the game starts to take a dark turn, you try to carefully thread your crosshairs between the ominous targets to what seems like a safe one, only for the text layout to force the exact misfire you were trying to avoid. Even if the player is not, in fact, a lesbian city slicker with dreams of becoming a cowgirl, the identification reinforced by the synchronicity between the text and the player's actions is enough to put you into that mindset, however briefly (Maragos).

This use of the crosshairs is particularly jarring in a narrative that includes significant eroticism and dialogue, two things not associated with game genres that typically ask players to look at the world through the lens of a gun. The game forces the player to be conscious of violence, and the potential for violence, throughout and asks the player to "holster" as a metaphor for inaction. Christine Love is particularly well known for her more visual works, such as *Digital: A Love Story* (2010) and *Ladykiller in a Bind* (2016), both built with Ren'Py, a more complex Python-driven game-making tool influenced by Japanese anime aesthetics and aimed at the development of visual novels. It is thus not surprising that she brings some of these aesthetics to her twine works, including *Magical Maiden Madison* (2013), a story that unfolds surrounding sexual tensions following a magical girl's battle with a tentacle monster (Love).

Another exemplar of camp twine with an explicit political emphasis is D. Squinkifer's *Quing's Quest VII: The Death of Videogames* (2014). Released as part of RuinJam, an event responding to the attacks on Zoë Quinn and the broader abuses of Gamergate, the game features an animated galactic background; bold, pink, and green text; and hover effects with animated links (refer back to figure 10). The game's text is similarly filled with references and commentary—the player finds themselves on a ship entitled the *Social Justice Warrior*, in reference to the derisive label given to feminist and queer influencers perceived as pushing for representation in games and other media at the cost of "quality" or "authenticity" (defined, of course, as fidelity to canons centered on the stories of straight, cis, white men). The character reflects on the "misogynerd" claiming of gamer identity at the expense of those already present, making games: "'Gamers.' That's what the misogynerds started calling themselves, once they invaded your planet. To make it worse, they act as if this is the way it's always been, as if Videogames was a planet that they alone discovered, as if your people hadn't been there first" (Squinkifer).

Ruberg responds to the queer experience of D. Squinkifer's *Quing's Quest* as encapsulating both content and aesthetics, noting that "the text shimmers and sparkles; upbeat lounge music plays in the background.... The game's message is ultimately one that mixes sadness and anger with hope" (Ruberg 219). Deeply embedded in classic hypertext and games, the aesthetics are both familiar and striking, but one reviewer describes the game's fundamental appeal as a power fantasy, bringing a twist to the video game mechanics the work resists: "In a game where your choices don't matter at all, it was strange to find myself feeling empowered at the completion. . . . I was left wanting to fist-pump and dance, full of renewed energy to fight the misogynerds I encounter everyday in my web space" (Reynolds). Notably, the type of power explored in all these examples is framed in terms of resistance—in particular, placing the bold, antihaters battle royal of *Cry$tal Warrior Ke$ha* alongside the dance battles and face-offs with "misogynerds" in *Quing's Quest* offers a commentary on the dull predictability of combat in most game systems.

Other exemplars of queer twine have less connection to camp aesthetic and instead push at the representational narratives of games. For example, Anna Anthropy's *Queers in Love at the End of the World* (to which we will return in chapter T-5) is a powerful example of a game that focuses on the moments leading up to an ending and thus recalls Shira Chess's work on the queer narrative potential of games that can "play in the middle spaces" rather than relying on the moment of climax

(Chess). Aesthetically, *Queers in Love at the End of the World* does not match the other Twine games discussed here—the palette is minimally altered from one of Twine's defaults, and the user's attention is drawn to the rapidly passing countdown of the ten seconds promised until the world ends. The ending of the game is always abrupt, and there's no way to get a sense of completion, only desperation. However, the game challenges expectations in another way: it takes the expected pace of hypertext and breaks it, pushing the user to frantic physicality as expressed through the few verbs available and the need for rapid action that is ultimately meaningless.

Anna Anthropy's *Twine and Punishment* collects some of her Twine games and is decidedly immersed in queer, camp aesthetics, including the sardonic work *The Hunt for the Gay Planet* and the prelude work *Keep Dreaming, Space Cowgirl* (Anthropy). *The Hunt for the Gay Planet* is particularly significant as a commentary on games culture, as the work engages with the lack of queer representation in massively multiplayer universes.

Sav Ferguson's *That Boy Is a Monstr* takes a fantastical spin on Grindr and makes more significant use of the aesthetic expressiveness of Twine for its mock-app interface, offering the player messages from characters with usernames from "AngryBear" to "xWereSelkiex." However, the messages the player encounters are quickly revealed to be darker. Sam's reflections shared with the player throughout the game are immediate and poignant, emphasizing a personal voice: "With a glance, he'd see band posters, polaroid's with friends, those little triangle things—bunting? rainbow and glittery, and fairy lights. Maybe if he got up and looked at the polaroid's, he'd see me with my old girlfriend. Or me pre-T. Or, what if he looks at the band posters too close and realises I just printed them myself? Is he gonna think I'm a hipster? God I hope not. AM I a hipster?" (Ferguson).

Aesthetically, the game includes pointers to its narrative—the trans flag colors inform the gradient background, visible even before the player is brought into the details of the character's struggle with rejection and discrimination from the other users of Monstr. The metaphor of monstrous bodies explored in Porpentine's work is made more literal and humorous through the character identities here. The game also employs a list of references as part of the credits, including an article serving as a point of inspiration: "More Americans claim to have seen a ghost than a trans person" (Williams).

The 2018 game *Pirate Queen* by twinegamesareboring is described on its itch.io page as "gay as hell" and lacks many of the aesthetics of the other examples profiled here but demonstrates some of the key opportunities for representation (twinegamesareboring, "Pirate Queen"). Another work by the same author, "Didn't," similarly offers representative play: "And remember when you were fourteen-years-old, and her hair was chlorine-bleached and her lips were blackberry-stained, and she kept asking is-there-something-in-my-teeth, and you wanted to kiss her, but you didn't?" (twinegamesareboring, "Didn't"). Such works are part of an ecosystem of personal, usually individually crafted games tagged as queer or LGBTQ on itch.io, a platform whose economics are primarily grounded in donations and a "pay what you can" system.

The visibility of *Cry$tal Warrior Ke$ha* and the other games discussed here in game publications reviews is part of its larger discursive impact and puts it alongside other queer, camp Twine games that use the medium to push back against all the dominant structures and assumptions that go with the word *game*. Importantly, the queer Twine games emphasized here were all originally released for free (although occasionally released later as part of paid collections) and thus are also not part of the traditional economics of game production. As Harvey points out, "Queerness acts as a destabilizing force, challenging norms of who gets to be a producer and what should be made, but it is wrought with the dangers and precarity of this position. Operating beyond hegemonic spheres of production and reproduction entails a number of real risks, and we should be careful not to equate emancipatory promise with poorly paid, insecure work and life below, on, or near the poverty line, dependent on the vicissitudes of crowdfunding" (Harvey 104). The larger discourse of games labor (and the binaries and hegemonies of the games industry) is being resisted through Twine but is far from dismantled.

The traditional economics of the game market leave little room for experimentation or diversity in representation, as Matt Conn points out in his discussion of the importance of GaymerX and queer gaming communities: "In the transition to 3D, as costs for game development skyrocketed in front of a hungry market, risks hit an all-time low and the nearly comically omnipresent white, straight, cisgendered, able-bodied, thin, classically handsome main character became a staple. Although there's nothing wrong with making a game about this guy, doing so over and over is akin to an entire fleet of artists all painting the same man" (Conn). Conn's words evoke the embodied avatars of nearly every shooter, the graphically enhanced but otherwise relatively unchanging bodies we've inhabited awkwardly as players through the decades.

Notably, that same transition to 3-D is often blamed for the death of other narrative game genres that Twine resembles—just as those genres have survived through alternative market modalities, so too has hypertext continued divorced from any models of clear profitability (Salter). The reconciliation of queer gaming and the current AAA labor market seems insurmountable. While queer narratives are making headways in film in indie productions (with notable recent standouts such as *Booksmart, Moonlight,* and *Call Me By Your Name* all receiving critical acclaim for coming-of-age stories of the type common to Twine as well), queer-centric videogames are still relatively absent. Indie successes such as *Life Is Strange, Gone Home,* and *Dream Daddy: A Dad Dating Simulator* (discussed in detail in *Playing the Outsider,* forthcoming from Bloomsbury) are outliers, receiving more critical acclaim than financial success and inspiring few commercial imitators.

Similarly, conferences such as Queerness and Games have been central to increasing the awareness and visibility of queer gamers, designers, critics, and scholars in games discourse (Pozo, Ruberg, and Goetz), while queer game studies is still even more marginal than feminist game studies in the field. Discussions of queer representation in electronic literature are even more unusual and not strongly embedded in the theoretical or aesthetic models of the field. At the same time, the designers of queer games resist some of the discourse of scholarship and criticism that can take a reductive approach. In 2015, Anna Anthropy exhibited a new piece entitled *Empathy Game* to comment on the trend of amplifying games by queer and marginalized creators as a way of "understanding." The game featured a pair of boots with a pedometer, with one mile of walking equating to a single point in the game. As Anna Anthropy described, "You can get a high score on that game . . . but you're probably not going to beat mine. You can spend hours stomping around in those boots and it will only bring you a fraction closer to knowing what it's like to be me, to be trans" (D'Anastasio). Anthropy's own work on indie game design (and particularly the need for inclusive, accessible, game design communities and tools outside of conventional commercial platforms) predicted a rise in personal game development that brought with it what Bo Ruberg called the "queer games avant-garde" (Ruberg 6).

However, that queer games avant-garde must be understood through the lens of attack and with an awareness of risk. In June 2019, at Narra-Scope, D. Squinkifer gave a talk entitled "How Making Videogames Turned Me into a Depressed Gay Communist" in which they addressed the making of videogames pre- and post-Gamergate through an interactive, choice-driven performance piece. The piece was augmented with a knock-off Google Glass that highlighted the uneasy relationship with technology that living in a "cyberpunk dystopia" evokes. They addressed Gamergate directly through the choice to talk about 2014, noting the lessons the hatred directed at designers left: "When you're part of any number of marginalized groups, fame is an occupational hazard. . . . Before, I used to believe in the fiction that there was no such thing as bad publicity. That it was important to be bold and brave and controversial. . . . But when the controversy isn't over your art or your ideas, but over your right to exist as a human being . . . What can I even say? It's terrifying."

D. Squinkifer acknowledged a complicated relationship with the concept of empathy, and indeed with the role of the personal in game-making, noting that many players had complained about the choice D. Squinkifer made to use the second person (a common interactive fiction trope) in their work: "When you write in the second person, and you bring in your own very specific experiences, people start to complain . . . you shouldn't have used you, you should have used I. So you continue to write in the second person, knowing this, being more deliberate in creating these disorienting feelings."

D. Squinkifer noted that inviting players into their experience is part of the goal of their work, even while resisting the idea that this type of understanding could be easily reached or that empathy for the marginalized was more than a "commodity" to players and the industry: "I'd also be lying if I said that getting people to understand me doesn't factor into why I make games. I make games based on my own lived experiences, in hopes that other people will relate to that experience in some way."

While Zoë Quinn has written about the impact of Gamergate on their life, and a few others have spoken publicly, even the act of speaking invites further silencing. The cycles of the alt-right that now occupy the attention of internet researchers both in the academy and on technical platforms are inescapable. As D. Squinkifer put it in their talk, the idea that "you will never be accepted, and this world has no place for you" is amplified. D. Squinkifer's performance is a reminder of the consequences of visibility—that exposure, the currency of the web, was fundamentally weaponized in Gamergate, and the awareness of that weaponization cannot be reverted. The consequences of Gamergate on game development (and its participants) are still not known and perhaps cannot be apprehended. Gamergate is not over. Indeed, as of 2019, Zoë Quinn left Twitter briefly following extensive harassment after recounting an experience of sexual harassment by a game designer who later lost his life to depression (Penny). As one critic powerfully recounted of the harassment without end, "Some days it feels like the whole world is being held hostage to male fragility. Sometimes it seems that there's no limit on what women, girls, and queer people are expected to tolerate in order to protect men from a moment's uncomfortable self-reflection. Sometimes I don't know who to trust anymore" (Penny).

In the face of this toxicity, the queer, camp Twine that persists is defiant in its very existence.

Works Cited

"American Visionary Art Museum—What Is Visionary Art?" American Visionary Art Museum, February 1, 2019. https://www.avam.org/.

Anthropy, Anna. "Twine and Punishment." itch.io, November 1, 2014. https://w.itch.io/twine-and-punishment.

Babuscio, Jack. "The Cinema of Camp (AKA Camp and the Gay Sensibility)." In Camp: Queer Aesthetics and the Performing Subject: A Reader, edited by Fabio Cleto. University of Michigan Press, 1999, 117–35.

Berens, Kathi. "Third Generation Electronic Literature and Artisanal Interfaces: Resistance in the Materials." Electronic Book Review, May 2019. http://electronicbookreview.com/essay/third-generation-electronic-literature-and-artisanal-interfaces-resistance-in-the-materials/.

Booth, Mark. "CAMPE-TOI! On the Origins and Definitions of Camp." In Camp: Queer Aesthetics and the Performing Subject: A Reader, edited by Fabio Cleto. University of Michigan Press, 1999, 66–79.

Chan, Casey. "Remember the Hilarious Horror of Geocities with This Website." Gizmodo, February 11, 2013. https://gizmodo.com/remember-the-hilarious-horror-of-geocities-with-this-we-5983574.

Chess, Shira. "The Queer Case of Video Games: Orgasms, Heteronormativity, and Video Game Narrative." Critical Studies in Media Communication 33, no. 1 (January 2016): 84–94. https://doi.org/10.1080/15295036.2015.1129066.

Conn, Matt. "Gaming's Untapped Queer Potential as Art." QED: A Journal in GLBTQ Worldmaking 2, no. 2 (July 2015): 1–5.

D'Anastasio, Cecilia. "Why Video Games Can't Teach You Empathy." Vice, May 15, 2015. https://www.vice.com/en_us/article/mgbwpv/empathy-games-dont-exist.

Espenschied, Dragan, and Olia Lialina. Digital Folklore. Merz and Solitude, 2009.

Ferguson, Sav. That Boy Is a Monster, Long, Complete. 2017. http://www.philome.la/TimesNTroubles/that-boy-is-a-monstr/play.

Fink, Marty, and Quinn Miller. "Trans Media Moments: Tumblr, 2011–2013." Television & New Media 15, no. 7 (November 2014): 611–26. https://doi.org/10.1177/1527476413505002.

Flores, Leonardo. "Third Generation Electronic Literature." Electronic Book Review, April 2019. http://electronicbookreview.com/essay/third-generation-electronic-literature/.

Gauntlett, David. "Digital Sexualities: A Guide to Internet Resources." sexualities 2.3 (1999): 327–32.

GeoCities. "GeoCities—Neighborhoods." Internet Archive, January 23, 1998. https://web.archive.org/web/19990129033446/http://www17.geocities.com/neighborhoods/.

———. "Geocities WestHollywood LGBTQ." Geocities.Ws Archive, 1999. http://www.geocities.ws/server2/.

Halperin, David M. "The Normalization of Queer Theory." Journal of Homosexuality 45, nos. 2–4 (2003): 339–43.

Harvey, Alison. "Twine's Revolution: Democratization, Depoliticization, and the Queering of Game Design." *GAME* 1, no. 3 (2014). https://www.gamejournal.it/3_harvey/.

Howard, Tanner. "How Geocities Suburbanized the Internet." CityLab, January 22, 2019. https://www.citylab.com/life/2019/01/geocities-archive-netscape-browser-first-web-suburbs-aol/580285/.

Hudgins, Amanda. "Haters Gonna Hate." Unwinnable, September 1, 2016. https://unwinnable.com/2016/09/01/haters-gonna-hate/.

Johnson, Jason. "Christine Love Explores Unbridled Expectations, Lesbianism, and Jilted Love in Even Cowgirls Bleed." *Kill Screen*, February 27, 2013. https://killscreen.com/articles/even-cowgirls-bleed-christine-love/.

Jones, Mat. "Indie Rock: Unravelling CHAOS JAM, a Twine-Only Game Event." Average Gamer, January 16, 2013. http://www.theaveragegamer.com/2013/01/16/indie-rock-unravelling-chaos-jam-a-twine-only-game-event/.

Kaye, Finch. "Beautiful Weapons." New Inquiry, June 25, 2013. https://thenewinquiry.com/beautiful-weapons/.

Keeling, Kara. "Queer OS." *Cinema Journal* 53, no. 2 (January 2014): 152–57. https://doi.org/10.1353/cj.2014.0004.

Love, Christine. "Love Conquers All Games." Tumblr, February 14, 2013. https://loveconquersallgam.es/post/43092144216/this-week-i-spent-the-day-making-a-game-in-twine.

M. "Cry$tal Warrior Ke$ha." Abnormal Mapping, January 1, 2014. https://abnormalmapping.wordpress.com/2014/01/01/cry-tal-warrior-ke-ha/.

Maragos, Nich. "Love Week: Twine." Gaming Intelligence Agency, September 13, 2013. http://www.thegia.com/2013/09/13/love-week-twine/.

Muncy, Julie. "Porpentine's New Twine Game Isn't Just a Twine Game." *Wired*, September 13, 2017. https://www.wired.com/story/porpentine-twine-game/.

Nellis, Krystina. "Kesha: Warrior." Drowned in Sound, November 30, 2012. http://drownedinsound.com/releases/17369/reviews/4145804.

Penny, Laurie. "Gaming's #MeToo Moment and the Tyranny of Male Fragility." *Wired*, September 6, 2019. https://www.wired.com/story/videogames-industry-metoo-moment-male-fragility/.

Phillips, LeAnne. "The Web of the Spider Woman." GeoCities, December 1, 1995. http://www.geocities.ws/server2/homestead/westhollywood/1027/.

Porpentine. *Cry$tal Warrior Ke$ha*. Self-published, January 12, 2013. http://slimedaughter.com/games/twine/kesha/.

———. "PORPENTINE." Tumblr, January 12, 2013. https://porpentine.tumblr.com/post/40366802882/porpentine-presenting-cry-tal-warrior-ke-ha-this.

Pozo, Diana, Bo Ruberg, and Chris Goetz. "In Practice: Queerness and Games." *Camera Obscura: Feminism, Culture, and Media Studies* 32, no. 2 (95; September 2017): 153–63. https://doi.org/10.1215/02705346-3925167.

Quinn, Zoë. "Zoe Quinn's Top 10 Games of 2013." Giant Bomb, December 23, 2013. https://www.giantbomb.com/articles/zoe-quinn-s-top-10-games-of-2013/1100-4813/.

Reynolds, Kate. "Twine Quing's Quest VII: The Death of Videogames!" Storycade, September 11, 2014. http://storycade.com/twine-quings-quest-vii-death-videogames/.

Ruberg, Bo. *Video Games Have Always Been Queer*. New York University Press, 2019.

Salter, Anastasia. *What Is Your Quest? From Adventure Games to Interactive Books*. University of Iowa Press, 2014.

Salter, Anastasia, and John Murray. *Flash: Building the Interactive Web*. MIT Press, 2014. http://books.google.com/books?hl=en&lr=&id=hhJmBAAAQBAJ&pgis=1.

Sontag, Susan. "Notes on Camp." In *Camp: Queer Aesthetics and the Performing Subject: A Reader*, edited by Fabio Cleto. University of Michigan Press, 1999, 53–65.

Squinkifer, D. *Quing's Quest VII: The Death of Videogames*. Self-published, September 1, 2014. https://games.squinky.me/quing/.

Twilite909. "Poet's Corner." GeoCities, October 20, 1996. http://www.geocities.ws/server2/homestead/westhollywood/5032/.

twinegamesareboring. "Didn't." itch.io, June 15, 2018. https://twinegamesareboring.itch.io/didnt.

———. "Pirate Queen." itch.io, June 15, 2018. https://twinegamesareboring.itch.io/pirate-queen.

Wallace, Amanda. "3 Twine Games to Introduce People to the Medium." Storycade, March 28, 2014. http://storycade.com/3-twine-games-introduce-people-medium/.

Wallace, Jonathan. "There Goes the Neighborhood." Ethical Spectacle, December 22, 1997. http://www.spectacle.org/cs/holly.html.

Williams, Joe. "More Americans Claim to Have Seen a Ghost Than a Trans Person." Pink News, December 18, 2015. https://www.pinknews.co.uk/2015/12/18/more-americans-claim-to-have-seen-a-ghost-than-a-trans-person/.

Too Much Twine

If we return for inspiration to their provocative 2014 Twine hypertext *Quing's Quest VII: The Death of Videogames*, D. Squinkifer takes on the specter of Gamergate by placing the player in a retro, animated-GIF-background-bearing space adventure where, driven from their home planet of Video Games, the hero expresses a longing to "build something again": "You were born to build things. As a member of the royal family of Videogames, building things is in your blood. You grew up apprenticing under your elders, whose queer, beautiful, complex structures you could only dream of coming close to emulating someday. You listened non-stop to their stories of the Golden Age of Videogames, envying the creative freedom and abundance they enjoyed" (Squinkifer).

D. Squinkifer's words are an invitation to learn from the elders, and in that mind-set, we look to several glorious, powerful, campy Twine works for inspiration throughout this and other practical sections. In this chapter, of all chapters, we cannot begin to tell you what to "build." If anything, camp Twine is the invitation to excess, and aesthetic play, which we will explore here as we explore existing techniques.

◊ As in other practical chapters, action items are boxed and set off with the symbol you see at left, in case you want to skip the contextual discussion.

Supporting materials for this chapter can be found online at https://github.com/AMSUCF/Twining. See our discussion at the beginning of chapter P-1 about using the .html and .txt files to follow along or adapt our code to your own purposes.

Example 4.1: End Times

In this making chapter, we will primarily be working with SugarCube, to continue our tour of Twine story formats. SugarCube builds on the most popular of Twine's first iteration story formats, Sugarcane, and thus has a legacy of useful macros built in to allow for versatile design. Start by creating a new story and selecting SugarCube 2.X.

The timed mechanics of *Queers in Love at the End of the World* create a sense of urgency that can lead to more frantic choice—such timers can be used within a work to add pressure to a conversation or pivotal moment, or they can envelop a work, offering the reader a limited amount of time in which to experience it (Anthropy). The Twine Cookbook includes iterations of this fundamental mechanic in every story format, which you can use to compare the complexity and approach of each format (Cox).

SugarCube allows us to embed passages within other passages easily, so we can think of our story as progressing in fragments. Note the characteristics of SugarCube: like HTML, SugarCube relies on < > to designate the beginning and end of tags but adds a second layer to differentiate from HTML itself. Thus HTML and SugarCube markup can comfortably coexist, as in this code:

◊ Let's start by creating a passage entitled "Countdown," where our ticking timer will lurk as the player progresses. Enter the following code into the passage:

```
<span id="countdown">Planetary implosion in
$seconds seconds</span>
<<silently>>
   <<repeat 1s>>
      <<set $seconds to $seconds--1>>
      <<if $seconds gt 0>>
         <<replace "#countdown">>Planetary
         implosion in $seconds seconds<</
         replace>>
      <<else>>
         <<replace "#countdown">><</
         replace>>
         <<goto "Lost">>
         <<stop>>
      <</if>>
   <</repeat>>
<</silently>>
```

In this code, several elements are at work: first, the *$seconds* variable holds the timer itself. Note that we haven't initiated a value for it here—we need to decide when our timer begins and declare it elsewhere. We might also change this variable to add complexity (for instance, if we want the reader to be able to influence or extend the timer through certain choices), so it's best to keep its value separate from the passage that displays its contents.

On its own, this passage doesn't do anything, but it provides the framework for counting time. Note the macros that are similar to those in Harlowe: *set* still assigns a value, and *replace* takes a parameter to replace the content. In place of Harlowe's *(go-to:)*—Chapbook has no equivalent—we use *goto*, which similarly takes the name of a passage and automatically reloads the page. This is similar to the two-second countdowns we used earlier during our hunt for the amulet in chapter P-2, but here we've isolated the timer so we can use it across multiple passages.

◊ Next, let's create the first passage of our narrative. We don't want to launch the timer immediately, so start by altering the first passage (designated, as always, by the rocket) to set up our prelude. Type the following into a first passage labeled "Beginnings":

```
You've come this far. The B Arc was full (too
many telephone sanitizers), first class was
always out of reach, and this hunk of junk
about to take off is the last ship off this rock
before it hits. If only you knew how to fly it.

[[Try.|Controls]]
```

Any need-driven quest will do for this conceit, or if you are feeling existential, a final countdown along the lines of *Queers in Love at the End of the World* is fitting (Anthropy). For now, stick with a single link on this page to avoid the need for multiple timer declarations—you can always add that complexity later by duplicating the code we'll place in the next passage.

◊ Create another passage titled "Controls." In this passage, initialize the timer and include the "Countdown" passage by typing the following code:

```
You're looking at buttons. Like, old school Wing
Commander, you're going to need a manual for
this, unlabeled buttons. You can hear your cell
phone beeping the warning alerts as you look for
something marked throttle.
https://media.giphy.com/media/CKRx4oUu3dzLa/
source.gif
<<set $seconds to 30>>
<<include "Countdown">>
[[Press the green button|Green]]
```

```
[[Press the yellow button|Yellow]]
[[Press the red button|Red]]
[[Look for an index|Search]]
```

Include works much the way *embed passage* does in Chapbook, inserting the passage where we've indicated. It's important to declare the variable sometime before we embed the countdown timer for the first time, as otherwise, you'll see an odd error. We don't need much text for any of these options—the player is going to need to make some fast, frantic decisions. We'll come back to fleshing out the paths in a moment, but first, let's set up a default ending for when the timer goes off.

◊ Create a passage entitled "Lost" and type the following:

```
The rumbling lets you know it's too late--that,
and the sinking feeling.

The flames are the last thing you see.
```

We'll also need to remove the user interface bar from the side of the screen to avoid players backtracking from this ending. You'll notice that many Twine works remove these user controls, particularly when it's important to eliminate backtracking.

◊ Open the story JavaScript file and type the following:

```
UIBar.destroy();
```

Reload and you'll see that the entire user interface bar has been removed—this takes away some of the story format's built-in functionality but also eliminates lots of design problems. This gives us a foundation, but it certainly isn't camp, and there's a lot of room to expand even within our short timer. We'll use this base for the next several exercises to start adding aesthetic enhancements and thinking about the role of audiovisual elements in how we work with Twine.

Example 4.2: Changing Styles

We've focused thus far on the text and functionality of Twine, not the look. However, Twine can integrate anything from the web experience—it's just a matter of figuring out how to mesh your desired elements with the story format you are using. Each story format has different strengths and weaknesses when it comes to bringing in visuals, styling, audio, and even video or animated elements.

Practically speaking, the more you know about CSS, the more control you'll have over Twine's aesthetics. In SugarCube 2, there are a few built-in tools to be aware of, including a foundational set of style sheet rules that give us more detailed control.

Let's start with something simple. We'll set each button link to display in the appropriate color, then change the background of the corresponding linked page to match by setting up passage style sheets.

◊ Tag each of the three colored-button passages with a corresponding color: red, green, and yellow. Open the story style sheet and type the following:

```
body {
    background-color: #A9A9A9;
    color: white;
    font-size: 200%;
}
a {
    color: purple;
}
body.red {
    background-color: red;
    color: white;
    font-size: 250%;
}
body.green {
    background-color: green;
```

```
      color: white;
      font-size: 250%;
   }
   body.yellow {
      background-color: yellow;
      color: black;
      font-size: 250%;
   }
```

Note a few oddities in this style sheet: the first two selectors control what you'll see on any passage that doesn't have a style tag. Most of this is straightforward CSS, using familiar elements of HTML—the body and *a*, or links. Even though we don't write links using <a> in Sugar-Cube, the markup we do write is translated forward to the standard HTML element, and all the usual properties apply. Note that we can use any color data format supported by CSS here—in this example, there are both hexadecimal codes and color names.

The tags we added to each passage are translated into class tags accessible as modifications to the body—thus, *body.red*, *body.green*, and *body.yellow* will each control the corresponding tag's styling. Test out your new design (be warned, it's a little garish). You'll notice that passages that are inserted into a tagged passage inherit the style of the page they are inserted into by default. This means we can use the countdown timer on any page, even as we add more complexity to the style sheets.

◊ Now let's add a bit more drama to the final page by adding CSS animations to fade out the text. Open the style sheet and add the following code:

```
.disappear {
    opacity: 0;
    animation-name: fadeOutOpacity;
    animation-iteration-count: 1;
    animation-timing-function: ease-in;
    animation-duration: 5s;
```

```
}
@keyframes fadeOutOpacity {
    0% {
        opacity: 1;
    }
    100% {
        opacity: 0;
    }
}
```

Currently, we have defined a new class, but we haven't applied it anywhere in the code, so you won't see any changes in the text. Let's break down this animation frame by frame: this is a simple fade-out that diminishes the *opacity* of the element from 1 (fully visible) to 0 (transparent) over time. It will only occur once (the *animation-iteration-count*) and will last for five seconds (the *animation-duration*). Depending on the impact you want, you can change the pacing by specifying an *animation-timing-function*. In this case, "ease-in" means it will start slowly and speed up as it disappears, while "ease-out" would do the opposite—try it and compare later. Importantly, the code *opacity: 0;* specifies the default state when the animation is not occurring—if we set this to 1, the text will abruptly reappear after the animation ends.

◊ Now we need to apply our animation to an element. Open the "Lost" passage and alter the text to match:

```
@@.disappear;The rumbling lets you know it's too
late--that, and the sinking feeling.

The flames are the last thing you see.@@
```

The @@ symbol is SugarCube's way of marking the beginning of inline CSS. The second iteration of the symbol indicates that this is where the in-line CSS ends. Anything that you can apply in CSS can be added using these properties, so it's a simple way to create emphasis—let's try it with font color directly by going back and altering the passage where the buttons are first introduced.

◊ Now open the story style sheet and add a new set of classes:

```
.greenLink a { color: green; }
.redLink a { color: red; }
.yellowLink a { color: yellow; }
```

We'll need to make corresponding changes in the "Controls" passage:

```
You're looking at buttons. Like, old school Wing
Commander, you're going to need a manual for
this, unlabeled buttons. You can hear your cell
phone beeping the warning alerts as you look for
something marked throttle.
<<set $seconds to 30>>
<<include "Countdown">>
Press the @@.greenLink;[[green|Green]]@@ button
Press the @@.yellowLink;[[yellow|Yellow]]@@
button
Press the @@.redLink;[[red|Red]]@@ button
[[Look for an index|Search]]
```

Note that there are several other ways we could approach this that just wouldn't work. It's important to reassign the link to surround just the word we want to impact (this also improves readability) and to use a class rather than trying to change the color directly with .color. Using .color directly creates the equivalent of a span with that color, which is great for changing nonlink text but is ineffectual within a link.

This is a highly visually motivated instance of using link color classes for impact, but changing link colors can also be a way to communicate meaning to the user that is commonly used in Twine. For instance, Porpentine's *With Those We Love Alive* opens with a message to the user:

Before living this life, have a pen or sharpie nearby, something that can write on skin.

Purple links change. Pink links move forward. The colorblind version is here. (Porpentine)

Importantly, this gives insight into the mechanics that assist in navigation. The monochromatic version, which is optimized to not rely on color, instead uses italics to assist in differentiating between links.

Example 4.3: Sound It Out

We've created the potential for drama with these changes, and you might imagine layering them further to enhance the impact. However, this is only the beginning of what we can do with Twine. Some of the most effective games incorporate audio, including *With Those We Love Alive*, which addresses the audio in the next line of the introduction: "There is music, so headphones are good. But it's okay if you can't" (Porpentine; text formatting preserved for clarity).

These disclaimers are also valuable reminders for our own design philosophies: while using Twine's full audiovisual potential is exciting, we can keep the work accessible by always providing other means of entry into any important information the user needs to progress in or understand the experience.

Some of the earliest examples of Twine audio integration made use of existing music—for instance, it's hard to imagine *Cry$stal Warrior Ke$ha* without the titular artist's track blaring in the background. Looping music of that type is typically declared outside of any particular passage, as it is intended to play uninterrupted as the experience progresses:

Audio is difficult to some extent in Twine for the same reason audio is difficult on the web—logistically, you'll need to host your own audio files to ensure that they will remain accessible. You may have the ability to record your own audio for an experience, but if you do not, Creative Commons licensed sound effects and music can give you a palette of sounds and atmosphere to play with.

The Creative Commons search engine (search.creativecommons .org) is currently optimized for images but is in the process of expanding to incorporate audio; in the meantime, their legacy search portal (available through the same page) links out to several searchable archives for media, although it is incumbent on the user to verify that the results are truly Creative Commons licensed. Freesound.org and Soundbible.com also have a large database of options, although again, it's important to verify the contents.

We'll play with two types of audio: atmospheric, which loops in the background throughout play, and effect audio, which is typically triggered when the player reaches a particular passage or moment in the narrative. First, we'll do a simple audio file embedded in a passage that plays as the end passage is triggered. We'll use a free sound effect called "Fire Burning Sound" recorded by JaBa and shared under a Creative Commons Attribution 3.0 license (which means we'll need to list it accordingly in the credits section of our game).

◊ For this exercise, it's important to use the offline version of Twine 2. You can create the audio macros in the online editor, but you won't be able to test them using the local sound files on your system. First, we'll need to load them in using a "StoryInit" passage. Create a passage with this name and type the following:

```
<<cacheaudio "fireburning" "Fire_Burning-JaBa.
mp3" "Fire_Burning-JaBa.wav">>
```

HTML5 audio is tricky—not every browser supports every audio file type, so when you have multiple versions available, it is best to preload them all by using *cacheaudio* to start the browser loading the audio files before you try to play a sound. The browser chooses which file type to load based on its preferences. If none of the file types are compatible, your sound won't play. The audio files must be right next to your .html file in the folder for the path structure in this example to work.

◊ Next, we'll actually play the audio. Open and edit the "Lost" passage. Add the following above the first line:

```
<<audio "fireburning" play>>
```

The *audio* element takes a reference to a cached audio file and reaches back to find the source file preloaded by the browser. The audio command to play will run as soon as the page loads, but it can also be embedded in a link. There are lots of modifiers available in SugarCube's robust audio macro library, which is one of the best-supported of any of the story formats. The closest functionality currently for Harlowe requires an external library, the Harlowe Audio Library (Chapel, "Harlowe Audio Library").

Let's try one of the modifiers to fade out our sound as we fade out our text. Modify the audio call to instead say the following:

```
<<audio "fireburning" volume 0.5 fadeoverto 5 0>>
```

The *volume* argument takes a number from 1 to 0 and plays the audio at the specified level relative to the source. Obviously, it can be difficult to modulate this without knowing how loudly your reader has set their speakers, so think about using the volume modulation for balancing different effects, such as ambient noises versus dramatic interruptions. The *fadeoverto* argument takes two numbers: The first is the number of seconds, which we've matched here to the number of seconds on the text animation. The second number is the level of the final volume.

Next, we'll add looping background music. We'll use a file of "Creepy Background" sound effects, recorded by Daniel Simon and shared under an Attribution 3.0 license.

◊ Start by caching the background audio files in the "StoryInit" passage:

```
<<cacheaudio "background" "background.mp3"
"background.wav">>
```

Next, we'll call the audio from the controls page of our story but loop the audio.

```
<<audio "background" loop play>>
```

To avoid collision, we'll also want to stop the audio loop before we start the fire effect:

```
<<audio "background" stop>>
```

Incorporating images into a text-driven platform isn't necessary, but it can be powerful and provocative. Let's finish out the audiovisual exercise of this Twine by adding some *image* elements and using SugarCube's markup to make the image active. Images can have three components—a *title*, which provides a text caption; a *link*, which points to another passage; and a *setter*, which activates when clicked and alters the state of a variable.

◊ We haven't done anything with the "find an index" page in our pathways, so let's start there. Open "Search" and change the passage text to include the following:

```
<<include "Countdown">>
You look for any text you can recognize,
but there's nothing helpful.
There are three well-worn buttons on the side of
the console, but instead of words, they only bear
symbols that you don't recognize. If they were
letters, they'd be been lost to oils and waste.

[img[shape.gif][one]]
[img[shape2.gif][two]]
[img[shape3.gif][three]]

You might as well press one.
```

As with audio, all the image files referenced need to be in the folder with the .html file for this structure to work. It's also possible to use the image tag as an alternative to traditional image markup within the CSS. This can be more convenient when you're already comfortable with SugarCube's markup.

◊ Let's try changing the background color on our main passages to a background image instead. Open the story style sheet and add the following code:

```
body {
    background-image: [img[stars.gif]];
    color: white;
    font-size: 200%;
}
```

Notice that this works with animated GIFs (as in this example, a set of animated stars), and by default, it tiles the image. This approach works best with retro background effects, which tended to use repeated patterns rather than stretching a single image to fit. Animated GIFs like this one are used in many Twine works and are usually most effective with a strong contrast to any text colors chosen.

Example 4.4: Tracery and External Libraries

External libraries for Twine extend the capabilities of Twine and frequently provide bridges for more easily pulling in traditional JavaScript to the engine. There are extensive options for SugarCube 2 macros online, including Chapel's Custom Macro collection, which includes particularly useful tools such as pronoun templants and mouseover macros (Chapel, "Custom Macros"). Macros frequently emerge when more scripting-inclined Twine creators want to solve a problem for one of their own works and choose to repackage and share their solution with the community. Frequently, those macros are integrated back into the core of story format projects when they prove particularly useful.

In this exercise, we'll pick one well-loved library to try. Note that combining external libraries can be difficult, as they may include conflict syntax or requirements. Let's take a look at Trice, a library that combines many elements into one (incobalt). Created by Michael Thomét and inspired by Matthew R. F. Balousek's earlier library Twincery, Trice is a 2.X SugarCube-specific wrapper for Tracery that allows us to play with generative techniques like those we explored in our previous chapter. It's easier to break down how Tracery's logic can be integrated with Twine by first approaching the two separately.

Tracery works with *grammars* that are constructed of *symbols* and *rules*: symbols are essentially arrays containing a set of possible values, and once inserted, they choose a particular value for that instance. Rules are more complex patterns that combine fixed works and symbols to generate text or images (more on that later).

> ◊ Let's break this down in a simple example before we combine Tracery and Twine. To work with this code on its own, try the online visual editor at https://beaugunderson.com/tracery -writer/ and type in the following:

```
{
"origin": ["#codeVerbs# the #craftNouns#,
#codeNouns# #craftVerbs#"],
"craftNouns":["album","backing","bargello","bark
cloth","basting","batik","batting","bearding","b
eading","betweens","bias","binding","stitch","ne
sting","bobbin","tension","chainstitch","emblem"
,"embroidery","frame","sash","gap","gapping","ho
op","hooping","lettering","mirror","monogram","n
eedle","nippers","pantograph","tape","puckering
","punching","density","design","thread","broadc
loth","block","border","calico","charm","die","f
lannel","feeddogs","paper","sleeve","foot","fabr
ic","loft","long arm","medallion","memory","moti
f","quilt","fiber","panel","patch","value","unit"
```

```
,"seam","fill","facing","hook","scale","satin","
punching"],
"craftVerbs":["appliqué","bind","sew","hem","bri
dge","fill","press","back","repeat","rotate","sta
bilize","thread","break","cut","tie","trim","ver
ify","glaze","label","layer","piece","corner"],
"codeNouns":["algorithm","application","bootstra
p","code","structure","data","framework","stack"
,"query","object","function","variable","binary"
,"bug","command","conditional","statement","patt
ern","server","parameter","grid","pixel","resolu
tion","user","flow","element"],
"codeVerbs":["decompose","debug","iterate","cont
rol","program","run","embed","influence","bounce"
,"optimize","mine","declare","edit","design"]
}
```

Syntax-wise, Tracery is built on JSON: curly braces indicate objects and thus surround the complete grammar, or all the rules and symbols that make up a particular iteration of Tracery logic. The hash marks indicate a substitution and must surround a string of characters that matches one of the symbols. Each symbol lists the name first (in quotation marks, which delineates a string), followed by the list of possibilities as an array. As with the generation we discussed in chapter P-2, this allows for emergent play and can result in combinations we don't anticipate. The output to this first iteration is fairly banal but demonstrates the simple generative potential:

```
optimize the lettering, pixel trim
edit the puckering, pattern bind
design the paper, function glaze
influence the barkcloth, structure repeat
```

When we bring Tracery into Twine, the base elements remain the same, but the syntax changes.

◊ The easiest way to work with Trice is to use their bundled starter code, which draws in all the required scripts. Download the repository from GitHub, and open trice.html through the "Input file" option in the Twine main menu. You'll see the Tracery code in the story JavaScript file, but that's not everything—in the example folder, you'll see a project set up with the Tracery libraries in a folder. Make sure you duplicate that same file structure when working on this exercise, or your code will break due to unmet dependencies.

Importantly, the full library won't be loaded in time for our first passage, so we'll need a title screen. Create a "Begin" passage and add text and a link:

```
Cut and Trace
```

```
[[Begin]]
```

Let's start by generating some individual symbols: each passage we create and tag with "grammar" will be part of Tracery's grammar. Create a new passage titled "gCraftNouns," tag it, and add one word per line to the appropriate wordset:

```
basting
mirror
lettering
foot
fabric
calico
loft
tape
hooping
bargello
sleeve
block
border
```

Note that you don't need any special characters; the paragraph break alone sets up the conversion. This eliminates the need for extensive syntax and, in doing so, cuts back on some of the more frustrating aspects of generative texts. Each passage can become a freewriting exercise, and elements can be added easily as you expand your code.

> ◊ Let's test that our grammar is connected by going to the "Begin" passage and generating a word:
>
> ```
> <<trace "gCraftNouns">>
> ```

Remember, you can't test through the Twine browser. Each time you test a trace, you'll need to export your file to .html—otherwise, the browser won't allow the files to access the necessary libraries, so Tracery won't run.

Note that whenever you invoke the library, you'll use *trace* to structure the command. This first simple stage just takes one symbol as input, using the string for the passage name, so make sure you type them exactly the same way. If you neglected to tag the passage as grammar, it won't import properly. Trace is a macro, so it provides a SugarCube syntax integration for the Tracery library. It's very flexible: it can be used to build entire rules and output full passages of generative text. Let's build a grammar with enough complexity that we can give this a try.

> ◊ Following the same pattern as the "gCraftNouns" passage, create a passage for "gCraftVerbs," "gCodeNouns," and "gCode-Verbs." Don't forget to tag each passage as a grammar. Next, we'll test by going to "Begin" and using a more complex trace:
>
> ```
> <<trace "#gCodeVerbs# the #gCraftNouns#,
> #gCodeNouns# #gCraftVerbs#">>
> ```

Notice a few changes from our simple call: if we are using more than one symbol, we need to integrate the full Tracery syntax with hash marks around each symbol's name. This also means we can start to integrate some of Tracery's more complex features, such as functions to make certain words plural or change the tense.

◊ Let's give this a try by extending our passage poetry further. First, we'll need some additional grammar passages. Add a grammar passage titled "gColor" and tagged grammar, and input the following text:

```
orange
blue
violet
yellow
pink
apricot
indigo
green
gray
black
white
```

◊ Next, edit the "Begin" passage to include the following:

```
<<trace "#gCodeVerbs# the #gCraftNouns#,
#gCodeNouns# #gCraftVerbs#">>
<<trace "#gCraftNouns.capitalize# is
#gCodeNouns.a# . . .">>

<<trace "#gColor.a.capitalize# #gCodeNouns#
#gCraftVerbs.s#">>
```

Output on the "Begin" passage will vary every time you revisit:

```
program the fabric, function back
Basting is a query . . .
An indigo stack threads
```

Note the modifiers from Tracery's library in play here: .*a* adds the appropriate article based on the starting letter of the modified word, *capitalize* changes the first letter of the modified word to capital, and .*s* pluralizes the word (usually—but not always—correctly, so watch this one). The trace macro isn't the only way to integrate Tracery: sometimes we want to generate text and save it for later. For that, we can use the trace function.

```
◊ Let's pick a noun and save it to a variable, and then we can
use it repeatedly in a generated text.

<<set $myNoun to trace("gCraftNouns")>>

$myNoun is $myNoun is $myNoun.
```

Now we can generate extensively within Tracery in text, keeping in mind examples such as Kate Compton's own stylistic play—for more ideas, take a look at her site. Generative content is also the emphasis of several communities of play, and GitHub is home to a growing "NaNoGenMo" collection of generated novels, made for National Novel Generation Month, which includes Tracery and other tools powering a range of works for inspiration.

Example 4.5: Mood Imagery

While generative text is endlessly playful, we can also use Tracery to assist in generative components for imagery. (This can also be accomplished without Tracery, but less efficiently!) Tracery is popular with the bot-making community for aesthetic bots, which are a Twine-adjacent form of computational creativity that can result in endless content. A great example is Kate Compton's Tiny Space Adventure bot (hosted @TinyAdv and powered by Cheap Bots Done Quick, an easy-to-use hosting service for Tracery bots), which results in content like the following:

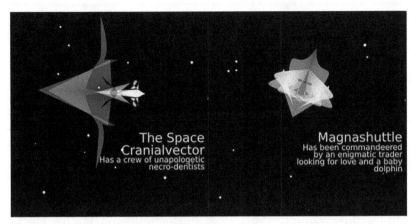

Figure 19: Examples of Kate Compton's Tiny Space Adventure bot

While the code for this is quite complex (and lives here: https://pastebin.com/YYtZnzZ0), looking at a fragment of it reveals how Tracery can be used to make substitutions in code:

```
"ship" : ["[gradID:#id#][bladeID:#id#]
[sideID:#id#]#gradient#<g
transform='translate(120, 100) rotate(#digit##
digit#)'>#shipSide#<g transform='scale(-1, 1)'>
<use xlink:href='\\##sideID#'></g></g>"],
"label" : "<text text-anchor=\"end\"
fill=\"\\#FFFFFF\" fill-opacity=\"0.4\" font-
size=\"12\" font-family=\"Verdana\" x=\"225\"
y=\"250\">#shipName#</text>",
"bg" : ["<rect fill='\\#000000' x='0' y='0'
width='300' height='300'/>#starField#"],
"star" : ["<circle fill='\\#FFFFFF' cx='#r255#'
cy='#r255#' r='#zeroone#.#digit#'/>"],
"starField" : ["#star##star##star##star##star#
#star##star##star##star##star##star##star##sta
r##star##star##star##star##star##star##star##s
tar#"],
```

```
"svgImg" : ["<svg viewBox=\"0 0 256 256\"
width=\"256\" height=\"256\">#bg##label##ship#</
svg>"],
"origin" : "{svg #svgImg#}"
```

Note particularly the SVG (Scalable Vector Graphics) element, defined in "svgImg" and including elements defined in succession: the ship is the product of much more complex code but is then added to the mix along with a label on top of a star field, which is generated from randomly placed and sized circles defined in the "star" symbol. SVGs are a web-friendly format defined mathematically and thus friendly to resizing and responsive design. Most people work with SVGs through graphical interfaces such as Illustrator, but it's also possible to work with simple or even complex SVGs directly through the markup of their code. SVGs are the heart of Tracery graphics. We'll continue with our code from exercise 4.4, since we're already set up for Tracery integration, and the language of code and crafting certainly lends itself to visual accompaniment.

◊ First, let's look at how SVGs work in SugarCube with some basic code. Add the following to your "Begin" passage:

```
<svg><line x1="0" y1="0" x2="200" y2="200"
stroke-width="1" stroke="white"/></svg>
```

You should see a diagonal white line beneath your text. SugarCube supports in-line SVG in this format natively, but only in some of its latest iterations—earlier examples and other story formats cause more problems with SVGs. *Line* designates the shape intended, and the two pairs of x- and y-coordinates indicate the beginning and endpoints of the line within the SVG. *Stroke-width* governs the width in pixels, while *stroke* sets the color.

◊ Now let's make it dynamic by first generating a color to save in a variable and then using a variable as an attribute within the SVG. To do this, we'll use another SugarCube macro, *print*, which will allow us to combine the HTML markup with a variable:

```
<<set $myColor to trace("gColor")>>
<<print '<svg><line x1="0" y1="0" x2="200"
y2="200" stroke-width="1" stroke="' + $myColor +
'"/></svg>'>>
```

Note that the code is mostly the same, but we need to use $ to designate the variable—and watch the placement of the single quotation marks to indicate when we're asking SugarCube to process the input versus just printing the HTML directly.

Let's build something more complicated. We're going to create graphics that might be used in a number of ways—they might be art that changes without warning when the player revisits a room or atmosphere background imagery to set the mood for a scene. Let's start by restricting our color palette to create a more unified aesthetic. For this, it's easiest to work with color-safe HTML codes if you also want to use the words in text, but you can also use hexadecimal colors.

◊ Create a new passage titled "gNum," and make sure to tag it as grammar. Add a set of numbers—the range will impact the size of the final line:

```
80
100
120
140
160
180
200
220
240
260
```

280
300

◊ Change the SVG code in "Begin" to the following:

```
<<set $myColor to trace("gColor")>>
<<set $myNum to trace("gNum")>>

<<print '<svg><line x1="0" y1="0"
x2="'+$myNum+'" y2="'+$myNum+'" stroke-width="1"
stroke="' + $myColor + '"/></svg>'>>
```

◊ Modify the contents of "gColor" to:

```
purple
blue
gainsboro
silver
gray
teal
navy
cyan
indigo
orchid
lavender
plum
```

◊ Now we'll need to create a more complex SVG to add dynamic design. This is going to require several symbols to control our shape's attributes, so create new passages for each of the following. The bolded lines should be the title of the passage, and every passage must be tagged as grammar:

gY
50

```
100
150
200
250
300
350
400
450

gX
100
200
300
400
500
600
700
800
900
1000

gOpacity
0.1
0.2
0.3
0.4
0.5
0.6
0.7
0.8
```

Each of these will be used to control the corresponding elements of a generative ellipse—assuming a canvas that is 1024 × 512 pixels, these numbers will let us distribute shapes along the x and y space of the SVG. The opacity will give us more dynamic colors through overlaps:

note that we're not using an opacity of 0, as that would disappear, or an opacity of 1, as that might lead to too abrupt of a layer. Our existing "gNum" and "gColor" will complete the shape's features.

◊ Now we're ready to add a Tracery rule as a passage. This time, let's use the SVG code for an ellipse and create a passage titled "gEllipse" tagged as grammar. Include the following code:

```
<ellipse cx=\"#gX#\" cy=\"#gY#\" rx=\"#gNum#\"
ry=\"#gNum#\" style=\"fill:#gColor#;stroke:#gColo
r#;stroke-width:2;opacity:#gOpacity#\" />
```

Creating a passage to hold the ellipse properties will make it easy to use Tracery to generate as many of these shapes as we want, so we can potentially fill the screen with a variety of overlapping ellipses. Notice how each property is inserted using the Tracery symbol markup, and all the quotation marks are escaped with \ to ensure the code syntax is preserved when we run our trace.

◊ We have all the components now to create ellipses from a passage. Instead of adding it to "Start," let's create a new passage to hold this SVG. Let's start by using Tracery to create a dynamic link to the new passage. In "Start," add the following code:

```
<<set $myLink to trace("gCodeNouns.
capitalize.a")>>
[[$myLink|Screen]]
```

Note that this reversal of the *capitalize* and *a* will result in capitalization on the word, not the *a*, which can be useful when you want a different rhythm to your style. It's also possible to use Trice directly to create rotating links that use the keywords of the grammar—just include the name of the grammar symbol in the link directly, like *[[gCodeNouns]]*—but this structure works best when you have a reason for using this dynamic link style, so we won't include it here.

```
◊ In "Screen," include the following code:

<<trace "<svg width='1024' height='512'>#gEllips
e##gEllipse##gEllipse##gEllipse##gEllipse##gElli
pse##gEllipse##gEllipse##gEllipse##gEllipse##gEl
lipse##gEllipse##gEllipse##gEllipse##gEllipse##g
Ellipse##gEllipse##gEllipse##gEllipse#</svg>">>
```

This can look a little overwhelming. Like Kate Compton's star field in the background of her spaceship bot shown earlier, we are using repetition of the generative element to create a layered effect. Note that the SVG size needs to be defined to ensure all our shapes display, so we declare the width and height first, again escaping the quotation marks to avoid errors. Watch the hash marks on repeating symbols, as it is easy to end up with an error in this section of the code. Note how we don't need to use print in this instance, as we are running the trace directly, eliminating the need to store every one of these properties as a variable prior to use.

The output should look something like this:

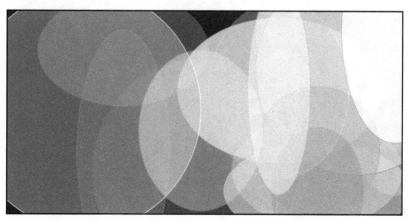

Figure 20: Sample output from our Tracery SVG generation

Note that this is only the beginning of what we can do with Tracery in Twine. SVGs can be scaled to fill the screen and can incorporate generative text as an overlay. They can be placed with CSS behind other elements to create a sense of mood-specific backgrounds. You can even invite the player to indicate a mood or color palette early in a play experience or shift the colors gradually to reflect changes in tone.

Consider how the colors set the tone of the opening decisions in Porpentine's *With Those We Love Alive*: the opening scene lives against a backdrop of turquoise fading into dark blue, reminiscent of the sea abstracted, with vivid pink links against it. This palette, not coincidentally, inspired some of the choices in this example. Note how every element is thoughtfully integrated, from the choice of link colors and fonts to the feel of the gradient across the page. It is harmonious with some of the later palettes in the same narrative, but those can be more immediately unsettling: a deep magenta fading toward a violet-black accompanies the words "Dead brown leaves cover inky black lake. / Something is rising from the lake" (Porpentine).

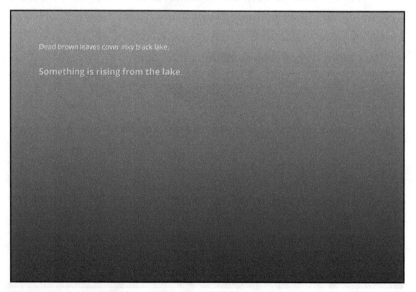

Figure 21: Screenshot from *With Those We Love Alive*

These visual choices can further be layered with the other elements we've discussed so far in this exercise. Consider how unsettling a deep color palette might be alongside a cheerful theme or how the alarming, unsettling aesthetics of Michael Lutz's more minimalist *My Father's Long, Long Legs* gradually alert the player to the wrongness of the family dynamics (Lutz). Whether constrained or over the top, atmospheric or full-on camp, the audiovisual elements of Twine are not necessarily secondary to the text.

Works Cited

Anthropy, Anna. "Queers in Love at the End of the World." itch.io, 2013. https://w.itch
    .io/end-of-the-world.

Chapel. "Custom Macros." TwineLab, 2019. https://twinelab.net/custom-macros-for
    -sugarcube-2/#/.

———. "Harlowe Audio Library." TwineLab, 2019, https://twinelab.net/harlowe-audio/#/.

Cox, Dan, ed. "iftechfoundation / twine-cookbook." 2017. GitHub, 2019. https://github
    .com/iftechfoundation/twine-cookbook.

incobalt. "incobalt /T rice." 2018. GitHub, 2019. https://github.com/incobalt/Trice.

Lutz, Michael. *My Father's Long, Long Legs*. Correlated Contents, September 23, 2013.
    http://correlatedcontents.com/misc/Father.html.

Porpentine. "With Those We Love Alive." Cambridge, MA: Electronic Literature Orga-
    nization, 2014. http://collection.eliterature.org/3/work.html?work=with-those-we
    -love-alive.

Squinkifer, D. *Quing's Quest VII: The Death of Videogames*. Self-published, September 1,
    2014. https://games.squinky.me/quing/.

CHAPTER T-5

Twine and the Critical Moment

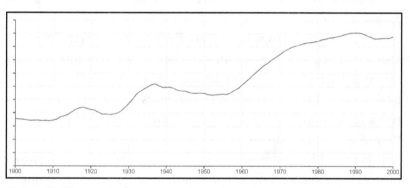

Figure 22: The previous century explained

What Crisis?

Centuries leave marks, such as the interesting signature of the twentieth century shown here. Despite its generally upward trend, this is not a world population graph, whose roughly 6:1 slope would be considerably steeper than the present line and whose curvature would be much more acute. A closer guess might be something like the gross domestic product for an industrialized nation, or perhaps the Dow Jones index—though, on closer inspection, we'd expect a sag around

1930, not the rise we see here. The steady ascent in the latter half of the graph looks familiar, though again the flattening after 1990 is at odds with the economic record.

The data mapped here are not financial but linguistic and, by extension, cultural. This chart shows the percentage share of the word *crisis* in relation to all words in the Google Books database of works in English. The values tracked are minuscule in absolute terms—about 0.0017 percent at the start, climbing to 0.005 percent around 1990—but the line's contours are revealing. The word grows about threefold in frequency over the century. There is a flat stretch in the twenties, spiking as we approach World War II, then a plateau in the postwar decade. From about 1960 to 1995, usage surges. During this period, there is a crisis at every turn: missile crisis, population crisis, energy crisis, hostage crisis, AIDS crisis, climate crisis, debt crisis, water crisis, crisis on infinite Earths, everyone's identity crisis, always in progress.

Since the graph stops just before the new millennium, it might seem of limited usefulness for thinking about developments that start ten years later. However, consider the last segment of the chart, the final decade of the old century. Occurrences fall off to an uncertain plateau. The word still has plenty of currency—how could it not in a time of growing economic and environmental unease?—but people have perhaps begun to have enough of it. With the keyword deployed in so many combinations, any fresh invention would face diminishing returns. On the evidence, we passed peak crisis three decades ago, about the time R.E.M.'s "It's the End of the World as We Know It" turned into a jejune earworm.

This chapter was first drafted before the coronavirus outbreak of 2019. Reread in the summer of 2020, those first paragraphs seem to tempt fate. Google's database stops at 2012, so we can only guess how the graph will look ten years from now. The decade from 2000 to 2010, not included in the graph, shows a pronounced downward hook. Perhaps by 2030, that trend will have reversed as *pandemic crisis* ripples through the record, possibly joined by other dire digrams. We are willing to bet, though, that the overall trend holds.[1] For a long while now, we've had all the crises we can stand.

Especially when combined with the adjective *existential*, the word *crisis* seems all too inevitably apocalyptic. As the human-driven Anthropocene morphs into what cultural critic Donna Haraway calls the "Cthulucene," visions of posthuman End Times overwhelm us (Haraway). At the beginning of the midcentury crisis boom, Stanley Kubrick and Terry Southern gave us *Dr. Strangelove, or How I Learned to Stop Worrying and Love the Bomb*, a film in which an insane Air Force commander triggers the end of civilization (Kubrick). Nearly a half century later, at the other end of the rising curve, Joss Whedon and Drew Goddard offered *The Cabin in the Woods*, in which something very similar happens, except the agent of doom is the "final girl" of a literally diabolical slasher film—the sanest and most moral person in the story (Whedon and Goddard). After peak crisis, our sense of an ending turns strange and more than a little toxic.

This chapter will eventually make its way, with some digressions, to one Twine writer's poignant response to this predicament—*Queers in Love at the End of the World*, Anna Anthropy's game of apocalypse. We will return inevitably to crisis—that's where we live these days—but we set out toward this destination with a deliberate swerve. Let's replace *crisis* with *critical*. Though technically this change just swaps adjective for noun, there is an important shade of difference. It is easy to imagine *crisis* as a final negative: no way out, no alternative, no future. In contrast, the word *critical* seems more negotiable, implying critical choices, critical practice, critical (and these days, literal) distance. It offers the chance to change the shape of certain curves. It leaves room to swerve. As Borges's labyrinth-novelist says, "I leave to various futures, but not to all, my garden of forking paths" (Borges 26). Some futures are more fortunate than others. In Twine work as in life, the ability to choose is crucial. Choosing *critical* over *crisis* lets us keep faith with the root word

---

1   In a nice bit of just-in-time journalism as this chapter was nearing completion, *Wired* posted a story titled "All This Chaos Might Be Giving You 'Crisis Fatigue'" (Simon).

krinein, which means *to decide*. This choice emphasizes difference, oppositional response, and the exploration of alternatives. It also connects powerfully to elective action, a crucial part of games and play.

Critical Moments

Unlike crisis, which at least implicitly dramatizes itself as a discrete event, critical moments can be flexibly invoked. Turn the calendar to the first weeks of 2019. We've already discussed the appearance of the *Black Mirror* "Bandersnatch" episode, with its Twine connection and an intriguing overture to branching narrative. A few weeks later, Netflix rolled out another show, the miniseries *Russian Doll*, with a radically different approach to story and play (Headland, Babbit, and Lyonne). Like "Bandersnatch," *Russian Doll* focuses on a game coder, the fabulously dissolute Nadia Vulvokov, who, like Stefan Butler, is dropped unwittingly into a garden of forking paths. In a way, both are under the control of a shadowy agency called Netflix, but Nadia's predicament does not involve viewer intervention. Somewhere in the course of every episode, Nadia suffers a bizarre or violent death—run over by a cab, fallen down stairs, poisoned, shot, attacked in the subway by killer bees—after which she returns to her initial position in the episode, staring into a bathroom mirror at a party for her thirty-sixth birthday. Nadia's work as a game designer offers a frame for understanding this iterative experience: like a character failing to complete her quest, Nadia is destined to keep replaying level 36.

Russian Doll deserves more detailed treatment both as a disrupted narrative and as part of the unfolding saga of binge TV, but we will confine ourselves to its juxtaposition with "Bandersnatch" (Slade). The scheduling was most likely coincidental, but all the same, it offers a meaningful contrast. For all that it restricts most player choice to a pair of alternatives, "Bandersnatch" subverts tele-cinematic storytelling. Any choice greater than one affects at least a small insurgency. *Russian Doll* reverses and atones for this rupture, even though it was probably not intended for the purpose. The series turns the ergodic breakpoint into a stylistic device. Instead of the relative openness of a game, it delivers what we might call a *closed, gamelike arc*, an appearance of randomness and contingency that in fact goes where television always goes, to singular narrative and moral resolution. We could gloss *Russian Doll* in many ways—*Groundhog Day* goes to Lower Manhattan, *Memento* with millennials—but it would not be inaccurate to call it a let's-play video with unusually high production values. It is one version of a game.

The pattern that emerges here is nothing new. Claude Lévi-Strauss identified the basic structure in the 1960s, back on the first step of our crisis escalator—a tension between contingency and static balance. In his view, this dynamic was as old as play itself:

> All games are defined by a set of rules which in practice allow the playing of any number of matches. Ritual, which is also 'played,' is on the other hand, like a favored instance of a game, remembered from among the possible ones because it is the only one which results in a particular type of equilibrium between the two sides. The transposition is readily seen in the case of the Gahuku-Gama of New Guinea who have learnt to play football but who will play, several days running, as many matches as are necessary for both sides to reach the same score. . . . This is treating a game as a ritual. (Lévi-Strauss 30–31)[2]

We can see a similar "transposition" in the swing from "Bandersnatch" to *Russian Doll*. The closed, gamelike arc treats game as ritual, preserving not harmony between neighboring tribes but the power structure of an executive culture, the singularity of authorized narrative that is part of what Ruberg calls "chrononormativity" (Ruberg 25). This complex is the target of that memorably self-parodic paranoid branch in "Bandersnatch," where the player makes Stefan aware that he is under the control of an entertainment network from the future. Welcome to videoland. Lévi-Strauss could have heard a similar message a year after his thoughts about game and ritual appeared in English. We imagine him nodding as he tunes in to an episode of *The Outer Limits*

---

2 Thomas Malaby, theorist of play and my colleague at University of Wisconsin–Milwaukee, discusses this insight from Lévi-Strauss in his article "Institutions in Play," to which I am indebted (Malaby).

(1963–1965), which began each week with a ritual message from the
"Control Voice":

> There is nothing wrong with your television set. Do not attempt to
> adjust the picture. We are controlling transmission. If we wish to make
> it louder, we will bring up the volume. If we wish to make it softer, we
> will tune it to a whisper. We will control the horizontal. We will control
> the vertical. We can roll the image; make it flutter. We can change the
> focus to a soft blur or sharpen it to crystal clarity. For the next hour, sit
> quietly and we will control all that you see and hear. We repeat: there is
> nothing wrong with your television set. (Wikipedia)

In many ways, the entire ergodic project, the reimagination of storytelling under procedural intervention, might be the afterlife of the
Control Voice. In one of the great ironies of human history, computing devices and the internet were developed as adjuncts to the
command-and-control culture campily evoked in that old broadcast
fantasy. As the public flooded into the new cyberspaces, "everting"
them, as Steven Jones says, from fantasy worlds to everyday habita-
tions, the original control culture was replaced by something we struggle to comprehend (Jones 2014). Computer games play a major role
in this understanding, so it is not surprising to find games intimately
concerned with both control and voices. We will have further thoughts
about voices with respect to Davey Wreden's *Beginner's Guide* in the
next part of this chapter. For the moment, there is more to say about
the object of control, which Lévi-Strauss describes as "equilibrium"
(20). Such dynamic balances are inherently fragile, especially under
the impact of radically destabilizing, disruptive technologies. There
may have been nothing wrong with our television sets—nothing the
old networks couldn't fix—but normativity cannot hold when video
screen meets game processor, and the network becomes an everted
internet.

There would inevitably be attempts to restore the supposed balance of forces between producer and consumer. The appearance of a
closed, gamelike arc in 2019 extends a long-running trend. Using similar

techniques, films like *Groundhog Day* (Ramis), *Lola Rennt* (Tykwer), and *Memento* (Nolan) fed a vogue for "mind-game" cinema in an increasingly game-obsessed era (see Elsaesser). Complex narratives were carefully channeled into the popular mainstream. Game ideas were adapted for all sorts of screens. The ultimate accommodation came in 2011, when the US Supreme Court ruled in Brown v. Entertainment Merchants Association, affirming the cultural standing of video games: "Like the protected books, plays, and movies that preceded them, video games communicate ideas—and even social messages—through many familiar literary devices (such as characters, dialogue, plot, and music) and features distinctive to the medium (such as the player's interaction with the virtual world). That suffices to confer First Amendment protection" (Brown v. Entertainment Merchants Association).

It may have seemed ironic that the author of his opinion was Antonin Scalia, the conservative archon. Yet the attempt to affiliate computer games with "books, plays, and movies" is definitionally conservative. Defying disruption, it affirms continuity between the present and the past. It envisions a living, changing culture. (Irony floods back in if we replace *culture* with *Constitution*.) In its way, the opinion is laudable, though the harmonious world it imagines was pure judicial fantasy. Even as Scalia wrote his ruling, the seeds of Gamergate were germinating. They would take roughly a year to flower into full evil, bringing backlash against those who wanted to use games for concerted expression rather than unreflective, unengaged *fun*.

By 2013, *fun* had become a fighting word. As Stephanie Boluk and Patrick Lemieux point out, this controversy had been a long time coming, starting the moment games converged with video: "In the same way that the British land enclosure of the eighteenth century transformed public land into private property, so too has the videogame industry worked to privatize the culture of games and play. Games have been replaced by videogames and play has been replaced by fun" (Boluk and Lemieux 8). Some might quibble about the analogy with land enclosure, but the rest of this observation is unimpeachable. The attempt to restore cultural equilibrium, to subordinate gameplay under rituals of consumption-oriented fun, would never succeed. Fun comes in far too many varieties. Ruberg remarks, "#GamerGate has gotten at least one thing right. It is no coincidence that this backlash comes at the same time that queerness is becoming a more central concern in games and the dialogues that surround them. As Katherine Cross has written, proponents of #GamerGate are driven by a fear that video games are changing, that they will no longer belong only to white, straight, cisgender men and boys. And that is true" (Ruberg 13).

There is a reason this chapter, like the previous chapter on Twine camp, returns inevitably to queer gaming and particularly to the work of Bo Ruberg, who has brought us the crucial recognition that video games "have always been queer," driven by a "core" impulse to explore "non-normative desires" that speaks to and proceeds from alterity (Ruberg 11). We embrace this idea because it does so much to explain the ineradicable difference that marks ergodic works. From the perspective of narrative normativity, they represent an unruly, uncanny other. They are fundamentally, deliberately, and joyfully abnormal. The critical moment of Twine owes much to queer people and their ideas, as so many have said before us. In learning to align our work as queer, some straight folk will find a strong sense of solidarity. This sentiment is deep but also hazardous.

Straight minds and bodies are not exposed to the traumas visited on queer people. Queerness is an important place to start—an essential "lens," as Ruberg says—but Ruberg adds a significant caution: "In using the word 'queer' itself, straight, cisgender subjects must remain aware that their experiences are never one and the same with those of LGBTQ people (who themselves bring their own individual perspectives to this work) and that their use of queerness as a lens must come with an acknowledgement of and respect for real, queer lives" (Ruberg 19). Both authors of this book operate in public spaces as white, able-bodied academics in heterosexual or straight-presenting relationships and thus are not subject to the challenges of, aggression toward, and harassment of those who are visibly queer, trans, or othered. For her feminist work, one of us has felt a share of that mistreatment. For his own unorthodoxies, the other has seen nothing worse than some bad reviews. Limits and obligations need to be made clear. The "lens" of alterity is invaluable. It requires "acknowledgement," respect, and more importantly, a commitment to shared struggle, which is the ethos to which this book aspires.

Normativities—economic, erotic, political, chrono-biological—can be powerfully opposed by discourses of difference—feminist, queer, nonwhite, neuro-atypical, anticapitalist. Ruberg's main claim, that video games have always been queer, implies a larger, ongoing struggle. As Boluk and Lemieux demonstrate, genuine play refuses the "enclosure" of pleasure in any hegemonic funhouse. In activating the reader as a player, all ergodic art forms—interactive fictions, game books, hypertexts, games—become at least fellow travelers in this insurgency. We need to consider a broader picture, one that will allow us to place queer games and Twine games in relation to other aspects of their critical moment. This will take us to a work that is outside of the Twine community and whose queerness seems at least debatable but whose questions about games and art are essential to our critical moment.

Turn Back from This Cave

For some, games are all about asking questions. Montfort affiliates interactive fiction with the ancient form of the riddle (Montfort 14). Every game in which we explore some baffling space poses ontological questions: *What is this world? Why is it the way it is? Who am I in this place? What do my interactions reveal?* All world-games are basically riddles; some are more direct than others in framing their enigmas. In his two major efforts so far, Davey Wreden has a way of putting the puzzles up front. *The Stanley Parable* begs the question, *parable of what?* (Wreden and Pugh). Similarly, coming to *The Beginner's Guide*, we might ask, *Guide to what practice, activity, or way of being? Just what are we beginning?* (Wreden).

Many players of *Stanley Parable* come away with plausible answers: the game is about free will and its paradoxical denial; the game explores the tension between structure and play or desire. These are not necessarily the best answers, but they are at least reasonably related to the experience of play. *Beginner's Guide*, by contrast, is harder to fix in a phrase. It's about a broken friendship, about the ethics of creativity, about the reasons for making game-based art. The work may tell us something about the nature and purpose of games. Which brings us to an important question: Is *Beginner's Guide* a game?[3]

The product is sold on Steam as a game, it has been reviewed as a game, and, like *Stanley Parable*, its playable spaces are assembled from components of other games (*Counter-Strike, Half-Life*). It seems to belong at least superficially to three divisions of the game market: independent games, B-games, and walking simulators. Yet the play experience of *Beginner's Guide* is about as railed-in as possible. As in *Stanley Parable*, there is voice-over narration keyed to our progress through each level. The plummy BBC announcer of the earlier game is replaced by Wreden speaking as "Davey," a character based on himself. Davey guides us through sixteen chapters and an epilogue, discrete levels ostensibly created by a shadowy figure called "Coda" between October 2008 and June 2011.

We will consider Davey and Coda fictional constructs, thus implicitly metaphorical—though what they represent is open to question.[4] The dates of Coda's efforts align neatly with the creative history of *Stanley Parable*, so some self-reference seems inevitable. *Beginner's Guide* seems ripe for interpretation as psychomachia, the struggle between halves of a divided self. At the same time, the work's slipperiness and complexity defy simplistic understanding. Is it a collection of "weird and experimental" game levels, or a unified production? (The presence of an epilogue—literally a coda yet outside of the Coda collection—strongly suggests the latter.) How should we characterize this effort? Is it a game or a piece of theater, a game-flavored monologue? Maybe *Beginner's Guide* is more video than game—a game collapsed into its own playthrough.

---

3 As we have said previously, this question has become infected by Gamergate and needs to be framed carefully, which I have tried to do in the article on which this section is partly based. See Moulthrop, "Turn Back."

4 Coda could be based on an actual person; Wreden has been coy on the subject, leaving us free to speculate (see, e.g., Klepek). The name has the appearance of a handle or *nomme de logiciel*—Coda, a coder. In music and writing, a coda is a final supplement, bringing a work to completion.

Beginner's Guide has important resemblances to machinima, game-derived linear video, but it also has features inconsistent with that form. As Davey reminds us in chapter 7 ("Down"), the work was built on the Source game engine. It is not delivered in a video format but as a playable download on Steam. Player action is allowed and often required. In chapter 1 ("Whisper"), we are told we can exit the game by stepping into an energy beam. As in *Stanley Parable*, we can refuse the narrator's suggestion—the beam will kill us—but unlike in *Stanley*, refusal has no interesting consequences; we just linger in a level we have already explored. In chapter 4 ("Stairs"), we are asked to press "Enter" to neutralize a speed limit that prevents us from quickly climbing a set of stairs. We can withhold the action, remaining in agonizingly slow ascent, or join in Davey's subversion of the original rules. These moments are paradigmatic: the system allows us to act, but only in ways that both move us along the rails and often violate an insanely dilatory design.

If *Beginner's Guide* is a game, it is arguably a queer one in the most general meaning of the word, an exploration of strange or deviant forms of play. Whoever or whatever he is, Coda is less game designer than conceptual artist. His levels carry absurd subtitles like "The Streetwise Fool," "Pornstars Die Too," and "Items You Love at Members-Only Prices." Coda appears to be a latter-day surrealist. His games subvert rational thought, substituting the inconsistent, associative flow of dreams. Many of the chapters feel like transcriptions of recurring nightmares—facing an audience across the footlights, or a lecture hall backed by a devouring black hole (been there), or a house with an endless cycle of cleaning chores (there also). Images of prisons, real and symbolic, occur with increasing frequency as the tour goes on.

There is also a sense in which *Beginner's Guide* is literally queer, or at least homo-antisocial. It is, after all, about the intense and ultimately toxic affection of one man for another. No sexual relationship is implied, and there seems no need to imagine one, but in Davey's account, which dominates until the final chapter, there is certainly intimacy. Davey cares deeply about his friend, whom he sees spiraling into a crippling depression. Coda's feelings are harder to describe, but in the early years, at least he seems willing to share his dream-games with Davey. In chapter 7, Coda pranks Davey with a zip file said to contain the ultimate game but which consists entirely of unopenable boxes—woebegone fan that he is, Davey tries each one. Even if it is actually the song of a divided self, the work deploys a fiction of relationship. We remember Ruberg's gloss of *Portal* as the story of a woman wandering through another woman's body (Ruberg 23). By analogy, *Beginner's Guide* shows us one man interfering with another man's imagination.

This recognition provides another reason to set *Beginner's Guide* apart from other works, even within the decidedly offbeat family of walking simulators. The work is not just queer but "weird" in the strict sense of the word: subject to irrational or inexplicable influences. *Beginner's Guide* is haunted. We could speak literally of Davey as an uncanny presence in Coda's games or vice versa, but there is also a ghostly influence from outside of the work. In 1962, Vladimir Nabokov published *Pale Fire*, a novel whose story unfolds through a series of annotations by a Russian émigré critic, Charles Kinbote, written into the manuscript of a poem by a recently deceased American writer, John Shade (Nabokov).[5] Kinbote is an iconic example of an unreliable narrator, a literary stalker who twists the dead man's poem around his personal delusions. One of the first scholars to explore the Nabokovian resonance, Berkan Şimşek, describes the novel as "a beginner's guide to *Beginner's Guide*" (Şimşek). There are very suggestive echoes—the parasitic pseudofriendship between artist and critic; misappropriation of an artwork; gradual exposure of the commentator's tampering with the work he describes. There are also important differences between the two stories. Kinbote is a madman who remains entirely within the grip of his delusions; Davey undergoes a crisis of recognition and achieves something like an epiphany. There are reasons to suspect Kinbote may have murdered Shade; all we have in *Beginner's Guide* is a very bitter breakup. Above all, there are no overt connections between the two works, no

---

5 The echoes of Nabokov were first brought to this writer's attention by Nathan Humpal, metadata librarian at University of Wisconsin–Milwaukee and game scholar nonpareil. Having made the connection himself, he found confirmation in Guido Pellegrini's "'The Beginner's Guide': Confessions of a Game Designer" (Pellegrini). I am also indebted to my student Ryan House, whose article on Wreden introduced me to *Beginner's Guide* (House).

allusions or intertextual references, no clear reason to suspect Wreden has read *Pale Fire*.

Whatever its resonances, the tension between Davey and Coda defines the work's descending narrative arc. At the outset, Davey tells us Coda has withdrawn from the game world. By publicizing Coda's genius, Davey hopes to encourage his friend to return to his art. As the tour of Coda's games proceeds, however, Davey's intrusions become more extensive and frequent and his commentary increasingly negative. Chapter 7 alludes to a debate between Davey and Coda over whether games should be playable. In chapter 9 ("Escape"), Davey warns that "this one is tough" and notes that Coda appears to be "unraveling" because he "lacks a voice to tell himself when enough is enough." In chapter 12 ("Theater"), Davey says Coda is "beginning to shut down," as iron bars repeatedly slam into the ground behind us. The text option that leads to the solution in chapter 12 ("Mobius") reads, "I can't keep making these." After this, Coda's supposed breakdown—or the demise of his friendship with Davey—proceeds to a climax. Chapter 14 ("Island") runs through a series of bewilderingly evocative dream images, ending with a fleeting glimpse of a naked, weeping figure glimpsed through prison bars. In chapter 15 ("Machine"), we play first as an interrogator putting hard questions to a machine that has stopped working. Eventually, we acquire a gun, which we can turn on an image of the machine. As its surface flies away, we see bits of computer code beneath.

Chapter 16 ("The Tower") is the last in the dated sequence. It is a "cold" level, Davey says. He tells us the game seems to despise its player. Reflecting on his attempt to celebrate meaning in Coda's games, he confesses, "I feel like I failed," and "I don't know this person." Crucially, Davey also reveals that he has made unannounced modifications to some of the levels and that bringing Coda's games to public attention has brought him fame and fulfillment. Finally, after ascending a series of twisty passages to the top of the tower, we enter a gallery space. In the display panels are messages from Coda to Davey accusing him of even deeper intrusion into his designs. Davey has added the lampposts we have seen in various levels, where they are

claimed as evidence of Coda's interest in coherent play. Coda specu-
lates that he has added solutions to some of his games under Davey's
influence. Above all, he indicts Davey for making his games public without his permission—in effect, stealing his work. He asks that
Davey have nothing further to do with him: "When I am around you,
I feel physically ill."

At this point, the game's central fiction collapses. Chapter 16 is followed by an epilogue whose status is eminently questionable. All the
previous Coda games have dates of composition. The epilogue has none.
It looks like another of Coda's compositions, but the link has been sev-
ered. Who dreamed this final dream, Davey or Coda? We cannot know
who these figures are to us now or if they were ever real. Davey's narration continues haltingly as we move through the first of several dream
transitions: railway station, tracks, great house, museum, salt mine,
station/museum again, finally into something that may be a sculpture
garden or a set of ruins. Davey is with us at the outset, talking more to
himself than to the player ("solution, solution, solution"). Eventually, he
gives up.

Coda's revulsion has shown Davey the awful depth of his vanity, of
his need for "more, more" doses of "external validation." He realizes
he has misunderstood Coda: "Maybe he just likes making prisons." He
apologizes for abandoning the player—"I know I said I would be there
to walk you through this"—but he has work to do now, presumably
the beginning of a new art no longer dependent on externalities. He
signs off abruptly, leaving us alone to make our way through a final set
of passages to something we have seen before: the energy beam from
chapter 1. When we stepped into the earlier instance, we found ourselves transported (in what Davey called a "glitch") through the ceiling
of the level, allowing us to look down on the maze we had just traversed.
Stepping into the final beam has the same effect, though the vast scale
of the maze we rise above suggests a city, a continent, or a planet—also,
strangely, the loops and whorls of a fingerprint. Above us is a starry
cosmos. The screen goes black.

But the game is not quite over, at least as we understand it. As is
often the case in ambitious games, there is a song to accompany the

credit roll. The singer is the Canadian vocalist Halina Heron. Music and lyrics are by Ryan Roth:

Turn back
Turn back from this cave
You said "let me prove that I'm brave,
Let me keep going."

But the cave goes for miles
And miles and miles
And you're so tired
But I know that you're strong

So turn back,
Turn ba-a-ack.

Strictly speaking, a song over credits is paratextual. We are not obligated to consider it part of the game's main business. However, after Coulton's incisive anthems for *Portal* and *Portal 2*, closing-credits songs have become more salient, particularly in Valve productions. There is good reason to suppose that, like "Still Alive" and "Want You Gone," the final song in *Beginner's Guide* was commissioned for the project. *Beginner's Guide* is dedicated "to R," who could be the writer of the song, Wreden's sometime collaborator and soundman Ryan Roth. Though the gameplay is over when we hear it, Roth's song needs to be considered in any attempt to understand the work—which is, after all, as much video (in this case, music video) as game.

Ever since Plato, caves have been associated in the scholarly mind with allegory. In *Gamer Theory*, McKenzie Wark restyles Plato's theater of sensual illusion into a game arcade. This imagined space summarizes the all-enclosing episteme of digital gaming (Wark 2). Perhaps this is the forbidden zone we are called on to reject. At the same time, sticking more closely to the terms of the Davey-Coda story suggests another interpretation. The cave might stand for the artistic catastrophe these two figures represent, the interminable contest between fame-seeking, public-facing expression (Davey) and an absolute formalism (Coda) that doesn't especially care if its prison-games can be played.[6] In this sense, the turn back is not a renunciation of gaming per se—though it comes at the end of an artwork that is not-quite-not a game—but perhaps a turn toward a better-conceived ludic future.

Maybe. The next offering by Wreden and Roth, *Absolutely: A True Crime Story*, does not seem especially promising in this regard (Wreden and Roth). Built in RPG Maker, the game is an ostensible "deconstruction" (Wreden's word) of Japanese role-playing games from the eighties and nineties. For some reason, it features a protagonist named Keanu Reeves, whom the player maneuvers around pixelated streets to prove he is not a serial stabber—unless we decide he is. Depending on our menu selections, he may also hand out dime bags of "the good stuff." This game seems less oriented toward a future aesthetic than toward the campy currency of games like *Cry$tal Warrior Ke$ha*—which have their virtues, though they hardly renounce external validation. As one reviewer noted, "For a meaningless parody project, *Absolutely: A True Crime Story* does a great job of showing just how compelling purposelessness [*sic*] referentiality can be" (Gach).

Perhaps Wreden's own turn back is not complete, or the maneuver may be more complicated than the song leads us to believe. There could be yet more moves in this dance—at this writing, Wreden is advertising for collaborators on another major project. Wark also imagines a turn away from the cave of gamespace, but conceptual dervish that she is, she continues the spin until she comes full circle, once more facing the cave: "The gamer arrives at the beginnings of a reflective life, a gamer theory, by stepping out of The Cave—and returning to it. . . . If the gamer is to hold gamespace to account in terms of something other than itself, it might not be that mere shadow of a shadow of the real, murky, formless that lurks like a residue in the corners. It might instead be the game proper, as it is played in The Cave. . . . The game shadows the real form of the algorithm" (Wark 19).

---

6 In a very humble way, we modeled this dilemma in our indefensibly ableist carousel game in chapter P-2, example 2.7.

Stepping back into the cave is the work of "gamer theory," which (as we hope this book demonstrates) involves as much playful practice as intellectual speculation. This theory-at-work asks for an understanding of the formal structures that underlie games: algorithms as well as the cultural logics, which Wark calls "allegorithms," in which these forms participate. In its most powerful form, we find gamer theory not in scholarly books but in games intended for experimental or deviant/devious play. Twine has been an important platform for efforts of this kind, and so it is to Twine games we make our way at last.

Ends of the Beginning

Updating Wark with the insights of Ruberg, Boluk, and Lemieux, we might say there are two possible avenues for allegorithmic criticism, or the therapeutic queering of games. One approach comes through theme or content: exploring divergent characters, settings, and situations. The thematic side of our critical moment is well represented in Twine games. Works like D. Squinkifer's *Quing's Quest VII*, discussed at length earlier, and Anthropy's *Hunt for the Gay Planet* (Anthropy, "Hunt") come at heteronormativity in game culture from the perspective of gay, trans, and gender-fluid characters. Porpentine's *Ultra Business Tycoon III* (Porpentine), Tom McHenry's *Tonight Dies the Moon* (McHenry), and Kris Ligman's *You Are Jeff Bezos* (Ligman, "You Are Jeff Bezos") satirize the obscenities of contemporary capitalism and the neoliberal orthodoxies of digital play. As Twine writers turn their attention to assumptions and operations of gameplay—the point where allegorithm meets algorithm—a second front of resistance opens.

This approach reinterprets games and play structurally, often at the level of basic player actions or game mechanics. The mechanics of intimacy discussed in earlier chapters present an opening to this strategy. Some years back, a Twine creator called neongrey pushed intimate mechanics across the species line in *Cat Petting Simulator 2014* (neongrey). We have already noted Porpentine's recruitment of the player's body as a writing surface in *With Those We Love Alive*. Neongrey extends this embodied aesthetic to the whole mammalian family. Petting a cat or some other friendly, furry creature reactivates primate grooming instincts lost long ago by naked apes. For humans not prevented by allergies or other conditions, petting can be a relaxing, centering, life-affirming experience. (Cats seem to like it too, though generally on their terms.) Until the arrival of something like William Gibson's "sims-tim," technologies can only represent this experience through images or symbols (Gibson). In conventional 3-D games, it would be a matter of a button-press and a resulting set of animations, maybe with a bass purr on the soundtrack. On a text-based platform like Twine, the representation can go deeper—not to mention more broadly in its implications.

In 2018 Ligman adapted neongrey's concept and crossed it with their own satiric agenda in *Pet Cats, Save the World* (Ligman, "Pet Cats"). The title itself could be considered as critique. Here is a game that calls out its play mechanic in its name. That move might not be original—the *Grand Theft Auto* series does something similar—but it prompts an interesting question: What if more games were named for their basic activities? The answer suggests GameStop shelves filled with seventies-style generic packaging sporting titles like *Shoot Shoot and Get Shot XXVII*, *Mutilate Undead Corpses LXV*, and *Jump Scare 4000*. If nothing else, Ligman's forthright title nicely frames player expectations: making some cats happy will adjust the moral arc of the universe. Here are three passages in sequence from the game:

> You take a sip of your drink and settle into your seat, allowing the delicious roasted warmth [of your favorite coffee] to spread through you.

> After a moment, you feel something brushing against your ankle. You look down to find that a long-haired smoky kitten of about 12 weeks has wandered over and rubbed against your leg.

> Pet the cat

> You reach down with your free hand and gently stroke a few fingers over the kitten's back.

> ICE has been dismantled.

<u>Pet the cat again</u>

The kitten rolls over onto their side for you, exposing their soft belly. You pet them while deftly avoiding the absolute terror zone.

In that same moment, a beloved old friend you've lost touch with suddenly texts you.

<u>Pet another cat</u> (Ligman, "Pet Cats")

And so forth, wonderfully. There are enough complications to keep the game interesting. Failing to optimize your textual choices for feline desire can result in a neutral ending; persist in petting against the grain and you can find yourself mauled and bitten at the bad end of the story. However, it is easy enough to reach the good end: a peaceful nap for you and your companion, with the state of the US government, the entertainment industry, and your character's finances much improved. Neongrey's earlier game became a refuge for people reeling from Gamergate, Brexit, and the 2016 US election. Ligman's satiric variation improves those psychic defenses.

Though in some ways just a modestly clever turn on a charming concept, *Pet Cats, Save the World* engages critically with game culture. Like neongrey's simulator, it explores an important alternative territory of desire, if not gender-queer then something like species-quaint.[7] In making this turn, the game attacks another idol of game culture, the fixation on epic or operatic narrative. Bogost has complained that so many games involve huge, existential threats to humanity and/or the universe, wondering why there are not more games about quiet, ordinary human experience (Bogost 18). *Pet Cats* answers this call with its own mechanic of intimacy, but Ligman's topical update of the earlier game adds an ironic spin. We indeed save the world, not with brutal heroics but through simple, animal bliss. Yet for all its undeniable delight,

---

7 Salter points out here the importance of games like *Catz* and *Dogz* in establishing interspecies affection as a theme of play. The Pokémon universe deserves mention also in this regard.

there is something bittersweet about this story. We may play ourselves into the ultimate catnap, but in real life, we will awaken to a broken universe where the effect of petting cats is only locally magical. Sadly, the most likely word after *wish fulfillment* is usually *fantasy*.

To fully understand Twine in its critical moment, we need to consider a game that reverses the polarity of desire in Ligman's sad, sweet ode to joy—a game that is in many ways a mirror image of his invention. This is Anna Anthropy's *Queers in Love at the End of the World* (Anthropy, "Queers"). Where *Pet Cats* offers instant gratification, this game inflicts equally swift and assured loss. In place of wish fulfillment, it gives us a blank but no less hyperreal apocalypse. In terms of its brief, broken diegesis, it is not a beginner's guide but a Dies Irae or hymn of endings. Yet this game is also a remarkably clear response to its critical moment. While it may not deliver the pleasures of a warm body—this is precisely what the game denies us—*Queers in Love* explains what it means to turn back, not so much from the cave of aesthetic crisis but from the horror of an impending future. In this respect, it may have its own strange message of difference, struggle, and hope.

Love and Permadeath

Electronic text replaces itself many times a second. Everything is wiped away and replaced either with the same screen state or a different one. Through its pattern of action and response inherited from both interactive fiction and hypertext, Twine invites both use and abuse of this effect. At its root, a digital computer is a logic processor, an adding machine—and a clock. Those who balk at identifying text-based works as video games because they generally lack graphics might remember that video, like cinema, is a technology of simulated motion. Motion implies time. As Bogost and Montfort showed in *Racing the Beam*, every video game is on the clock (Montfort and Bogost). This includes games of electronic text. McDaid's delta-t's turn the time. Ligman's enchanting cats change the world, averting an apocalypse. Other works, however, take apocalypse by the horns. In Pierre Chevalier's *Destroy / Wait* the player is given those twin options with a series of objects:

cities, trees, love (Chevalier). Choosing *wait* temporizes, extending the narrative. *Destroy* iterates the nightmare of history—and this option always comes at the end of each chain of evasion. The dark fatalism of that game is not the last word in this line, however. *Queers in Love* spares us the waiting.

Queers in Love at the End of the World plays with time across two registers. As its title indicates, it is set in an End Times where we are doomed to read a fatal sentence: "Everything is wiped away" (Anthropy, "Queers"). The nature of the apocalypse is never spelled out—not that we need it to be. Our time is filled with threats—as promised, we've come back to crisis in the end. Some of us live in the knowledge that the virus now rampant will likely kill us, and people we love, if we cannot avoid infection. Other agencies of doom are easy enough to imagine: climate convulsion, fascist holocaust, nuclear war—or perhaps, to return to fiction, just writerly imperative, driven by the sense that this world can't last.

If one hand of Anthropy's clock sums up millennia of human history, the second hand is just that: a counter that works through a ten-second interval, graphically depicted as a closing circle inside which we see how little time we have left. This is a text game that diabolically permits almost no time for reading, an engine of frustration and distraction. Long ago, somewhere in Anna Anthropy's early childhood, this writer produced a hypertext fiction called *Hegirascope* (Moulthrop, "Hegirascope"), which gives readers thirty seconds to select an outbound link before it chooses for them. At its debut, Michael Joyce called this work "the hypertext that reads itself" (Joyce). By analogy, *Queers in Love* would be the hypertext that withholds itself, even more steadfastly refusing our desire to read, among other desires. It gives us a mechanic not of intimacy but of stymied gratification—specifically so because the story it lays out describes desperate passion: "In the end, like you always said, it's just the two of you together. You have ten seconds, but there's so much you want to do: kiss her, hold her, take her hand, tell her."

Each of the verbs is hyperlinked, forming a fourfold gate that promises further development of this poignant scene. Here is one way the story can unfold:

[2—take]
You take her hand in yours, giving it a squeeze.

Look into her eyes.
Kiss her.
Put your hand up her skirt,
Just hold her hand.

[3—Just hold her hand]
Your fingers <u>twine</u> between hers. After all the forces that tried to keep you and her apart, maybe just holding her hand is <u>enough</u>.

[4a—twine]
What a powerful form of expression.

[4b—trying again, this time taking the link on "enough"]
Maybe it's enough to know that they lost.

[5—No onward link; time runs out]
Everything is wiped away.

That final phrase is both diegetic and procedural or ludonarrative: it announces the erasure of the lovers and their world and at the same time a clearing of the textual record. The final act in this game is *permadeath*, a halting state that erases all traces of previous progress (Juul 86).[8] However, the fatal passage includes two links, "Afterword" and "Restart." The first leads to a final statement, closing off the game. The other offers a fresh try from the initial passage ("In

---

8 This account is basically accurate, though it elides some details. Once "everything is wiped away," the player is locked into the terminal passage. Before this point, it is possible to use the browser "Back" button, making previous states of the reading technically accessible. Thus a record of play is indeed lost at the ending, constituting permadeath. While it remains, however, the usefulness of this record is tenuous. Using the "Back" function on any passage except the first or last spawns a new ten-second clock that runs concurrently with the original. The resulting fragmentation of the game's time scheme is more likely to produce bewilderment than coherent reading.

the end . . ."). In the record mentioned earlier, the fatal passage comes after we have completed the narrative line—twice actually, as we explore both branches from the third passage. As we will explain later, this reading was not produced entirely within the game. The wiping-away passage will appear whenever the ten-second timer runs out. In actual gameplay, this is likely to happen before the player reaches the end of even a four-passage story line, and some lines are longer. Thus until patience gives out, players are likely to take the restart option multiple times, reentering the hypertextual maze in an attempt to retrace previous steps.

Ruberg and Claudia Lo, who each read *Queers in Love* with notable insight, de-emphasize the deathwardness of the narrative, legitimately concentrating on the larger, processual aspects of play experience. For Ruberg, the game exemplifies the queering of "chrononormative" in-game death, a concept they call "permalife" (Ruberg). Lo makes a revealing comparison between Anthropy's game and so-called slow cinema:

> Expressing something as simple as recalling several memories at once is a complicated affair that requires at least four separate playthroughs. The ten-second limit actually serves to stretch out time rather than compress it. Like the lingering camera of slow cinema, the game spins out time in an indulgent manner. Slow cinema focuses on the unbelabored body, and its gaming counterpart is the unresponsive body incapable of acting quickly enough, or drastically enough, to satisfy the player. To know what is happening, the player must put in the work of reading, remembering, and racing against the timer. If slow cinema redeploys boredom in order to draw attention to "that genre's insistent disarticulation of the body onscreen from the body offscreen," then *Queers* redeploys panic in a similar way. In short, the panic and anxiety of the player is contrasted with the calm certainty of their character. (Lo 190)[9]

---

9 The included quotation is from Schoonover's article on slow cinema (Schoonover).

Lo's reading is remarkable in several ways. She understands hyper-textual multiplicity with a clarity that has eluded older critics. Bringing in the discourse of embodiment from slow-cinema theory once again illuminates the mechanics of intimacy. She also suggests, importantly, the potential of this game to deconstruct its form and medium.

We will work toward a similar end with perhaps a bit more emphasis on the discontinuity of the action, in contrast to its (quite real) para-cinematics. We take Lo's point about embodiment, though we will contextualize it differently. Given the likelihood of repetition, we describe the fatalities of *Queers in Love* as little permadeaths, after the French metaphor for sexual ecstasy. This suggestion eroticizes play and reading, but *Queers in Love* is, after all, a work of disrupted erotic fiction—many traversals are considerably more explicit than the one given earlier. As the title announces, the desire in play here is specifically queer. We can take this marking in its biopolitical sense, noting how the game's second-person address interpellates the player as someone who desires a queer partner. Anthropy's use of she/her pronouns for the lover is interesting, as it throws interpretive smoke at those still indoctrinated by patriarchy, where the feminine object may look deceptively like the default of straight, male poets. That history has no purchase here. Straight people must imagine themselves as lesbian—or better, recognize that gender reference and amatory choice are no longer governed by binaries.

While its grand themes may be love and loss, along the way, *Queers in Love* works through frustration and satisfaction of desire. As *Hegirascope* tried to do in its day, *Queers in Love* interrogates an ever-accelerating attention economy. Any simple transcript of the work will fail to capture its dynamic effects—something Ruberg and Lo also make clear. As we have noted, the representation of game narrative shown earlier does not record a single, uninterrupted play session. Though it may look like what Montfort calls a "traversal," a completed run through an interactive fiction, what you see here only simulates such a procedure (Montfort 32).

To reach almost any conclusion, players will most likely finesse or bypass the game's primary rules of play. In the case of the pseudotraversal, we reached the end of the story line by repeatedly restarting the game and taking screenshots of successive passages. Players with quicker hands and eyes might manage without such maneuvers, effectively speed-running the game; though, given the strict economy of attention, this style of play must limit comprehension. Playing through four passages in ten seconds leaves 2.5 seconds for each—plenty of time to read a quick sentence or phrase, but probably not enough for a reflective choice among the four links in the second passage or even the dual set in the third.

With this queering of play, Anthropy brings together the discourses of *ludus* and *eros*. Reading about acts of desire makes us desire to keep reading, holding to that middle state of narrative arousal or hypertextual possibility from which the circling clock inexorably excludes us. We can refer to Ruberg's chrononormativity and the ways queer games oppose it. Ruberg acknowledges the role of player death in disrupting traits like singularity and authority, though with appropriate skepticism, since player death can also be a component of reactionary fun (Ruberg 206). Arguably, Anthropy's disruptive design, with its *petite-permadeath*, falls squarely on the side of critique. This will be clear if we align her work with the examples used earlier in discussing chrononormativity: "Bandersnatch" and *Russian Doll*. The former is a genuine, if flawed, game, the latter a closed, gamelike arc converting game to ritual. We can try to fit *Queers in Love* into this binary scheme, perhaps on the game side, but despite its context (Anthropy wrote it for the Ludum Dare game jam in 2013), *Queers in Love* really belongs neither to the pole positions nor anywhere between. It is neither game nor ritual but *antigame*.

It is worth considering the several ways in which this description applies. First, while the possibility of winning is not an absolute requirement for games (see Juul), its absence is often significant. Diegetically, *Queers in Love* is unwinnable. Even if you reach the end of a narrative line before the clock winds down, you will meet the same fate as more dilatory players: everything will be wiped away. For all that the endings represent glorious *Liebestode*, they are also, symbolically speaking, versions of the same event, the great permadeath of "everything." We could apply the same analysis on the ludic side. Does winning mean optimal performance, speed-running to the end of a narrative line with only hasty glimpses of its contents? This would seem a strange requirement for a text game. Or should we define winning in completist terms as exploration of all possible story lines, an anthology or autopsy of all the game's possibilities? This solution shows more respect for Anthropy's prose, but what about the gameplay?

It is tempting to label *Queers in Love* an antigame because it is deliberately unplayable, designed to exhaust conventional ludic engagement. In fact, though, this work may be too playable. Wark at one point defines the goal of gamer theory as "to play at play itself, but from within the game" (Wark 019). She has in mind a turn back to the cave of gamespace duly informed by allegorithmic insight. It is possible to understand Anthropy's game in these terms: recognizing the game's insanely apocalyptic time scheme, we speed-run or screen-shoot to "play at play." However, there are other opinions on the playability of play. David Myers, whose neoformalism contrasts sharply with Wark's approach, says this about the hierarchy of playful forms: "If you play with a simulation, it becomes a game; if you play with a game it becomes just play; and if you play with play—well, you can't play with play: *play pwnz*"[10] (Myers 26; emphasis in original). Play is an absolute; we can play *at* playing (theory-play), but if we attempt a twist on play itself, we find ourselves played.

Arguably both *Queers in Love* and *Beginner's Guide* lie at the far end of Myers's second division. Beginning as simulations (of apocalypse in the first instance, of a gamer's portfolio in the second), they run through the territory of game, emerging into a liminal zone on the other side. They are in a way two expressions of a similar artistic crisis. Both share a sense of divided purpose, encapsulated in Wreden's Davey/Coda pairing. Davey is biographer and interpreter, social animal and extrovert, seeker of human truths. The Davey side of *Queers in Love* shows in its story lines the doomed desires of the fated lovers. Coda is a

---

10 That last word is hopelessly infected by its origins in toxic gamer culture. I quote it not for its ideology of dominance but because it marks in stark linguistic terms the limits of theory.

maker of impenetrable prisons and unwinnable games, an uncompromising, hermetical formalist. The Coda aspect of *Queers in Love* is its diabolical dynamic, the time-lock that repeatedly slams down a barrier, sealing us out.

Crisis is decisive, transformative, a point of decision or choice. Played to its logical and artistic conclusion, neither work remains simply a game, but the ways they resolve their crises are diametrically different. The ultimate guidance of *Beginner's Guide* is "turn back." The work is only nominally a game, using affordances of digital play mainly to advance its underlying monologue. It has more than half collapsed from game to gamelike arc, or from game to ritual. *Queers in Love*, on the other hand, manipulates game mechanics so radically that for many players, the experience transforms into pure, subversive play. We jump out of the game and play back against its structures.

In a way, *Queers in Love* also turns us back from the endless cavern of game-simulation-play, but with an important difference. In its queering of gameplay, this work turns crucially from crisis to critical practice. Davey deserts us in the cave, headed off to forge the uncreated conscience of his art. The creator of *Queers in Love* makes no such departure. She does not need to. Her work is already intensely engaged with its moment. It is, after all, a relentless deconstruction of apocalyptic thinking. To understand Anthropy's achievement, it is useful to slide back down the crisis-banister of the previous century, back to the heyday of TV's Control Voice—though the testimony we seek will come not from television but a visionary novel:

Taking and not giving back, demanding that "productivity" and "earnings" keep on increasing with time, the System remov[es] from the rest of the World these vast quantities of energy to keep its own tiny desperate fraction showing a profit: and not only most of humanity—most of the World, animal, vegetable, and mineral, is laid waste in the process. The System may or may not understand that it's only buying time. And that time is an artificial resource to begin with, of no value to anyone or anything but the System, which sooner or later must crash to its death, when its addiction to energy has become more than the rest of the World can supply, dragging with it innocent souls all along the chain of life. Living inside the System is like riding across the country in a bus driven by a maniac bent on suicide. . . . He is waiting beside the door of the bus in his pressed uniform. . . . As he nods you by, you catch a glimpse of his face, his insane, committed eyes, and you remember then, for a terrible few heartbeats, that of course it will end for you all in blood, in shock, without dignity—but there is meanwhile this trip to be on. . . . Over your seat, where there ought to be an advertising plaque, is instead a quote from Rilke: "Once, only once . . ." One of Their favorite slogans. No return, no salvation, no Cycle. (Pynchon 480)

These words were written between 1966 and 1971, on the cusp of the first oil shock, though they track with depressing accuracy our even later stage of capitalism and ecological trauma. They come from a work of fiction, *Gravity's Rainbow*, that in some ways epitomizes the late-twentieth-century counterculture, crying out for return, salvation, and Cycle against extraction and dissipation. Like our later game-fictions, the book was a crisis work, a push against artistic limits. Its narrative famously collapses into fragmentation and self-denial. It is also, in the root sense of the word, an apocalypse or revelation, its final scene a vision of extinction whose last word is replaced by a traumatic dash.

Despite the structural similarity of their abrupt endings, there is a considerable difference between the novel and the game. Pynchon's bus rider will die in "blood, shock, without dignity." Anthropy elides agony in her erasures and in many instances finishes her story lines with an affirmation: "When she kisses you back, she's telling you your needs are real." Or "So many people and institutions tried to pull you two apart. They all failed." Though in a millennial context, they/them becomes an alternative pronoun choice, Anthropy's usage in this last case reminds us of the old 1960s *Them*, oppressors of *Us*, and thus of the fact that we are still, in the new century, deeply concerned with systems. Pynchon's System—capitalized in every sense of the word—appears as "a bus driven by a maniac bent on suicide." While we are still on that terrible trip in the new century, we have access to other kinds of systems: computing machines, platforms, networks, games.

The system of 2013 differs crucially from its counterpart in 1973. We may not own or control it in any ultimately satisfying way, but we can at least try some strategic interventions. Anthropy's queer-critical perspective endows her with the core wisdom of counterculture—namely, that time is an artificial resource "of no value to anyone but the System" (Pynchon). As Lo's cinematic reading makes clear, time is negotiable. Time is in play. Anthropy's small-*s* system—the queer loops of her Twining—values time in its own nonnormative way. This new system is iterable: we can restart the game. It is also permutable: we are invited to jam or hack the game when it exceeds the bounds of play. With whatever odds against success, we can even attempt to play play itself. These ludic maneuvers amount to a major critical achievement.

Queers in Love at the End of the World deconstructs apocalypse, putting the terrible fatality of that all-too-present event literally under erasure. Pynchon's imperfect sentence comes on the last page of a book. It delivers, even as it fails to deliver, a final word. When "everything is wiped away" on the self-replacing screen of a video game, there is always the possibility of Cycle—sixty or so per second in fact—of reboot, of return to the mischievous dominion of play. We may yet be on that gas-guzzling bus of doom, its maniac driver at the national wheel, but we dream of difference and we have begun to express ourselves in the queer medium of games. At the very least, we can take down that plaque They hung over our seat. In place of "Once, only once," we can write—on our own flesh if need be—the graffito that is Anna Anthropy's afterword:

WHEN WE HAVE EACH OTHER WE HAVE EVERYTHING.

Works Cited

Anthropy, Anna. "Hunt for the Gay Planet." Cambridge, MA: Electronic Literature Organization, 2013. https://collection.eliterature.org/3/work.html?work=hunt-for-the-gay-planet.

———. "Queers in Love at the End of the World." itch.io, 2013. https://w.itch.io/end-of-the-world.

Bogost, Ian. *How to Do Things with Videogames.* University of Minnesota Press, 2011.

Boluk, Stephanie, and Patrick Lemieux. *Metagaming: Playing, Competing, Spectating, Cheating, Trading, Making, and Breaking Videogames*. University of Minnesota Press, 2017.

Borges, Jorge Luis. *Labyrinths: Selected Stories and Other Writings*. Translated by Donald Y. Yates. New Directions, 1962.

Brown v. Entertainment Merchants Association, 564 U.S. 786 (2011).

Chevalier, Pierre. *Destroy / Wait*. Lilinx, accessed June 2, 2020. http://lilinx.com/destroywait.

Elsaesser, Thomas. *Puzzle Films: Complex Storytelling in Contemporary Cinema*. Blackwell, 2009.

Gach, Ethan. "The Beginner's Guide Creators' New Game Is about Keanu Reeves Stabbing People." Kotaku, November 28, 2017. https://kotaku.com/1820805627.

Gibson, William. *Neuromancer*. Bantam Spectra, 1984.

Haraway, Donna J. *Staying with the Trouble: Making Kin in the Chthulucene*. Duke University Press, 2016.

Headland, Leslie, Jamie Babbit, and Natasha Lyonne, dir. *Russian Doll*. 2019. Netflix.

House, Ryan. "The Author Interface: Rethinking Authorship through Ludoliterary Analysis of *The Stanley Parable* and *The Beginner's Guide*." *Paradoxa* 29 (2017): 99–122.

Jones, Steven. *The Emergence of the Digital Humanities*. Routledge, 2014.

Joyce, Michael. Private conversation. October 1995.

Juul, Jesper. *The Art of Failure: An Essay on the Pain of Playing Video Games*. MIT Press, 2013.

Klimas, Chris. *Twine Past, Present, Future*. Cambridge, MA: NarraScope, 2019.

Kubrick, Stanley, dir. *Dr. Strangelove, or How I Learned to Stop Worrying and Love the Bomb*. 1964. MGM.

Levi-Strauss, Claude. *Savage Mind*. University of Chicago Press, 1962.

Ligman, Kris. "Pet Cats, Save the World." itch.io, 2018. https://direkris.itch.io/pet-cats-save-the-world.

———. "You Are Jeff Bezos." itch.io, 2018. https://direkris.itch.io/you-are-jeff-bezos.

Lo, Claudia. "'Everything Is Wiped Away': Queer Temporality in *Queers in Love at the End of the World*." *Camera Obscura* 32, no. 2 (2017): 185–92.

Malaby, Thomas. "Institutions in Play: Practices of Legitimation in Games." In *Playful Participatory Practices*. Edited by P. Abend and V. Ossa. Springer, 2020, 15–30.

McHenry, Tom. *Tonight Dies the Moon*. Self-published, 2015. https://tommchenry.itch.io/tonight-dies-the-moon.

Montfort, Nick. *Twisty Little Passages: An Approach to Interactive Fiction*. MIT Press, 2003.

Montfort, Nick, and Ian Bogost. *Racing the Beam: The Atari Video Computer System*. MIT Press, 2009.

Moulthrop, Stuart. "Hegirascope 2." *New River* 3 (1997). http://www.cddc.vt.edu/journals/newriver/moulthrop/HGS2/Hegirascope.html.

———. "'Turn Back from This Cave': The Weirdness of *The Beginner's Guide*." *Journal of Gaming and Virtual Worlds* 12, no. 1 (2020): 91–103.

Myers, David. *Play Redux: The Form of Computer Games*. University of Michigan Press, 2010.

Nabokov, Vladimir. *Pale Fire*. G. P. Putnam's Sons, 1962.

neongrey. "Cat Petting Simulator 2014." itch.io, 2014. https://neongrey.itch.io/pet-that -cat.

Nolan, Christopher. *Memento*. 2000. Newmarket Films.

Pellegrini, Guido. "'The Beginner's Guide': Confessions of a Game Designer." PopOptiq, accessed June 2, 2020. https://www.popoptiq.com/the-beginner/.

Porpentine. *Ultra Business Tycoon III*. Self-published, 2013. http://slimedaughter.com/ games/twine/tycoon/.

Pynchon, Thomas. *Gravity's Rainbow*. Penguin, 1995.

Ramis, Harold. *Groundhog Day*. 1993. Columbia Pictures.

Ruberg, Bo. "Permalife: Video Games and the Queerness of Living." *Journal of Gaming and Virtual Worlds* 9, no. 2 (2017): 159–73.

Schoonover, Karl. "Wastrels of Time: Slow Cinema's Laboring Body, the Political Spectator, and the Queer." *Framework: The Journal of Cinema and Media* 53, no. 1 (2012): 65–78.

Simon, Matt. "All This Chaos Might Be Giving You 'Crisis Fatigue.'" *Wired*, June 4, 2020. https://www.wired.com/story/crisis-fatigue/.

Şimşek, Berkan. *The Beginner's Guide for Play Fire: The Medium's Effects on Fictional Works*. Academia, accessed June 2, 2020. https://www.academia.edu/34959760/The _Beginners_Guide_for_Play_Fire_The_Mediums_Effects_on_Fictional_Works.

Slade, David. "Bandersnatch." *Black Mirror*, 2018. Netflix.

Tykwer, Tom. *Lola Rennt*. 1998. Prokino Filmverlein.

Wark, McKenzie. *Gamer Theory*. Cambridge, MA: Harvard University Press, 2007.

Whedon, Joss, and Drew Goddard. *The Cabin in the Woods*. 2012. Lionsgate.

Wikipedia. S.v. "The Outer Limits (1963 TV Series)." Accessed June 2, 2020. https://en .wikipedia.org/wiki/The_Outer_Limits_(1963_TV_series).

Wreden, Davey. *The Beginner's Guide*. Everything Unlimited, 2015.

Wreden, Davey, and William Pugh. *The Stanley Parable*. Galactic Cafe, 2011.

Wreden, Davey, and Ryan Roth. *Absolutely: A True Crime Story*. dualryan, 2017.

Conceptual Twining

In our fifth practical chapter, we turn from the technical to the conceptual. In previous practicals, we built up a repertoire of capabilities. You learned to do increasingly sophisticated things with Twine: linked storytelling, textual variation, formulaic text generation, and inclusion of other media. We experimented with Harlowe, SugarCube, and JavaScript. This chapter, which will rely exclusively on Chapbook, will mainly use coding techniques we have already presented, so it serves at least partly as a capstone, reviewing and consolidating the work so far. Our emphasis here is on using Twine in the service of various schemes and ideas—what we call *conceptual Twining*.

The word *concept* can be hard to define with precision and easy to toss around loosely. "Reality—what a concept!" as Robin Williams's Mork used to say. For the purposes of this chapter, *concept* refers to an expression or design that operates simultaneously on two levels. One of these is direct or literal. In our five examples, we will build more or less familiar Twine texts: fragmentary stories, little games, riddles. Aside from whatever dubious charm these texts may have in themselves, they invite further reflection on Twine and its uses and perhaps on stories, games, and language generally.

> ◊ We continue the typographic conventions of earlier practi-
> cal chapters, where invitation/instructions to type in code frag-
> ments are boxed and marked with the symbol you see here.
> You can, of course, skip either the typing or the intervening
> explanations, though, in a chapter dedicated to concept, those
> explanatory bits are especially important.

Supporting materials for this chapter can be found online at https://
github.com/AMSUCF/Twining. See our discussion at the beginning of
chapter P-1 about using the .html and .txt files to follow along or adapt
our code to your own purposes.

Example 5.1: *Labyrinth*

This project has a history. In 1991, Stuart wrote *Victory Garden*, a
long-form hypertext fiction developed with an authoring tool called
Storyspace, which was then under development by Jay David Bolter
and Michael Joyce. In those days, many fewer people knew about the
internet (then called "Internet" with a big *I*), and the World Wide Web
was, no kidding, *an application program*, what we would today call a
web browser—only nobody in those days ever said, "the Web," with
or without capital letters. Like text adventures a decade or so earlier,
hypertext was a fresh concept. No one knew exactly what could be
done with it, though a few people had ideas.

The conception for *Victory Garden* was a big, tangled mass of stories
intersecting at various points. This was by no means an original invention, as anyone up on their George Eliot, John Dos Passos, or Richard
Linklater will tell you, but its application to digital media up to then
had belonged mainly to parser-based games. With all respect to that
form, some of us, including Michael Joyce and Judy Malloy, wanted to
try something different—*a story that would change each time you read
it*, as Michael said—shifting the stress from game to story.

Given that emphasis, readers needed to enter the narrative thicket
as unpredictably as possible, but the early version of Storyspace made
this difficult—it had no capacity to choose a passage at random. With

randomness unavailable, the author reckoned the next best thing might be confusion, so he designed an elaborate set of passages with bifold links—a verbal labyrinth—in which it was hoped readers might productively wander toward the main events, discovering various predefined ways to get there.

To make this process of discovery more meaningful, the labyrinth asked participants to build a sentence one word or phrase at a time. At each place in the story, readers chose between two candidates for the next word in the sentence. The succeeding place repeated the sentence as it currently stood and either offered another pair of choices or came to a conclusion. That conclusion was a complete sentence that somehow stamped the reader's ticket for the ride that followed.

Three decades is a long time, in which interactive storytelling has made considerable progress, but we think the old labyrinth concept remains useful. Our first project in this chapter implements the labyrinth in Twine.

◊ Start a Twine story, change the story format to Chapbook if necessary, and give it any title you like, though *Labyrinth* seems an obvious suggestion. Change the name of the default first passage to "Origin" and enter the following text:

```
In the

>[[green bag]]
>[[vicinity of metaphor]]
```

Close this passage and have a look at your structure view. You'll see two linked passages, both so far unwritten. We'll get to one of them shortly, but for the moment, a note about those right angle brackets (greater-than signs) at the left of each link. In Chapbook, these symbols identify a *fork*, a choice of two or more options that are set off typographically when the passage is displayed.

To keep this chapter from growing tedious, we'll only explore one branch from the initial prompt—only one course of the labyrinth, in technical terms. You are free to develop the rest of the maze in your own way. The online materials include a completed version of this project with all possibilities written out, and we'll discuss a few before we're done. For the moment, let's pursue the green bag.

◊ In the passage labeled "green bag," type the following:

```
In the green bag

>[[we found]]
>[[it was possible]]
```

As you can see, each phrase plausibly extends this rather strange sentence, and at the start of each passage, we display the sentence as currently composed. The fork construction gives us another two links and another pair of auto-generated passages. Like spectators at a magic show, we applaud the Amazing Klimas every time this trick comes off. We'll go with the first one, "we found."

◊ In the passage labeled "we found," type the following:

```
In the green bag we found

>[[the recipe for Detroit]]
>[[a rich deposit of language]]
```

Once again, we have a fork and a pair of resulting passages—though don't worry, we're nearly at the end of this line. This time, we'll choose the top bunk.

◊ In the passage labeled "the recipe for Detroit," type the following:

```
In the green bag we found the recipe for Detroit
```

What follows from this declaration is negotiable. We have a suggestion, but you can do differently if you like. You'll note we haven't added terminal punctuation to our nearly finished sentence. You could put in a period and then write more sentences to follow, making this the first full passage of a branching story in prose. Something like this: "In the green bag we found the recipe for Detroit. 'Put that back this instant!' the Chief Investigator thundered. Which we did, but not before committing the contents to memory."

Links out of such a passage, or a different passage of your own invention, would then be up to you. Before we wrap this project up, we'll mention a variant outcome that turns the labyrinth concept to another purpose. What if the completed sentence functions not as the first line of a story but as the title of a poem? All the other possible outcomes from the labyrinth might work likewise so that the word-maze would function as a hypertextual framework for a collection of poems. There's a lovely coincidence here: in the print tradition, such a collection is often called a *chapbook*. Here's our version of the recipe for Detroit:

> *cars the size of cars*
> *implying*
> *a continent of erasure*
> *in the scattering of a people*
> *plus two ideas,*
> *unpromising,*
> *and the given name of an advertised lawyer*
> *featuring seven types of ambiguity,*
> *overlooking a sunrise, and*
> *one sad invention*
> *with statistics,*
> *disaggregated,*
> *with a warm place to put the results.*

Poem notwithstanding, here is the structure map of our verbal maze:

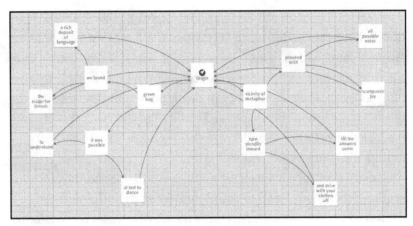

Figure 23: Structure map of the *Labyrinth* project

As you can see, our labyrinth offers seven other sentence trajectories:

> In the green bag we found a rich deposit of language
> In the green bag it was possible to understand
> In the green bag it was possible at last to dance
> In the vicinity of metaphor turn steadily inward till the answers
> come
> In the vicinity of metaphor turn steadily inward and drive with
> your clothes off
> In the vicinity of metaphor proceed with all possible noise
> In the vicinity of metaphor proceed with encompassing joy

In the completed version, there's a bit of free verse or prose poetry at the end of each one. We have used this labyrinthine model in various classes over the years, and our students have come up with many interesting applications of the stepwise-approach concept: as introductions for other sorts of creative work, such as video or music; as a test of attitudes or preferences; and of course, the inevitable guessing game with one or more ostensibly right answers. Every game a riddle, as we'll see in our final example. Meanwhile, let's continue with overtures and opening acts.

Example 5.2: *Spooky*

This example bears a certain resemblance to the first in that it, too, is designed as a preamble or entry point for further fiction. This one works more in generalities or atmosphere instead of the specificity of a title or first line. The concept here is mood-setting, foreshadowing, or coalescence—a distillation or inspiration of horror. In addition to reviewing our familiar method of randomized text selection, this example also demonstrates an approach to page layout that works around some basic limitations of Chapbook. No art without constraints.

The first step of this exercise can take place either in or out of Twine, as you like. You need a list of words and phrases that might either come from or be associated with a tale of horror. If you've read Mary Shelley or Poe or Lovecraft or played *Call of Cthulhu*, this will be a cinch. You could write your list on paper, in a convenient word processing document, or in a Twine passage. If you're going to do the last, perform this first step before writing.

> ◊ Open a new story and name it *Spooky*. If you're using the default passage to write your list, you may want to name it "List." Otherwise, name your first passage "wordcloud."
>
> Write the list as previously described. The length is up to you. A set of ten items is probably minimal; twenty-five feels like more than enough.

As you have probably guessed, we'll use that word list as a database for random selection with the substitution grammar technique we demonstrated in chapters P-2 and P-3. It should be very familiar by now.

> ◊ If you didn't designate or set up a passage called "wordcloud" in the previous step, do that now. Open that passage and type the following:
>
> ```
> words: []
> --
> ```

We've started a variables section for the "wordcloud" passage, and in that section, we have declared an array variable called "words." Fill in (the technical term is *populate*) that array with the words and phrases in your list, being careful to enclose each one in single quotation marks, separated by commas. There's no comma following the last item. For reference, here's a selection from our version of the array:

```
'groan','splatter','apparition','testament','Ab
igail','unliving','rupture','invasion','ovuloid
','pulsing mass','pullulating','unquiet','blood-
chilling','viscera','abomination','immense','b
eyond the veil','partly decomposed','unnatural
fusion','funebrous','rotting fruit','spoiled mea
t','shambling','shade','axehead','severing','unr
easoning','revenant','shrieks'
```

◊ Now we'll add one more line to our variables section, immediately below the definition of the array:

```
theLink: words[Math.floor(random.fraction*words.
length)]
```

Be careful to leave in place the two dashes that close the variables section.

You've seen this code before, but it's sufficiently complicated to make a review worthwhile. We're declaring a variable, *theWord*, to hold a selection from the *words* array. Selections from an array are made by putting a number into [square brackets]. The complicated expression inside the brackets will be processed into a convenient number—you'll remember the process. The *random.fraction* expression is from Chapbook. It returns a decimal number between zero and one. Multiplying that number by the length of the array gives us another decimal greater than zero. We use the *floor* method of the JavaScript *Math* object to round this fraction down to the nearest integer, which will be between zero and the length of the array minus one. All arrays are numbered beginning with zero, so the last item has a number one less than the overall length. That's what we mean by convenient number.

◊ Now that we have *theLink*, let's serve it up. After the two dashes closing the variables section, type the following:

```
{theLink}
```

This insert calls on Twine to display whatever value is stored in "theLink."

Make sure "wordcloud" is identified as the start point of your story, then run or test your project several times. You should see one word or phrase from your shop of horrors every time you restart. Since nothing prevents repetition, you may see the same selection on successive tests, so be patient. The more words and phrases in your array, the lower the chance any item will repeat—though larger sets increase your exposure to mistyping.

In case of repetition, we generally try up to five times before assuming an error. If you see nothing on-screen, check to be sure you entered the line in the previous step properly, using curly braces, not square brackets. Assuming no mistake there, check the definition of your array. It's very easy to forget a quotation mark or comma.

This might be a good time to reread our section on debugging in chapter P-2. If you're struggling to find the problem, copy the contents of your array to a temporary passage and replace them with one or two test words. Once you've found the bug, or if your code was fine in the first place, you are ready to proceed.

This project is designed to do a bit more than display one word or phrase at a time. If you look at the completed version in the online materials, you'll see it presents a scattering of words across the screen, each a live link. Clicking on any of the horror words refreshes the screen with a new set of links, likely at different positions, the better to emphasize the randomness of the effect.

Making all this happen requires more than what we currently have in the "wordcloud" passage. Let's start by getting just one of these horrifying links to appear.

◊ In the text body of "wordcloud"—the part below the double dashes—take out the line we added in the previous step and replace it with this:

```
[[{theLink}->wordcloud]]
```

This line has a lot going on, typographically. It starts with double square brackets, the fundamental Twine convention for creating a hypertext link. Inside the brackets, there's a set of curly braces around the name of our random-phrase variable, "theLink," and then the familiar basic syntax of a stylized arrow -> pointing to the destination passage "wordcloud." Yes, that means this link reloads the passage that contains it, a trick we've seen previously.

Now it's time to test or run. You should see a single word or phrase from your array as before, but this time hyperlinked. Clicking on the link should change what is displayed, though remember our earlier advice about possible repetition. If you find errors, use the procedure we recommended to root them out. If all is well, proceed.

So far, we haven't done anything to introduce the scattered or floaty design aesthetic that appears in the finished version. We'll add those pieces now.

◊ Edit the text body of "wordcloud," adding lines above and below the single line that is there presently, ending up with this:

```
<br /><br />
<div style="text-align: 5em">
[[{theLink}->wordcloud]]
</div>
```

If what you just typed looks like part of a web page, congratulations, you know something about HTML, the basic construction kit of the World Wide Web. More people should be like you. We've pointed out that Twine is made of JavaScript, which is also part of web infrastructure. It's the scripting language that extends the functionality of web pages, and Twine stories are delivered in that form. Just as we can slip JavaScript expressions into Chapbook en passant, we can also turn to HTML when needed. The first HTML effect we use here is the line break tag *
*. Two of these tags in sequence, as we have here, create a skipped line or vertical space on the screen.

Next, we introduce a division, or *DIV*, using the paired tags or *container <div></div>*. A DIV is a block-level element of a web page—or in this case, Twine passage—one that is set off from previous elements as paragraphs are. (We could also have used the *P* or paragraph container here.) Notice the tag that introduces our DIV. It contains some added information:

```
<div style='text-indent: 5em'>
```

This tag calls on the third major element of web technology, CSS. That invocation happens in the expression *style=*. A style sheet, technically an *inline style sheet*, in this case, modifies the appearance of the DIV to which it is attached. Here we call for that element to be indented five ems from the left margin. If you're a graphic designer or typographer, you know an em is the width of an em dash, like this one—which varies with the font family and size being used. Web designers prefer these relative measurements nowadays. For our purposes, let's just say it's a unit of horizontal space. (It's a game of ems, not inches.)

If you run and test now, you should see your randomly selected link offset from both the top and left of the window. This is part of the effect we're aiming at, but the full concept involves multiple, randomly chosen links, placed differently on the screen at each reload. We can get this to happen with the tools at our disposal—HTML, CSS, and

Chapbook—but we'll need to blend them into a slightly more complicated cocktail. Let's handle the vertical spacing first, as that's the more familiar part of the recipe.

◊ Once again edit the text body of "wordcloud." Replace the pair of *br /* tags with what you see here. Leave everything else alone.

```
{vSpace}
<div style="text-align: 5em">
[[{theLink}->wordcloud]]
</div>
```

You've just replaced those *br /* tags with a variable that doesn't yet exist, so let's take care of that. In your variables section, below the line that defines *theLink*, add the following:

```
breakers: ['<br />','<br /><br />','<br /><br
/><br />']
vSpace: breakers[Math.floor(random.
fraction*breakers.length)]
```

The *breakers* array contains three collections of *br /* tags, which when applied will set our DIV at variable distances from any element above it or from the top of the screen. The *vSpace* variable contains one of these collections (or strings). If you test your project at this point, you should see the randomized link appearing at a variety of vertical positions.

We could use the same array-selector strategy for the initial DIV tag, using different values for the em spacing, but this would involve a whole lot of repetitive typing. The only thing we really need to change is the number that precedes "em." We achieve this effect by using a variable for vertical spacing and using the Chapbook *random* function when we generate that variable. Here's the way it works:

> ◊ In the variables section of "wordcloud," below the material
> you added in the previous step, type in the following:
>
> ```
> hSpace: "<div style='text-indent:" + random.d10
> + "em'>"
> ```

Pay superclose attention to the placement of single and double quotation marks in this line—we need to use both. We take the familiar inline style sheet and cut it apart where the number occurs. Instead of that number, we insert the expression *random.d10*, which generates an integer between 1 and 10, inclusive. Notice we need the string 'em' and the closing angle bracket at the end. All this is enclosed in a set of double quotation marks because it is a string, a sequence of words and numbers treated as text. When we invoke this string variable, it is added to the code of our passage and treated by the browser as an HTML expression, which is how browsers treat any text containing angle brackets.

If you test your project now, your randomized link should appear at unpredictable locations both horizontally and vertically. At this point, we've built the core pieces of the project, but there are still important elements missing. So far, we only have one link in play, but we want several. We'll handle that feature next.

It might occur to you that all we need to do in order to include more links is duplicate the code that brings in the first link. That's partly right, but we need to adjust things a bit because of a certain feature of Chapbook. That story format allows us to define variables only once, when the passage loads into memory. So if we use our *hSpace* and *vSpace* variables for additional links, they'll have the same vertical and horizontal offsets as the first one. That's not what we want. Here's the work-around, beginning with the vertical spacing:

> ◊ In the variables section of "wordcloud," find the section that
> handles vertical spacing. You can leave the line that defines the
> *breakers* array as it is, but replace the line that follows, the one
> that defines *vSpace*, with the following:

```
vSpace1: breakers[Math.floor(random.
fraction*breakers.length)]
vSpace2: breakers[Math.floor(random.
fraction*breakers.length)]
vSpace3: breakers[Math.floor(random.
fraction*breakers.length)]
```

You can copy the original definition of *vSpace* and paste it in three times to define its new companions. Be sure to add the numerals that make these three variables individual.

This new code creates a trio of variables, each with a selection from the *breakers* array. Two or more of them may have the same selection, but that's not a problem for this project. We only have room for a limited amount of vertical spacing, anyway. Next, we'll handle horizontal spacing:

◊ Replace the line that currently defines *hSpace* with this set:

```
hSpace1: "<div style='text-indent:" + random.d10
+ "em'>"
hSpace2: "<div style='text-indent:" + random.d10
+ "em'>"
hSpace3: "<div style='text-indent:" + random.d10
+ "em'>"
```

Copying and pasting will work here as well, since the only difference in these lines, as in the vertical spacing, is the numeral that makes each horizontal spacer unique.

In order to support our scheme, we'll also need three servings of our link text. By now, the procedure should be familiar:

◊ Replace the line that currently defines *theLink* with this threesome:

```
theLink1: words[Math.floor(random.fraction*words.
length)]
theLink2: words[Math.floor(random.fraction*words.
length)]
theLink3: words[Math.floor(random.fraction*words.
length)]
```

Copying and pasting is fine, but once again, be sure you've added the numbers to the variable names. No other changes are necessary—we're making three unique selections from our *words* array, using the same procedure each time, but with potentially a different random selector.

Now we need to adjust the contents of the text body in "wordcloud" to support three floating-horror links.

◊ Again, remember that we're in the text body this time and not the variables section. The code that currently conjures up our solo link looks like this:

```
{vSpace}
{hSpace}
[[{theLink}->wordcloud]]
</div>
```

Veteran web coders may find this a bit disturbing because having a closing tag like *</div>* without an initial *<div>* tag is ordinarily an error. However, that initial tag is loaded into the *hSpace* variable, so we're fine.

If we want three links, all we need to do is copy and paste our link construction two times, making necessary adjustments:

```
{vSpace1}
```

```
{hSpace1}
[[{theLink1}->wordcloud]]
</div>

{vSpace2}
{hSpace2}
[[{theLink2}->wordcloud]]
</div>

{vSpace3}
{hSpace3}
[[{theLink3}->wordcloud]]
</div>
```

Do not forget to change all three variable invocations—for vertical spacing, horizontal spacing, and link text—in each of the three segments. The numbers in the variable names are crucial.

You can test at this point. You should see three live links, randomly planted on your screen, in an arrangement that changes each time you reload. Clicking any of the links will cause a reload. If that's what you're seeing, you are ready to proceed to the final stage of construction: offering the reader a chance to leave the horrifying word cloud and enter the story proper. We'll specify that we may not make this offer every time the passage loads, and if we do offer the exit, we'll do it only once per iteration. We'll build these features in four steps. The two in the middle are a bit detailed, but the last is very simple, as is the first:

◊ Let's add one final asset to our variables section. This variable could be introduced anywhere in the section, but we'll put it below everything we currently have. Add this line:

```
exitPos: random.d4
```

> As you'll remember, *random.d4* returns a value of 1, 2, 3, or 4. We actually only need a range of 1 to 3, but that would require a bit more tedious typing. Using the virtual d4 slightly reduces the chances of our exit link appearing, but this won't be a problem.
>
> If you want to improve the odds for the exit link, you could use this instruction instead:
>
> ```
> exitPos: Math.ceil(random.fraction*3)
> ```

The *exitPos* variable determines which of our three horror links will be replaced by a link to the main story. Remember, though, that we want the possibility of the escape link not appearing in any given iteration. Doing that will involve one last piece of detailed coding, described in our second step:

> ◊ In the main text body of the "wordcloud" passage, find the first of the three link units. Delete it and replace it with the following:
>
> ```
> {vSpace1}
> {hSpace1}
> [if exitPos===1 && random.coinFlip]
> [[Begin]]
> [else]
> [[{theLink1}->wordcloud]]
> </div>
> [continued]
> ```

The first two lines in this section are the same as in the previous version—we're still invoking the strings that create randomized horizontal and vertical spacing. After that, there are some changes. We introduce an *if* condition that makes the display of our link to the "Begin" passage depend on two factors: *exitPos* being 1, and the value of *random. coinFlip* being true. There is a one in four chance of the former condition (if we use d4) and a one in two chance of the latter. That means a one in eight chance our first link will be replaced with the story exit.

After the standard link to the "Begin" passage, there's an *else* statement, after which the rest of this code chunk is as it was in the beginning, except for the *[continued]* statement at the very end. This statement terminates the *if/else* logic and lets us treat the next link segment independently.

You might want to test at this point. Keep trying until you see your first link replaced by the link to "Begin." If that doesn't happen after about ten attempts, you probably have an error. Hopefully, this procedure will go fine, and you can proceed to the third and penultimate step:

◊ Modify the remaining two link segments to have a similar structure to the first, though remember to change the crucial numbers—the value of *exitPos* and the numbers of the spacer variables—as indicated. Here's what you should have:

```
{vSpace2}
{hSpace2}
[if exitPos===2 && random.coinFlip]
[[Begin]]
[else]
[[{theLink2}->wordcloud]]
</div>
[continued]

{vSpace3}
{hSpace3}
[if exitPos===3 && random.coinFlip]
[[Begin]]
[else]
[[{theLink3}->wordcloud]]
</div>
```

You don't need to include *[continued]* after the third option, as nothing follows it.

Now there's just one easy thing to do, which we won't bother writing out as a formal instruction. Go back to your structure map and find the new passage called "Begin." Write something unspeakably spooky there. For testing purposes, you might also want a link back to "wordcloud."

And so our maleficent mechanism is complete. On a technical level, this project shows how to weave semi-intricate cobwebs of code, grafting disembodied bits of HTML into Chapbook with diabolical abandon. One code-packed passage ("wordcloud") can support endless cycles and iterations or as many as your reader can stand. Conceptually, this example builds on the tension between anticipation and action—a main component of horror—or between a fitful, recursive flow of possibilities and the forward progress of conventional storytelling.

Like the labyrinth of our first example, the evocative links of example 5.2 could be applied to other genres and purposes besides the one suggested here. The links in our example are based on a somewhat arbitrary collection of words, but as we hinted, they might be drawn directly from the text they precede. Readers in the waiting room would thus encounter hints and teasers for what awaits beyond the entry. Taking this concept further could bring us back to the original motivation for the labyrinth in *Victory Garden*—randomized beginnings. Suppose each of those brief quotations from the work contained a live link to the passage where its word or phrase occurs. In a sizeable work, there could be a large constellation of starting points. If that kind of sprawl is not desirable, various prefatory links might cluster around a more limited number of options. The alternation between link-scattering and reading ahead might also be used between sections of a multipart work. Possibilities abound. The horror . . .

Example 5.3: *Active Measures*

Let's start this one with a disclaimer: we have nothing against text adventures. Both authors of this book have been significantly influenced by games of this kind, one of us before the advent of computer graphics, the other afterward. We belong to communities like ELO and IFTF, where turn-based, procedural stories are treated with love and respect. The Inform programming language, to which we have frequently referred in this book, means much to us. One of us, no kidding, has been known to dream in it.

However, as we pointed out all the way back in chapter P-1, there are two ways to think about procedural storytelling. One approach favors procedure, the other story. You will recall we discussed contrasting ways to treat links in Twine, either by separating them formally from the narrative, in the manner of interactive fictions and game books, or by planting the links in a single narrative stream, as in hypertext fiction. The distinction is largely arbitrary, and many writers do both, but this next exercise pits one mode against the other. It's a concept.

> ◊ Start a Twine story, remembering to use the Chapbook story format, and call it *Active Measures*, or what you will. Change the name of the default first passage to "Action!" Yes, Twine allows exclamation points in passage names, and you can name the passage something else if you like, provided you make relevant changes as we go. Enter the following text:
>
> ```
> verbs: ['Take','Drop','Examine','Eat']
> theVerb: verbs[Math.floor(random.fraction*verbs.
> length)]
> --
> ```

Here it is again, our inevitable grammar of substitution. Do we know how to do anything else with code? Maybe—see the bonus practical chapter in the appendices. Do we *want* to do anything else? Not all that much, apparently.

Note that we're working on the variables section of our passage, that's what those two dashes on the final line indicate. The topmost line of this code chunk declares an array, which in this case is a comma-separated list of words (strings) in a specific sequence. The second line defines a variable called *theVerb* and assigns it a randomly chosen item from the *verbs* array. But you knew that!

There's quite a bit more to do with "Action!," but we should first say a few things about the design of this project. The "Action!" passage will hold data and logic we'll use to generate randomized phrases on demand—again, something we've done in many previous exercises. There will be two other passages in this project, one calling back to "Action!" in a self-perpetuating loop, and the other representing the way out of that loop: the same pattern we used in the previous example. We'll come to these passages eventually. Meanwhile, let's build more of the "Action!" passage. It's pretty extensive.

◊ Enter three blank lines ahead of the double dashes. Move your cursor up one line and type in the following. There's a lot of typing here. If you want to shorten any of the arrays, feel free. You could also expand them without causing any problems.

```
nouns: ['eyedropper','skillet','cleaning
robot','fishbowl','phrasebook']
theNoun: nouns[Math.floor(random.fraction*nouns.
length)]

IVerbs: ['Jump','Cry','Scream','Wait','Pass','Br
eathe','Exist','Persist','Think']
theIVerb: IVerbs[Math.floor(random.
fraction*IVerbs.length)]

directions: ['north','east','south','west','back
','forward','up','down','nowhere','anywhere','si
deways','to pieces']
theDir: directions[Math.floor(random.
fraction*directions.length)]

askTell: ['Ask','Tell','Notify','Enlighten','In
form']
theAskTell: askTell[Math.floor(random.
fraction*askTell.length)]
```

```
persons: ['Mr. Jones','Starbird','Flux Man','Jim
my','Otto','Maisie','Hermione']
thePerson: persons[Math.floor(random.
fraction*persons.length)]

topics: ['astrometry','fine wines','outwitting
the Troll','contents of the box','the
key','stuff']
theTopic: topics[Math.floor(random.
fraction*topics.length)]
```

As always, you do not need to put in these lines exactly as they appear. You can (should!) substitute your own words in any of these lists, provided yours are of the kind that is called for—singular nouns in the *nouns* array, proper names in the *persons* array, and so forth. As indicated, you can delete or add items. Because we use the *length* parameter of the array, you can change the size of the array without breaking the code. Do be careful to use single quotes around every word and make sure the commas go outside of the quotation marks. In the selection lines, the ones that invoke the *Math* object, pay close attention to the succession of parentheses and square brackets.

You are building the raw materials for several generated sentences or phrases. The next chunk of code contains the templates for those phrases.

◊ Still within the "Action!" passage, below the last line you typed before, enter the following:

```
phrase1: theVerb + ' the ' + theNoun
phrase2: theIVerb
phrase3: "Go " + theDir
phrase4: theAskTell + " " + thePerson + " about
" + theTopic
phrase5: "Give the " + theNoun + " to " +
thePerson
```

```
phrase6: "Take the " + theNoun + " from " +
thePerson
```

There are six variables, each containing a phrase generated from the arrays and variables you previously defined. As you can see, five of these phrases are multiword combinations. Be careful to type spaces where they are called for, around words like *to* and *from*. Notice that *phrase2* simply invokes the premade selection from *IVerbs*. That's because this phrase consists of a single word, an intransitive verb like *Jump* or *Wait*.

That was quite a lot of detail, though we're only about halfway done with "Action!" Don't worry, the rest of the project is less verbose. After resting eyes, wrists, and fingers, once more unto the breach.

◊ Still within the "Action!" passage, after the line that defines *phrase6*, make a new line and type the following:

```
theRoll: Math.ceil(random.fraction*6)
```

This line generates a random number between 1 and 6. Chapbook offers a perfectly good way to do this—*random.d6*—but we'll eventually want to roll a seven-sided die, which Chapbook does not provide for directly. That's why we're using *random.fraction* rounded up with the Java-Script *Math* object. Now one more push to finish the "Action!" passage.

◊ Find the double dashes that mark the end of your variables section. If you inadvertently took them out at some point, put them back. Below those dashes, type the following:

```
[if theRoll===1]
[[{phrase1}->Scene]]
[if theRoll===2]
[[{phrase2}->Scene]]
[if theRoll===3]
[[{phrase3}->Scene]]
[if theRoll===4]
```

```
[[{phrase4}->Scene]]
[if theRoll===5]
[[{phrase5}->Scene]]
[if theRoll===6]
[[{phrase6}->Scene]]
```

If you can already tell what these lines do, congratulations—you're a Twine master! If they're a mystery, read on. What we have here is a sixfold chain of *if* conditions, tracking the possible values of our virtual dice roll. You may recall that in Chapbook, the *if* condition may be used only outside of the variables section and only to control the display of text. We're meeting both requirements here, though the text we're displaying—contents of one of our phrase variables—will show up within a passage other than the one we're working on here. Don't freak, we'll explain that in a bit.

Meanwhile, a bit more detail of the step you just completed. The line following each of our *if* conditions contains a hyperlink whose verbal content is one of our variables. You saw this design pattern in the previous example. Each of these links goes to the "Scene" passage. It's time to write that passage.

◊ The passage called "Scene" will be added to your structure as soon as you close the "Action!" passage. Open "Scene" and type what you see here:

```
{embed passage: 'Action!'}
```

```
{embed passage: 'Action!'}
```

```
{embed passage: 'Action!'}
```

```
{embed passage: 'Action!'}
```

Yes, it's the same instruction four times, embedding four instances of the "Action!" scene. Embedding opens or activates the passage, so we get different content each time. It's as if we had a room containing doors that let us enter varying versions of another room. If this idea isn't working for you, you're not watching enough *Doctor Who*.

Science fiction aside, we can also explain this in terms of programming. As we've seen, embedding is a superpowerful technique that lets us keep all our gnarly code stuff in one place, the better to refine it. If you've worked with object-oriented programming, you'll know the importance of functions or methods, which are bits of code that can be reused (or *invoked*) flexibly as a program operates. An embedded, code-intensive passage does much the same thing as a custom method in JavaScript or Objective C. Chapbook is great for beginners but equally useful for more ambitious coders—which you now are.

We're almost ready to test our project, though we need one slight change. By default, the passage marked as the start of our story is "Action!" because it was created first. While having an embedded passage so marked will not cause your project to break, it also won't put anything on the screen. Select the "Scene" passage, hover your mouse over it, and click on the three dots at the right of the pop-up, which causes a menu to appear. Select "Start Story Here." Now play or test your story.

You should see four links, each displaying a phrase composed by the generator code in "Action!" Click on any link and the current view will refresh with four new links. So far, all we have is another version of our text-generation demos from chapter P-3 or example 5.2—though with perhaps a twist on the content. However, we have one more trick to add.

◊ Close the passage called "Scene" and reopen "Action!" Find the line in the variables section that defines *theRoll*. Change the 6 to a 7. You should have this:

```
theRoll: Math.ceil(random.fraction*7)
```

This is a small change, but important. We're now rolling a (virtual) seven-sided die. Note our use of the *ceil* function to round fraction to integer—this function rounds up to the maximum value, eschewing zero. We'll use this difference for an important feature of the work.

◊ Right after the line you just worked on (the one defining *theRoll*), add the following:

```
escapes: ['Refuse all further action','Prefer
not to','Declare an adventure strike','Stop
suspending disbelief','Stop putting up with this
noise','Have about enough of this']
theEscape: escapes[Math.floor(random.
fraction*escapes.length)]
```

This is one final array-and-selector combination, allowing us to generate a phrase that will be uniquely useful. Meanwhile, at the very bottom of "Action!," below the sixth *if* condition, add a seventh condition as follows:

```
[if theRoll===7]
[[{theEscape}->Escape]]
```

We now have the possibility of throwing a lucky seven. When that happens, the link that will come up in the "Scene" passage will contain one of our "escape" phrases, and it will be linked to a new passage called "Escape."

Close "Action!" and open that new passage. Type anything you like there. We have:

```
And so our story begins for real.
```

You can test the project at this point. When "Scene" comes up, you should see four links. There is a one in seven chance one of these links will contain an "escape" phrase. Clicking on a nonescape link refreshes "Scene" with four more links.

Technically speaking, you have just built a recursive hypertext with the possibility of aleatory termination—look at you! More to the point, you've participated, we're ashamed to admit, in a send-up of the adventure-game idiom. All the nonescape options are based somewhat loosely on the actions that may be taken in a text adventure. "Take," "Go," "Ask/about"—even "Jump" and "Wait"—are either valid or plausible verbs in systems like TADS or Inform. If one were inclined to make fun of text adventures, insinuating that true story is more like old-fashioned fiction, this might be one way to do it. There's your concept. Whether this is something that needs to be done, we leave to the reader's judgment. If done at all, it must be with affectionate understanding—sibling rivalry or something equally childish. The next time someone shows us a text adventure that makes fun of hypertext fiction, we promise to smile. Yes, Sis, those links are as ridiculous as flared pants.

Of course, it is entirely possible to flip this binary script and write a version of this concept where the real fun lies with the action links—maybe they could do something other than just refresh the screen. The conventional narrative in this version might serve as the obstacle or distraction from the proper story of player action.

Though this chapter is devoted more to concept than technique, we can't resist some technical reflection on the exercise we've just completed. The "Action!" passage uses code far less efficiently than would a comparable structure in Harlowe or JavaScript. As we've seen in chapter P-3, JavaScript permits the use of a structure called *switch* to select one of several phrase templates on each run. Here we have to generate all seven possibilities each time "Action!" is embedded, or twenty-eight times every time "Scene" is accessed.

Why don't we care? Because we're spoiled, twenty-first-century code monkeys who casually toy with machines their grandparents could barely imagine. For us, knocking numbers around is cheap and easy. It's worth remembering that computation implies *heat*—every mathematical operation uses energy—so if playing with Twine makes you interested in learning more ambitious programming, be advised that the world beyond the playground makes harsher demands.

Example 5.4: The Tumblers,
or a Tune Out of Season

This project has two inspirations. One is Thomas Pynchon's attribution of "high magic to low puns" (Pynchon 95) The other is Walt Kelly's comic strip *Pogo*, in which we gamboled through postwar America with the laid-back critters of Okefenokee Swamp. Kelly also knew the power of puns: he lampooned the corrosive Spiro T. Agnew as a snorting, fuming "A. Gnu." As we will see, he also had a certain way with holiday songs:

> *Deck us all with Boston Charlie,*
> *Walla Walla, Wash., an' Kalamazoo!*
> *Nora's freezin' on the trolley,*
> *Swaller dollar cauliflower alley-garoo! (Kelly 9)*

Seasonal mondegreenery[1] will figure a bit later in our project. First let's consider the concept, which we admit has more to do with hackery than even midrange magic. As in previous examples, we'll be introducing no new Twine features, relying mainly on the *cycling link* modifier we used in chapter P-3. Keeping that feature in mind, we start with three recognitions:

1. A cycling link is much the same thing as a *tumbler*, the numbered cylinder of a combination lock.
2. In the right context, numbers and words are conveniently interchangeable.
3. A certain low pun comes to mind.

---

1 A *mondegreen* is a misheard lyric, such as "and Lady Mondegreen" for "and laid him on the green" in "Barbara Allen," or "'scuse me while I kiss this guy" in Jimi Hendrix's "Purple Haze." The actual reading there is "kiss the sky," but what's life without variety? We're also hugely fond of another of Walt Kelly's festive mondegreens, "Good King Sauerkraut look out, on your feets uneven . . ."

The mise-en-scène, or situational framing, is especially important in this example. Let's get to it.

◊ Start a new Twine story called anything you like—for instance, *Tumblers*. Name the default first passage "A Tune Out of Season." In this passage, type the following, or any variation you prefer:

```
Lunch with insufferable Uncle Buster in the
Tumbolia Room. You would do anything to
escape. "Why was Ten glancing so warily up the
numberline?" the old man asks, you suppose you
should say rhetorically, though that's far too
nice a word. "Because . . . ?"
```

Do your best to stifle that groan if you know the punchline. Yes, it's an insufferable-uncle thing. It is also the absurd structure on which we will build our not-so-high concept.

◊ Add a new paragraph to "A Tune Out of Season":

```
Meanwhile, some conventioneers at the bar are
attempting a seasonal song, though it is the
middle of {cycling link for: 'month', choices:
['June', 'July', 'August']}. They have some odd
ideas about the lyrics:
```

We'll get to those lyrics in a bit. First, a review of the *cycling link* modifier. You'll remember it designates a variable—in this case, *month*—for which we supply choices as a comma-separated list enclosed in square brackets. Yes, that's the same form used to define an array because the option list of a cycling link is indeed an array. However, instead of selecting from this array at random, which is our usual method, we'll let Twine do what it does with cycling links, presenting them in sequence. Each time the player clicks the linked month, it will move ahead to the next of the three options, looping back to June from August. The solution to this puzzle—don't make us say it—consists of three integers. We could offer all twelve months, but the story says the song is out of season, so we're using only the summer months.

◊ Now let's fill in what the chorus is singing in the next room. This time we'll use the full range of options:

```
"{cycling link for: 'song', choices: ['12
mummers slumming', '11 typers griping', '10
Fords a-beeping', '9 maybes branching', '8
trades a-bilking', '7 swamps a-brimming',
'6 tweets a-braying', 'FIVE OLD SPRINGS!',
'4 appalling nerds', '3 clenched pens', '2
hurtful shoves', 'AND A CARTRIDGE WITH A GAME
FREE!']}."
```

Feel free to write your own variations. For the final line, we considered "A SMART FRIDGE WITH SOME SPARE PEAS" and in true *Pogo* idiom, "SOME CARTILAGE FOR YOUR TEARED KNEE." The words matter less than their ordinal position, which is why our convention-goers are singing a sequential carol at the wrong end of the calendar. By now, you may know the final number in our virtual combination, though we have one more alphanumeric trick to play:

◊ Add the following new paragraph:

```
To further unsettle your sanity, the folks at
the next table have started flinging breadsticks
at one another. They are about to proceed to the
cutlery. "Let me put this in a language you will
understand," one of them is saying: "{cycling
link for: 'word', choices: ['MEIYOU','NE','NAY',
'NAE','IIYE','NON','NIX','NEM','NEIN']}!"
```

You can have more or fewer options for *word*, but we're looking for a particular number, *nein*? With the final tumbler in place, we need to make the combination testable.

◊ Add this link at the bottom of "A Tune Out of Season":

```
[[Solution?]]
```

Close the passage and return to the structure map, where you'll find the new passage "Solution?" That's where we'll check out the settings of the three cycling links. (*Three cycling links, two drop-downs, and a . . .* sorry, that's another song.)

◊ In the passage titled "Solution?," enter the following:

```
[if month === 'July' && song === '8 trades
a-bilking' && word === 'NEIN']
"Is that the time?" you notice. "Gosh, late for
that root canal!" And out the door.
```

If our player has set the three cyclers to the correct set of values—really, don't make us say it—our hero gets to flee Uncle Buster and his abominable puns. However, there are 323 possibilities for a wrong answer—$(3 \times 12 \times 9) - 1$—so we need to allow for incorrect solutions.

◊ In the passage titled "Solution?" add the following:

```
[else]
You're stuck here until you solve the stupid
riddle. [[Keep trying->A Tune Out of Season]]

Hint: three numbers in sequence, horrible
pun . . .
```

If you want to be especially kind to your player, you could build an escalating series of hints, like so:

```
[else]
You're stuck here until you solve the stupid
riddle. [[Keep trying->A Tune Out of Season]]

[if passage.visits === 1]
Hint: three numbers in sequence, horrible
pun . . .
[if passage.visits === 2]
Hint: three numbers in sequence, horrible pun,
numerical cannibalism . . .
[if passage.visits === 3]
OK, enough hints: BECAUSE SEVEN ATE NINE!
```

And there it is. This is, of course, an entirely nonserious application of the combination-lock concept, but there's no reason it couldn't be used less foolishly. The options in the cycling links don't have to contain or imply numbers, for instance. The point of the game might be to choose the right sequential settings, presumably in response to some reasonably useful hint, with the cycling options sending the narration or dialogue in meaningful directions. Say we're in a story called *Room 112*, set in a motel, and the combination for each successive passage is the next address along the hallway (114, 116, 118, and so forth), with the correct settings of the cyclers advancing the story, revealing complications among the characters and other things. Or the combinations for successive passages might be permutations of the original, or products of some mathematical operation implied in the text. Or there could be only one cycler in each of many passages, with a final challenge to match some extended series of digits across all of them. Also, of course, it's possible to generate a fresh solution each time the story runs—we leave further word-number permutations to your imagination.

Example 5.5: *Twine Box*

Like the first project in this chapter, this last one has a history, though its origin is more recent than that of the old labyrinth. *Twine Box* was written in the pandemic spring of 2020, just as much of the world was entering lockdown.[2] No surprise that the project is about an enclosed space and the contents of a box. It is also yet another riddle-text. The concept for this project is not simply thematic, though—it is also geometrical. Any box or cube can be flattened into the pattern of a *T*:

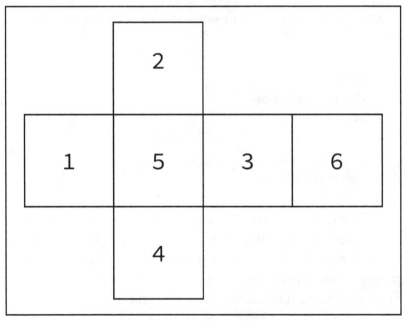

Figure 24: Conceptual diagram of the *Twine Box* project

The six cells represent the sides of the box. You could print this diagram, cut out the image, and fold it into a cube. This image of a deconstructed box led to the architectural scheme for our story: six rooms,

2 The completed version of this project included in the online materials, *Twine Box*, was the basis for a somewhat different story called *Dread Box*, built on the same six-room architecture. It appears in the first issue of *Digital Review*. See http://thedigitalreview.com/issue00/dread-box/begin.html.

each with four transitional links leading to adjacent faces of the cube. You can add the links to the diagram. Starting at the left edge of cell 1 and working clockwise, you might label these links *A* through *D*. Each link has a counterpart on the cell to which it is joined in the cube. Link A connects to the right-hand edge of cell 6, the top of the box. Link B connects to a matching link on the left edge of cell 2. Link C goes on the shared edge with cell 5, and link D, at the bottom of cell 1, matches its partner on the left edge of cell 4. The same logic will define the link pairs in the remaining cells. If you're extending the alphabetic series, as we suggest, your last link pair will be labeled *L*. There are twelve pairs in all.

Moving from geometry to story, let's identify the six rooms as follows:

1 Lecture Hall
2 Committee Room
3 Writers Room
4 Lunch Room
5 Scary Basement
6 Top of the World

These are, of course, fanciful assignments. When it comes to Twine, some of us have a hard time sticking with realism. Through a certain dream-logic, each of these rooms is intended to be a place where our player character can encounter suggestive traces of language—which is to say, clues to the riddle. Let's get started on the build.

◊ Start a new Twine story, making sure your format is set to Chapbook, and name it *Twine Box*, or what you will. Name the default passage "1 The Lecture Hall." Create five more passages and name each according to the aforementioned scheme. In passage "1 The Lecture Hall," enter the following text:

```
Oak paneling, mangled chair-desks, lingering
aura of angst and ennui. At the battered podium,
a vile cigar smokes itself out. The ancient
```

chalkboard could use scrubbing. You can make out
some words there:

Repeat for each of the five other passages. Here are recommended
texts for each:

The Committee Room
The door opens just enough to admit the owlish
mug of the deputy assistant secretary. "Private
meeting," she informs you. Inside, you hear
privileged voices saying:

The Writers Room
When you attempt to peek in, an associate
producer rumbles, "GO PLAY IN THE STREET" and
tosses a wad of ill-considered passages toward
your person. "CAN'T YOU SEE WE'VE GOT AN I.F.
TO FINISH HERE?" As the door slams, you hear
unstable voices shouting:

The Lunch Room
For some reason, nobody in here has any clothes
on. Guess we forgot to tell you it's a Naked
Lunchroom! All eyes stare at your overdressed
self. As you back out the door, you hear people
muttering, "In your dreams." Also:

omygosh It's the SCARY BASEMENT!
An ancient bulb flickers feebly and surrenders
to the darkness. The room is filled with uncanny
shapes . . . canopic jars . . . eldritch
apparatuses . . . a cleaner of vacuum. A voice
like an old cigar wails, "BEGONE!" You are about
to do just that when a hovering presence appears,
scrawling words across the skin of reality:

```
Top of the World
It's a cross between one of those revolving
restaurants and the bridge of some uncanonical
starship. The reception droid takes your
soulprint and shows you to a mediatronic
terminal. You idly thumb some flashing red
indicators and jettison the city's antimatter
core. Diners at nearby tables murmur:
```

Eventually, there will be text following the colons in each of the six passages, but before we come to that, let's take care of the navigational links.

◊ Open the passage "1 The Lecture Hall." Below the existing text, skip a line and add the following:

```
<div style="text-align: center">
[[3 Writers Room]] [[6 Top of the World]] [[4
Lunch Room]] [[5 Scary Basement]]
</div>
```

There are more elegant ways to arrange these links, but we'll let function win over form for once. Our only concession to formatting is an HTML DIV with centered alignment. We require the player to visit all six rooms, which means you need to be careful about the placement of links, making a full traversal possible. Here are the link sets for the five other passages:

```
2 Committee Room
[[3 Writers Room]] [[5 Scary Basement]] [[4
Lunch Room]] [[6 Top of the World]]


3 Writers Room
[[6 Top of the World]] [[1 The Lecture Hall]]
[[5 Scary Basement]] [[2 Committee Room]]
```

```
4 Lunch Room
[[5 Scary Basement]] [[1 The Lecture Hall]] [[6
Top of the World]] [[2 Committee Room]]


5 Scary Basement
[[3 Writers Room]] [[1 The Lecture Hall]] [[4
Lunch Room]] [[2 Committee Room]]


6 Top of the World
[[3 Writers Room]] [[2 Committee Room]] [[4
Lunch Room]] [[1 The Lecture Hall]]
```

Make the necessary additions to each passage and test your project. You should be able to move from room to room, and if you're keeping track, you should visit all of them eventually. Before we're finished, each room will offer a set of clues about the answer to the riddle, the contents of the conceptual box. In order to ensure exposure to these clues, we want the player to visit every room at least once. When all rooms have been entered, we'll display a new link in each of the rooms to a seventh passage called "INSIDE," representing the interior of the box. Because there's a tedious amount of text involved in the *if* condition for our inside link, we'll set it up as an embedded passage.

◊ Create a new passage and name it "tracker." Enter the following:

```
[if r1 && r2 && r3 && r4 && r5 && r6]
GO [[INSIDE]]
```

We haven't yet created any of those variables starting with *r*—we'll do that in the next step. An explanation about the syntax first. Our r-series variables will be Booleans, with possible values of *true* or *false*. Saying "if *r1*" asks if *r1* has the value *true*. We could write out "if *r1* === true," but that's more typing. Remember, the double ampersands stand for the logical *and* operator, which means all six subconditions much be true for the main condition to be met.

When you close the "tracker" passage, you will see a new passage called "INSIDE," which we'll leave blank for the moment. First, we need to make sure our r-series variables (*r* stands for *room*) are properly taken care of. We're designing our system so that all six variables need to be checked whenever we enter a room. For that to happen, Twine needs to know about those variables. So far, it doesn't. There's only one proper solution to this problem: create a new starter passage.

◊ Make a new passage and name it "And . . . box." (Yes, there's a mixed metaphor here.) Enter the following into this passage:

```
r1: false
r2: false
r3: false
r4: false
r5: false
r6: false
--
TWINE BOX

[[begin->1 The Lecture Hall]]
```

This is a title passage, with our six tracking variables initially declared and set to *false* in the variables section. Doing this will get us off on the right foot with "tracker."

Next, we have to allow each of our room-tracking variables to become *true*.

◊ Open the passage "1 The Lecture Hall." Insert two blank lines in front of its current contents. Add the following variables section:

```
r1: true

--
```

Make similar changes to the other five room passages, changing the number part of the variable each time (r2 for the second
room, r3 for the third, and so on).

Next, we need to embed the "tracker" passage in the link options
for each room.

◊ Open the passage "1 The Lecture Hall." In the text body, below
the existing series of four links, add the following:

```
{embed passage: 'tracker'}
```

Place this line within the HTML DIV container—before the *</div>*
tag. Repeat this procedure for each of the other five room passages. You'll be inserting the same line in the same position
for each.

Now the rules of our game are largely implemented. Each time we
visit a room, the "tracker" logic will check to see if we have visited all six
rooms, in which case it will display the link to "INSIDE." Each passage
records its visited state in its *r* variable. You should test your project
at this point, visiting each room. When you come to the last unvisited
room, you should see the "INSIDE" link.

We'll continue to defer work on that climactic passage because we
need to provide the clues we want the player to encounter in each room.
In order to make this game minimally playable, we'll pick our clues
randomly from large sets, using our substitution grammar. However,
we'll want clues of two kinds—right and wrong—so we'll need two sets.
Again, we'll handle this feature with embedded passages.

◊ Create a new passage and name it "right." Enter the following:

```
rt: ["thing with feathers","fairey
obama","ancient funnyman bob","and
change","fingers crossed"]

theText: rt[Math.floor(random.fraction*rt.
length)]
--
{theText}
```

The basic scheme here should be entirely familiar: define an array, then a variable that holds one randomly selected item from that array. Both of those things happen in the variables section. In the main text body of this passage, we display the contents of our selector variable. We've included only a small selection from the array used in the finished version of this project. You will want many more than five options for both the "right" and "wrong" clue sets. You can have as many as you want. As for the word those clues indicate, you can probably figure that out, especially if you remember a certain story from Greek mythology. Now let's take care of our not-so-helpful clues.

◊ Create a new passage and name it "wrong." Enter the following:

```
wt: ["seventh of six","if you can read
this","this is not a clue","time fades away","is
time emits I","I is another","you are not
reading this"]

theText: wt[Math.floor(random.fraction*wt.
length)]
--
{theText}
```

The form of this passage is identical to the "right" passage. You'll want to expand the set of options considerably. The wrong-headed clues can be any misleading or nonsensical expression. Technically, they should not lead to the right solution, though as you'll see, it's not a huge problem if they inadvertently do. Now that we've set up our two clue sets, we need to make use of them. We'll do that in the next steps.

◊ Open passage "1 The Lecture Hall." In the main text body, following the sentence that ends in a colon, skip a line and add the following:

```
{embed passage: 'cluetrain'}
```

Add the same line in the same position in the other five rooms.

Our "cluetrain" passage will take selections from the "right" and "wrong" clue sets, put them in a certain order, and make them ready to appear in each of our rooms. Here's how all that is done:

◊ Create a new passage called "cluetrain"—embedding a passage does not create that passage—and enter the following:

```
<div style="text-indent: 2em">
[if random.coinFlip]
{embed passage: 'wrong'}
[continued]

{embed passage: 'right'}

[if random.coinFlip]
{embed passage: 'wrong'}
[continued]

[if random.coinFlip]
{embed passage: 'wrong'}
[continued]
</div>
```

Inside our familiar HTML DIV container you'll see a series of *embed passage* inserts. Yes, you can embed passages in an embedded passage—just don't embed a passage in itself, as we've already cautioned. The player never suspects how much bed-hopping is going on behind the scenes. In the "cluetrain" passage, the first, third, and fourth embed the "wrong" clue generator. The second embeds the "right" generator. However, we add a coinflip *if* condition to all our wrong-way clues, so they each have a fifty/fifty chance of appearing. Notice we add a *[continued]* modifier to terminate the *if* condition each time. Don't omit that detail.

According to this scheme, our right-leading clue will always appear, though it will sometimes be the first and perhaps only clue. When the coin lands the right way for the initial "wrong" embed, it will be the second clue. This arrangement gives what we consider a minimally interesting amount of variation, though that's a subjective judgment.

It's time to test the project again. You should see between one and four clues following the introductory sentence each time you visit a room. If all is well, you are ready to begin the final stages.

◊ Because it is referenced in a conventional link, the passage called "INSIDE" should already exist. (If it doesn't, go back and check the step in which you set up the link to that passage in the embedded "tracker" passage.) Open "INSIDE" and enter the following:

```
**~~inside the box~~**
So here we are--turning outside in--reaching the
heart of the matter--coming down to core.

Moment of truth . . . or not: _**what's in the
box?**_
```

Those double asterisks and tildes, as well as the underscores around the final phrase, are formatting characters. Lots of dramatic effect here. The payoff is in the selection, for which we'll use a familiar device:

◊ Below what you typed in the previous step, enter the following:

```
{cycling link for: 'answer', choices: ['puzzle',
'nothingness','illusion','ignorance','secrecy','
concealment','hope']}

_**[[REVEAL]]**_
```

Because of the basic scheme of the cycling link, the options will always be presented in the order you code them. The complete version of this project uses *random.d6* to branch among six variations of the cycling link, each with the right answer in a different position. In this version, there are also different wrong options in each version of the cycler. For our purposes, though, let's stay with the simple solution. Now it only remains to test the outcome.

◊ The passage "REVEAL" should have been added to your structure. Open it and enter the following:

```
[if answer==='hope']
Always.
[else]
The box retains its mystery. {restart link,
label: 'Play on'}
```

Besides revealing the answer to the riddle of the "Twine Box" (but you knew), this final piece of code uses a Chapbook feature we first saw in chapter P-2: the *restart link* insert. As the name suggests, a restart link erases all system and custom variables in play, including our *r* series of trackers, and takes us back to our launch passage, which we called "And . . . box." Our six tracking variables are redeclared there, reset to *false*, and we are ready to begin anew.

We've made the design choice to have a fresh start after a wrong guess, requiring the player to receive clues in all six rooms before the "INSIDE" link appears again. If we wanted to be more generous, we could have avoided the restart link and used an ordinary link back to the lecture hall or any of the other rooms.

And so the secrets of the mystery box have all been revealed, and with that, our tour of conceptual Twine comes to an end. We've dwelt heavily on riddles and puzzles in these five exercises, but as we've seen in preceding chapters, Twine can be used for many more purposes—creative, expressive, analytical, persuasive, and even therapeutic. What you find inside the Twine box, or what you decide to put there, is entirely up to you.

At this point, we're also very near the formal end of *Twining* itself—the conclusion awaits—though as you might expect from such a rambling and rambunctious enterprise, even that final chapter will not really be the end. We invite you to carry on with the appendices, including the interview with Chris Klimas with which this project started and the talk with Dan Cox that guided its growth. For those who still haven't had enough code tinkering, there is even a bonus practical chapter that finds its way "Beyond Twine."

Though if you're like us, you can always find a bit of Twine somewhere around the place.

Works Cited

Kelly, Walt. *Deck Us All with Boston Charlie*. New York: Simon & Schuster, 1963.
Pynchon, Thomas. *The Crying of Lot 49*. Philadelphia: Lippincott, 1966.

Conclusion

Forever Twine

Twine has been around for more than a decade now. There have been two formal releases of the core software, coordinated with four major story formats. Based on download statistics, Twine has thousands of users around the world, clustered largely in game development, academia, and entertainment (Klimas). Major media outlets have noticed the role of *Depression Quest* in Gamergate (see Hudson) and Charlie Brooker's use of Twine for the "Bandersnatch" treatment. Something looking suspiciously like a Twine game appeared in an episode of Cartoon Network's *Adventure Time* in 2016 (Han and Ito). However, as we have previously noted, the best measure of Twine's cultural impact may be *Videogames for Humans*, the massive compendium of Twine writers playing and commenting on one another's games that we have already mentioned (merritt k). We could also point to the increasing prevalence of Twine pieces in portfolios of aspiring game designers and the platform's formal relationship with the IFTF, founded to assure continuity in the tools and institutions of the text-based game community (Interactive Fiction Technology Foundation).

These developments give reason to look forward another ten years or more. The idea of doing creative things with hypertext links and related scripting seems an indelible part of digital culture. Twine supplies an important tool for this work, so we imagine a future Twine, even a forever Twine. This book has concentrated notably on works appearing between (roughly) 2012 and 2018, which we might consider a heyday or first harvest. We carefully avoid the term *golden age*, which has a way of making those tagged with it feel antique before their time. For true believers, at least, Twine is timeless. We feel the work will go on, in and out of game, art, and literary worlds. Twine or Twine-like efforts a decade hence may be notably different from the games and fictions we have profiled. In ten years, works in the Twine line could be mainly auditory (see the next section), or graphical, or generally used for psychotherapy, or written exclusively by machines.

Before dreaming any further, however, we need to check our perspective. Each author of this book has several decades of intellectual, artistic, and personal investments in digital storytelling across multiple platforms. Where Twine is concerned, we teach with it and we make things with it. Lately, we may have begun to think with it. We also have our own oblique connections to the circumstances of Twine's creation: Anastasia explored theirs in chapter T-2; I will say more about mine at the end of this chapter. As writers of a book meant to promote Twine's use and appreciation, we have an obvious bias.

If You Can Read This . . .

Consider a more objective view. In 2017, the artist and critic John Cayley, a field leader in digital literary arts, called for a change of direction. In an article called "Aurature at the End(s) of Electronic Literature," he proposes a fundamental move from visible text to sound—the aural delivery of words spoken or synthesized using currently emerging home entertainment platforms, so-called smart speakers like Amazon's Echo (Cayley, "Aurature"). Paradigm shifts are inherently rivalrous. When you are trying to open a new path, it's necessary to point out the errors of other ways. Accordingly, Cayley deprecates several electronic writing practices, including some with roots in his own academic program. When he comes to Twine, he is more dubious than dismissive, though he raises serious questions: "In the case of expressive hypertext—with choose-your-own-adventure gaming capabilities—we can now point to Twine as a platform still gaining significant popularity. But will it ever end up supporting Twine-writers and designers commercially, or as prominent literary practitioners?" (Cayley, "Aurature").

Cayley acknowledges Twine's popularity, and he notes Twine's attachment to game culture. Beyond this, he seems unimpressed, though that sentiment is understandable if one knows the history. The reference to "expressive hypertext" points back to earlier days of Cayley's academic program, before his arrival at Brown University, when figures like Robert Coover, George P. Landow, and the computer scientist Andries Van Dam made that university's writing program a center of literary and scholarly hypertext. This project flourished from the early 1980s to the mid-1990s, but its success was limited at best. Alice Bell's generally sympathetic account of hypertext fiction concedes that such works were rarely read outside of college courses (Bell 166). Seeing in Twine a hypertext revival, Cayley reasonably wonders if this platform will suffer the same fate that befell earlier systems, such as Brown's Intermedia and Eastgate's Storyspace. However, his uncertainty about commercial viability or popularity is tied to a deeper objection on aesthetic grounds, a problem Cayley sees in other forms of electronic writing as well. He calls this "the challenge to reading":

> Formal bewilderment discourages reading and readers. Reading is a learned practice; it is not innate to the human animal. Asking readers to learn new forms is asking them to extend their learning rather than immediately offering them aesthetic experience. Of course, some formally innovative artifacts will be of a quality or importance that necessitates and rewards extra learning and effort. Literary culture moves on. But how will readers pick and choose amongst forms when every artifact is formally distinct if not entirely outside of any pre-existing formal categories? And how are they to discover any quality or importance for the language of the work if formal bewilderment makes it difficult or impossible for them to read? (Cayley, "Aurature")

Twine works are not the only subject of this critique. Plenty of baffling, often bafflingly beautiful work exists in other systems and contexts. Cayley names no names, but we could cite a few examples: Mez Breeze's linguistically mutant m[ez]ang.elle (see Raley), Nick Montfort and Stephanie Strickland's oceanically vast *Sea and Spar Between* (Montfort and Strickland), Jason Nelson's trippily fractal *Sydney's Siberia* (Nelson, *Sydney's Siberia*). Cayley does mention *Pry*, the groundbreaking text/video app for Apple iOS, one of whose developers came from Brown (Cannizarro and Gorman). Though he concedes the brilliance of this work, he worries that it, too, is a one-off. Like the surrealist game levels of Wreden's *Coda*, these projects push against any number of common expectations about language and text. Most are either singular experiments or self-contained series. They invent new categories rather than fall in with old ones, partly in response to an explosion of technical possibility, possibly also because tradition, canon, and even genre are to some extent tainted by toxic ideas of hegemony.

Twine works bring new transgressions and their own challenges to reading. We have just been looking at Anthropy's *Queers in Love at the End of the World*, which deliberately makes conventional reading extremely difficult. The work sabotages its own hypertextuality, tantalizing players with clusters of links they can barely register, let alone explore, before final erasure. This is undeniably a challenge to reading—though as we and others have argued, its intentional disruptions deliver an experience that works toward cultural critique. Though *Queers in Love* is an extreme instance, it nonetheless shows how Twine works may answer Cayley's challenges.

Conceived as textual games, Twine works are far less formally bewildering than other forms of digital writing, such as "expressive hypertexts." One last comparison between *Queers in Love* and its paleozoic ancestor *Hegirascope* may be helpful here. In an evocation of early web browsing, the older work jumps across many narrative lines, constantly decentering the reader's attention. Perhaps because she has grown up in a web-saturated culture, Anthropy feels no need to mimic this diffusion. She keeps her player focused on variations of a single scenario even as she diabolically contracts the time frame. The result is still narratively disruptive, but it confronts the player with fragments of a single encounter, not pieces of a world.[1] Crucially, this difference can be linked to the influence of game culture. *Queers in Love* was built during a game jam whose theme is circulation or sharing—*ludum dare*, to give (the world) a game. For all its tricky difficulty, Anthropy's work is still intended for a certain kind of play—subversive and self-canceling, perhaps, but play nonetheless.

In embracing games as an aesthetic framework, Twine makers take up a coherent cultural identity, even as they resist and transform it. Twine games may split off from other forms of game culture, but they belong to increasingly well-defined alternative communities centered on independent games, narrative games, and interactive fictions. These domains include "pre-existing formal categories" that support critical judgment. In chapter T-3, we cited Short's revealing first response to *With Those We Love Alive*. That review was written as part of the annual Interactive Fiction Competition, a tradition of critical reception and recognition with more than thirty years of history. Interactive fiction, which either contains or overlaps with Twine work, is in fact the most critically informed type of electronic writing.

However, would recognition by Short, Montfort, Andrew Plotkin, Aaron Reed, or some other authority from the interactive fiction world make someone, in Cayley's terms, a "prominent literary practitioner?" Much depends on the way we define each item of this phrase.

Concerning prominence or recognition, Bell argues that hypertext fiction and other digital literary practices must break out of "niche" status (Bell 92). It might be objected that most kinds of literature—and these days, even most forms of popular entertainment—fall into niches of various sizes (Moulthrop). But some niches are more accessible to nonmembers than others. Fiction writers outside of *the genres* (crime, thriller, science fiction, fantasy, romance, Westerns) tend to do readings at bookstores in cities and suburbs. At the peak of celebrity, we see them on TV talk shows with large viewerships. Genre writers are more likely

---

1 Among Twine works that negotiate this problem somewhat differently, we should mention Dan Weber's *A Kiss*, which has one of the more compelling formal maps included in Twine stories: http://logolalia.com/hypertexts/hypertextscreencap.gif.

to appear at community-focused conventions (cons) that do not attract what is quaintly called a general audience.[2]

Likewise, makers of Twine games show up largely at game jams and conferences, either industry-oriented or academic. A writer can certainly be "prominent" in these circles—known and respected by a few hundred people, many of them other Twine writers. There are stirrings of wider recognition. The website for the 2015 launch of *The Late Show with Stephen Colbert* featured a Twine game, and there are the *Adventure Time* and *Black Mirror* connections. Porpentine has had a game commissioned by the Museum of Contemporary Art in Chicago, and her games have been shown in other museums. Anthropy has been interviewed about her work on National Public Radio. If prominence requires being known to millions, through Twitter, television, or some other megamedium, the prize remains elusive—but is this a problem?

As we have already hinted, the answer to that question is implicated in how we understand the term *literary*. In general, thanks to the efforts of people like N. K. Hayles, Dene Grigar, Scott Rettberg, and Cayley himself, academia seems more ready to accept electronic writing now than it was in the 1990s. There were cracks in the wall of resistance even then. Two early hypertext fictions, Joyce's *afternoon* and J. Y. Douglas's *I Have Said Nothing*, were included in W. W. Norton's *Postmodern American Fiction* anthology (Geyh, Leebron, and Levy). ELO has been a presence at the annual MLA conferences for years and in 2018 was formally recognized as an affiliated organization. Marjorie Perloff, a defining figure in modern poetics, has written about the significance of digital work in contemporary poetry (Perloff). Hayles, among the first academic critics to recognize electronic literature as a continuing project, sees it as part of a reformist expansion of literary tradition (Hayles 4–5). Rettberg, one of ELO's first founders, suggests a more progressive view: "Those waiting for the first '#1 bestseller' of electronic literature are largely missing the point: electronic literature is not about

---

2 Gen Con, the venerable tabletop gaming convention, had attendance of more than seventy thousand in 2019; San Diego Comic-Con regularly draws twice that number. Their audiences are both large and diverse by several measures. The "general audience" seems increasingly mythical.

replacing print literary culture, it is instead about extending storytelling and poetics to the contemporary digital environment and creating literary experiences specific to this cultural moment. Electronic literature is experimental literature that generates productive tests of particular admixtures of literature and technology, but it is also fundamentally about a sense of play and a sense of wonder" (Rettberg 203).

Despite these rapprochements, academic creative writing programs still generally identify with poetry, literary nonfiction, and the unmarked genre of nongenre fiction. Twine work, and game culture generally, may be recognized as a parallel or related activity, but it is not usually part of the curriculum.[3] We have already expressed our ambivalence about Twine and literary tradition in chapters T-3 and T-4. Twine work can connect to established forms and practices, but it may just as genuinely go its own way. Perhaps, as Rettberg says, we should simply celebrate experiment and play.

In chapter T-4, we explored the influence in Twine work of alternative, anti-elite aesthetics: retro-stylish kitsch and fan-based camp. Twine carries forward an unruly, experimental impulse last seen in the first decade of the World Wide Web. This agenda has no strong regard for long-standing tradition and may in fact subvert it—recall Xalavier Nelson's first take on *legacy*, noted in chapter T-3. To some extent, the queer-gaming insurgency explored in chapters T-4 and T-5 reflects a similar attitude. Given the tensions between Twine's outsider ethos and traditional culture, *literary* may not be the identity most Twine writers aim for. A certain social distance may be good for both sides. In the famous words of Marx, "I DON'T WANT TO BELONG TO ANY CLUB THAT WILL ACCEPT ME AS A MEMBER" (Marx 321).

Cayley's third term is *practitioners*. Writers are by definition practitioners, but Twine writers (or creators, designers, developers) use practices that differ markedly from the ones Cayley advocates. In at least its first

---

3 There are always exceptions. In 2018, Christopher Macalester Williams received his doctorate in English with a concentration in creative writing from the University of Wisconsin–Milwaukee. His dissertation included an epic poem called *The Wrong Sky*, with both a conventional print and a Twine component. Dr. Williams is now an assistant professor teaching literature and creative writing.

stages, his "aurature" involves the development of "skills" for Amazon's digital assistant, Alexa. An Alexa skill is a software application the system can run in the background or in response to a user's spoken request ("Alexa, ask the listeners about . . ."). Cayley's demonstration project for aurature, called *The Listeners*, uses an impressive range of design and production techniques, including interactive sequencing and processing of sound (Cayley, "*The Listeners*"). Twine entails a much smaller and less sophisticated range of activities: simple hypertext linking, textual substitution, maybe some work with substitution grammars, all usually intended for screen display—though as we saw in chapter P-4, other media types can be used as well. Building a Twine game generally presents a lower technical barrier to entry than developing an Alexa skill.

Most important, Twine is an open-source application supported by a noncommercial community. While the programming tools used to develop an Alexa skill are not proprietary, the considerable infrastructure on which it depends—the system of digital monitoring and response behind the Echo device—is intellectual property held by one of the wealthiest corporations on the planet. This brings us to the most difficult of Cayley's hard questions: Can Twine sustain its creative community commercially or economically?

Twine and Hard Times

Before taking up this question, some important concessions are in order. The invidious distinction between proprietary and open-source software needs at least partial correction. Nobody loves a Puritan, and we do not claim or wish to be software saints. In art and everyday life, we use proprietary systems. The world is big enough for both commercial and noncommercial approaches to art. There are good reasons to criticize Amazon's desire to place live microphones in our living rooms, but the disapproval of academics will not make them go away. If we believe in technological realpolitik, Cayley's call for change is important. Taken more sympathetically, aurature could allow artists to infiltrate Amazon's collective unconscious. (Alexa, delete the last record.)

Further, we admit that Cayley's economic skepticism about Twine is hard to rebut. Like hypertext fictions before them, most Twine works circulate in the public domain and carry the curse of a gift economy. Once the public comes to expect free access to art or entertainment, it is exceptionally hard to return to a cash basis. Paywalls infamously fail. Many of us do not believe in them in the first place, though it is easier for tenured academics to aspire to such virtue and feel an obligation to share freely. Those closer to the rope-end of precarity may do what Anthropy and an increasing number of Twine writers do: include a link inviting financial support on the title pages of their projects. Those who find that work important, especially in teaching, need to give as generously as possible. Patreon and related subscription schemes are another expedient, though Klimas recently disclosed that his income from this channel amounts to less than the minimum wage in his home state (Klimas).

Could these dismal conditions change? If the "Bandersnatch" possibility ever yields something more than a mirage, crossovers with emerging markets could be facilitated by IFTF, which gives common identity and purpose to those interested in parser games (especially on the Inform platform), Twine work, and other branching narrative systems. IFTF is not primarily academic and welcomes interest from the entertainment industries. While waiting for other opportunities, collaborations among the current interactive fiction emphases might be equally important. Twine/Inform hybrids could be intriguing, along with various ventures to connect Twine and other platforms to the Unity game system, particularly with an eye to mobile applications. In her software development role at Spirit AI, Short continues to explore the integration of artificial intelligence with interactive narrative. Poet and system designer Daniel C. Howe recently joined Tender Claws, the independent software studio that created *Pry*. Howe's new system, *Tendar*, like Spirit's *Ally*, focuses on algorithmically generated interaction, with important implications across the field of interactive fiction. IFTF could provide a crucial framework for the integration of developments like these.

Visions of possibility aside, however, economic prospects for Twine, in both infrastructure and artistic practice, remain deeply

uncertain—yet of what can this not be said? Independent game development is as tenuous as any garage-based art form. Developers may
find refuge in academia, more likely in game or media studies programs
than in older departments, but the state of higher education throughout
the developed world is parlous, with humanities programs especially at
risk. At this writing, the stresses imposed by the coronavirus pandemic,
both on enrollments and state budgets, raise this risk to new levels.

Culture-war politics are implicated in this instability, especially
when it comes to public institutions, and attacks on academics involved
in game studies have been a part of Gamergate and the larger alt-right
movement of the US in particular (see Chess and Shaw). But the root
of the trouble is the continuing fragility of postindustrial economies.
This insecurity may at first seem paradoxical. Twine's first decade co-
incided with the longest economic expansion in the history of the US.
That party may now be over, and the benefits of the expansion were
notoriously concentrated in any case. If the current disaster exposes
fundamental weakness like the banking crisis of 2008—say, in student
loans, the retirement system, or international trade—we may face a
long and devastating economic depression.

Long ago, at the beginning of the last boom before this one, Neal
Stephenson published a novel of speculative fiction featuring a global
virtual-reality system with a social center called "the Street." (The
GeoCities of old may have been among his inspirations.) Being essentially a realist, Stephenson salts his Tomorrowland with some sobering
observations: "In the real world–planet Earth, Reality, there are somewhere between six and ten billion people. At any given time, most of
them are making mud bricks or field-stripping their AK-47s. Perhaps
a billion of them have enough money to own a computer; these people
have more money than all of the others put together. Of these billion
potential computer owners, maybe a quarter of them actually bother to
own computers, and a quarter of these have machines that are powerful
enough to handle the Street protocol" (Stephenson 24–25).

It is interesting to reread this passage in the 2020s. Stephenson's
informed guess about world population holds up, though the explosion of smartphones has blown out his forecast of a billion computer

owners by a factor of three. More salient is the allusion to the have-nots, those folks with the bricks and assault weapons. In its day, the remark registered, no doubt cynically, the economic inequalities that accompanied early phases of the information revolution. There were strong concerns about a so-called digital divide. Today, we are more concerned with wealth gaps. "These people have more money than all of the others put together" remains a true statement, but the size of the apex class has greatly contracted. Also, the folks with the AK-47s and AR-15s are no longer in mud-brick hinterlands but in our state capitols and our nondigital streets. At this writing, some of those streets are patrolled by National Guard units in armored vehicles.

Instead of Stephenson's Metaverse and Street, we have Facebook, Twitter, Instagram, and other stretches of the social media hellscape. The world those forces engender may be very like the neoliberal inferno described in *Snow Crash*, though it is hard now to imagine anything like the entrepreneurial happy ending Stephenson gives that book. That was another century. In this one, we face not only economic instability but the subversion of democracies, driven in the first instance by racists and gangsters and exacerbated in some measure by refugee flows and, most recently, by a worldwide biothreat. How long, it must be asked, before we're no longer the people with computers but the ones with the rifles and wall-building bricks?

It's not just institutions of popular art and education that are imperiled—the entire civilization seems palpably at risk. (These words, first written before the pandemic, seem even more appropriate in 2021.) In such a dire context, why does the future of Twine matter? True, the social martyrdom of a Twine writer, Zoë Quinn, was the precipitating event for a battle in the culture wars that laid down the pattern for many to come (Warzel; see also LaFrance). Twine is implicated in a critical moment that goes far beyond game culture, but since that moment counts as a genuine crisis, with outcomes that may include the end of the world as we know it, we need to justify our perverse interest in computerized games and clever ways to tell stories.

Can Twine save our world? No way! However, here is a quick list of other things that offer no immediate and total remedy:

mumblecore
crowdsourcing
ukuleles
food porn
live streaming
Lin-Manuel Miranda
polar bears
psilocybin
quantum gravity
Donna Haraway
the flightless cormorant
life on Mars (whatever that means to you)
the Five Virtues
slavery reparations
universal basic income
petting cats

This list, which takes off from the "litanies" of Bruno Latour and Ian Bogost, is unordered and eminently debatable (Bogost 38). Some of its items might seem potentially redemptive, depending on one's understanding of the world's problems. Many will not. The point of this list, like all lists, is to assert totality over singularity. The list contains no answer; the list is the answer. Which is to say, as Anthropy teaches, the best way to stave off the moment when everything is wiped away is to make the case for everything, almost. No saviors, no panaceas, but many things may be helpful in some fashion. Let us consider some ways in which a world with Twine in it is preferable to one without. In an epitome of this book itself, we offer three arguments: conceptual, practical, and finally personal.

Maps and Algorithms

Plato and McKenzie Wark had their caves. The cultural critic Fredric Jameson found allegory in a different sort of cavern, the lobby of the Westin Bonaventure Hotel in Los Angeles, circa 1984. Many who visited grand hotels in the 1980s had similar experiences of disorientation and procedural uncertainty—*where do you suppose they've put the front desk in this one?* Jameson laid out the full implications of this experience, which was always more than a complication of check-in protocol. As Plato's cave allegorizes the world of phenomena, the Westin lobby brings home the contours of late capitalism:

> This latest mutation in space—postmodern hyperspace—has finally succeeded in transcending the capacities of the individual human body to locate itself, to organize its immediate surroundings perceptually, and cognitively to map its position in a mappable external world. It may now be suggested that this alarming disjunction point between the body and its built environment—which is to the initial bewilderment of the older modernism as the velocities of spacecraft to those of the automobile—can itself stand as the symbol and analogon of that even sharper dilemma which is the incapacity of our minds, at least at present, to map the great global multinational and decentered communicational network in which we find ourselves caught as individual subjects. (Jameson 39)

Not knowing where to check in is a signature of postmodern experience, an effect produced by spaces, real or hyperreal, that defy understanding. Never mind hotels: think of the "decentered communicational network"—these days, we call this thing the web, or the Twitterverse, or as advertising types say with ominous familiarity, *social*. In response to mutating hyperspace, Jameson calls for "an aesthetic of cognitive mapping" (Jameson 44). That project has many moving parts, but game culture is clearly one of them. Wark's gamer theory, exposing the allegories of power behind algorithm, makes an obvious contribution. The same might be said for Galloway's insight that playing *Civilization III* teaches us how that game's algorithms intersect historical understanding (Galloway 92). We have already noticed Burden and Gouglas's observation that *Portal* exemplifies the making of art from "algorithmic experience" (Burden and Gouglas).

As spatialized occasions for narrative, games literally involve cognitive mapping. "Thinking with portals," as Burden and Gouglas explain, deconstructs Euclidean geometry as well as the conventional, recti-linear design of game levels. That operational geometry is also a key subject in *Beginner's Guide*, where Davey and Coda struggle, in their curiously passive-aggressive way, over the need for mazes to have solutions. As Wreden's work demonstrates, there is much more at stake in this contest than the pragmatics of level design. Coda's prisons are as much existential as architectural. They are "analogons," to borrow Jameson's word, of Coda's dubious desire for privacy and interiority. This is where the cognitive part of the mapping project comes in.

Though many decades have elapsed since its discovery, we still occupy something like the "hyperspace" Jameson named. Gameplay illuminates the complexity and irrationality of that space. Games can also bring to consciousness several features of cybernetic infrastructure, the reliance of our virtual environments on algorithms and logical transactions. Through the mechanisms of player death and regeneration, games bring home the power of iteration or cyclic repetition, showing us in experiential terms the form of software loops. By incorporating randomized behavior, games make us aware of stochastic outcomes, predictable but uncertain. By presenting complicated simulations involving multiple agents, games demonstrate the dependency of elements in a system and the way such dependencies can lead to emergent or unforeseen consequences. Above all, computer games model contingency, the ability of situations to evolve differently over multiple encounters. They reveal a world of complex, systematic, but unpredictable possibility.

Jameson believed an aesthetic of cognitive mapping would be essential to politics in the twenty-first century. In order to address injustice, oppression, and ignorance, we need to understand, in the deep way art makes possible, the baffling structures of a world that is too large, too fast, and too intricately detailed for ordinary human witness. To put this much faith in imagination involves a huge dose of utopian chutzpah, but we might venture some hypotheses anyway. Perhaps a generation of gamers will be less inclined to call for regime change in regions traumatized by imperialism; or route tank trains full of volatile hydrocarbons through major population centers; or mine the tar sands that fill the bomb cars in the first place; or otherwise deny the fragility of our critically damaged ecosystem; or fail to grasp that, ironically, iteration only applies in software, so we can't reboot the West and replay from 1955 or 1820.

Coming to Code

Maybe, just maybe, playing and making computer games can help us map the catastrophe, jam the machines, hijack the bus of doom before everything is wiped away. The help in question may be small—more in the way of ukuleles than reparations—but it is something we can articulate. The essayist Joan Didion was once asked to write on the abstract subject of morality but swerved away, declaring, "My mind veers inflexibly toward the particular" (Didion 160). We follow her mental taillights. Our conceptual/political argument was framed broadly to take in a large swathe of game culture. Twine and its productions belong to that domain but in a very peculiar way. Multimedia extensions aside, Twine is fundamentally a text technology. Like Inform, TADS, and other parser-driven platforms, Twine draws on the considerable power of the written word to evoke and manage playable spaces. We can make a second, more pragmatic case for the importance of Twine, along with other forms of interactive fiction, based on its engagement with writing.

Interactive fiction is connective tissue, a ligament anchoring the skeleton of language and literature to the musculature of computing. (Flip those anatomical metaphors if you wish.) We invoke the living body, since that is what culture feels like to us, but we could also have gone to geology, thinking of stratified bands in sediments and the interlayers between them. That metaphor brings the advantage of history, which is important here. As another major critic, Alan Liu, has argued, a major task of humanist work in this century is reassertion of cultural memory in the face of amnesiac market forces (Liu 72). Twine and its interactive fiction companions are helpful in this regard, connecting practices from the precomputer world to those that have evolved more recently. It is probably no coincidence that Jay David Bolter, an important early advocate of hypertext, and

Short, perhaps our greatest writer of interactive fiction, both started as classicists.

After its very early days, game development has followed the organizational scheme of cinema: production involves fairly large groups overseen by a lead designer. This is necessary when the work involves many specialized skills, such as AI programming, 3-D modeling, motion capture, interface design, sound and voice production, and so on. Because they do not take the exit ramp to graphics but stay on the old textual blacktop, interactive fictions and Twine games especially require no such division of labor. Most of the Twine games we have discussed in this book are the work of one or two people. As Anthropy says in her manifesto for the independent game movement, *Rise of the Video Game Zinesters*, text-based and simpler graphical platforms allow artists to express radically personal visions (Anthropy, *Rise* 18–19). Independent game creation hearkens back, as we have said, to an earlier moment of digital technology, when imaginations were less constrained by mainstream expectations and corporate economies. Solo and small-group work is not inherently virtuous, of course. For every Anthropy or D. Squinkifer, there may be many versions of Wreden's Coda, pursuing visions that will never connect with a wider audience. By the same token, large-scale corporate teams can make thoughtful and genre-redefining games, from *Katamari Damacy* and *Portal* to *Legend of Zelda: Breath of the Wild*, *Animal Crossing*, and *Death Stranding*. Meanwhile, there is a sweet spot between solo and large-team efforts, where games like *Gone Home*, *Firewatch*, and *80 Days* flourish. However, single authorship and very small collaborations have one important advantage: they open development to people at the margins of game culture.

This opening involves another kind of identity as well—it bridges the cultural divide between programmers and nonprogrammers, between those conversant with computer code and those whose main expressive mode is natural language. The leading contribution to this unification is Graham Nelson's revolutionary rewriting of the Inform language, Inform 7, which uses something like English syntax (Nelson, "Inform 7"). We have already said some things about Inform 7 back in chapter T-1, noticing the way its code tends to converge with ordinary language.

In Inform 7, statements are passed to a compiler program, which in turn generates much less readable code that establishes and populates a game space. At the same time, these statements are also understandable as sentences in the traditional sense. Playing on this ingenious overlay of linguistic registers, writers from the interactive fiction world have composed verses consisting entirely of well-formed Inform 7 expressions. Here is one by a writer who goes by the tag "Adjusting" (Adjusting). It riffs on Noam Chomsky's famous example of formal nonsense, *colorless green ideas sleep furiously*:

> *Chomsky is a room.*
> *A thought is a kind of thing.*
> *Color is a kind of value.*
> *The colors are red, green and blue.*
> *A thought has a color. It is usually Green.*
> *A thought can be colorful or colorless. It is usually colorless.*
> *An idea is a thought in Chomsky with description "Colorless green ideas*
> *sleep furiously."*
> *A manner is a kind of thing.*
> *Furiously is a manner.*
> *Sleeping relates one thought to one manner.*
> *The verb to sleep (he sleeps, they sleep, he slept, it is slept, he is*
> *sleeping) implies the sleeping relation.*
> *Colorless green ideas sleep furiously.*

"It compiles," one slightly skeptical commenter observes. "It just doesn't do much"—except compile, of course, which the final line will not do in the absence of the lines that precede it. The observation is correct as far as the compiled game goes—there's not much to do in the room called "Chomsky"—but placing the exercise in a larger context, we very much beg to differ. Wrapping Chomsky's famous example around the twin poles of poetry and programming language is, culturally speaking, a whole lot indeed. It demonstrates how the structure of language, which Chomsky's sleep of reason is meant to reveal, can be not emptied out but doubly loaded—deeply Inform-ed, as it were.

Twine is less formally ambitious than Inform 7. Because Twine games branch off not from rule-based text adventures but from link-based game books and hypertexts, they generally have simpler infrastructures than parser games—though a glance back at our discussion of *With Those We Love Alive* in chapter T-2 complicates this claim. In its own way, Twine also allows for relatively seamless connections between natural and cybernetic language. The foundational double-bracket convention for linking, with its automatic expansion of the structure map, offers a prime example of this effect. The Chapbook story format, intended to simplify Twine writing for beginners, extends the principle throughout the authoring process.

If we think about Inform 7 and Twine not just as clever, marginal improvements to game development but as interventions in literacy itself, their importance is evident. Socially speaking, both platforms allow people without programming backgrounds—often people alienated by the cognitive and ideological signatures of conventional game design—to build things with code. Even writers who never go beyond simple linking schemes are introduced to the structure editor. Working with this directed graph both underscores the dual nature of digital production, scriptonic content set within a textonic framework, and emphasizes the possibilities for complex expression, a challenge to both writers and programmers. In our classroom experience, a significant number of beginners move beyond basic hypertext, at the very least to conditional linking and textual variation, both techniques that implicate aspects of code such as variables and Boolean logic.

Outside of the classroom, where Twine writers are driven mainly by aesthetic exploration, there is a clear path from the basic Chapbook repertoire of links, forks, modifiers, and inserts to more complex approaches like embedded JavaScript. More venturesome creators may also find their way to Harlowe, Snowman, and SugarCube, with their broader arrays of programming tools. At each of these points of advance, Twine users will find online references, examples, and explanations in places like Cox's Twine Cookbook (Cox), Melissa Ford's *Writing Interactive Fiction with Twine* (Ford), Anna Anthropy's *Make Your Own Twine Games!* (Anthropy), and Emily Short's blog (Short). Like other forms of interactive fiction, Twine can be an effective gateway experience for those who may not have otherwise thought of themselves as coders. Of course, not everyone is obligated or destined to make such a cultural crossing. For those who carry on happily with older forms, Twine and interactive fiction extend the ambit of literacy to include cybertexts. They expand the field of expression and indeed of reading. In this way, Twine and its cousins serve that highest function of writing, literary and otherwise: they advance the language itself.

What's in Your Heart

Language is always two things at once: a vast, intergenerational cultural project—what Ferdinand de Saussure called *langue*—and individual human utterance, or *parole* (de Saussure 91). While it may be important to speak of cognitive mapping or new horizons for literacy, the most powerful argument for the importance of Twine is simply personal. In the introduction, Anastasia told a version of her Twine story. In telling my own, I will add a character, a scene, and a crucial piece of dialogue.

In 2008, Klimas, Salter, and I were all associated with the School of Information Arts and Technologies at UB. If, as one woebegone troll suggests, this was anything more than coincidence, credit the invisible hand of history, that ultimate conspirator. Chris and Anastasia were graduate students; I was on the faculty. Eight years earlier, I had cofounded the school (which most places would call a department) with my partner, Nancy Kaplan, who directed its graduate programs. As Anastasia has written, Chris had begun building Twine on the foundations of TiddlyWiki. He had also taken some classes toward our MS in interaction design and information architecture. He had spoken to Nancy, and briefly to me, about using the development of Twine as his thesis project. We encouraged him, but there was a hitch.

Constraints of time and budget restricted Chris to one class per semester. At that pace, it would take several years to complete the degree and probably even longer to release Twine. So one evening, with next-semester registration looming, Chris came to Nancy's office to ask a difficult question: Should he carry on with the MS program or stop and concentrate on bringing Twine into the world? What Professor Kaplan said to him deserves to be remembered in the annals of Twine and possibly also in any history of electronic literature because it was exactly what she said to me in the summer of 1991 when I was agonizing about taking time from an academic project to write a long-form hypertext called *Victory Garden*. Her words: "You have to do what's in your heart."

Chris and I both decided to step off, or around, the academic adventure line. I've had no regrets and I hope the same for him. Over the next decade, I have encountered other people who have drifted crosswise through the cultures of software and higher learning, people with their hearts set on new forms of writing—Anastasia and Chris—and lately a constellation I have yet to know well or in most cases even meet—Anna Anthropy, Dan Cox, Cara Ellison, Porpentine, Kitty Horrorshow, merritt k, Christine Love, Kris Ligman, Michael Lutz, Xalavier Nelson Jr., D. Squinkifer, and too many more to list.

Twine was in my heart long before there was Twine, when, circa 1986, someone told me this thing I thought I was inventing had a name already—it was called hypertext, and there were people who knew about it: Mark Bernstein, Jay Bolter, John Cayley, Robert Coover, Yellowlees Douglas, Carolyn Guyer, Terry Harpold, Michael Joyce, George Landow, Judy Malloy, Cathy Marshall, John McDaid, and first of all, Ted Nelson. Hypertext was a thing for a few years, but creative attention eventually drifted from nodes and links toward graphics and animation and platforms like Flash (see Salter and Murray). Electronic literature became its own thing, and then Rettberg and Robert Coover went and Organized it, but by that time, I was trying to learn enough about video game design not to feel completely embarrassed teaching it. Somewhere my links back to hypertext broke down, or so it seemed, and by 2010, hypertext fiction felt enough like ancient history that Grigar and I had to start digging it up and putting it in archives (Moulthrop and Grigar). Game culture, meanwhile, was on its way to crisis.

At the same time, Twine was happening, in ways that only in retrospect seem completely reasonable. Even Chris professes himself surprised with what Anthropy and merritt k and D. Squinkifer and Porpentine were doing on the platform—making games, making noise, making a difference. Reconnecting with Twine made me feel a lot like McDaid's Glass Man, a vagrant scuffling across time tracks. Didn't we disappear somewhere in the nineties? Bones of old men, indeed. Back in the heyday of hypertext, my generation consisted mainly of academics with an attitude, skulking in basement Macintosh labs—the labs were *always* in the basement—fondly dreaming about the end of print. That end came, sort of, and in an important way did not. Meanwhile, there were other changes. The culture war about which I fabulated in *Victory Garden* erupted in harsh reality. The skin my cohort had in the game was nothing compared to what Quinn and others, including my coauthor, have had to risk in the endless aftermath of Gamergate. The older generation was out to change college composition, creative writing, and perhaps publishing, not the multibillion-dollar video game industry. What did we know? All commitment to the struggle, all respect to the youth.

So now here we are, friends and strangers, writers and aca-fans, all wound up in this project that threads through our lives in so many weird, queer, and astounding ways. As the oldest Twine writer in the world—because I was writing Twine before there was Twine, also because I am old—I will say this entanglement feels, in a way it has never felt before, really good. As Rettberg says, the play continues. For all the anger and suffering and thickening darkness, something important is happening. We are all part of a significant unfolding of language, ideas, and human possibility—may it last. May the future of Twine be glorious and full of righteous trouble, and may we all live to see it.

Never give up what's in your heart.

Works Cited

Adjusting. *I7 Chomsky*. June 17, 2007. https://groups.google.com/forum/#!topic/
rec.arts.int-fiction/2pHd-vPfAVY.

Anthropy, Anna. *Make Your Own Twine Games!* Penguin-Random House, 2019.

———. *Rise of the Video Game Zinesters*. Seven Stories Press, 2012.

Bell, Alice. *The Possible Worlds of Hypertext Fiction*. Palgrave Macmillan, 2010.

Bogost, Ian. *Alien Phenomenology, or What It's Like to Be a Thing*. University of Minnesota Press, 2012.

Burden, Michael, and Sean Gouglas. "The Algorithmic Experience: 'Portal' as Art."
Game Studies 12, no. 2 (2012). http://gamestudies.org/1202/articles/the_algorithmic
_experience.

Cannizarro, Danny, and Samantha Gorman. *Pry*. Tender Claws, 2014.

Cayley, John. "Aurature at the End(s) of Electronic Literature." Electronic Book Review, February 2017. https://electronicbookreview.com/essay/aurature-at-the-ends
-of-electronic-literature/.

———. "*The Listeners*: An Instance of Aurature." *cream city review* 40, no. 2 (2016).
http://io.creamcityreview.org/40-2/cayley/.

Chess, Shira, and Adrienne Shaw. "We Are All Fishes Now." *DIGRA: Transactions of the
Digital Games Research Association* 2, no. 2 (2016). http://todigra.org/index.php/
todigra/article/view/39/91.

Cox, Dan, ed. "Welcome to the Twine Cookbook." Twinery.org, 2019, https://twinery
.org/cookbook/.

de Saussure, Ferdinand. *Course in General Linguistics*. Philosophical Library, 1959.

Didion, Joan. *Slouching toward Bethlehem*. Farrar, Straus and Giroux, 1968.

Ford, Melissa. *Writing Interactive Fiction with Twine*. Que, 2018.

Galloway, Alexander R. *Gaming: Essays on Algorithmic Culture*. University of Minnesota Press, 2006.

Geyh, Paula, Fred G. Leebron, and Andrew Levy. *Postmodern American Fiction*. W. W.
Norton, 1994.

Han, Bong Hee, and Elizabeth Ito, dir. "Five Short Tables." *Adventure Time*. 2016.
WarnerMedia.

Hayles, N. Katherine. *Electronic Literature: New Horizons for the Literary*. University
of Notre Dame Press, 2008.

Hudson, Laura. "Twine, the Video-Game Technology for All." *New York Times*, November 19, 2014. https://www.nytimes.com/2014/11/23/magazine/twine-the-video
-game-technology-for-all.html.

Interactive Fiction Technology Foundation. "Our Mission and Goals." 2020. https://
iftechfoundation.org/mission/.

Jameson, Fredric. *Postmodernism, or, the Cultural Logic of Late Capitalism*. Duke University Press, 1991.

Klimas, Chris. *Twine Past, Present, Future*. Cambridge, MA: NarraScope, 2019.

LaFrance, Adrienne. "How QAnon Is Warping Reality and Discrediting Science." *Atlantic*, June 2020, 27–38.

Liu, Alan Y. *Laws of Cool: Knowledge Work and the Culture of Information*. University of Chicago Press, 2004.

Marx, Julius. *Groucho and Me*. Da Capo Press, 1959.

merritt k, ed. *Videogames for Humans: Twine Authors in Conversation*. Instar Books, 2015.

Montfort, Nick, and Stephanie Strickland. *Sea and Spar Between*. Dear Navigator, 2010. https://nickm.com/montfort_strickland/sea_and_spar_between/.

Moulthrop, Stuart. "For Thee: A Response to Alice Bell." Electronic Book Review, January 2011. https://electronicbookreview.com/essay/for-thee-a-response-to-alice -bell/.

Moulthrop, Stuart, and Dene Grigar. *Traversals: The Use of Preservation for Early Electronic Writing*. MIT Press, 2017.

Nelson, Graham. "Inform 7." 2006. www.inform7.com.

Nelson, Jason. *Sydney's Siberia*. Accessed August 20, 2019. http://www.secrettechnology .com/sydney/.

Perloff, Marjorie. *Unoriginal Genius: Poetry by Other Means in the New Century*. University of Chicago Press, 2012.

Raley, Rita. "Interferences: [Net.Writing] and the Practice of Codework." Electronic Book Review, September 2002. http://electronicbookreview.com/essay/ interferences-net-writing-and-the-practice-of-codework/.

Rettberg, Scott. *Electronic Literature*. Polity Press, 2019.

Short, Emily. *Emily Short's Interactive Storytelling* (blog). Accessed March 4, 2020. www .emshort.blog.

Stephenson, Neal. *Snow Crash*. Bantam Spectra, 1992.

Warzel, Charlie. "How an Online Mob Created a Playbook for a Culture War." *New York Times*, August 15, 2019. https://www.nytimes.com/interactive/2019/08/15/opinion/ what-is-gamergate.html.

Appendix I

Interview with Chris Klimas

This interview took place between the authors of this book (AS and SM) and Chris Klimas (CK) via Skype on April 6, 2017. Our work was in the early stages, and the exchange helped us understand much about the origins and circumstances of Twine. It also confirmed our commitment to multiple agendas—historical, personal, critical, and creative—because as Chris makes clear, the Twine phenomenon has all those dimensions. The conversation was notably free ranging. We have used a light editorial hand in order to preserve the flow of ideas.

AS: Circa 2009, people may have tended to think of hypertext as more of an appliance than an area for active software development. What made you interested in the concept?

CK: Of hypertext . . . ? [bemused] wow.

AS: . . . of building something in hypertext . . .

SM: If that's in fact what you were thinking—I don't know—did you think of [Twine] as something else?

CK: I don't know, actually. I think so. I think that [hypertext] was a fair characterization. . . . I think at that point, I had done a lot of experimentation with parser IF, and I had done a couple of games myself, but I felt sort of frustrated with the medium . . . how *object-y* it is . . . very world-model-based . . . and that felt like an obstacle, I guess. That was when I started messing around with stuff that was, more . . . hypertext-y. You just have tons of exposure to the idea of hypertext. For me, it was more the web. I hadn't played or experienced the stuff from the early nineties or whenever you want to date that particular period.

I ran across this technology called TiddlyWiki, and it was this really clever thing [that created] a self-modifying web page. You download it to your computer, you can edit it, it's like a wiki, but there's no server component to it at all, and so it's like a very simple . . . DIY hypertext. And so I started editing and playing out stuff in there and experimenting with that medium.

It just got very disorienting, actually, to try to edit [a TiddlyWiki story] from inside . . . where I'd click links, and follow them, and it's like—*where am I?* I'd get lost in my own stuff, and that was the genesis: *I want to build a tool that will help me do this better.*

SM: What was your process [of development and invention] like? When did you first think you were building Twine?

CK: There were a couple of abortive attempts. Before [there was Twine] it started as Twee . . . and they all started with "TW" because they came from TiddlyWiki . . . and this was just a plain old text format and compiler, the sort of programming environment you expect out of traditional programming.

That worked OK, and I wrote some stuff with that . . . and then I thought . . . I should make something web-based because I wanted more people to get into it . . . because there were so few things at that point on the web that were . . . literary hypertext, I guess.

I was always trying to convert people to the cause [of branching stories]. I thought, I should try to win over [some of my] friends who are writers . . . to have them try this out. And of course, if you give them a compiler, they're like, *What is this?*—so I tried building a web-based thing, but it was just a web front end to the compiler . . . which I called . . . TweeBox . . .

I had all these attempts to try to build something [along these lines], and I always had this idea, actually while I was in the UB IDIA program [University of Baltimore, Interactive Design and Information Architecture], where I was on track to do a master's, and I was thinking this would be an interesting thesis project . . . and then I got really impatient because I was doing it part-time, taking one class at a time, so I was at least two years away from even starting on [the thesis]. I remember just deciding, I'm going to do this and try it out, and that's where the genesis of [Twine] began.

I had always hesitated to build an actual GUI behind it . . . and then I was like, there's never actually going to come a moment where somebody tells me, *You should go ahead and do that*—so I just did it. And that's how it started.

SM: [Ironically] Why wait for permission?

AS: Since you did mention Twee . . . It's always been interesting to me that you've included Twee in the releases, that it's stayed a part of Twine. Do you see people still using it? Is there a following for Twee or a motivation for you in keeping Twee part of the platform?

CK: I wouldn't say that I actively develop [Twee]. . . . For a long time, I did, and then I lapsed working on it. I came back to Twine. . . . Twine 2.0 was very much for me like, let's think about what succeeded here, what didn't, and rethink assumptions. . . . That was when I actually stopped working on Twee. It seemed like kind of a done deal. [Twee] does what it needs to do.

[There's] sort of this pendulum swing between programming and writing. . . . I am building larger projects now and I need to merge stuff together, so I wrote a bunch of JavaScript, it's an NPM module called twine-utils that includes a tiny little compiler. . . . There have been quite a few Twine competitors that have sprung up in its wake. . . . I don't remember all of the names. . . . The guy who does TextAdventures .co.uk has one—Squiffy, I think it was called?—it seemed like for a while, every day there was someone who said, I have a better way to do Twine . . . and they all had [a] programming language, like, *Here's a text file* . . . [something like] Raconteur, which is based on Undum.

To me, the hard problem has always been the interface. It has never been, like, I need something really sophisticated in terms of functionality. It's actually the ease of use, from my point of view, so it's a useful substrate.

Beyond that . . . the people who are into programming, who come at it from a programming angle, it's more comfortable to them, like I definitely hear about people in the community who are like, *Oh man, I just want to be able to use my text editor*, and that's great, go for it, you know? . . . [Twee] was a useful stepping-stone. . . . To be honest, I still use it from time to time, for programming utility kinds of things, but I don't see it as a big deal.

SM: This is a shift-focus question . . . Have you always thought of Twine as a free platform, or have you thought at any point of monetizing, commercializing?

CK: One of the core tenets of my thoughts on [Twine] is that it should be free, and I think, to be honest, that is a large reason why it succeeded in the first place . . . because obviously Storyspace existed, and as I learned later on, there's this product called AXMA Story Maker . . . but it's not the price tag so much as the open-source thing.

I do cling to hippyish beliefs about open-source, and I read Slashdot back in the day, which is I think where I got indoctrinated. . . . I still sort of pine for that period . . . the early 2000s, where the web was . . . much less a social-media, TV-like experience . . . and I think that is important, one of the foundational things. . . . Obviously it would be nice to be paid for my work, but it has never made economic sense to me. The people who are using [Twine] are, by and large, not the kind of people who are going to pay fifty dollars or more for what we [for some reason still] call a boxed product.

AS: Given the commitment to open-source, have you had any notable successes, challenges with that, taking that model, maintaining the Twine code base, especially as you handed it off?

CK: I did a talk at a conference called NoShowConf, which talks about me burning out on the project and some of the history too. . . . When I gave the talk, which was maybe 2014 . . . it was definitely a moment to reflect. . . . So yeah, I totally burned out on [Twine], to be honest. . . . It was ironically just as [Twine] was taking off that I burned out . . . and it's hard because you get a lot of support requests and bug reports.

The Twine user base often is not particularly technically savvy, which is cool most of the time, but it also means that people will write in bug reports like *It just doesn't start.* Which is very frustrating because, you know, you feel bad because there's no information to actually fix [whatever the problem is] . . . and people often have an expectation that . . . it's a program like Office and Word, so if it doesn't work right, it's a travesty . . . and some people get angry about it. I guess that's just human nature, but to be on the other side of it gets frustrating, and I've had to learn and am still learning how to manage my time with the project . . . and also my emotional well-being.

I used to have . . . a [Twitter] TweetDeck column . . . for people talking about Twine games . . . or I'd have this very convoluted search term to see what people are saying on Twitter about Twine . . . and it was . . . kind of a terrible idea, actually. . . . This was just when Gamergate happened, so I had to close it down because the flow was just too much.

I still have a Twitter account, which I mainly oversee, though I just brought on someone else to help with it . . . and people will just tweet at me, "Your software sucks" [laughs] and it's like, thanks! And that's tough, and I guess that's also . . . living a little bit in the public eye, in the internet sense of the word. People are going to have opinions about what you do, no matter what. That is the major challenge, trying to keep Twine afloat while maintaining a full-time job elsewhere.

The truth is, the number of people who work on [Twine] in general is very small. There are people who do . . . drive-by pull requests, which is good. . . . Like yesterday, somebody came in with a request. . . . He wanted to add a thing for adding force touch, like when you push very hard on a trackpad, to do stuff with that. . . . But the problem with any open-source project is there's a judgment call. . . . You are adding a functionality to this thing that I have no way of testing myself . . . so if it breaks, I am going to be the guy who fixes it, probably . . . and is that a decision I'm willing to make? . . . I'll bet that's pretty typical for an open-source project.

SM: Are there particular contributors to the code base who are memorable or rank as among the most important?

CK: Yeah, definitely. Leon Arnott is a guy who lives in Australia. . . . I don't know much about him otherwise, which is also really interesting. . . . Leon developed a lot of macros, things you can add to your story to make it do stuff, back in the Twine 1.X days. He had done a lot with it, and when I was looking at version 2, I thought, this is going to be too much for me, to do both the editor and the runtime at once, and [Arnott] seemed to have thought hard about what people were doing or wanted to do with Twine stories, so I asked him to work on Harlowe, which is the default [story] format [in Twine 2]. . . . Leon's interesting to chat with. He works at a different speed and thinks about things very differently than I do, which makes for interesting conversations.

The other guy is Thomas Michael Edwards. . . . He is the maintainer for SugarCube, which is the legacy [format], so if you're used to using Twine 1 . . . SugarCube takes what I did in 2010 or so and builds on it quite a lot. It's a very mature kind of format.

Those are the two [people] I could go to just off the top of my head in terms of programming, though obviously the community goes much wider than that.

AS: Shifting into the community itself, what are some of the things you see in terms of Twine extensions like community-generated code that's not necessarily part of the format choices that you've found most interesting? Anything that's surprised you?

CK: A lot of it is . . . one-off things. People do really surprising things with Twine, in the sense of . . . content, obviously, but there've been instances where I've seen like, wait, oh, kind of taking it and twisting it. . . . It reminds me a little of [the way] Andrew Plotkin did an implementation of Tetris in the Z-machine. . . . That level of stuff that serves no practical purpose, and it's not necessarily even like a big artistic statement in terms I understand, but it's more like technically playing with what you can do.

There's this guy . . . the only thing I know him by is his Twitter handle . . . such is internet life. . . . His Twitter handle [is] *lectronice*. . . . He did this really amazing thing where it looked very much like a Japanese RPG, with little dialogue boxes and such. . . . People are always trying to build RPG games out of [Twine] . . . which is always to me . . . a giant quagmire because there are a million ways you could potentially do that . . . lots of little modules or extensions or plug-ins or whatever.

People came up with this idea for cycling text, which may well have antecedents way before Twine that I'm not aware of . . . but the idea that I'm clicking and the text changes . . . you're not moving, the text just changes to a different adjective, or something like that. That was always interesting to me, and something I hadn't seen before.

AS: I think that's the extension I use most.

CK: Yeah, it's fun to do. At least for me, there's the fear that . . . you know, with [disjunctive] hypertext, you're like, if I click here, will I be able to get back to where I was? Am I about to jump off a cliff? Whereas if I click on a link and [the current text] just changes, and that's it, that's kind of pleasant, in fact.

SM: My students have impressed me a lot with timed effects [using the (*live:*) macro in Harlowe] . . . that thing where you say, *If I wait another five seconds, maybe it'll do something . . . or maybe he set it up to wait FIVE HOURS!*—and then you have to crawl the code [to figure it out]. What do you think about timed effects?

CK: One of my favorite Twine things is *Queers in Love at the End of the World* [by Anna Anthropy], which has the ten-second thing, but it's tricky because in the IF community, people were very against the idea of having text appear slowly, even, or making [the reader] wait at all. . . . I remember this big debate back in the nineties on USENET. . . . David Cornelson was writing this suspense story, and he wanted it to play out [so that] the text would appear like you're reading it on a really old modem, and everybody in the community was like, *That's a stupid idea! I'm going to hate it!*—or whatever. And we've come so far, I feel that people have let go of that and . . . let text appear one character at a time but also play with time in an interesting sort of way. It's cool. I don't know. A game that requires you to wait five hours would be . . . challenging . . . but interesting at the same time.

SM: I have a question I've been dying to ask since you sort of answered it earlier. I'll ask it again, nonetheless. You know Darius Kazemi, right?

CK: I've met him a couple of times.

SM: I was talking Twine with him about a year ago, and I wondered, Should I say, "Twine games," or should I say, "Twine fictions?" And [Kazemi] said, "Well, these days the kids just say 'Twines.'" [General amusement.] So let me ask you, where would you go with that?

CK: Well, it's interesting. To sort of sidebar a little . . . I'm a member of the board of the Interactive Fiction Technology Foundation, [a] nonprofit that's about community infrastructure . . . and one of the things we're exploring is possibly trademarking Twine . . . so then it gets real muddled if we start saying, like, *Oh yeah, it's a Twine.*

To be honest, it's a struggle every time [I ask myself], Is this a Twine game? Is this a Twine story? And both times, people might not like your description, so my internal stylebook is, I just write *Twine works.* . . . "This is a work of Twine." . . . That was the one middle ground I could find. I don't really so much care. At the same time, I like the idea of people saying, *Oh, I made a Twine*—even inasmuch as that is a problem, legally speaking, potentially. [It's nice that *Twine*] is a term, and people know what you're talking about.

AS: You talked a bit about trying to convert your literary friends and people writing in a more linear way when you were talking about the audience for this platform, and Stuart has just touched on the age-old "games versus stories" debate. So given all of that happening in the various spaces of *serious writing*, which sometimes tends not to engage . . . when serious writing goes digital, it means they made a PDF . . . over to games. Where do you see Twine fitting in this larger culture?

CK: I see it as this thing that confounds people. I really like that aspect of it. I initially thought of [Twine] as this thing that was for . . . serious writing, I guess, though *serious writing* is obviously a loaded term. It wasn't that I thought [Twine work] was somehow better than a game; it was more that I couldn't see how you build a game out of it, originally. And then everybody came along and proved me wrong, basically. And that was the other piece of it. I had zero awareness of the indie game scene at the time.

[The importance of indie gaming] was the thing that Anna Anthropy really recognized, I think. I honestly credit her . . . fifty-fifty for Twine's success. Because she saw something and was in a digital community I had no relationship to.

Personally, I think you can build stories with Twine; you can build games with Twine. I think that's fine. I think there are things that I wouldn't call games that I've experienced with Twine. . . . The problem is that a lot of people see [the claim that] *this is not a game* as an insult [laughs]. And I see how people do that. . . . At the same time, I wish we could return to a world where it's not a value judgment—where people just say, *Eh, this is a game, according to my own personal rubric, and that's not*, and that's the end of it. Unfortunately, now it's just so fraught. I like the fact that there are things people build in Twine that are . . . aspects of both, and people can argue about it.

I suppose that's my own hell-raiser tendencies: let us disrupt these somewhat stuffy debates.

SM: I agree with that. I wanted to ask further about the Interactive Fiction Technology Foundation.

CK: It turns out the acronym [IFTF] is the same as the one for the Institute for the Future . . . which I'm pretty sure is unintentional. [Much amusement.]

SM: Show up at their conference!

CK: The president and the ringleader is Jason McIntosh, who is part of the parser IF community, mostly. He's run the IFComp for the last couple of years now. He reached out to me when he was getting it set up. It's been in existence since July of last year [2016]. Its real purpose is . . . there are all these projects run by people in the community, there's the IFDB, there's the IF Archive, there's the IFComp. . . . All these things are done because people are interested in them, and it's great to have that level of enthusiasm, but the danger is if people burn out, like I did, or just want to move on, then all this stuff could just completely fall apart.

Right now, [IFTF] is trying to help out with projects that need people to look at them. [For instance] right now, the parser IF interpreter situation on Mac OS is terrible. All the ones that used to work don't work anymore on [Mac OS 10.12] Sierra. And it's a real problem. . . . I don't know that I can play . . . the only thing that works right now is a thing called Lectrote. . . . One of the things we're working on right now is to have people fix up this interpreter called Gargoyle, which had been working really well for a long time. So [IFTF] is about adoption of projects, and eventually, hopefully, to fund-raise to help grow stuff . . .

SM: So this gets to the metaquestion I want to ask: What kind of community has Twine become, what kind of community does it belong to, and it sounds like you're saying it's part of the general interactive fiction community?

CK: I believe so. You may get different answers from different people, but as someone who is more steeped in that community, I think of it that way.

SM: Could you tell me how you think of the IF community? How does it fit into the culture generally?

CK: It's an interesting question because [the IF community] has changed so much over time. When I first got internet access . . . when I first went to college, which would be have been in 1998 or so . . . I trawled around in USENET and found the news groups . . . and so, through the nineties . . . I don't exactly know when they died out. . . . It was this very, very tiny community, relatively speaking, of people who were really, really dedicated to it. . . . Looking back on it now, there was always that thread in Infocom's advertising of *Text-based games are inherently superior to graphical games because your mind is the best graphics engine ever* . . . or whatever. Which I kind of believe, though not necessarily to the exclusion of graphical games.

There's this online term, *Amiga persecution complex* . . . you feel you have this superior thing but the world doesn't recognize [it]. [The IF community] had that vibe to it, for a time, but at the same time, people were doing really interesting stuff. . . . The other thing I hear people say is that everything interesting going on in the gaming world at large happened in the IF community ten years before. Which is a bit of an overstatement, but I believe a lot of that is actually true.

I never really intended it to be this way, but Twine became this existential threat [to parser-based games], at least among the old guard. . . . People [said], *We have this very strict definition, and we clung to it because it was part of our community identity: you have to type in words and you get back text in return, and you can't even show graphics*—[or], God forbid—sound! I clued into this way late, but there were people in the wider world [saying], *Twine games aren't games*, and people in the IF community saying, *Twine games aren't IF.*

Carl Muckenhoupt, who was the guy behind Baf's Guide to the IF Archive, one major review site, wrote this article that explained it really well, though I thought his view was incorrect. . . . [Muckenhoupt said], it's like, you're really into jazz, and you keep going to this one jazz club that is preserving your particular definition of jazz, and all these young upstart kids show up and start ruining it with their new jazz.

I'll bet this is a pattern that repeats in every subculture . . . where people come around and challenge things, and the old guard hate it . . . and it's funny to me because I came from that [traditional] part of the community, and I never intended [Twine] to be this massive, subversive, destructive tool, but I also like to think that at this point, people have chilled out a bit and realized we can coexist in peace.

There's the IFComp and then there's the Xyzzy Awards, and people look at how many parser games versus how many choice-based games are in both, and because the community's a little bit nerdy, there's graphs, and stuff like that, and trend lines, and people freak out and post detailed analyses. . . . It's a little overblown, obviously, but people have started to relax. . . . An equilibrium is starting to be achieved. . . . I forget what the numbers were last year, but it was about equal [between parser and Twine entries].

This is a little bit grandiose to say, [but] I think that without Twine, the [IF] community would have continued to be a small thing. There are definitely people who pick up parser games now, even so. I was at PAX East in 2011 and they had an IF meet-up, and there was a girl who must have been about seventeen who showed up at the meet-up, and I was walking back with her to the main area, and I asked how she found out about IF. I said, "You are the youngest person I've ever met who's into it." And she said, "Oh yeah, I found [interactive fiction] on the [Apple] iOS Store and just started playing the games." So there's some longevity to [IF].

And it's not just Twine, actually. Choice of Games had a similar issue, and their communities were much bigger, and there was an eruption of controversy over . . . I forget which Xyzzy Award. . . . One of their games was nominated for it, and a bunch of their fanbase came over to the forums and voted for it, and everybody panicked because normally a thing you'd see 200 votes for was getting 1,500, and so everybody was [thinking], *You must be cheating.* But then people mellowed out about it and realized it was not this big existential threat.

AS: Since you've talked about Twine as an existential threat in the context of IF . . . you and I talked about this during Gamergate—what do you think about the ways Twine has disrupted mainstream gaming culture?—the way the legacy of *Depression Quest* hangs over us . . .

CK: That is sort of the go-to example. [That game approaches its subject] both in terms of form and content. Overall, I think there's bias toward procedural-ness—this has to be hard to program in order for it to be good, artistically. There's obviously parallels in other mediums, even from super-photo-realism to stuff that's more impressionistic, where people say [on one end], *Oh, I can do this*—people say that about everything.

I think it was either TotalBiscuit or someone even worse who said . . . Twine games are great because you can make them without knowing how to make games . . . [to which I say] YES, I AM ON BOARD WITH THAT! I think he was actually meaner. I think he said you can [make Twine games] without any skills—which I am in favor of—or talent, which I disagree with [laughs] and so there is that aspect, where it has to have 3-D graphics to be a game, or something like that.

There are a lot of historical reasons for that, and a lot of them happened by accident, where you look at how journalists cover games, to see how that came out. . . . The way I talk about it, when I give talks, is that the content of *Depression Quest* is really interesting, too, because there are very few games that talk about mental illness in a very non-gimmicky kind of way . . . but that obviously got lost completely in the whole controversy.

I think long term what Twine might really be remembered for is for broadening the scope of what a game can be about . . . and allowing more personal narratives. . . . It's hard to build graphical games unless you're a very skilled artist. . . . It's hard to build a one-off; there's more effort involved in something that will take twenty minutes to play or read through. That's why the confessional Twine genre is such a thing: there's a more immediate payoff to it. Say I want to build a Unity game based on the way I feel today. . . . You're going to be done next month, where you're going to be done with it in Twine, hopefully, that same day.

SM: I still feel that way about [HTML] and JavaScript things, where I'll say, *I really want to do this thing* . . . and it's going to take three weeks, but I won't feel this way in three weeks.

CK: Yeah.

SM: You've just touched on where you think Twine will be in the near future, or the even further future. Could you expand on that? If you could think twenty years out, what do you think happens to Twine?

CK: I'm a pessimist by nature. . . . I think Twine will no longer . . . I think it will always have a place, but at the same time, I think it won't have as prominent a place as it has right now. I see some game companies are taking Twine writing samples, which is pretty cool, and that argues for more longevity among the world at large. But at the same time, I'm mindful that . . . Twine becoming popular was . . . sort of an accident.

Nothing I tried [made the difference] . . . other than building it in the first place, which was [laughs] NO BIG DEAL REALLY! As far as making it popular, I feel like I was very not-responsible for that. . . . It was really Anna [Anthropy], among others, who managed to make that happen, and it seems equally likely that if [Twine] remains popular . . . it will be for reasons I have no idea about.

I'm trying to keep myself a little rooted on the ground and to realize nothing is forever, especially in the software world. It would be nice [for Twine] to persist as a standard-ish format. . . . I still want to be working on it. . . . I think it was Judy Malloy who was writing about . . . her own hypertext engine that she'd been working on since the eighties . . . and that's amazing because that amount of time . . . it would be really interesting to see what that looks like. . . . There are very few software projects out there on which people spend more than a decade, really.

I don't see myself ever losing interest in [Twine], exactly. . . . It will always be a thing for me, but I'm not sure it will always be as big of a deal as it is right now, and that's OK . . . and that's the thing that I'm trying to prepare myself for, I guess. I keep wondering, What is the next Twine going to be? and if I knew, I guess I would build it.

The one thing I think it's not so great at, and people have tried to improve on is . . . I was talking to people at the Mozilla Foundation because I was looking for a home for Twine, and [the man from Mozilla asked], *Well, what's the mobile story for Twine?* And I [thought] I don't really have one because I hate typing on a phone, and I feel like that's the one aspect that someone could really improve on. The other thing would be making it better at collaboration. . . . I know Stuart and I have talked about that in the past. . . . That's something I want to try to do.

SM: This is going to stop being [an] interview and start being an ordinary conversation, but have you ever thought about people being able to just talk to the phone and compose orally?

CK: Mmm . . .

SM: As you were talking, I was thinking about [the IF programming language] Inform 7 and [its] natural-language interface. I kind of hated the idea until I started working with it, and now I want everything to be in English, or whatever [Inform 7's idiom] is. . . . If you think about being able to create powerful structure with almost gestural simplicity . . . that might be really cool.

CK: Yeah, I agree. I think that . . . it needs to embrace text, but also embrace the fact that it's on a phone and on a relatively small screen . . . and swiping or any kind of gesture is much more natural on a phone or any kind of touch screen than it is on a track pad or moving stuff around with the mouse—that kind of thing.

AS: What do you think about the future of interactive fiction? We pick up the odd seventeen-year-old who finds it on the iOS store, and that's good, but what do you think more broadly about the future of the interactive fiction community?

CK: [The Inkle game] *80 Days* is my really short answer. It'll be things that people don't even think of as IF, or like [the mobile game] *Lifeline* [from Big Fish Games]. Stuff like that. I have a lot of respect for Andrew Plotkin, who's also on the board of the IFTF, and he's trying really hard to make the parser thing work on a phone and elsewhere, but I ultimately think it's going to be something else that keeps the principles of the medium and not necessarily the trappings.

If you ask people what kind of game *80 Days* is, I don't think anybody will say it's interactive fiction. Part of it is that *interactive fiction* feels sort of esoteric. . . . The community held on to the definition of IF with a really tight grip . . . and this orthodoxy emerged . . . and to me, it's better to, like, let it go a little bit.

I was talking to Brian Moriarty [of Infocom], and he seemed a little bit perplexed by the worship of parser [games] by people he ran into still . . . because he [was thinking], *How do we adapt this?* He told me about . . . a voice-driven [storytelling technology] . . . which is interesting because I certainly listen to a lot of podcasts now, when I drive, and so I could see, like, talking back to it, potentially . . . [and] in general, speech seems to be the next big thing as far as technology goes.

You can draw on a ton of IF things. . . . Emily Short and Aaron Reed are now working at a company called Spirit AI. . . . I don't know their elevator pitch, exactly, but it seems like they are taking a lot of the principles behind IF and applying them to . . . designing a traditional AAA kind of game, where it's like, *Our company will help make your AI better* . . . or make your conversation trees better, and stuff like that. To me, it's like this hidden substrate to [IF], where you're using it, or playing it, but not necessarily thinking of it as such.

AS: I think Aaron Reed is also working on that.

CK: Yeah. There's also an NYU professor . . . Mitu Khandaker-Kokoris. . . . I don't know much about their technology, but . . . Emily is a really smart person, so I figure there must be something there. And Aaron is too, but I'm less acquainted with him. . . . I really like the Inform 7 book he wrote.

SM: Yeah, I love it. [I've taught with it so much that] my copy is now completely shot. [General laughter.]

CK: I like *Sand Dancer*, the game he has in the book. . . . So anyway, there's a lot of talent there [at Spirit AI], so I'm interested to see what happens, and obviously Inkle, they're kind of a big deal, too, but their new game that they just announced, [*Heaven's Vault*], is moving more toward a graphic novel feel than a text-based one. . . . I'm interested to see what they do with it.

AS: That definitely will be interesting. And you have companies like Netflix supposedly doing a choose-your-own-adventure concept.

CK: We'll see. Sam Barlow is the guy I try to pay attention to on that stuff because I really liked *Her Story*, which was really innovative . . . and I forget the company that he's with, but I feel that he will come up with something really interesting. . . . I'm not so much convinced about Netflix.

AS: If they have any sense, they'll hire [Barlow].

CK: Hopefully! Brian Moriarty has this amazing talk about the history of interactive cinema, and having learned from that, [I realize that] this is a really old concept and nobody has really changed much about it since the very beginning, and it's always been kind of a novelty; it's never gotten any traction, it feels like. And so it seems, the Netflix thing sounds exactly like this . . . but we'll see.

AS: A lot of folks from interactive fiction are going off and working for companies and founding start-ups right now. Are you thinking of doing anything with this background of everything you've done?

CK: I would love to. I've talked with folks, but I've never found the right fit. I've been really hesitant to get into the game industry per se. Back when Zynga—East, I think it was?—had a Baltimore-based branch, I talked to folks from there, [but I thought], *This is Zynga*, and I'm not sure my values are compatible with yours.

SM: And they lasted about eighteen months too.

CK: I guess I dodged a bullet there. I would have switched careers and immediately gotten laid off. Which I guess would have been an instructive experience in the game industry, right there. It's very tough right now because all the companies are like five people.

And I have my own two-person company. It's called Unmapped Path, and the first client work that we've done is for Andrew Schneider, who's written this incredibly long (by my standards, at least) about 150,000 words . . . this interactive story about Robin Hood. We're building that for him. It's supposed to be coming out June-ish . . . and we're working on our own projects as well.

The idea is to leverage Twine to build games for mobile. And that goes back to the problem of Twine not having a good story on mobile. If I play Twine games on my iPad, it's a little bit janky, to be honest. . . . I keep meaning to come around and improve on it. If I tap on a link, it's like for some reason the whole thing highlights. . . . So we are leveraging the content creation aspect of Twine to build games that feel like text adventures but hopefully have a little bit more mass appeal.

This is the boring part where I say that we don't have anything to announce yet, but there's something we're working on that we hope to have an announcement about soon as far as games go. Because I see the role of Twine as like a Photoshop or a Unity. The interesting part to me is not so much the tools but the content. I would like tools as much as possible to be open-source, but I don't feel the same way about games or content per se. I'm more comfortable buying a book than a software program, but I guess that's just my deal.

[Around this point, Chris asks about the book we are writing, which is our chance to say we don't have anything to announce yet . . . and brings up the subject of books about Twine.]

CK: I was at Games for Change a few years ago, and Merritt Kopas [now known as merritt k] was speaking with Austin Walker and Naomi Clark from NYU, and I came up to them after the talk, and Merritt actually gave me a copy of her book, *Videogames for Humans*, and it was like, wow, when you have a book written about something you made, and it's just sort of astonishing. So when there's a book out of all this, it will occupy a place of honor on my bookshelf.

SM: Well, we hope so. [General amusement.]

CK: See, I'm not even saying *if*, I'm saying *when*.

AS and SM: Thanks.

Appendix II

Interview with Dan Cox

November 3, 2017, at HASTAC in Orlando, Florida

SM: Can you talk about what drew you to Twine, or your lead-up to Twine? How did you get started?

DC: I first ran into Twine in November 2012, which is when Porpentine's *Cyberqueen* was submitted at Ludum Dare. Which I was a part of, and when you take part in them, you participate as a judge, so I saw it right then. I think I started posting stuff late December 2012 for the first time.

SM: So via Porpentine?

DC: Yes.

SM: What is Ludum Dare?

DC: Ludum Dare is a twice-a-year game jam that has a random theme, picked sometimes hours before. It's usually forty-eight hours, although sometimes they change the rules—that's been going for years now.

SM: So via the personal game community to Twine? What other things were you working with before Twine?

DC: I did Flash games for a little while; I did C++ before that. Two to three years before that would have been middle of high school for me. I'm in my early thirties now.

SM: It's appalling how old people are who seem very young to me now. This will happen to you eventually. People will say they are in their early thirties and you'll realize there's this whole swatch of things that happened before you were born.

SM: I noticed that people like Porpentine or Anna Anthropy use pen names or screen names that have almost become a signature of Twine. What's your screen name?

DC: Videlais.

AS: Do you see Twine as belonging to the game space, the interactive fiction space, the web space, or belonging to some other tradition?

DC: I would say it belongs to the interactive fiction space, since that opens more doors than it closes. It has its roots in wikis, but I don't think it [does] anymore: for the longest time, it was built on Tiddly-Wiki, from when Chris originally built it. If there's any of that left, it's just the barest of bare bones. 1.3.4 and 1.4.2 still are on that, but 2.X, as far as I know, is not based on that.

SM: This is continuity with our interview with Chris, when I asked him, "So why did you build a hypertext system?" and Chris replied, "I didn't think that's what I was doing, I was much more thinking about interactive fiction."

DC: I will just say, especially sort of post Gamergate—well, Gamergate's not really over—I'm way more open to applying things like *developer* and *gamer* to things in Twine because of the hideousness that came out of that, and especially conversations I was a part of right before that where people were sort of dismissing it. Even before *Depression Quest* was around, there were huge conversations about "Twine stories aren't games, they aren't developers."

SM: You've in fact anticipated another question from our list—should we say *Twine game* or *Twine story*, or *Twine fiction*? I put this to Darius Kazemi, and he said, "The kids just say Twine."

DC: I've seen that in a number of places. I should put it to the committee and see what they say. I have at various times said *Twine fictions*, *Twine stories*, myself.

SM: When we mentioned "Twines" to Chris, it raised the question of trademarking Twine, which apparently has been discussed.

DC: Yes, it still is.

AS: Let's talk about some of the things you've been working on, like the Twine Cookbook. What motivated that project, and where do you see it going?

DC: A not-small amount of it is me being sort of selfish in that I've got five years' worth of Twine tutorials and videos that are somewhere around ten hours' worth of content and I still get comments from people looking at stuff that was recorded around four years ago and going, "Hey, this doesn't work anymore." And I'm like, "Yes, because it was for three versions ago, for systems that don't exist anymore."

When I joined the Twine Committee, I proposed something similar, and they said they had had something like it on the backburner and asked if I'd like to take it over. And I said yes because I've got years and years of examples. We had discussions about how those examples would go in and become a part of it. It's still an ongoing conversation, and I think I just did something yesterday, planning a meeting on how to move forward.

AS: Why GitHub?

DC: This was an interesting problem. We wanted to be as open as possible and traditionally—and I say *traditionally* in that it started with Twine 2—most Twine documentation has been on BitBucket. Chris's stuff is there, Leon's stuff is there, most of the story formats live there.

The problem with BitBucket is that a lot of the people who contribute to projects are just more familiar with GitHub from a brand perspective. So with GitHub, it's easier for those who don't have accounts to navigate. Given we were considering moving to GitHub anyway, this was a good test, starting on one of IFTF's private accounts, to let us play with some things. We're trying GitHub out to see if it works as well to support open-source and offer a better way to let people contribute.

SM: And you're committed to the open-source aspect—it has a wiki feel, so users will be updating and making changes?

DC: Yes. That was a Chris suggestion. He'd been looking at GitBook, which is the format we use, and I played around with that—it's weird because my memory of it extends before it was public, and we tried other things. But we liked GitBook for the free export to a range of formats.

SM: Could you give us a little gloss on the IFTF? We heard a little bit from Chris about it.

DC: My understanding of its rise is it came about from a number of different problems. The Interactive Fiction Competition (IF Comp) wanted a place to keep track of code and funding and other things. Simultaneously, Chris was feeling the pull of the Twine community exploding and not being able to keep up with a lot of the development. There's also a bit of a history here in that 1.3.5 was Chris, but 1.4.2 sort of wasn't, in that it was Leon and a couple other people who had moved into that space. Eventually, those people took over a story format, and then they all moved into development for Twine 2.

IFTF came about as a confluence of wanting to keep track of a bunch of interactive fiction efforts and give them a place, and a nonprofit, and to pool funding and resources. I've really only been a part of it for a few months now, but my understanding was we've got all of these different funding sources and this was a way to put it all under a single nonprofit to protect their future.

SM: Do you have a sense that this is a formalization of the IF world, that this might be a starting point to look for money?

DC: That's in fact going on right now. We have an asynchronous meeting this week, and we've started the conversation on *If we find funding, what do we do with that?* And simultaneously, there's been conversations about formalizing specifications, like the Twee specification, which is currently informal. It doesn't have an ISO or IEEE format or anything. There's been ongoing conversations about how we might standardize to help people—the Twee stuff's not documented anywhere, for example.

SM: From my perspective sitting in the dinosaur world of higher ed, this feels like the arrival of the mammals. As our institutions die out, here's maybe a way to keep the things we care about alive. Good luck to you.

AS: Switching gears, we've discussed the open-source aspect of Twine: How's that model working for you, and what do you see as the successes and challenges?

DC: My own experience with the open-source communities, which has extended to three or four of them now, is that it tends to be the eighty-twenty problem, where 20 percent of the contributors are doing 80 percent of the work.

Right now, at least within Twine, there is a great deal of support coming out of the committee and less work coming out of the community, which isn't doing technical work. They're producing a lot of interesting things, but they don't always contribute back to the technical documentation, which is a problem right now. Chris told me after I joined that the push for me to be on the committee was driven in part by my history documenting Twine stuff and the need for a champion for that. I've made it my mission to do the work of trying to document story formats. As an example, Snowman hasn't had any formal documentation for a year and a half. I personally wrote a lot of it, and Chris checked it for me to make sure it was right. That went up on the wiki a few weeks ago, and before that, we had some Google documents I had created.

These efforts are me trying to collect community knowledge, and in doing that, I learned that a number of people had been doing that already—Keegan Long-Wheeler, for instance. So community reception has been very positive, but it's also turned out that a lot of people have been doing this work but none of it is standardized or formalized. We're just now trying to get it on the site, which has been an interesting open-source problem.

The successes and problems, at least as I've been dealing with documentation and standardization, have been interesting in the push and pull about how best to document code when we have existing documentation on different websites. How do we make it easier for people to see that? One of the problems right now is that to see the documentation of story format, you have to know that you can change story formats and then click a link to an outside site, which is three or four more steps than it should be, but it's been the traditional way. We're trying to figure out UI/UX stuff at the same time as we improve documentation, and solve parts of the problem with the Cookbook, and figure out what the future solution might look like. There's a whole lot of stuff in the air as we're trying to figure that out.

SM: Given this range of formats, do you think there's any chance of Twine having a schism where a format takes off on its own?

DC: Away from Twine?

SM: Like, there was Twine, but now there's Harlowe. We don't hold for Snowman.

DC: I don't think there's been official talk of that, but yes, my personal feeling precommittee was that I was seeing people get annoyed when I made videos supporting one story format over another. Anyone who has looked at them over time realizes I do a run of like a dozen on one format, and then I switch and do a run on another, but I have seen that in places. I think it's more because of the weird functionality overlaps and disconnects. For instance, for a while, Harlowe didn't do arrays, but now it does—SugarCube did them better, so if you wanted to do anything with arrays you would use it. And then, of course, Snowman hasn't had documentation in forever. Generally, they try to be on par and support similar things, so I don't think it would be purposeful.

AS: From an educational perspective, this is why it took me so long to get on board with Twine 2—the variance in story formats, particularly in syntax, creates a lot of [confusion] for students. Do you think the formats will ever reconcile?

DC: I wish they would. I will say that while trying to write the Cookbook stuff, I've gotten complaints that "I'm doing this wrong" on parts, and it's in part because [of] the transition between thinking in different story formats—the difference in variable scope between formats, for instance.

SM: When people make up a language from the same root as yours that *isn't* yours, you're in trouble.

DC: We had a whole conversation about whether we should make things as close as possible to one another—if we're using the replace macro here, should we change it, or try and match the different functionality in the story format? Link replacement in Harlowe and SugarCube works slightly differently, and Snowman doesn't have link replacement at all. I wish they would come together, but I don't anticipate them ever doing that.

SM: How well are Twine folks connecting with the parser-driven Inform 7 community, for instance? It's almost like we've got different congregations in our church, but then there are other churches.

DC: I will say on our IFTF Slack, the general channel is open to anyone, and I've seen conversations between Chris and Zarf (who does IFComp/Inform stuff), and I've seen groups gather and start general conversations connected to past projects, such as the Inform Recipe Book.

SM: History is a factor here, as we're discovering.

AS: We talked a little about Twee and its documentation. What do you see as the motivation and future of Twee?

DC: I can talk a lot more about the future of Twee than I can talk about the past, since I don't know the motivation behind the decisions Chris made with Twee or the community's view previous to me. I was aware it existed, and my feeling is that they wanted a format that they could exchange between versions and import and export. With Twine 2, the ability to import from HTML, and thus to import anything that was made after Twine 2, in any story format, was essential.

As for the future of Twee, I haven't been an active part of these conversations, but as part of the committee, I've been observing them. The story format editors, along with Chris and a couple of other people, are trying to figure out a way to standardize it so that other people can build editors for it or tools that export it. One of the things we've found is that people want to use parts of Twine in Unity and other engines, so Twee has been a format bridge to help people with that. There's no specification for it, so you usually just have to go ask people, "Does this work?"

As part of this, we've learned there's no way to do commenting internal to Twee code either. You can do HTML comments in Harlowe [and] JavaScript comments in SugarCube and Snowman. This turned into a Cookbook problem: How do you put comments in the code to show people on a website? I don't know if anything will come of it this year, but there is an active conversation about it and where we put comments. For the future, I think the hope is to build something that can move toward a visual interface.

AS: So moving out of the code and into the community, what has surprised you the most in how people are using Twine? What do you most admire?

DC: I would say the anti-Twine response has been the most interesting, particularly since 2012. One of the things I've gotten the most angry about with individual people is people saying Twine stuff's not games, or Twine stuff's just projects, or even people going as low as to say women can't code, or we don't want people of color, or we don't want queer people—a whole [lot of] homophobic, racist, misogynist responses—which blew up during Gamergate. It makes sense in a weird way that it blew up around *Depression Quest* because of Quinn's use of Twine. There's a lot of silent hatred that was bubbling and exploded in its wake. My first response is, "Who cares—like, what are you, the game police?"

AS: Which was, of course, a Twine game.

DC: My response pre-Gamergate would have been to say that you're not Chris, so who are you to say what Twine is? But in a positive way, I've seen Twine embraced in academia, which I did not think was ever going to happen—your Chronicle posts and mention of my videos, which is where we met. Previous to that, I was told by people at my current institution that Twine was a waste of time. I'd been doing the videos for a while, but I don't talk about Twine a whole lot outside of Twitter. I was told Twine was a waste of time, it was never going to catch on, and that I should stop doing the videos, and eventually that I should just take the videos down. My feeling from that was "Oh right, no one in academia is ever going to care about Twine." It has been adopted by academia in a number of surprising ways in the last year.

Based on the initial negativity, I'd decided not to talk about Twine at conferences, as my thought was of course, *Everybody hates Twine, so I'm just not going to talk about it.* Last year, I introduced myself in a workshop as the guy who does these videos, and everyone went, "Oh, it's you," because they'd only ever heard my voice and didn't know what I looked like. "You're Dan."

When I started making videos in 2013, Anna Anthropy's guide to Twine already existed, so Twine being embraced by the personal game community was not very surprising. It had been that way for as long as I've known it. But the hatred? I've never understood it.

To turn to your next question, what have I admired? I tried my hand at personal games, and I found that I have the teacher bug more than I have the developer bug. I'm really good at explaining things, not particularly good at creating things. The people I admire are those who can imbue wonderful and personal stories into Twine. I'm sometimes jealous of that, when I'm moved by a game that's amazing. I admire people who do weird things with Twine, like when Porpentine's done something new, like a jQuery experiment pre–Twine 2 for a proto-MMO with multiple players in the story. She always does wonderful, delightfully weird things. *Even Cowgirls Bleed* by Christine Love was really cool and inspired a whole lot of conversations around whether we should try to enable that in Twine 1. I was excited to see a lot of that come into Twine 2, like events and mouseovers suddenly were enabled.

A lot of student work is also great. My teaching experience with Twine has been very strange—entirely online for five years. I've never taught it in a classroom. My experience with my students is that someone would email me a question, I'll try to answer it, and then they will disappear. There's a couple people that have been very nice and a year later or so will email me a "Thanks, Dan" and put me in the acknowledgments or something. It's usually triage. Student projects have always been my favorite.

AS: From your perspective, what's Twine's place in larger culture? You've talked about it finding more of a space in academia, and of course there's the more literary world, the IF world—do you see Twine as belonging, or really being its own community?

DC: My increasing feeling over the last few years is it doesn't really matter as long as people are using it and doing good work—and good work here defined as *not hate speech*. Over the last five years, I've felt a very strange connection to the community, in that at times, I feel like I'm very, very close to it, and it feels like there are maybe fifty people who are the main contributors and that I basically know the names of them. Porpentine, Anna Anthropy, [and so on]. And then there's times when I'll discover there was a whole other community producing hundreds of works that I knew nothing about.

The other day, when I put a call out on Twitter for teaching resources, I found a community that had been using Twine for years. They had a ton of personal projects, tutorials, student projects—all archived—that I couldn't believe I hadn't seen. And still they said, "Thanks, Dan." And I'm just in a room by myself, talking to myself for hours at a time, trying really hard to say things like "the value of the variable" and not screw that up.

AS: Is there anything you would like to see from Twine in the future?

DC: Someone once asked me, "What can Twine do? Is it anything a web browser can do?" And I said yes, and I'm going to forever tell that story because the answer is always yes. The possibilities are endless. This includes things like game controllers—I've seen some projects use game controllers. I've seen stuff integrate video, audio, like your thing at SIGDOC last year. What haven't we tried? Well, what hasn't games explored? Every time I think games cannot do that, someone comes out with a game like *Blindsight* (all audio) or *Hidden Agenda* (using mobile phones to play and vote on a story).

AS: So where do you think it's headed in the next decade?

DC: I think it's easier to say in the next year what I'm hoping will happen: documentation and standardization, which is sort of a double-edged sword—formalization also cuts. My hope is that standardization will help more than it hurts. As for the second decade, I have no idea. I did not anticipate Twine 2 existing. I didn't even know Chris was working on it, and then, hey—Twine 2. Harlowe has changed a whole lot. if you'd asked me if Sugarcane would become SugarCube, I'd have no idea, so in a decade—I have no idea. I've seen with Flash and HTML5 projects, they're around because there's a niche for them, and then when there isn't a niche, they fall. Will the web browser be around? Or is the web browser the computer? I don't know.

I will say, when I mentioned Inform the other day in a workshop, someone laughed and said, "People are still using that?" And I laughed and said, yes—me.

Appendix III

Bonus Practical Chapter: Beyond Twine

One of the major virtues of Twine, especially with the Chapbook story format, is the way it connects smoothly to other kinds of software practice. In this encore practical chapter, we look beyond Twine into the coding world we've briefly glimpsed in previous chapters. The projects in this chapter do not use Twine at all but depend instead on HTML and JavaScript, the associated coding language supported by all modern web browsers. We make this departure from Twine not because we've exhausted its possibilities but to serve two complementary purposes. On one hand, we explore some design techniques Twine does not readily support. At the same time, this excursion into the wilderness may put into welcome relief the things Twine makes easier. You may come away from this chapter with a renewed appreciation for Twine, especially if your interests lie mainly with storytelling and turn-based interaction.

This chapter might not be for everyone. As we said all the way back in chapter P-2, code work can be daunting. Twine spares its users significant drudgery and detail, including things like spelling, capitalization, syntax, order of operations, and some basic math. The projects in this chapter involve only very modest code structures, but they do raise the bar of complexity slightly above even our more code-intensive

Twine practicals. If you are willing to trade design constraints for relative simplicity, skip this wilderness tour and stay in the civilized precincts of Twine. It's an eminently livable environment. If you're tempted but uncertain about the exploring that lies ahead, here are some questions for the boarding ramp:

1. Have you ever built your own web page or site, without using a code-generating tool like Dreamweaver?
2. Are you considering working with more sophisticated game design systems such as Unity?
3. Do you like making things that break conventions?

Answering yes to any of these questions qualifies you for the trip. Of course, you may also proceed if you don't have a choice—maybe this chapter has been assigned for class—or if you're just the kind of person who always does things they're told to avoid. We warned you.

Tools and Procedures

Even though this chapter does not work with Twine, supporting materials can be found online at https://github.com/AMSUCF/Twining. You're as welcome to adapt the code examples here as in the other practical chapters. You won't be able to import our .html pages into Twine, obviously, but you can do something just as useful: use the "View Source" feature of your web browser to see our code. If for some reason your browser makes this difficult, we've provided the code in text files with notes in cases where the code is meant to be placed anywhere other than the HEAD division of a web page (mentioned later).

Instead of the Twine application, you will need two other pieces of freely available software: a web browser and a text editor. Any reasonably current browser will do except Microsoft Edge, which for some ill-considered reason makes opening local web pages very hard. At this writing, Google's Chrome browser is generally preferred by web professionals. When we say *text editor*, we do not mean a word processing program like Microsoft Word but a simpler program designed to produce plain text or ASCII files. If you have a Windows system, type "Notepad" into your search window. You should have an application by this name. On a Mac OS computer, the equivalent program is *Text Edit*. For Linux users there is *VI*. Because we spend significant time writing code, we use a commercial product called *TextPad*, available for Windows and Mac OS. This program adds many useful features but is by no means required.

Do not attempt to build any of the exercises in this chapter with Word or another word processor, even if you choose the text-only save or export option. Word processors often add unseen formatting information that can cripple a web file. In fact, because the level of detail in code structures of these projects is high, you may not want to type what you see at all. You're better off downloading the digital version of this chapter, or even better the complete finished code, from the *Twining* website (https://github.com/AMSUCF/Twining). Open one of these files in a text editor and you can modify and tinker as you like. Because of this recommendation, we'll modify the visual convention of previous chapters. Code fragments will be boxed, but we've omitted the ◊ prompt for text entry.

The kind of DIY web coding we describe here is a two-window experience. You need your text editor and your browser both running. (Two windows does not mean two monitors; you can toggle back and forth.) You need the same file open in both applications—doing this will not cause a crash. The taskbar is your friend. The typical development process starts with entering some code into a web page file, which is a text-only document with the extension .htm or .html. *The extension is not optional.* If you try to open what you think is a web page in a file having any other extension, such as .txt or .rtf, all you will see is the page markup, not what the markup is supposed to produce. Once you've saved your changes in the text editor—*make sure to save*—switch over to your browser and open the page file locally.

If you wonder what *open the file locally* means, we have some news for you. (Also, consider replacing that Microsoft browser.) Browsers mainly pull in data from the internet at large by communicating with computers called servers via HTTP. However, all web browsers—even Microsoft bleeding Edge—can obtain data by opening a document on the computer on which they are running—which is to say, locally. Civilized browsers allow you to do this by selecting something like "Open" or "Open Local" from the file menu or equivalent. The keyboard shortcut in Windows and Linux is usually CTRL+O (or on Mac OS, Apple key and O). You may need to traverse your file structure to find your page file, which brings us to another important point: *always know where your files are!*

In these Cloud-y days of remote and virtual storage, this principle may need reinforcing. Before starting any web project, we recommend two things. One, put your phone down, or set it aside because it may come in handy if you need to look for help at some point—but *a smartphone is not a coding tool.* Two, a minimum requirement for coding is access to a main directory or, ideally, a graphical desktop. You'll need the other kind of computer, a desktop or laptop machine. (Netbooks are acceptable.) This brings us to the other basic procedure: create a folder (or directory) on your PC desktop—by which we mean the level of file storage you see when you log into your computer—and save your work there. Now we come to the contents of your web page, which will eventually get us to code—but first, one more preparatory section.

Basics of Page Coding

The most important elements of a web page are three *containers*, one called HTML, the second called *head*, and the last called *body*. In terms of *markup*, which is another word for HTML code, a container is a pair of *tags*. A tag is a statement within a set of angle brackets, or a less-than and a greater-than sign:

```
<HTML>
    <HEAD></HEAD>
    <BODY></BODY>
</HTML>
```

The closing tag of a container always begins with a forward slash. Eventually, we'll introduce some other containers, including the all-important container *<script></script>*, within which almost all our JavaScript code will reside.

With these basics out of the way, let's look at the structure of a blank web page. You can type this into your own blank text-editor document, making sure you've saved your file with the extension .htm or .html. There's enough complexity here that you might want to download from our website rather than transcribe.

Here's the page code before any JavaScript happens:

```
<!DOCTYPE HTML PUBLIC "-//W3C//DTD HTML 4.01
Transitional//EN">
<html>
<head>
    <meta charset="utf-8"/>
    <title>A page needs a title</title>
    <style type="text/css">
        div{ font: 18pt Cambria; padding: 20px; }
    </style>
    <script>
        //JavaScript goes here
    </script>
</head>

<body>
    <div id="out"></div>
</body>
</html>
```

If this were a book on HTML and general web coding, we'd go into detail about various features of this markup—the document type definition, the meta declaration, and the CSS style sheet, for instance. We might also point out that though web code ignores white space, it's important for readability to keep tags on separate lines whenever you can. We should also note that this page has a preconfigured style sheet for the projects we intend to build. That style sheet contains a rule for the page element called *DIV*, specifying that any text found within such a container will be in eighteen-point Cambria with twenty pixels of padding around it. You can see a blank DIV container within the body container. This DIV has an ID attribute (informally speaking, a name), which is the word *out*.

We direct your attention primarily to this pair of tags:

```
<script>
</script>
```

This is a script container. It's where all our JavaScript code will be installed. Though you can put a script container at several points in the markup, we'll always place it within the head container. Putting it there ensures that all the page elements we reference are loaded into memory before we start doing things with them.

With this quick tour of page infrastructure done, we can proceed to our first coding project.

Bonus Example 1: JavaScript Text Selector

If you notice a certain resemblance between our first two projects here and example P-3.3, you're paying attention. We'll base all our projects in this chapter on the same kind of substitution grammar we used in chapter P-3, though we'll move on to other techniques besides text generation. In the JavaScript context, we can streamline text generation in a couple of important ways. The first of these improvements is the use of specialized functions, or as programmers call them, *custom methods*. We'll come to the second major refinement, the use of a switch structure, in bonus example 2. For the moment, consider three small but momentous bits of code. If you were typing along, we'd have you enter them into the script container of our blank web page, yielding this:

```
<script>
    function r(range){
        return Math.floor(Math.random()*range)
    }

    function g(source){
        theArray = source.split(",")
        return theArray[r(theArray.length)]
    }

    function outIt(what){
        document.getElementById("out").innerHTML =
        what
    }
</script>
```

As we've mentioned earlier, a function is a set of code statements that can be put flexibly into action or *invoked* as needed. Functions can be invoked by *handlers* when a page loads or some other event takes place in the browser. They can also be invoked by other functions, which is what puts the *fun* in functions. Our three functions are called *r*, *g*, and *outIt*. The writer of a function can use any name not reserved by JavaScript and the browser. The name *r* refers to random numbers. The name *g* suggests "generate" or possibly "gimme." The name *outIt* refers to output or display. As you can see, in each of our custom methods, the name is followed by a word in parentheses. This word is called a *parameter*. It is a special kind of variable that passes a value from the invoking code to the function.

In *r*, the parameter is called *range*, and as you can see, it is used to set a maximum value for the generation of a random number, using the same call to the JavaScript *Math* object we used (somewhat liberally) in chapter P-3. The *r* function supplies a random number between 0 and (because it rounds down) a value one less than the range parameter. This arrangement is perfect for working with arrays, which are series of items numbered from 0 to a number that is one less than the number of items—for an array of 6 items, 0 to 5. The *return* statement converts the chosen number into output so that if we write *r(5)*, the expression may translate as 0, 1, 2, 3, or 4.

The parameter for g is called *source*, and unlike the range parameter of r, it will be the type of variable called a string—which is to say, a non-mathematical series of letters and numbers such as "hooey" or "44 A.D." or, closer to our context here, "firefly,omnivore,beauty." That last example is a comma-separated string. The g function accepts a string and does two things with it. First, it uses the built-in *split* method to convert the comma-separated list into an array. So "firefly,omnivore,beauty" yields the following array:

```
firefly
omnivore
beauty
```

"Firefly" is item 0, "omnivore" is item 1, "beauty" is item 2, and the length of the array is 3. Next, the *g* function calls the *r* function to generate a random number between 0 and the length of the array, which it uses to make a random selection from the array via square bracket notation. The result is again turned into output using the *return* statement.

The *outIt* function does not use a *return* statement but instead modifies a page element directly. JavaScript can do that! In fact, this is what JavaScript was invented to do. The *outIt* function changes the *innerHTML* property of the DIV we created with the ID of "out"—our display DIV, in other words. To achieve this, *outIt* traverses the DOM of our web page. All pages automatically have such a model, which is a listing of all the various elements they contain along with their names and, in some cases, numbers. The traversal uses something called *dot notation*, which is a familiar convention in web coding. It uses the *getElementById* method of the *document* object to find a DIV called "out." When found, said object's *innerHTML* property—what it contains—is changed from something (or in this case, nothing) to something else.

The custom methods *g* and *r* create a basic framework for randomly selecting from comma-separated strings of text. We can show how they work by adding a few more pieces to our page markup. First, let's build a string with which to test our random selector. We'll add this line at the top of the script container:

```
testSource = "firefly,omnivore,beauty,greeble,Prov
o,whimsical,flatiron,Mme. Ortega y Bullfrog"
```

The final item of this test string shows our system will work even with multiword phrases and punctuation marks, so long as they don't include commas. Notice the final item is not followed by a comma.

Next, also within the script container, we'll add a fourth function immediately after *outIt*:

```
function writeUp(){
   for(var i=0; i<5; i++){
      outIt(g(testSource))+ " "
   }
}
```

This function contains a *for* loop—we've mentioned this element before. It's a way of repeating an instruction a specified number of times and keeping track of the repetitions. We'll see something like it in our further examples. *For* loops are enormously useful. Notice also we've appended a space to our output, using the + operator, which is smart enough to know that it's dealing with strings (because " " is a string) and not numbers. The line within the loop is the key to the show: it calls the *outIt* function, passing it the result of the *g* function, which is passed the test source string to work with. The result on each iteration of the *for* loop is a randomly chosen word from *testSource*, with a trailing space added.

Finally, we need to invoke this new *writeUp* function. We do this by adding an *onLoad* handler to the initial body tag of our page, which is outside of both the script container and the head container. The body tag will now look like this:

```
<body width: 800px onLoad="writeUp()">
```

When we load the page in our browser, we may see something like the following:

firefly omnivore Mme. Ortega y Bullfrog greeble beauty

Though much more likely, we'll have something like this:

firefly omnivore flatiron greeble flatiron

Repetitions! Yes, well, remember the orange wheelbarrow. As you'll recall, getting a random number generator to avoid repetition takes some work, and for the sake of simplicity, we won't bother this time. Instead, we'll move on to a more sophisticated application of the substitution grammar technique.

Bonus Example 2A:
JavaScript Generator (Sequential)

As we said in the previous section, switching to JavaScript and the DIY web brings two major benefits for our text-generation project. Custom methods are the first. The second is a very powerful programming structure called *switch*. In this example, we'll show how to apply this technique. First, some setup. Assume we've opened a new copy of the template web page introduced in the "Tools and Procedures" section. The script container is blank.

In this container, we'll install our three core functions—*r*, *g*, and *outIt*—exactly as they were in the previous example. (In the next example, we'll see a way to avoid this duplication of text. For clarity, we'll hold off on that for the moment.) At the top of our script container, ahead of our core functions, we'll add the following lines:

```
numOptions = 5;
switcher = 0;

function writeUp(){
        for(var i=0; i<numOptions; i++){
                outIt(generate())
        }
}
```

The first two lines are variable declarations. The *numOptions* variable declares the number of grammar options we will have in our switch statement (we're coming to that). The *switcher* variable is a counter we'll use to cycle through our options in sequence. The *writeUp* function resembles its counterpart in the previous example, with two small variations. First, the limit set for the loop is whatever value we assign to *numOptions*. We could simply have put a 5 here, but referring to the variable makes adding grammar options easier. If we add more options, we can just increase the number assigned to *numOptions*. Second, the function called for generating text is not the *g* function directly but a new function called *generate*, which we'll proceed to define. We'll start by roughing in the bare outlines of this function:

```
function generate(){
t = "";

    switch(switcher){

        case 0:
                //you wake up
                break

        case 1:
                //somewhere nearby is the sound of
                a chainsaw
                break
```

```
    case 2:
            //you can smell woodsmoke
            break

    case 3:
            //you remember there was a bonfire
            break

    case 4:
            //go back to sleep
            break
    }

}
```

Before we come to our switch, structure let's briefly discuss the first line, which defines a variable called *t*. *T* is for text—this variable will hold the text of the sentence we are generating. We'll build it up step by step. When we're done, we'll turn it into output with a *return* statement. All that will be explained later.

First, let's discuss the switch structure. As the name suggests, it's a mechanism for directing the operation of the program to certain lines depending on the value of its parameter, the variable named in the parentheses that follow the word *switch*. For this version of our project, we'll use a sequential counting variable, *switcher*. A switch structure has branching options called *cases*. A case is identified by that keyword followed by a value or an expression and a colon. Here we're using integer values, so you see a series of numbers. Switch cases can also be written on strings or logical expressions.

Following each case line are two indented lines. The indentation is required by JavaScript—one of the few cases where it matters. Right now, there are only two lines indented for each case. We'll come to the first one momentarily. For the moment, let's consider the second, which is the single statement *break*. This very powerful command tells Java-Script to break out of its current operation—marching through a series of statements in a switch structure—and go to the next line outside of that structure. In other words, *break* breaks the action. Every case in a switch structure must have a break statement. Technically, the final case doesn't need one, but you should put one in just in case you decide to add more cases, as you can do if you like.

The other element in our switch structure is a series of sentences preceded by double slashes, one for each case. The // indicates that the following text is a *comment*, material that will be skipped by the JavaScript interpreter when the script is run. A comment introduced by // continues to the end of its line. (There's another construction for multi-line comments, but it's not relevant here.) Our comment sentences are, strictly speaking, optional. Each one indicates a template or grammar we'll use for variation. We put them in as a mnemonic device to remind us of the pattern we are matching. For the human writer, they are not optional. You don't have to set things up this way; it's just one model, though it's served us well on many occasions.

We flesh out the switch structure by adding conditions under each case. We'll discuss the first in detail, then look at the completed structure. Case 0 is our first option—programmers like to count from zero. We'll flesh it out as follows:

```
case 0:
        //you wake up
        t += "you " + g("think you're
        awake,cease to dream,open your good
        eye")
        break
```

That new line is kind of monstrous, but it's very useful. It starts by adding to the *t* variable: that's what "+=" means. Technically, we could have just said "=" at this point because the *t* variable is empty when this line executes—it was declared that way. Since later cases will have multiple assignments to the *t* variable, when we'll need to add rather than replace, we've used "+=" for the sake of uniformity. The first thing we add to our *t* variable is the word *you* followed by a space. All variations of our sentence will start this way. This brings us to the variations.

Remember, our *g* function takes in a comma-separated string, splits it into an array, and then chooses from the array at random. We're passing along just such a list, consisting of a series of phrases that could follow *you*. There are only three options in our string. That's strictly for convenient readability. You can add as many variations as you like without any change to the *g* function. The function always knows how many options to choose from, no matter how many or few you throw it. In setting up the string passed to *g*, which contains our variations, some very careful typing is required. We have to remember to add no spaces around the commas, to put the quotation marks around the whole series and not single items (as we'd do for an array), and to make sure there are "+" signs connecting all pieces of the template. Let's just say it's easy to get all this wrong.

After a whole bunch of careful typing—or after much sloppy typing and some grumbly debugging—we end up with this completed version of our switch construction:

```
switch(switcher){
   case 0:
      //you wake up
      t += "you " + g("think you're awake,cease
      to dream,open your good eye")
      break;

   case 1:
      //somewhere nearby is the sound of a
      chainsaw
      t += "somewhere " + g("nearby,far away,not
      here")
      t += " is the " + g("sound of a
      chainsaw,smell of mahogany,country of
      smiles")
      break;
```

```
    case 2:
        //you can smell woodsmoke
        t += "you can smell " +
        g("woodsmoke,begonias,an elephant")
        break;

    case 3:
        //you remember there was a bonfire
        t += "you " + g("forget,remember,imagine")
        t += " there was a " + g("bonfire,search
        party,barn raising")
        break;

    case 4:
        //go back to sleep
        t += "the " + g("chaplain,barista,walrus")
        t += " says " + g("go back to sleep,dream
        more carefully,walk on")
        break;
}
```

Again, there are just three options at each substitution point, mainly to make the example marginally readable. You may add more without making any changes to the script. Just add a comma at the end of any of the sequences and type in your additional text. Be sure to preserve the closing quotation marks. You can also add template options by putting more cases into the switch structure. If you do that, however, be sure to increase the value of *numOptions*. If you forget, though the script will run successfully, you'll never see your new sentences.

Speaking of running the script, we need three more lines to make this possible. They go outside of the curly brace that closes the switch structure—the last character you see in the aforementioned block—but before the curly brace that closes the *generate* function as a whole. Here are those final instructions:

```
switcher ++;
if(switcher == numOptions) switcher = 0;
return t;
```

The first command increases the value of switcher by one. The second checks to see if switcher has reached the number set in *numOptions*—in other words, have we run through all five of our grammar templates? Finally, we return *t*, the string variable in which we've been building our variant sentence. (If a function contains a return statement, it must always be the last statement in the function.)

With these details in place, we can run the example and observe the output, which ought to look something like this:

you cease to dream
somewhere not here is the country of smiles
you can smell woodsmoke
you remember there was a barn raising
the chaplain says go back to sleep

or this:

you think you're awake
somewhere nearby is the smell of mahogany
you can smell begonias
you imagine there was a barn raising
the chaplain says dream more carefully

There's enough structure here—the unvarying sequence of those five sentences, designed to read as a certain kind of narrative—to balance the variations, which are written carefully enough, unlike our free-verse excursions in chapter P-3, for at least an approximation of coherence. For our next trick, we'll make some key changes to the example we've just completed to convert it from a sequential generator to a random-access generator.

Bonus Example 2B:
JavaScript Generator (Randomized)

Only a few changes are required to convert the sequential generator to random operation. First, delete two of the lines we added to the bottom of the script at the end of the previous example:

```
switcher ++;
if(switcher == numOptions) switcher = 0;
```

Do *not* delete the third line, containing the return statement! We're just dispensing with that sequential counter, the variable called *switcher*. While we're at it, we can also delete this line from the top of the script:

```
switcher = 0
```

Nothing bad happens if you don't delete this line, but it's good practice to eliminate useless lines, as they can be confusing when you try to understand your code later on.

Next, change the parameter at the beginning of the switch structure so that it looks like this:

```
switch(r(numOptions))
```

Now, instead of marching through the sequence of sentence templates, we're choosing one on each pass, as randomly as we choose any number in this chapter, using our faithful *r* function. After completing these changes, the output looks like this:

the barista says walk on
somewhere not here is the smell of mahogany
you think you're awake
the barista says dream more carefully
you can smell an elephant

or this:

> *somewhere not here is the smell of mahogany*
> *somewhere not here is the country of smiles*
> *the chaplain says walk on*
> *you can smell woodsmoke*
> *you imagine there was a bonfire*

Once again, our little machine seems to hold up pretty well. The repetitions look almost deliberate (which they are, in an indirect way). The narrative scheme, such as it is, is impressionistic enough to survive the imposition of randomness.

Externalizing the Generator

As we move toward our final three examples, we'll need to make one more important change to our text generator: moving it to an external script file. As it happens, JavaScript need not be written into a script container on a single page. We can move JavaScript code to a separate text file with the file extension .js. To set up our last examples, we will do this, copying the complete contents of our script container into a new text document, which we name "generator.js." In that new document, we delete the lines <script> and </script>. Externalized Java-Script doesn't need a script container.

Why do we move our work to an external file? As you may suspect, it's so we can use the same instructions flexibly in multiple projects without having to cut and paste or (mercy!) type them in. Once a set of functions have been moved to an external file, we can invoke them from within JavaScript code on any other page, so long as we include this special script container in our new page:

```
<script src="generator.js"></script>
```

An important detail here: the *src* ("source") attribute added to the initial script tag takes as its argument the location of the external file. As the tag is written here, that file must be in the same directory as the page that is loading it. Put everything into one folder and you'll be fine. Note, however, that you can access external JavaScript pages from anywhere in your local system or indeed from any point accessible to the web. Our use of an external script demonstrates two important principles: *modularity* and *dependence*. A program is a composite or assemblage of distributed parts. The parts depend on one another; they interoperate. If you plan to use more sophisticated game development tools like Unity, or if you think you might want to learn programming on a more serious basis, you'll need to understand these concepts.

Now back to our example. In effect, this blank container is filled, at least virtually, with the contents of the external file. (We're not sure that's technically accurate, but it feels that way.) Web pages can have more than one script container, as it happens, and in our next examples, we'll build additional containers and scripts that coordinate with our original text generator.

Bonus Example 3: An Everlasting Scroll

When we discussed Montfort's *Taroko Gorge* in chapter P-2, we noted the importance of its limitless operation. Like the gorge, the poem keeps unfolding (or in terms of its code, folding back on itself). What we see is an infinite scroll. There may be no way to achieve such an effect in Twine without slipping into JavaScript. (More on that possibility at the end of this section.) It's certainly not possible within the basic script affordances of Chapbook, which includes no loop structures. There are timed effects in Chapbook and Harlowe, but they are meant to run only once and have generally limited function.[1] Generally speaking, the Twine idiom assumes that changes will follow player action, not occur automatically.

We can break that taboo easily enough with JavaScript. All we have to do is look away politely when a function invokes itself. We've

---

1 We have not experimented with SugarCube, a story format with robust support for programming.

been using this technique for many years now without problems, so until Skynet sends a robot assassin from the future, we'll assume it's safe.

We start again with a blank version of our template web page. The first thing we do is add, above the existing script container, the reference container for our externalized text generator:

```
<script src="generator.js"></script>
```

We'll be using the feed from the text generator as content for our endless scroll. This is, of course, an arbitrary choice, but it has the virtue of tying our examples together and showing a remote script in operation. Note that the reference container does not do anything in itself because the script we brought over has no activating instructions. If you remember, its operation was triggered by an *onLoad* handler written into the body tag of the page, which is not part of the external Java-Script. So our generator code just sits in memory until we ask some bit of it to do something—which we will, directly.

Before we discuss the fresh code for this example, let's explain what we're trying to do and how we'll go about it. We want text to scroll constantly. We'll decide that the new text should appear at the bottom and disappear at the top of the window, because *Star Wars*. (It's easy enough to reverse the effect if desired.) We're adding to our scroll in discrete units, one sentence at a time. This makes the job a bit easier.

We need a data structure that will let us keep track of items in a numerical sequence, with the ability to add new items to the bottom of the sequence and delete from the top. This is why JavaScript gave us arrays. By now, you're very familiar with arrays in both Twine and JavaScript. We'll be using two built-in functions of the JavaScript array object, *push* and *shift*, which perform the needed addition and trimming. Since the code for this project is refreshingly compact compared to our text generator, we'll just show it complete and then discuss its features. Everything you see here sits inside the main script container.

```
textArray = new Array();

function writeUp(){

    //push on a new line
    textArray.push(generate());

//trim top line
    if(textArray.length==10) textArray.shift()

//output
document.getElementById("out").innerHTML = ""
    for(var i=0; i<textArray.length; i++){
        outIt(textArray[i]);
    }

    //don't stop
    theTimeout = setTimeout(writeUp, 1000);
}
```

First, we declare *textArray* to hold our generated sentences. We use the keyword *new* (technically called a *constructor*) to generate an array. The empty parentheses mean the array has nothing in it and an undefined size or length.

Next, we define the lone function in this example, called *writeUp*. You could call it anything you like. As you can see, we've marked off the four parts of this script with descriptive comments. To add to the bottom of our array, we use the *push* function, and what we push onto the array is the output from *generate*, our randomized, template-based sentence generator that is sitting in the remote file generate.js. (See how this works!) Next, we set an instruction to trim off the top line of the array once the array contains ten elements. That number is an arbitrary design decision, entirely changeable. It determines how many sentences will be visible in your scrolling window. You may want to keep this value low enough to fit the entire stack onto a typical screen. This could be accomplished mathematically by bringing in some parameters about the browser window and the line height, but we'll rely on guesswork for simplicity.

Next comes output, where we write the updated contents of *textArray* to the screen. Before we can do this, we remove any version that may have been displayed on a previous pass through this script—it's designed for repetition, remember? So we replace the *innerHTML* of our "out" DIV (in effect, the display window) with the null value, signified by two quotation marks without a space between them: "". At this point, you might wonder why we don't use the *outIt* function that is handily sitting in our remote script. We will use it later, but we can't do so here. That's because *outIt* is designed to add to the contents of the display DIV using the "+=" operator. Passing it a null value would just add a null value. We need to replace, not add. If we wanted to be clever, we could either write a second function (say, *blankIt*) or, even better, change *outIt* to accept a second parameter determining whether it adds or replaces. These improvements would have made the example more complicated, so we leave them to your imagination.

With the board erased, we're ready to write. You might think we could just pass *textArray* to our *outIt* function. If you try this, you'll see your sentences all jammed together, separated by commas, which is not what we want. We need to peel each of our sentences off, one at a time. That's what a good old *for* loop is for. It marches through the array from 0 to the last value before its length (which is the last item), referring to the item in question with the loop's built-in counter variable *i*. Notice we don't need to add <*br* /> at the end of our sentences because that's included in *outIt*.

Now we come to the final piece of the code, thoughtfully labeled "don't stop." This function reactivates itself. Generally speaking, programmers do not recommend that practice, but Montfort does much the same thing in *Taroko Gorge*, and he has advanced degrees in computer science and computational linguistics. As we said, this is technically an infinite loop, but it does not crash the browser, destroy the internet, or open any wormholes that we know of. The simplest way for a function to invoke itself is, of course, simply to write, on the last line of *writeUp*,

```
writeUp()
```

We could do that, but only at the expense of reading. Without some delay, the function will simply spew sentences up the screen, iterating several times a second. To avoid this, we wrap the reinvocation in a *setTimeout* function, which formally requires us to create a new variable called *theTimeout* and invoke the delay from there. The number parameter used is a value in milliseconds. One thousand milliseconds equal one second. You can change this value if you like. The effect of *setTimeout* is much like the delay factors in Chapbook and Harlowe: it holds operation until a certain amount of time has elapsed. The difference here is that the function it eventually invokes sets up another timer at the end of its run and so forth ad infinitum, if you can wait that long.

The result is an eternal scroll, filled with a constantly changing (and only occasionally repeating) series of sentences from our now familiar generator. As in *Taroko Gorge*, you won't see the scroll effect until enough lines have appeared to start the trimming process. After that, the business runs as long as you stay on the web page. As we've said, Montfort's poem may tell us something about the infinite complexity of the natural world. What this little example says about anything except coding is probably beside the point.

Finally, a further note on what can and can't be done with Twine. Because Chapbook supports both JavaScript code and HTML elements like DIVs with IDs, we can in fact port almost every piece of this project back to Twine and produce a passage (not page) with an endless scroll. We could mix this feature with other affordances of Twine for a richly hybridized experience. The only thing we can't do in this context is move our key functions to an external JavaScript page. Actually, that might be possible, but it would be necessary to know more about the inner workings of Twine than you probably want to learn right away. The hybridized Twine story is included in our online examples as bonus example 3A. We won't go through the code because it's essentially what you've seen already.

Bonus Example 4: Drifting down the Screen

For our next set of tricks, we'll explore another feature of the computing environment that has no obvious place in the Twine world: animation. From the start, we should point out that HTML and JavaScript
are less-than-ideal platforms for motion graphics. Yes, you can watch
movies through your browser, but you generally do so in a video window running a specialized resource called a *coder/decoder* (codec) or
sometimes a browser enhancement called a *plugin*. Back in the day,
before someone decided it should no longer be supported, there was a
famous plugin called Shockwave Flash, designed to run content developed by the two Adobe products of those names. You may recall our
mention of those programs in chapters T-1 and T-4. Those applications and their plugin handled animation very, very differently than
we can or will, depending on just the resources of your web browser,
unplugged. Nonetheless, these two simple exercises will at least give
you a taste of poetry in motion.

Let's begin with a single falling object. We start, as always, with a
fresh copy of our starter web page, to which we add the reference container to link up generator.js. Next, we go to the style sheet—the style
container found within the head just before the script containers. The
style container is blank. We add the following:

```
div{
    font: 18pt Cambria; padding: 20px; position:
    absolute;
}
```

The font and padding specifications are familiar from earlier examples. Note that last item, though: it declares that the position of any
DIV in our document will be mathematically fixed, not determined in
relation to other page elements. Animation won't work without this
declaration.

Next, we open the main script container of the page and add two
functions. The first of these is called *setUp*. It's designed to run once

when the page loads, so we also go down to the *onLoad* handler in the body tag and set it to activate *setUp*. Here's what *setUp* looks like:

```
function setUp(){
      theDIV = document.
      getElementsByTagName("DIV")[0]
      theDIV.innerHTML = generate()
      theLeft = r(600)
      theDIV.style.left = theLeft + "px"
      theTop = 0--r(100)
      theDIV.style.top = theTop + "px"
      animate()
}
```

The first line introduces a variable called *theDIV* and assigns it a value. The construction we use here looks a bit like the one with which you're probably familiar, *getElementById*, though actually, it's the cousin of that method, *getElementsByTagName*. Note it says "Elements," plural. This method of the *document* object can be used to reach out to a single page element, as we do here, but it first situates that element within a set of similar elements—the *collection* of DIV elements on our page. You'll see why we do this when we get to our next example. For the moment, have a look at the arguments we pass to the *getElementsByTagName* method: a tag name in parentheses ("DIV") followed by a number in brackets [0]. This is the same notation used to identify elements of an array—and, indeed, a document object collection is a bit like an array, though it does not have all the features of that object. Why do we say *0* here? Because our page only contains one DIV, and programmers always start with nothing (or count from zero). So item 1 (and only) is item 0.

Why do we attach this laborious identification to a variable? Strictly for convenience, because we are going to operate on our one and only DIV in ways that require us to name it. Our variable *theDIV* acts like a pronoun, saving much bothersome typing. What we're doing, specifically, is placing our DIV at a specific point on the screen. Yes,

JavaScript, the DOM, and HTML can do that. That's what makes animation possible.

Any DIV, or block-level page element, has properties called *top* and *left* that indicate where its respective edges are located within the browser window. To move the element, we reset those properties. They are actually subproperties of a more general *style* property, so we address them in dot notation as *style.top* or *style.left*. There are some further complexities beyond this. First, we can't modify the values with a statement like the following:

```
theDIV.style.top ++
```

For arcane reasons, the values of geometric properties must be expressed with metrics—for instance, *100px*, which means one hundred pixels from the top of the window. We need to append the text string "px" to the number, which means we first extract the number, assign it to a variable—*theTop* and *theLeft*—modify the variable as we wish, append the metric, and then bang the result back in. This is quite baroque, and we've never understood the reasoning behind it, but so be it. You'll see that for the left position of the DIV (x-axis), we're asking good old *r* for a value between 0 and 599, which assumes the browser window is at least six hundred pixels wide. (Here's hoping.) For the top position, we do something that may seem strange: we ask for a random number between 0 and 99, subtracting that number from 0 to make it negative. That's because we want our DIV positioned *above the top edge of the browser window*. And yes, we can do that. This way, we start with a blank screen, and our drifting DIV can make a dramatic appearance.

Let's get to the drifting part, which is the business of our second function, *animate*—which, you'll note, is invoked at the end of *setUp*. Here's the code:

```
function animate(){
    theDIV = document.
    getElementsByTagName("DIV")[0]
```

```
theTop += 5
theDIV.style.top = theTop + "px"
if(theTop > 500){
        setUp()
}
else{
theTimeout = setTimeout(animate, 50);
}
}
```

We're repeating that step from *setUp* where we identify our DIV and assign it to a pronoun-like variable. There are ways to avoid this inelegancy, but they would complicate the conversion of this one-DIV example to a multi-DIV example in the next section, so we do it again, somewhat mysteriously. The variable *theTop* comes into play again in the next statement. Until we modify it here, it has whatever value it received in *setUp*. Our modification increases it by five, meaning we move our DIV five pixels down the screen. We assign the modified value in the same way you saw in *setUp*. Notice we don't change the left position of the DIV. We're only animating in one axis, though you could use two (or even three) if you wanted.

Now we come to that *if* test. Once our drifting DIV passes line 500 of the browser window, we want it to go through the *setUp* routine and reposition at the top of the screen. We use an inequality (>) because we're using increments of five, and it's possible for our DIV to exceed 500 without ever having that value—for instance, if its position changes from 499 to 504, which is possible. Remember, the vertical position of the DIV is assigned randomly in *setUp*, so we don't know the exact value (and don't really need to). We're actually using an *if/else* construction here because we want another thing to happen if our DIV has not yet dropped offscreen. In that case, we start a *setTimeout*, just as we did in our eternal scroll, using a delay factor of fifty milliseconds. Higher values slow the animation, lower ones speed it up. Experiment as you like. Once again, we have a function that calls itself. What's a little recursion among friends?

If all the pieces are properly assembled, this example drifts a randomly generated sentence down the screen, followed by another and another, at various horizontal locations. It's about as simple as animations get. In our next and final example, we'll make it just a bit more interesting.

Bonus Example 5: It's Raining Story

For our final example, we'll multiply the floating DIVs to give greater visual (and maybe narrative or poetic) interest to the project. To do this, we'll need a way to animate, track, and reset several page elements independently. Now you'll see why we started referring to our single DIV via its place in the DIV collection. We'll need the whole set in play for this one.

Since we modified our basic page template slightly for the previous example, we'll start this one by making a copy of that page file, renaming it, and erasing the contents of the main script container—the two functions we created in example 5.4. We'll end up rebuilding some of that code, but there are enough differences to reward a fresh start. Before we start on the JavaScript, we'll go down into the body portion of the markup and make two changes. We'll add an *onLoad* handler to the body tag:

```
<BODY width: 600px onLoad = "startUp">
```

Next, we'll replace the single DIV that's sitting in the body container with a stack of five:

```
<BODY>
    <DIV></DIV>
    <DIV></DIV>
    <DIV></DIV>
    <DIV></DIV>
    <DIV></DIV>
</BODY>
```

These DIVs need neither IDs nor contents. There do need to be five of them, however.

Now for the scripting. At the top of our pristine script container, we'll declare and initialize three very important arrays:

```
leftNum = new Array(0,0,0,0,0);
topNum = new Array(0,0,0,0,0);
DIVSpeed = new Array(0,0,0,0,0);
```

You'll remember that arrays can be set up with initial values, as we do here. Those zeroes will be replaced with nonzero numbers when the script starts up. We could have used any number, so long as it's an integer. We need to start with integers here, since that's what we'll be storing in these arrays as we go.

You'll recall that in bonus example 4 we had a function called *setUp*. This time we'll have one called *startUp*. It's a bit different from our previous *setUp* function:

```
function startUp(){
    for(var i=0; i<5; i++){
        reset(i);
    }
    theInterval = setInterval(animate, 50);
}
```

Here's a familiar five-step *for* loop, but all it does is call a function called *reset*, passing it a number from 0 to 4. We'll build reset next. Before we do, have a look at the final line of *startUp*, which uses the first cousin of *setTimeout* called *setInterval*. The *setTimeout* method runs once; that's why we need to keep reinvoking it in our earlier examples. By contrast, *setInterval* repeats automatically as long as the page is loaded and the interval is not canceled by some other instruction.

When we only had one falling object, we could have it restart its animation function every time it passed offscreen. However, this time we'll control five DIVs with one function. Under that scheme, it's easier to start the animating engine once and let it run. Before we can get to animation, however, we need to create our reset function:

```
function reset(which){
   theDIV = document.getElementsByTagName("DIV")
   [which]
   DIVSpeed[which] = 3 + r(5)
   theDIV.innerHTML = generate()
   leftNum[which] = r(600)
   theDIV.style.left = leftNum[which] + "px"
   topNum[which] = 0--r(100)
   theDIV.style.top = topNum[which] + "px"
}
```

This is the function called five times by *startUp*. Much of it will look very familiar from bonus example 4. There are two main differences. First, this function takes a parameter called *which* (it could be called anything). This parameter is an integer between 0 and 4, inclusive. Notice that in our DIV-identifier (*theDIV*), we use this number to say which DIV we're addressing. Remember, all the DIVs are numbered in the collection. (This scheme assumes our animating DIVs are the first five to appear in the markup. If you change the page in a way that breaks this pattern, the animation won't work.) The second variation here is the reference to that third array we created, *DIVspeed*. This array stores an integer value for each of our five animating DIVs, setting the amount of downward displacement that will occur on each cycle of the animation—in effect, the speed at which they fall. We require a minimum of three pixels but add to that a random selection on a range of five, meaning the maximum amount is seven. You can experiment with different values here. The important thing about this feature is that it can give each DIV a different rate of descent. The effect is very important visually.

The final element of this project is the *animate* function, which goes into operation at the end of the *startUp* function, activated on page load. Here's the code:

```
function animate(){
  for(var i=0; i<5; i++){
    topNum[i] += divSpeed[i];
    theDIV = document.
    getElementsByTagName("DIV")[i]
    theDIV.style.top = topNum[i] + "px";
    if(topNum[i] > 500) reset(i);
  }
}
```

The bones of this function should be familiar from the previous example. Here we have a five-way *for* loop that addresses each of our falling objects in sequence (so quickly it seems instantaneous). We do all the usual business of updating the top location of the DIV, handing it off to the reset routine when the DIV passes the five-hundred-pixel line. But notice that the value passed to reset is just the number of that particular DIV. This animating routine manages each element separately.

The result is a shower of sentences or a variable story crossed with a confetti machine. What that might amount to, beyond an excuse to practice JavaScript coding, is the subject of our very last section.

Conclusion

You'll notice something conspicuously missing from the five examples presented in this chapter: interactivity. All five are focused on display. They presume a reader, or perhaps a viewer, but not really a player. Should we conclude therefore that moving from Twine to JavaScript/ HTML means leaving behind interactive fiction and games? Is web coding primarily a replacement for the cinematic aesthetics and poetics of dear, dead Flash?

Beware of hasty conclusions. It's easy enough to see how some or all of these examples could be harnessed for story-centered games. For all three of our final examples (scroll and falling texts), imagine a stack of clickable prompts (words, names, faces, symbols) that call on alternative text generators, allowing the reader/player to steer the unfolding

story in specific directions. Adding features like these to the demonstra-
tions would make the code-crawling unbearably tedious. The drawback
of simple examples is simplicity. We invite you to think beyond them.

Figure 25: Salter and Blodgett's *ALT-RT: Ctrl+A; DEL* (2017)

Both authors of this book have built creative works that use HTML,
JavaScript, and other web resources to design evocative interfaces and
tell salient stories. Salter and Blodgett's *ALT-RT: Ctrl+A; DEL* creates a
simulated tweetstream drawn from a database of actual and invented
material to capture the nightmare of social media (Salter and Blodgett).
It combines quasi-randomized text sampling with selectable options
for self-preservation. These selections have meaningful consequences,
making the work legitimately interactive. Its experience has a distinct
ending and alternative outcomes, making it very gamelike. Moulthrop's
Emaji Naratgee Marakka, born of similar inspiration, renders trollish
tweets as a visually accreting mass that the player can suppress or erase
completely by doggedly choosing acts of resistance (Moulthrop). Successfully wiping out the troll-storm (if only for a moment) earns the
reader an installment of a fable. Once this chunk of story has been
read, the tweets return, growing ever more deranged. To reach the end
of the fable, the reader must repeatedly fend off the troll, then pen-
etrate a few final mysteries of cryptographic text. Both of these works

are hypertextual, narrative, and gamelike; both depend on affordances (database access; animation) not easily supported in Twine.

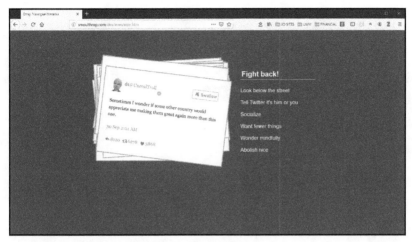

Figure 26: Moulthrop's *Emaji Naratgee Marakka* (2018)

Twine is not the only way to make interactive fictions. However, as the extent and density of even the modest code examples in this chapter will show, there is a significant trade-off between the broad creative scope of hand-built web work and the elegance, stability, and community of Twine. As always, creators and communicators should understand the range of possibilities implicit in these tools and feel empowered on any platform.

Works Cited

Moulthrop, Stuart. *Emaji Naratgee Marakka*. Work in progress, 2018. www.smoulthrop .com/lit/enm.

Salter, Anastasia, and Bridget Blodgett. "ALT-RT: Ctrl+A; DEL." *Persona Studies* 3, no. 1 (2017). https://ojs.deakin.edu.au/index.php/ps/article/view/656.

9 781943 208241